CHICAGO PUBLIC LIBRARY
4455 N. LINCOLN AVE. 60625
DISCARD

CHICAGO PUBLIC LIBRARY - MURL GRANT
P9-ARL-816

Blacks in Antiquity: Ethiopians in the Greco-Roman Experience

Blacks in Antiquity

Ethiopians in the Greco-Roman Experience

Frank M. Snowden, Jr.

The Belknap Press of
Harvard University Press
Cambridge, Massachusetts
London, England

ELEVENTH PRINTING, 1995
ISBN 0-674-07626-5
Library of Congress Catalog Card Number 70-88812
Printed in the United States of America

To Elaine

Preface

Among the many peoples who entered the Greco-Roman world were the dark- and black-skinned Ethiopians of Africa. The experiences of these Africans who reached the alien shores of Greece and Italy constituted an important chapter in the history of classical antiquity. An examination of the resultant intermingling of these peoples enables us to study an early encounter of white Europeans with dark and black Africans.

Following the practice of the Greeks and Romans, I have applied the word "Ethiopian" to the several dark- and black-skinned Africans whom the Greeks and Romans designated as Ethiopians. The classical evidence relating to physical characteristics, geographical location, and tribal identification demonstrates that the Greeks and Romans classified as Ethiopians several physical types of dark and black peoples inhabiting different parts of Africa. However classified by modern scholars, to Greeks and Romans these peoples were *all* "Ethiopians." A very large portion of these Ethiopians comprised peoples considered by anthropologists today as Negroes. In fact, the Negroid type, both in classical art and literature, was in a sense the most frequent example of the Ethiopian in Greco-Roman usage. The Ethiopian, especially the Negroid type, was the yardstick by which antiquity measured colored peoples. The Ethiopian's blackness became proverbial. The Ethiopian, together with the Scythian, was a favorite illustration of a physical type differing from the Greeks and Romans. Some Egyptologists and Africanists prefer the term "Kushites" for the inhabitants of certain areas south of Egypt, and some scholars reject the term "Ethiopian" to avoid confusion with the modern nation of Ethiopia. I have chosen "Ethiopian," however, for the simple reason that it was the word used by the Greeks and Romans themselves. I have not included Asiatic Ethiopians except for purposes of clarification. Eastern Ethiopians (exactly who they were and where they came from are not certain) differed physically from African Ethiopians, according to Herodotus, only in that those of Asia were straight-haired and those of Africa the most woolly-haired of all men.

An important constituent part of the evidence is that provided by the numerous representations of Negroes depicted in classical art. Since archaeologists differ as to the criteria they use in classifying a depiction as Negro, archaeological reports are often misleading, especially when unaccompanied by photographs. Hence, a first-hand examination of relevant materials in museum collections was indispensable. In classifying art-objects as Negro or Negroid I have followed the guidelines of modern anthropologists. Although using Ethiopian whenever it appears in the ancient evidence, in referring to art-objects I have employed Negro or Negroid.

I have attempted to set forth the facts as precisely as possible on the basis of the ancient evidence — literary, epigraphical, papyrological, numismatic, and archaeological. The material has been presented topically, each topic chronologically as far as practicable when such an arrangement was necessary for the most effective presentation of my findings. I have focused on the Ethiopian from the Homeric period to the age of Justinian; on what the Greeks and Romans said, knew, and felt about the Ethiopian both in the lands of his origin and in various parts of the Greco-Roman world. Only a few ancient authors dealt with the Ethiopians in some detail; the works of several writers reported to have visited Ethiopia are lost. For a comprehensive picture, therefore, the countless scattered notices had to be examined. In addition to classical sources I have used pertinent findings of Egyptologists, especially for the Meroïtic period of Ethiopian peoples.

Scholars have treated one or more limited aspects of the Ethiopian in the Greco-Roman world; yet no comprehensive study has appeared. As a result, important specialized investigations have not had the advantage of the perspective derivable from a broad picture of the Ethiopian in Greek and Roman civilization. For example, even though some early archaeologists foresaw the significance of the archaeological evidence, scholars have not always related properly the literary notices and the archaeological materials. The most detailed treatment of the Negro type in Greek and Roman art — *The Negro in Greek and Roman Civilization: A Study of the Ethiopian Type** by Mrs. G. H. Beardsley — recognized the importance of considering the lit-

*Baltimore and London: The Johns Hopkins Press, 1929.

erary evidence. This pioneer work of forty years ago, however, gave only scant treatment to the Ethiopian in Greek and Roman literature.

Even more serious are two other consequences of the absence of a comprehensive study. First, unwarranted generalizations have been made and repeated by generations of scholars. The view, for example, that classical references to Ethiopians glorify an unknown, mysterious people needs to be modified in light of what is known of these peoples from the findings of Africanists. Or, to designate certain depictions of Negroes as caricatures is to overlook the anatomical curiosity of the artist similar to the scientific interest of the Greek environmentalists. Second, classical texts have often been misinterpreted because scholars have mistakenly attributed to antiquity racial attitudes and concepts which derive from certain modern views regarding the Negro. I considered it essential, therefore, to acquire some familiarity with modern anthropological and sociological research on pertinent racial and intercultural problems. For an interpretation of the Greco-Roman attitude toward the dark and black peoples of Africa designated as Ethiopians this excursus into nonclassical disciplines has been valuable. Having lived in Egypt, Greece, and Italy for substantial periods of time, I have noticed similarities between the ancient and modern views of colored peoples in these areas of the Mediterranean. Two personal experiences illustrate this point. During my last visit to Athens, the taxi driver who drove me from the airport, upon observing my dark color, exclaimed with confidence "Αἰθίοψ!" (Ethiopian) — a happy coincidence and an encouraging introduction for an investigator in pursuit of classical representations of Ethiopians in Athenian museums. I once encountered in Sicily an interesting parallel to the ancient confusion between Indians and Ethiopians, between east and south. A colleague and I had spent some pleasant moments with the local custodian of an archaeological site. Finally the Sicilian's curiosity prompted him to inquire of me "Are you *Chinese?*" I have acquired some unexpected insights, therefore, from my sojourns among the descendants of the people whose literary documents and art are the subject of my study.

"Africa is always producing something new" was a Greek proverb, preserved by Aristotle and Pliny. This proverb has a certain applicability to my study. A fresh and comprehensive look at what the Greeks and Romans had to say about Ethiopians from Africa has perhaps yielded something new.

In the preparation of this book, I owe much to many. I am grateful to William L. Westermann, who long ago discussed some of my findings with me and suggested that I develop and publish them and to Mason Hammond, who has encouraged me over the years. I acknowledge my gratitude for the leisure and financial assistance provided at various intervals by a Fulbright fellowship and by research grants from the American Council of Learned Societies and the Howard University Research Fund. I have enjoyed the generous hospitality of the libraries of Harvard College, Dumbarton Oaks, the Center for Hellenic Studies, and the American Academy in Rome. I have many individuals and museums to thank for the courtesy of photographs and permission to publish them and for the kindness in helping me study the objects themselves. Certain chapters of this book are either based on or are developments of ideas expressed in articles which I have published. Some portions are the same as in the articles in question but in general have been modified or enlarged by the inclusion of additional material. My thanks are due, therefore, to the editors of the *American Journal of Philology*, *American Anthropologist*, *L'Antiquité Classique*, and *Traditio* for permission to make use of material which has appeared in these journals. I am also grateful to the many scholars who have generously answered my questions on knotty points. Colleagues at Howard have been very helpful — Leon E. Wright and Gene Rice in the chapter on early Christianity; Mark H. Watkins, in anthropological matters; J. Edwin Foster, in photographic guidance; Eva Keuls, in proofreading; and members of the Department of Classics as well as other departments, in their willingness to hear me and advise.

I am deeply obliged to my secretary, Mrs. Gladys Clemmons, who cheerfully typed draft after draft, and to Mrs. Natalie Frohock of the Harvard Press, who patiently edited this volume. Finally, I can never express sufficient gratitude to my wife for her assistance and encouragement along the way.

Unless otherwise noted, all translations are my own.

F. M. S., Jr.

Washington, D.C.
February 1969

Contents

Illustrations

Figures 1-77 follow page 29.
Figures 78-120 follow page 218.

1. Stone figures of Negroes from Ayia Irini, Cyprus, ca. 560 B.C. Photo: Courtesy E. Gjerstad et al., *The Swedish Cyprus Expedition, Finds and Results of the Excavations in Cyprus: 1927-1931,* vol. II. Plate CCXXXIX.

2. Negro participant in a dancing scene, detail from an Apulian askos, ca. 380-360 B.C. Ruvo, Jatta Collection, 1402. Photo: courtesy Deutsches Archäologisches Institut, Rome.

3. Terra-cotta head of woman with cicatrices, probably from the Fayum, Roman period, the author's collection.

4. Heracles and Negroid attendants of King Busiris, from a scene on a red-figured pelike, fifth century B.C. Athens, National Museum, AP9683. Photo: courtesy National Museum, Athens.

5a–b. Steatopygic women on marble relief from tomb near Ariccia, early second century A.D. Rome, Museo Nazionale, 77255. Photos: courtesy Gabinetto Fotografico Nazionale, Roma.

6. Pygmy with protuberant stomach on Kabeiric skyphos. Boston, Museum of Fine Arts, 99.534. Photo: courtesy Museum of Fine Arts, Boston.

7a–b. Front and side views of a terra-cotta mask from Agrigento, late sixth century or early fifth B.C. Agrigento, Museo Nazionale Archeologico. Photos: courtesy Soprintendenza alle Antichità, Agrigento.

8. Laver-handles decorated with Negroes, from Centuripe, Sicily, sixth century B.C. Oxford, Ashmolean Museum, 1890.222. Photograph Ashmolean Museum.

9. Attic head-vase, 6th-5th century B.C. West Berlin, Staatliche Museen, F4049. Photo: courtesy Staatliche Museen, West Berlin.

10. Mask-like terra-cotta head of a Negro from Salamis, fifth century B.C. Photo: from J. Sieveking, *Die Terrakotten der Sammlung Loeb,* I (Munich 1916) plate 29.

11. A faience vase in shape of Janiform heads of Negro and bearded barbarian from Cyprus, late seventh century B.C. London, British

Museum 47 8-6 20. Photo: courtesy the Trustees of the British Museum.

12a–c. Views of white-ground kantharos in shape of Janiform heads of a Negro and a white from Tarquinia, ca. 510 B.C. Rome, Villa Giulia Museum, 50571. Photos: courtesy Soprintendenza alle Antichità dell'Etruria Meridionale, Roma.

13. Aryballos in form of conjoined heads of a Negro and a white, end of sixth century B.C. Paris, Louvre, C.A.987. Photo: courtesy Louvre. Paris.

14. Views of kantharos in form of conjoined heads of Heracles and a Negro, ca. 480-470 B.C. Rome, Vatican, Museo Etrusco Gregoriano, 16539. Photo: Anderson, 42090.

15a–b. Negro (Memnon?) and two Amazons in scene on black-figured neck-amphora and detail of the Negro, ca. mid-sixth century B.C. Brussels, Musées Royaux du Cinquantenaire, A 130. Photos: courtesy Musées Royaux du Cinquantenaire, Brussels.

16a–b. Negro and Amazon depicted on fifth-century B.C. alabastron. West Berlin, Staatliche Museen, 3382. Photos: courtesy Staatliche Museen, West Berlin.

17. Warrior on interior of red-figured kylix, from Poggio Sommavilla, ca. 520-500 B.C. Paris, Louvre, G93. Photo: courtesy Louvre, Paris.

18. Detail of Memnon and Negroes from black-figured neck-amphora, ca. 530 B.C. New York, Metropolitan Museum of Art, 98.8.13. Photo: courtesy the Metropolitan Museum of Art, Gift of F. W. Rhinelander, 1898.

19. One of Memnon's Negro companions from black-figured neck-amphora, ca. 540-530 B.C. London, British Museum, B209. Photo: courtesy the Trustees of the British Museum.

20. Soldiers coming to the assistance of King Busiris, scene from Caeretan hydria, ca. 530 B.C. Vienna, Kunsthistorisches Museum, 3576. Photo: courtesy Kunsthistorisches Museum, Vienna.

21. Warrior lifting shield from ground, from a polychrome lekythos in Six's style from Cumae. Naples, Museo Nazionale, 86339. Photo: courtesy Soprintendenza alle Antichità della Campania, Napoli.

22. Negroid trumpeter on shield of warrior from fifth-century B.C. red-figured amphora from Vulci. Würzburg, 302. Photo: from A. Furtwängler and K. Reichhold, *Griechische Vasenmalerei,* Series II, Plates (Munich 1908) plate 104.

23. Woman on sard scarab, fifth century B.C. Boston, Museum of Fine Arts, 23.581. Photo: courtesy the Museum of Fine Arts, Boston.

24. Gold ornament in form of a Negro head hanging from gold necklace, ca. fifth century B.C., from Canusium. London, British Museum, 2272. Photo: courtesy the Trustees of the British Museum.

25a–b. Negroid diphrophoros contrasted with white figure in a grave scene from a white-ground lekythos from Eretria, fifth century B.C. East Berlin, Staatliche Museen, 3291. Photos: courtesy Staatliche Museen, East Berlin.

26a–b. Ethiopians in scene from Andromeda myth and detail of one of the Ethiopians on a red-figured hydria from Vulci, fifth century B.C. London, British Museum, E169. Photos: courtesy the Trustees of the British Museum.

27a–b. Front and profile views of a vase in form of Negro's head from Vulci, fifth-fourth century B.C. West Berlin, Staatliche Museen, F2970. Photos: courtesy Staatliche Museen, West Berlin.

28. Vase in form of Negro's head, fifth-fourth century B.C. Paris, Bibliothèque Nationale, Collection de Janzé, 149. Photo: courtesy Bibliothèque Nationale, Paris.

29. Negro-head oinochoe, from near Viterbo (?) fourth century B.C. New York, Metropolitan Museum of Art, 03.3.1 (GR 615). Photo: courtesy the Metropolitan Museum of Art, Rogers Fund, 1903.

30. Etruscan Negro-head mug, fourth century B.C. New York, Metropolitan Museum of Art, 56.49.2. Photo: courtesy the Metropolitan Museum of Art, Gift of El Conde de Lagernillas, 1956.

31. Plastic Etruscan vase in form of Negro head, second half of fourth century B.C. Ferrara, Museo Nazionale Archeologico, 1909. Photo: courtesy Museo Nazionale Archeologico di Ferrara.

32. Etruscan vase in form of Negro's head, fourth century B.C. Oxford, Ashmolean Museum, 1947.147. Photograph Ashmolean Museum.

33. Negro and crocodile, south Italian (Apulian). London, British Museum, F417. Photo: courtesy the Trustees of the British Museum.

34a–b. Front and side views of Apulian head-vase, second half of the fourth century B.C. or later. Ruvo, Jatta Collection, 1113. Photos: courtesy Deutsches Archäologisches Institut, Rome.

35. South Italian lekythos with profile of Negro head, fourth century B.C. Paris, Louvre (N. 2566). Photo: courtesy Louvre, Paris.

36. Negroid Circe and Odysseus on Kabeiric skyphos. Oxford, Ashmolean Museum, no. G.249. Photograph Ashmolean Museum.

37. Askos in form of a boy bent over to the ground from Boeotia, fourth century B.C. Oxford, Ashmolean Museum, 1922.205. Photograph Ashmolean Museum.

38. Askos in form of a boy seizing a goose from south Italy, fourth

century B.C. New York, Metropolitan Museum of Art, 41.162.45. Photo: courtesy the Metropolitan Museum of Art, Rogers Fund, 1941.

39a–b. Gold phiale with concentric circles of Negro heads and detail from Panagurishte, middle of fourth century B.C. Plodiv (Bulgaria), National Archaeological Museum. Photos: courtesy National Archaeological Museum, Plodiv (Bulgaria).

40a–b. Terra cottas of Negroes from Egypt, largely Greco-Roman. Photos: P. Perdrizet, *Les Terres cuites grecques d'Egypte de la Collection Fouquet,* II Plates (Nancy, Paris, Strasbourg 1921) plates XCVI, XCVII and courtesy Berger-Levrault, Paris.

41a–c. Negro mahouts on bronze coinage from central Italy associated with Hannibal's Italian campaign. Photos: from P. R. Garrucci, *Le monete dell'Italia antica: Raccolta generale del P. Raffaele Garrucci,* pt. 2 (Rome 1885) plate LXXV and E. Babelon, "L'Eléphant d'Annibal," *Revue numismatique* XIV (1896) 1, fig. 1.

42. Black steatite statuette of a crouched boy with rings around legs, Alexandrian. Boston, Museum of Fine Arts, 01.8210. Photo: courtesy the Museum of Fine Arts, Boston.

43. Bronze statuette of a standing beggar, Egypt, Alexandria (?), first century B.C. Cleveland, The Cleveland Museum of Art, 63.507. Photo: courtesy the Cleveland Museum of Art, Purchase, Leonard C. Hanna, Jr. Bequest.

44. Bronze statuette of a boy, Hellenistic. New York, Metropolitan Museum of Art, 18.145.10. Photo: courtesy the Metropolitan Museum of Art, Rogers Fund, 1918.

45. Terra cotta of Negro Spinario from Priene, ca. second century B.C. West Berlin, Staatliche Museen, TC 8626. Photo: courtesy Staatliche Museen, West Berlin.

46. Terra cotta of a boy sleeping beside amphora, Hellenistic. Oxford, Ashmolean Museum, 1884.584. Photograph Ashmolean Museum.

47. Limestone figure of a sleeping boy from Ptolemaic period. Copenhagen, Ny Carlsberg Glyptotek, ÆIN 1597. Photo: courtesy Ny Carlsberg Glyptotek, Copenhagen.

48. Bronze figure of sleeping boy, perhaps Hellenistic original. Copenhagen, Ny Carlsberg Glyptotek, ÆIN 2755. Photo: courtesy Ny Carlsberg Glyptotek, Copenhagen.

49. Terra-cotta statuettes of boxers, late Hellenistic. London, British Museum, D84 and D85. Photo: courtesy the Trustees of the British Museum.

50. Marble relief of a charioteer from Herculaneum, ca. first century A.D. Naples, Museo Nazionale, 6692. Photo: Alinari, 34314 and courtesy Soprintendenza alle Antichità della Campania, Napoli.

51. Marble statue of an acrobat, Roman work in Hellenistic style. Rome, Museo Nazionale, 40809. Photo: courtesy Gabinetto Fotografico Nazionale, Roma.

52. Bronze upper bust of a diver holding a *pinna*, Roman. London, British Museum, 1674. Photo: courtesy the Trustees of the British Museum.

53. Small bust of a Negro, Roman, from Ostia. Ostia, Museo Ostiense, 3558. Photo: courtesy Gabinetto Fotografico Nazionale, Roma.

54. Bronze vase in form of head of an Ethiopian chieftain or ambassador, Roman. Paris, Bibliothèque Nationale, Collection de Janzé, 1018. Photo: Bibliothèque Nationale, Paris.

55. Bronze vase in the form of a Negro head, Roman. Paris, Musée du Petit Palais, Collection Auguste Dutuit, 83. Photo: Bulloz, Paris and courtesy Musée du Petit Palais, Paris.

56. Marble statuette of a youthful bath attendant, Trajanic-Antonine periods. Rome, Museo Vaticano, 2752. Photo: courtesy Archivio Fotografico dei Musei e Gallerie Pontificie, Vatican City.

57. Silver pepper caster in the form of a sleeping old man, Roman, second century A.D. from near Montcornet (Aisne). London, British Museum, 145. Photo: courtesy the Trustees of the British Museum.

58. Black marble statue of a boy, from Hadrumetum, second century A.D. Photo: courtesy Director of the National Museums and Embassy of Tunisia, Washington, D. C.

59. Glass cup molded in form of a Negro head, Roman, first-fourth centuries A.D. New York, Metropolitan Museum of Art, 81.10.226. Photo: courtesy the Metropolitan Museum of Art, Gift of Henry Marquand, 1881.

60a–c. Bronze statuette perhaps of a street singer and details of head, Hellenistic. Paris, Bibliothèque Nationale, Collection Caylus, 1009. Photos: courtesy Bibliothèque Nationale, Paris.

61. Small bronze bust of a young child, Hellenistic. London, British Museum, 1955 — 10-8-1. Photo: courtesy the Trustees of the British Museum.

62. Small bronze bust of Nilotic type, Hellenistic. Florence, Museo Archeologico, 2288. Photo: courtesy Soprintendenza alle Antichità dell'Etruria, Firenze.

63. Bronze of a Negroid jockey, Hellenistic, ca. 240-200 B.C. from Cape Artemisium. Athens, National Museum, 15177. Photo: courtesy National Museum, Athens.

64. Bronze statuette of a boyish orator, Hellenistic-Alexandrian. Boston, Museum of Fine Arts, 59.11. Photo: courtesy the Museum of Fine Arts, Boston.

65a–b. Front and side views of a bronze statue of a boy, Hellenistic, second or first century B.C. from Bodrum. Bodrum, Archaeological Museum, 756. Photos: courtesy Archaeological Museum, Istanbul and Turkish Embassy, Washington.

66. Bronze statuette of a lamp-bearer, late Republican or early Imperial Rome, found at Perugia. London, British Museum, 1908-5-15-1. Photo: courtesy the Trustees of the British Museum.

67. Marble statue of a Negroid woman, personification of Africa (?) from lower Egypt, end of first century B.C.–first century A.D. Photo: from *Fondation Eugene Piot: Monuments et memoires publiés par l'Académie des Inscriptions et Belles-lettres,* XXII (1916) plate XVI, and courtesy Presses Universitaires de France, Paris.

68. Marble bust of an African with Negroid admixture, Augustan or Julio-Claudian period. Boston, Museum of Fine Arts, 88.643. Photo: courtesy the Museum of Fine Arts, Boston.

69. Yellow limestone head of a Negro from Meroë, Roman, ca. 100 A.D. Copenhagen, Ny Carlsberg Glyptotek, ÆIN 1336. Photo: courtesy Ny Carlsberg Glyptotek, Copenhagen.

70a–b. Small marble head of woman from Agora, Trajanic period. Athens, Agora Museum, S 1268. Photo: courtesy American School of Classical Studies at Athens.

71a–c. Views of an over-life-sized basalt head of a man from Egypt, perhaps the Fayum, 80-50 B.C.–Trajanic period. Alexandria, Graeco-Roman Museum, 3204. Photos: courtesy the Corpus of Late Egyptian Sculpture, the Brooklyn Museum, and the Graeco-Roman Museum, Alexandria.

72. Marble head of a Negroid woman, probably Hadrianic period. Rome, Museo Nazionale, 49596. Photo: courtesy Gabinetto Fotografico Nazionale, Roma.

73. Marble head of Memnon, pupil of Herodes Atticus, found in Thyreatis, ca. 160-170 A.D. East Berlin, Staatliche Museen, SK 1503. Photo: courtesy Staatliche Museen, East Berlin.

74. Black marble head of a youth from Asia Minor, second century A.D. East Berlin, Staatliche Museen, SK 1579. Photo: courtesy Staatliche Museen, East Berlin.

75. Marble head of a young man from Agora, ca. 250-260 A.D. Athens, Agora Museum, S 435. Photo: courtesy American School of Classical Studies at Athens.

76. Pygmy fighting with crane, scene from top of red-figured rhyton, Leningrad, Hermitage B.1818 (679). Photo: courtesy Hermitage, Leningrad.

77. Scene from a Pompeiian fresco of pygmies hunting crocodiles and hippopotamus. Naples, Museo Nazionale, 113195. Photo: Alinari, 12027.

78a–b. Cast from a mold found at Naucratis, fifth century B.C.: Oxford, Ashmolean Museum, G96. Photographs Ashmolean Museum.

79. Black granite head of King Taharqa, Egyptian. Copenhagen, Ny Carlsberg Glyptotek, ÆIN 1538. Photo: courtesy Ny Carlsberg Glyptotek, Copenhagen.

80. Plate with Negroid warrior from Taranto, fifth century B.C. Taranto, Museo Nazionale, I.G.4424. Photo: courtesy Soprintendenza alle Antichità della Puglia, Taranto.

81. Alabastron with Negroid warrior crouching and reaching for his shield, fifth century B.C. Athens, National Museum, 412. Photo: courtesy National Museum, Athens.

82a–b. Negroid mahout and elephant and detail of the mahout, terra cotta from Pompeii. Naples, Museo Nazionale, 124845. Photos: courtesy Soprintendenza alle Antichità della Campania, Napoli.

83. Bronze head of Augustus found at Meroë. London, British Museum, 1911 9-11. Photo: courtesy the Trustees of the British Museum.

84. Bronzes of prisoners, early Empire. East Berlin, Staatliche Museen, Misc. 10485-86. Photo: courtesy Staatliche Museen, East Berlin.

85. Negro and Libyan herms in black limestone from Carthage, middle of second century A.D. Photo: from G. Picard, *Carthage* (New York 1965) plate 2.

86. Negroid(?) soldier on Arch of Septimius Severus in Roman Forum. Photo: courtesy Deutsches Archäologisches Institut, Rome.

87. Marble sarcophagus, ca. 180-200 A.D., depicting triumph of Bacchus, with two Negro boys astride a pair of panthers. Baltimore, Walters Art Gallery, 23.31. Photo: courtesy the Walters Art Gallery, Baltimore.

88. Negroid victory driving a chariot and a seated Heracles, scene on a red-figured oinochoe (from Cyrenaica) of the late fifth or early fourth century B.C. Paris, Louvre, N3408. Photo: courtesy Louvre, Paris.

89. Woman tortured by satyrs, scene from Attic, black-figured lekythos, fifth century B.C. Athens, National Museum, 1129. Photo: courtesy National Museum, Athens.

90. Ethiopians and the Andromeda myth in a scene from a red-figured pelike, ca. 560 B.C. Museum of Fine Arts, Boston, 63.2663. Photo: courtesy the Museum of Fine Arts, Boston.

91a–b. Heracles and Negroid Busiris and attendants of Busiris on red-figured stamnos, ca. 470 B.C. Oxford, Ashmolean Museum, 521. Photographs Ashmolean Museum.

92. Negroid attendants of King Busiris, on column-krater, ca. 470-460 B.C. from near Naples. New York, Metropolitan Museum, 15.27. Photo: courtesy the Metropolitan Museum of Art, Rogers Fund, 1915.

93. Plastic vase in form of conjoined heads of Negro and satyr from same mold, fourth century B.C. New York, Metropolitan Museum of Art, 06.1021.204. Photo: courtesy the Metropolitan Museum of Art, Rogers Fund, 1906.

94. Dancing Negro woman and satyr, participants in a dance with a phlyax and menads, a scene from an askos from Ruvo, Apulian, ca. 380-360 B.C. Ruvo, Collection Jatta, 1402. Photo: from A. Furtwängler and K. Reichhold, *Griechische Vasenmalerei,* Series II, Plates (Munich 1906) plate 80, no. 4.

95a–c. Scenes from Kabeiric skyphoi. Athens, National Museum, Ap. 12547, 427, and 10425. Photos: courtesy National Museum, Athens.

96. Mitos, Krateia, and Pratolaos on Kabeiric skyphos. Athens, National Museum, AP. 10426. Photo: courtesy National Museum, Athens.

97a–b. Non-Greek, perhaps Negroid Aphrodite and Hera, in scene on Kabeiric skyphos. Boston, Museum of Fine Arts, 99.533. Photos: courtesy the Museum of Fine Arts, Boston.

98. Life-sized terra-cotta mask, perhaps from Sicily, mid-fourth century B.C. London, British Museum, D361. Photo: courtesy the Trustees of the British Museum.

99. Small terra-cotta Roman mask, first century B.C. Rome, Villa Giulia Museum, 52393. Photo: courtesy Soprintendenza alle Antichità dell'Etruria Meridionale, Roma.

100. Terra-cotta statuette of phlyax, Hellenistic, from Taranto. Taranto, Museo Nazionale, I.G.4077. Photo: Carrano Gennaro and courtesy Soprintendenza alle Antichità della Puglia, Taranto.

101. Terra-cotta statuette of a juggler from Thebes. East Berlin, Staatliche Museen, 8327. Photo: courtesy Staatliche Museen, East Berlin.

102. Bronze of a dancer(?), Hellenistic, from Carnuntum. Bad-Deutsch-Altenburg, Museum Carnuntinum, 11949. Photo: H. Kral and courtesy Museum Carnuntinum, Bad-Deutsch-Altenburg.

103. Bronze statuette of a dancer, Hellenistic, from Erment, Egypt. Baltimore, Walters Art Gallery, 54.702. Photo: courtesy the Walters Art Gallery.

104. Bronze dancer from Herculaneum, Hellenistic. Naples, Museo Nazionale, 5486. Photo: courtesy Soprintendenza alle Antichità della Campania, Napoli.

105. Scene of dancing and clapping from a marble relief from Ariccia, early second century A.D. Rome, Museo Nazionale 77255. Photo: courtesy Gabinetto Fotografico Nazionale, Roma.

106. Hellenistic terra cotta of an athlete, perhaps a boxer, from J. Sieveking, *Die Terrakotten der Sammlung Loeb,* II (Munich 1916) plate 84.

107. Acrobat poised on crocodile, Roman after an Hellenistic original. London, British Museum, 1768. Photo: courtesy the Trustees of the British Museum.

108. Bootblack in bronze, ca. 460 B.C. London, British Museum, 1676. Photo: courtesy the Trustees of the British Museum.

109. Bronze of a worker pulling a cable(?), Alexandrian. Paris, Bibliothèque Nationale, 1010. Photo: courtesy Bibliothèque Nationale, Paris.

110. Laborer standing among vines and working an Archimedean screw with his feet, terra cotta, after 30 B.C. London, British Museum, 37563. Photo: courtesy the Trustees of the British Museum.

111. Lamp-bearer in bronze, Roman. Budapest, Museum of Aquincum, 51344. Photo: courtesy Museum of Aquincum, Budapest.

112. Standing bronze figure from Reims, Roman. Saint-Germain-en-Laye, Musée des Antiquités Nationales, 818. Photo: courtesy Musée des Antiquités Nationales, Saint-Germain-en-Laye.

113. Terra-cotta lantern-bearer from Egypt, early Empire. Alexandria, Graeco-Roman Museum 23100. Photo: courtesy Graeco-Roman Museum, Alexandria.

114. Young reveler attended by a slave carrying a lantern, from Alexandria, terra cotta, after 30 B.C. London, British Museum, 37561. Photo: courtesy the Trustees of the British Museum.

115. Life-sized marble bust of an ambassador or hostage, Flavian period. Rome, Villa Albani, 209. Photo: courtesy Deutsches Archäologisches Institut, Rome.

116. Life-sized white marble statue of an actor or singer of the second century A.D. from the vicinity of Naples. Naples, Museo Nazionale. Photo: courtesy Soprintendenza alle Antichità della Campania, Napoli.

117. Black diorite or marble statue of a bath attendant or *Isiacus,* Hellenistic, from Aphrodisias. Versailles, Gaudin Collection. Photo: courtesy Professor Kenan T. Erim, New York University.

118. Dark Isiac cultists from Herculaneum wall painting, Neronian age. Naples, Museo Nazionale, 8924. Photo: Alinari, 12035.

119. Isiac scene from Herculaneum fresco. Naples, Museo Nazionale 8919. Photo: Brogi (no. 14311) — Art Reference Bureau.

120a–b. Black marble head (bust modern) of a woman (front and profile), second half of second century A.D. Naples, Museo Nazionale, 6428. Photos: courtesy Soprintendenza alle Antichità della Campania, Napoli.

Blacks in Antiquity: Ethiopians in the Greco-Roman Experience

Abbreviations

AJA	*American Journal of Archaeology*
AJP	*American Journal of Philology*
Apophth. Patrum	*Apophthegmata Patrum*
AthMitt	*Mitteilungen des deutschen archäologischen Instituts, Athenische Abteilung*
CCL	*Corpus Christianorum, Series Latina*
CIG	*Corpus Inscriptionum Graecarum*
CIL	*Corpus Inscriptionum Latinarum*
CJ	*Classical Journal*
CP	*Classical Philology*
CSEL	*Corpus Scriptorum Ecclesiasticorum Latinorum*
GCS	*Die griechischen christlichen Schriftsteller der ersten drei Jahrhunderte*
GGM	*Geographi Graeci Minores*
JEA	*Journal of Egyptian Archaeology*
JHS	*Journal of Hellenic Studies*
JRS	*Journal of Roman Studies*
Karanòg	*Karanòg: The Romano-Nubian Cemetery*
Kush	*Kush: Journal of the Sudan Antiquities Service*
MGH	*Monumenta Germaniae Historica*
MonPiot	*Monuments et mémoires publiés par l'Académie des Inscriptions et Belles-Lettres, Fondation Piot*
PG	*Patrologiae Cursus Completus, Series Graeca*
PL	*Patrologiae Cursus Completus, Series Latina*
PFlor	*Papiri fiorentini, documenti pubblici e privati dell'età romana e bizantina*
RE	Pauly-Wissowa-Kroll, *Real-Encyclopädie der classischen Altertumswissenschaft*
REG	*Revue des études grecques*
REL	*Revue des études latines*
Sammelb.	*Sammelbuch griechischer Urkunden aus Ägypten*
SHA	Scriptores Historiae Augustae

I. The Physical Characteristics of Ethiopians – the Textual Evidence

The Greeks and Romans knew a great deal about the physical features of the peoples whom they called Ethiopians. Their writers described the Ethiopian type in considerable detail. From the hands of their artists we have received an even more copious evidence which shows in a vivid manner the racial characteristics of many Ethiopian inhabitants of the Greco-Roman world. Hence, it is surprising that modern scholarship has virtually ignored Greek and Roman anthropological knowledge of the Ethiopian. E. E. Sikes and C. Kluckhohn, for example, comment on the absence of biological racism and of color prejudice among Greeks and Romans, yet cite little of the available data in support of their observations.[1]

A failure to relate both archaeological and literary materials and to use the total evidence has at times resulted in questionable conclusions as to Greco-Roman attitudes toward the physical characteristics of Ethiopians. In a recent study of Greeks and barbarians, for example, A. Dihle postulated for classical antiquity a "child-psychological theory" which regarded black skin as unpleasant and a widespread popular belief which discredited the black man's color. Such a conclusion does not seem to be supported even by Agatharchides' statement that fear of Ethiopians ceases at childhood, and is much more questionable in light of the total Greco-Roman image of the Ethiopian, which includes numerous examples of the classical attitude toward the Ethiopian's color. W. den Boer has rightly questioned such an analysis and has concluded that, as far as the study's observations on skin-color are concerned, modern views have vitiated the interpretation and have attributed anachronistically to antiquity a nonexistent racial discrimination.[2] Further, some scholars have interpreted as caricature or as evidence of a penchant for the ugly the portrayal of Negroes which obviously reflected either the aesthetic interest of the artist or the scientific curiosity of a period.[3] Although we know from art Ethiopians who might well be described as *Aethiopes capillati*[4] (long-haired), scholars, who should have looked to art or anthropology for assistance, have excogitated fanciful explanations of this phrase. Or, to say that one should not expect to find Negroes in Carthage because the races of northern Africa were totally distinct from Negroes of central Africa[5] ignores the literary and archaeological evidence which demonstrates clearly that Negroid types lived not only in sub-Egyptian Africa but also in various other parts of the Greco-Roman world. To determine more precisely, therefore, what physical types the Greeks and Romans had in mind by the use of the word Ethiopian, a detailed examination of the literary and archaeological materials is essential.

Greek and Roman Descriptions of Ethiopians

The color of the skin. Color was obviously uppermost in the minds of the Greeks and Romans, whether they were describing Ethiopians in the land of their origin or their expatriated congeners in Egypt, Greece, or Italy. The distinguishing mark of an Ethiopian was the color of his skin. Though not unaware of other physical characteristics of the Ethiopian, the Greeks and Romans classified as Ethiopians those having in common a certain pigmentation which they attributed to environment, especially the heat of the sun.[6]

Ethiopians were the yardstick by which antiquity measured colored peoples. The skin of the Ethiopian was black, in fact blacker, it was noted, than that of any other people.[7] Indians were dark or black but not all of them to the same extent as Ethiopians. Herodotus mentions some Indians who resembled the Ethiopians in color.[8] The Indians whom Alexander visited were said to be blacker than the rest of mankind with the exception of the Ethiopians.[9] Indians south of the Ganges were described as browned by the sun but not so black as Ethiopians, whereas northern Indians resembled Egyptians.[10] The Asphodelodes, an African people conquered by a lieutenant of Agathocles at the end of the fourth century B.C., were described as similar to the Ethiopians in color. The practice of using an Ethiopian yardstick by which to judge dark peoples was perhaps reflected also in Leucaethiopes and Melanogaetuli, names which have been interpreted as suggesting mixed peoples of Ethiopian descent.[11] Ethiopians were most frequently selected to illustrate blackness of color. Mention is made, for example, of a flower as dark as an Ethiopian and of tanning the skin until it resembles an Ethiopian's.[12] The prominence of color in the Greek and Roman view of Ethiopia and Ethiopians bears a resemblance to a somewhat similar emphasis on color appearing in the later French usage of *l'Afrique noire* and *les noirs.*

The most common Greek words applied to the Ethiopian's color were μέλας and its compounds — μελάμβροτος and μελανόχροος.[13] αἰθαλοῦς, κελαινός, and κυάνεος were also found.[14] In Latin the adjective most frequently used for this purpose was *niger.*[15] Used also were *ater, aquilus, exustus* (*perustus*), *fuscus,* and *percoctus.*[16] νυκτίχροος and *nocticolor* (night-colored) also appeared as equivalents of the various adjectives used to describe the Ethiopian's color.[17]

Though describing Ethiopians as black or dark, the ancients recognized that these peoples differed in pigmentation and took considerable pains to record the observed differences. Ethiopians may have looked alike to Philostratus[18] but not to most Greeks and Romans. Even Philostratus himself described Memnon as not really black because the pure black of his skin showed a trace of ruddiness.[19] When Statius spoke of red Ethiopians, he was perhaps revealing the accuracy of the Roman's knowledge of the Ethiopian type. Negroes of a red, copper-colored complexion are known among African tribes.[20]

Some Ethiopians were obviously an intense black and much darker than others. The Acridophagi (locust-eaters), for example, were described by Agatharchides and by Diodorus as exceedingly black.[21] The peoples who inhabited the regions about Meroë, according to Ptolemy, were deeply black in color and were pure Ethiopians.[22]

The Romans developed a variety of ways to express degrees of Ethiopian blackness. An intense black was denoted in Plautus by the intensive *per-*, which Lucretius also used in his description of black men south of Egypt, thoroughly baked by the sun.[23] The superlative indicating intensity of blackness was applied to auxiliaries who, according to Frontinus, were employed by the

Carthaginians in their encounter with Gelon of Syracuse.[24] A deep black was described in a series of images in which Martial celebrated a lady "blacker than night, than an ant, pitch, a jackdaw, a cicada."[25]

Philostratus observed that as one proceeded south of Egypt up the Nile one found that the inhabitants were darker. Those dwelling near the boundaries between Egypt and Ethiopia were not completely black but were half-breeds as to color, in part not so black as Ethiopians but in part blacker than Egyptians.[26] Interesting in this connection is the Barberini mosaic at Palestrina depicting Egyptian landscape and the Nile in flood. The figures in the foreground are whites, while hunters on a mountain at the top of the mosaic, representing the southernmost figures up the Nile, are blacks.[27]

In their comments on the gradations of color observable among Ethiopians, the ancients did not overlook the changes in color resulting from racial mixture between blacks and whites. The child of a white mother and an Ethiopian father was *decolor* (*discolor*). These two words were often used to describe the skin-color of the peoples of India and Mauretania. Hence, the Roman usage of these words to describe children born of Ethiopian and white parents suggests that the children of such unions resembled in color the lighter Indians and Mauretanians. In other words, such black-white crosses were neither *nigri* nor *fusci*, adjectives applied to Ethiopians, but *decolores*, corresponding perhaps to modern usage of the word "mulattoes."[28]

In light of the importance the ancients attached to the color of the skin as a means of classifying the Ethiopian, it is not surprising to find that μέλας, *niger*, and similar words denoting blackness were often used interchangeably with or as the equivalent of Αἰθίοψ or *Aethiops*. Several references to the descendants of black-white racial mixture either indicate clearly or imply that μέλας was used as the equivalent of Αἰθίοψ.[29] A similar usage is suggested in a passage describing the slaying of Antilochus by the Ethiopian Memnon, who, according to Philostratus, seemed to inspire terror among the Achaeans by the novelty of his race, since before Memnon's time black men were myth only.[30] Memnon was described in some instances as *Memnon Aethiops* and as *Memnon niger* in others.[31] Paralleling an antithesis common in the contrasted white and Negro heads of Janiform plastic vases, frequent racial contrasts between white northerners and black

Ethiopians also point in the direction of an "Ethiopian-black" equivalence.[32] Such an equivalence appeared also in the notes of scholiasts and lexicographers.[33]

It is clear, therefore, that both μέλας and *niger*, and perhaps *fuscus* at times, were used as equivalents of Ethiopians. Such a usage raises the question of the extent to which these adjectives, either when used singly or when accompanied by significant anthropological details, designated Ethiopians. In some cases the context leaves no doubt as to the intent of an author.[34] In view of the frequency of a proved "Ethiopian-black" equivalence, however, adjectives denoting black, even in the absence of other evidence, must have indicated Ethiopian extraction. Pausanias, for example, was perhaps making a "white-Ethiopian" contrast of the type referred to above when he described a figure of a woman holding in her right arm a white and in her left arm a black child — a portion of the design on the chest of Cypselus, the tyrant of Corinth.[35]

Blackness and the Ethiopian, therefore, were in many respects synonymous. The Ethiopian's blackness became proverbial and gave rise to the expression Αἰθίοπα σμήχειν, "to wash an Ethiopian white." Lucian used the proverb in an illustration of the futility of advice to the ignorant book-collector on the proper use of books: counsel is wasted, or in the words of the proverb, efforts are as futile as an attempt to wash an Ethiopian white.[36] It is apparent that the paroemiographers used the expression frequently of unending or futile labors.[37] A similar view is expressed in the Aesopic fable concerning the Ethiopian who was vigorously washed and scrubbed to no avail — a demonstration that nature does not change.[38] The inseparability of the Ethiopian and his color was used allegorically by the early Christians. The virtuous life of the black Father Moses of the desert of Scetis was a demonstration that the proverb Αἰθίοπα σμήχειν can be reversed.[39]

Other physical characteristics of the Ethiopian. Although color of the skin, we have seen, was the feature most frequently used to identify dark peoples known as Ethiopians, the Greeks and Romans were obviously not unaware of other physical characteristics of Ethiopian types. As early as Xenophanes, the first European known to apply to Ethiopians a physical characteristic other than color, the flat nose of the Ethiopian was subject of comment.[40] Though noting the Ethiopian's blackness, Agatharchides, without supplying details, observed that the Ethiopian differed from the Greek in external appearance.[41] The idea that a white man could "pass for" an Ethiopian merely by blackening his body was ridiculed, for, Petronius pointed out, artificial color would only dirty the body without altering it. A complete Ethiopian disguise would require thick lips, curled hair, cicatrices on the forehead, and bowlegs.[42]

The majority of the Ethiopians, especially those who dwelt along the Nile, according to Diodorus, were black-skinned, flat-nosed, and woolly-haired.[43] Scybale, the only helpmate of the rustic Simylus, was "African in race, her whole figure proof of her country — her hair tightly curled, lips thick, color dark, chest broad, breasts pendulous, belly somewhat pinched, legs thin, and feet broad and ample."[44] One version of the life of Aesop described the fabulist as Ethiopian — black, flat-nosed, and with protruding lips.[45] These three notices, together with the above-cited Petronian requirements for a complete Ethiopian disguise, provide somewhat detailed descriptions of the blacks known to the Greeks and Romans.

The hair of the Ethiopian evoked considerable comment. In the language of the Greeks, Ethiopians were ulotrichous, their woolly hair at times described as thick.[46] The black skin of the Ethiopian, it will be recalled, was used as a norm for judging the skin of other dark peoples; a similar normative use was made of the Ethiopian's hair. The Ethiopians of Libya were the most ulotrichous of all men.[47] Southern Indians resembled the Ethiopians a great deal except that they were not so flat-nosed or woolly-haired.[48] Like the color of his skin, the Ethiopian's hair was explained by climate. The curliness of his hair, for example, was described as the result of crookedness caused by heat, in the same way as bowlegs resulted from distortion by heat.[49] The woolly hair of the Ethiopian was frequently contrasted with the straight hair of whites.[50] Herodotus found the only difference between the eastern and Libyan Ethiopians to be in the straight hair of the former and the woolly hair of the latter.[51]

In describing the Ethiopian's hair the Roman employed greater variety than the Greek, who used only one word, οὖλος (woolly).[52] This may mean either that the authors of the Latin descriptions were acquainted with a wider variety of Ethiopian types than the Greeks or that the Romans were attempting to describe more accurately what they saw. At any rate, Scybale had tightly curled hair ("torta comam")[53] as did the Ethiopians ("aliter tortis crinibus")[54] present at the opening of the Colosseum. Cleopatra's dark-skinned attendants were described similarly ("pars sanguinis usti / torta caput").[55] One commentator observed that to "convert" non-Ethiopian to Ethiopian hair a curling iron was necessary.[56] Pliny the Elder, on the other hand, mentioned Ethiopians with frizzly hair ("capillo vibrato"),[57] and Petronius spoke of long-haired Ethiopians ("Aethiopes capillati").[58]

Flatness of nose was apparently so pronounced in one tribe of Ethiopians as to justify the designation *Simi.*[59] The platyrrhiny of the Ethiopian, like his color and his hair, was the norm for anthropological comparisons. Regarding beauty as relative, Sextus Empiricus noted that the Ethiopian preferred the blackest and most flat-nosed; the Persians, the whitest and the most hook-nosed.[60] Arrian observed that Southern Indians were not so flat-nosed as Ethiopians.[61] The everted lips of certain types received notice in a few instances. One account characterized Aesop's lips as protruding or prominent (πρόχειλος).[62] Ethiopians were twice described as "puffy-lipped."[63]

The legs of Ethiopians were described by some as thin, by others as bandy. One account attributed the bandy-legs of Ethiopians and Egyptians to the heat and explained that bodies are distorted by heat just as logs of wood, when dry, are warped.[64] Two sources commented on the breasts of Ethiopian women. The author of the *Moretum* describes Scybale as *iacens mammis*, "with breasts low lying," and Juvenal asks "Who in Meroë would marvel at a woman's breast bigger than her fat infant?"[65]

Summary of Greek and Roman Anthropological Observations on the Ethiopian

Frequent references to color indicate that the word Ethiopian designated persons of varying degrees of blackness. Furthermore, the association of various combinations of other physical characteristics with the Ethiopian suggests that the Greeks and Romans were describing at least two types of people whom anthropologists today would classify as subtypes of the Negroid race. Even if we lacked the evidence of art, it would be clear from classical texts alone that such Negroid types were well known to the Greeks and Romans and were referred to as Ethiopians.

Traits of the Negroid race in their most marked form appear in a subtype that anthropologists have designated as the "true" or "purest" type of African Negro. This group possesses, among others, these characteristics: color varying from reddish-brown to deep brownish-black; tightly curled and wiry hair described as woolly, frizzly, or kinky; a broad, flattened nose; thick lips, usually puffy and everted; prognathism, often marked in the subnasal region.[66]

Another subtype of Negro known to the ancients apparently resembled a group described variously by anthropologists as Nilotic, Hamitic, or Nilo-Hamitic (designated hereafter as Nilotic).[67] This type is black or bluish-black in color, has reduced prognathism (often absent), less platyrrhiny, and lips probably less thick or everted than in the "true" Negro, with hair, according to M. J. Herskovits, ranging from less tightly curled to almost straight, and with long narrow faces. Acquaintance with such a type is suggested particularly by certain observations on the hair, such as Herodotus' distinction between straight-haired eastern and woolly-haired Libyan Ethiopians and by Roman references to frizzly or long-haired Ethiopians as distinct from Ethiopians with tightly curled hair.[68] Furthermore, certain references to color or to color and hair of Ethiopians, without mention of lips and nose or of either, may mean that the commentators did not consider the nose and lips worthy of anthropological notice. In other words, though dark in color and woolly or frizzly-haired, certain persons described as Ethiopian were perhaps not so flat-nosed and thick-lipped as other Ethiopians. Such individuals may have been a subtype of Negro resembling the so-called Nilotic Negro or the descendants of a black-white cross.[69]

Anthropologists note that the Negroid race includes the tallest groupings of mankind as well as pygmies. The Greeks and Romans were also acquainted with these extremes. The Ethiopians against whom Cambyses sent troops were, Herodotus tells us, the tallest men in the world.[70] One group of Ethiopians, the Syrbotae, was reputed to have been some twelve feet in height—obviously an exaggeration, but no doubt based, like the Herodotus statement, on a knowledge of extremely tall Ethiopians.[71] The many references to pygmies in ancient literature and the frequent depiction of pygmies in classical art are evidence of acquaintance with this type.[72]

The description of the woman in the *Moretum* provides the most complete, single anthropological portrait of a Negro in classical literature. Eight physical characteristics are mentioned, all of which are noted by modern anthropologists in classifications or discussions of the African Negro. The author of the *Moretum,* who described Scybale, would be rated today as a competent anthropologist. His portrait of a Negro woman bears a striking resemblance to modern summaries of the outstanding features of the Negroid division of mankind. Table A compares the Negroid characteristics appearing in the *Moretum* and as listed by two modern anthropologists.

The author of the *Moretum* did not include all the features mentioned by the two moderns with whom he has been compared. He did not, for example, mention the flat nose which was noted in some ancient descriptions.[73] No classical writer refers to prognathism (unless protruding or prominent lips imply subnasal prognathism[74]) or gives details of bodily structure except mention of the height of certain Ethiopians. It must be kept in mind, however, that the author of the *Moretum* was writing poetry, not anthropology. And what he included is good anthropology; in fact, the ancient and modern phraseology is so similar that the modern might be considered a translation of the ancient.

Except for the omission of anthropometric data, certain descriptions of the Ethiopian parallel modern classifications of the Negro in a most remarkable way. In noting the color of the Ethiopian's skin, the ancients, like the anthropologist, used skin-color as the most important distinguishing criterion. Though even the anthropologist of today experiences great difficulty in attempting to deal with color scientifically, the ancients, by calling attention to gradations of color in Ethiopians, anticipated the moderns who have pointed out that the color of African Negroes ranges from an intense black to a light yellow.[75] The ancients did not overlook the form of the Ethiopian's hair, and in so doing used a basis most frequently employed for a primary classification of present-day human groups. The only form of lip that is racially distinctive is the Negro's — a fact that did not escape the notice of Greek and Roman commentators. All but one of the physical characteristics which the ancients included in descriptions of Ethiopians appear in modern classifications of the Negro. Al-

Table A. A comparison of the Negro as described in the *Moretum* and by two modern anthropologists

Traits	*Moretum*[a]	*E. A. Hooton*[b]	*M. J. Herskovits*[c]
Color	Dark color ("fusca colore")	Integument rich in color	Reddish-brown to deep brownish-black
Hair	Tightly curled hair ("torta comam")	Tiny curls	Hair wiry, tightly curled and lying close to the scalp
Lips	Puffy lips ("labro tumens")	Thick lips (Hooton elsewhere uses the terms puffy and everted)	Lips thick
Shoulder or pectoral area	Broad chest ("pectore lata")	Omitted	Broad shoulders
Waist	Belly somewhat pinched ("compressior alvo")	Omitted	Narrow waist
Legs	Thin legs ("cruribus exilis")	Thin legs	Arms and legs slender and long in proportion to stature
Feet	Broad and ample feet ("spatiosa prodiga planta")	Flat feet	Omitted
Breasts	Pendulous breasts ("iacens mammis")[d]	Omitted	Omitted
Other	Omitted	Wide noses, narrow heads, round foreheads, protruding jaws and receding chins, integument poor in hairy growth	Broad nostrils, high cheekbones; prognathous faces, with an acute facial angle; short stocky build and heavily muscled, triangular shaped torso

[a] 31-35.
[b] Hooton, *Ape* 619-620 in listing the outstanding features of the specialized Negroid division of mankind.
[c] Herskovits, *Negro* 193 in a description of the characteristics of the true Negro.
[d] J. H. Lewis, *Biology* 77 mentions the accentuated breasts in African women.

though anthropologists describe the legs of Negroid types as thin and their calves as poorly developed, I have found no mention of a trait that seems to correspond to what some ancients described as "bandy-legged."[76]

Afer, Indus, and Maurus as Equivalents of Aethiops

Although Αἰθίοψ or *Aethiops* is by far the most common generic word which the Greeks and Romans used to designate a Negroid type, *Afer* (African), *Indus* (Indian), and *Maurus* (Moor) are at times obviously the equivalents of *Ethiopian*. The *Moretum* passage uses *Afra* of a woman about whose racial identity there can be no doubt.[77] This usage of *Afra* is evidence that *Afer*, which generally indicates African or Libyan origin, may refer also to a racial type that is unquestionably Negroid.[78] In spite of a common ancient confusion between east and south, both Vergil and Ovid seem to have applied *Indi* to Ethiopians, that is, African Negroes. The former refers to the Nile pouring down from the colored Indians; the latter, to Perseus' bringing Andromeda from the black Indians. *Ab Indis*, appearing in both cases at the end of a dactylic hexameter, seems to be a poetical tag, a convenient substitute for an intended *Aethiopibus*, metrically unsuited.[79]

Mauri was also used at times both as a poetical equivalent of *Aethiopes* and as a broad term which included Ethiopians. S. Weinstock notes that the meaning of *Mauri* is not sufficiently clear and considers impossible the association which some ancients made between *Mauri* and the color of the people or the words for black.[80] Manilius, for example, says that Mauretania received its name from the color of its inhabitants.[81] Further, Isidore preserves a similar tradition and adds that the Greeks designated *nigrum* by μαῦρον.[82] Martial's *retorto crine Maurus*,[83] a phrase clearly suggesting the kinky or frizzly hair associated with the Negro, however, and perhaps Juvenal's *nigri . . . Mauri*[84] provide classical corroboration of a tradition which Weinstock rejects. Claudian speaks of all the Moorish tribes ("omnes Maurorum . . . populos") who lived beneath Atlas and of those whom the excessive heat of the sun cut off in the interior of Africa.[85] Early Christian literature, as Den Boer has emphasized, also uses μαῦρος in the sense of *Ethiopian*.[86] Most pertinent in this connection is the phrase Αἰθίοπα μαῦρον ὡς ἡ ἀσβόλη (an Ethiopian black as soot), which has the proverbial force of the classical Αἰθίοπα σμήχειν.[87] Further, a sixth-century A.D. papyrus from Hermopolis pertaining to the sale of a Μαύρα, a twelve-year-old girl, seems to point to the practice of equating Μαῦρος and Αἰθίοψ.[88] In short, the Greeks and Romans on occasion grouped colored peoples together loosely on the basis of color and, ignoring certain other physical characteristics, used *Maurus* as a comprehensive term for various colored peoples of Africa; and from the first century A.D. onwards at times also used *Maurus* as an equivalent of *Aethiops*.

The Names of Ethiopians

A consideration of nomenclature is also pertinent for whatever light the names borne by Ethiopians may throw on the question of physical characteristics. Conclusions as to racial identity or provenance based on nomenclature, however, must be reached with the greatest caution. In some cases, for example, there may be no relation between the name of a slave and his provenance.[89] Further, names denoting color such as *Niger*, *Fuscus*, and *Melas*, type of hair such as *Iras*, or shape of nose such as *Simus*, although sometimes perhaps given to Ethiopians by their masters, by no means necessarily implied Ethiopian extraction and may have referred only to the spread of physical characteristics observable in white races.[90] In addition, just as today Mr. Blackman may be a white man and Mr. White a black man, the same was true in the ancient world. Finally, it should be noted that the descendants of Ethiopian-white unions in the second or third generation would in many instances be physically no different from Greeks and Romans and, hence, names such as *Aethiops*, *Niger*, or *Iras* would not be applicable.[91] The Greeks and Romans had no category such as "sociological Negroes," that is, whites defined as Negroes because of one Negro great-great grandparent, regardless of the number of white ancestors, nor did they establish "Negroes" as defined in the laws of some southern states.[92]

In spite of a much needed caution in the examination of Ethiopian nomenclature, there are certain patterns observable in classical antiquity with respect to the names of Ethiopians. Evidence suggests that some slaves received from their masters names related to their physical characteristics. Nigra, whose appeal is celebrated in a Pompeiian graffito, and perhaps Julia Nigra, appearing on a tombstone of a Negro woman near Carthage, seem to point to such a practice.[93] Martial speaks of Marsus' dark ("fusca") Melaenis.[94] The epigrammatist's flippant comment on black ("nigra") Chione's frigidity may point to the practice of giving humorously the name of white or snow to blacks.[95] St. Jerome records a similar custom when he notes that it was common practice to call Ethiopians silver boys.[96] Iras, one of Cleopatra's faithful women who remained with her to the end, was no doubt an Ethiopian whose woolly hair was responsible for her name (Εἰράς), for Lucan tells us that among Cleopatra's attendants were some who had black skins and woolly hair.[97]

On the basis of the Greco-Roman usage of *Aethiops*, we may safely assume that bearers of that cognomen were of a physical type denoted by that word. That Meroë should have been given as a name to some Ethiopian slaves is what would be expected in light of the importance of the Ethiopian capital of the same name. Such a practice is suggested by an epigram in which Ausonius referred to a tippler who received her name Meroë, not from the black color of those born in Nile-washed Meroë, but from her capacity to consume pure wine, unmixed with water.[98] Although the Meroë in question may have owed her name to a capacity for imbibing her drinks straight, there is no reason to doubt that other Meroës were so named because of their black color and origin in Nilotic Meroë. The association of *Afer* and *Maurus* with unquestionably Negroid types suggests that the cognomina *Afer* and *Maurus*, though frequently given to non-Negroid types, might also have been used of Ethiopians. An interesting commentary on *Maurus* as a cognomen for dark persons is found in Ausonius' observation that his grandmother was given the name Maura by her childhood friends because of her dark complexion.[99] Neither *Afer* nor *Maurus*, however, should be equated with *Aethiops* unless there is additional evidence in support of such an identification.

In addition to names related to physical characteristics and provenance, our sources have preserved a few Egyptian, Hebrew, and Ethiopian names.[100] And finally, as with other foreigners in the Greco-Roman world, Ethiopians carried Greek or Latin names, although those preserved in texts and papyri that can be identified with reasonable certainty are by far predominantly Greek, with only a few Latin names extant. An appendix at the end of this chapter gives a list of names illustrating the practices mentioned above. Although some names are obviously fictive, they are included for whatever light they throw on Ethiopian nomenclature.

Summary of Criteria for Determining Whether a Given Passage Refers to a Negroid Type

In consideration of the Greek and Roman acquaintance with the Negroid type as revealed by the literary evidence, and in view of the use of the word Ethiopian, it is reasonable to assume that a given passage refers to a Negroid type in the following instances:

(1) whenever the word Αἰθίοψ or *Aethiops* is used, with the knowledge, however, that the word comprehended different Negroid types — (a) the "true" or "purest" type of African Negro, with Negroid traits in their most marked form; (b) the Nilotic or mixed type with less pronounced characteristics, such as reduced prognathism and platyrrhiny, and with hair ranging from less tightly curled to almost straight; and (c) modifications thereof — differences in pigmentation and various combinations of Negroid physical characteristics;

(2) whenever a consideration of the evidence indicates that *Afer*, *Indus*, or *Maurus* is the equivalent of *Aethiops;*

(3) whenever μέλας and *niger* (*fuscus*) are used as the equivalent of Αἰθίοψ and *Aethiops;*

(4) whenever an individual is designated as belonging to one of several Ethiopian tribes such as Blemmyes, Megabari, Troglodytes, Nubae, et cetera;

(5) whenever a passage mentions two or more of the physical characteristics included by modern anthropologists in their classification of Negroes;

(6) whenever contextual or other evidence indicates that an Ethiopian or Negroid type is intended.

Appendix to Chapter I: Names of Ethiopians in the Greco-Roman World

The usages employed with respect to names borne by Ethiopians permit a classification of several categories. In light of the caution necessary in the treatment of names, a brief explanation of the reasons for inclusion is provided in each case. The list includes only those names which meet the criteria I have suggested as valid for assuming that a given passage either designates or may refer to a Negroid type.

Names related to physical characteristics.

Chione — the practice of naming Ethiopians by opposite physical characteristics, Martial 3.34.1-2.[1]

Iras — a reference to the woolly hair of Cleopatra's faithful servant, Plutarch *Antonius* 85.4, and Lucan 10.131-132, who describes some of Cleopatra's attendants as *pars sanguinis usti / torta caput;* W. Pape, *Wörterbuch der griechischen Eigennamen*[3] (Brunswick 1863-1870) s.v. Εἰράς.

Melaenis — described as *fusca*, Martial 7.29.8.

Nigra — Nigra, *CIL* IV 6892, and perhaps Julia Nigra, *CIL* VIII 19888.[2]

Names related to provenance.

Aethiops — the most common generic word denoting a Negroid type: ai-ti-jo-qo (Aithiops), one of the landowners mentioned several times in the Pylos tablets (for a discussion of this ai-ti-jo-qo see Chapter III and n. 6); Aethiops, a spendthrift from Corinth, associated with the founding of Syracuse, Archilochus, T. Bergk, *Poetae Lyrici Graeci*[4], II (Leipzig 1882) *Frg.* 145 [126]

p. 428, and Athenaeus 4.167d (see Chapter III for a discussion of this Aethiops); and Aethiops of Ptolemaïs, one of the pupils of Aristippus of Cyrene, Diogenes Laertius 2.86.

Afer — the evidence of the single, most detailed anthropological description of a Negroid type from classical antiquity: Publius Terentius Afer and Helpis Afra, a name appearing in a Pompeiian graffito (*CIL* IV 2993zγ).[3]

Meroë — the suggestion of Ausonius that Ethiopians were named after the capital city of Nubia, *Epigrammata* 41.9-10.

Ethiopian, Egyptian, or Hebrew names.

Abratoi — who visited Philae on behalf of his father, the Ethiopian king in 260 A.D., *CIG* IV 4915 C (p. 1224); F. Ll. Griffith, *Catalogue of the Demotic Graffiti of the Dodecaschoenus*, vol. I, text (Oxford 1937) 11, 116, 118; D. Dunham, *The Royal Cemeteries of Kush*, vol. IV, *Royal Tombs at Meroë and Barkal* (Boston 1957) 3.

Amasis — appears as Amasis or Amasos on vases of Exekias depicting Negro attendants of Memnon (W. Technau, *Exekias* [Leipzig 1936]) = no. IX of *Bilder griechischer Vasen* edited by J. D. Beazley and P. Jacobsthal, nos. 23b and 26a. C. Dugas "Note sur l'origine d'Amasis et de quelques peintures de vases," *Mélanges Gustave Glotz* I (Paris 1932) 336-337 states (1) that Amasis, as his exotic name suggests, was not Athenian but Egyptian or half-Egyptian, perhaps the son of a Greek settler in the Delta and of an Egyptian woman, whose features revealed his ancestry and (2) that Exekias by placing the name Amasis above Ethiopians was humorously referring to his rival's mixed blood and caricaturing him as a Negro. J. Boardman, "The Amasis Painter," *JHS* LXXVIII (1958) 1-3, and *The Greeks Overseas* (Penguin Books 1964) 169, pointing out that Amasis was a common name in Egypt and that Amasis (Boardman is inclined to regard Amasis as potter-painter) was a metic, a swart or dusky-skinned descendant of a Greek and Egyptian woman and brought up most likely in Naucratis, questions Dugas's contention that Exekias was humorously giving the name Amasis to the two Negroes on his vases and suggests that Exekias surely had in mind his swart Athenian rival as well as Amasis, the king of

Egypt. Since Exekias gave the name Amasis to the Negroes he depicted, there is no reason to doubt that Negroes were named Amasis, a Grecized form of an Egyptian name. If Exekias, as Dugas and Boardman argue, is referring also, either humorously or otherwise, to Amasis, the allusion may indicate that he was not merely swart or dusky-skinned as Boardman suggests but Negroid. Cf. M. Robertson, *Greek Painting* (Geneva 1959) 67.

Aron — whose name, designated as Νουβα(ῖος), appears in the temple of Philae, from the Christian period, J. Kraus, *Die Anfänge des Christentums in Nubien* (Mödling 1931) 117.

Charachen — a "basiliskos" of the Blemmyes of perhaps the sixth century A.D., L. Mitteis and U. Wilcken, *Grundzüge und Chrestomathie der Papyruskunde* I (Leipzig and Berlin 1912) no. 7, pp. 13-14 and F. Bilabel, ed., *Sammelbuch griechischer Urkunden aus Ägypten* [hereafter abbreviated as *Sammelb.*] III (Berlin and Leipzig 1926) no. 6257. See Chapter V and n. 57.

Chello — a Nubian, from Upper Egypt under Ptolemy IV (221-205 B.C.), W. Spiegelberg, "Demotische Kleinigkeiten," *Zeitschrift für ägyptische Sprache und Altertumskunde* LIV (1918) 115.

Ela Atzbeha (Ellatzbaas, Hellestheaeus, Elesboas) — king of the Axumite Ethiopians, who, with the aid of ships supplied by Justin I, defeated Dhu Nuwas, who had been persecuting the Himyarite Christians; for sources and details, see Chapter IX.

Harmais — a Blemmys (?), from Apollinopolis Magna, 220/219 B.C., son of Harpaêsis and Wen-ese, W. Spiegelberg, *Die demotischen Papyri Hauswaldt* (Leipzig 1913) no. 6; for blacks in the Ptolemaic period, see F. Heichelheim, *Die auswärtige Bevölkerung im Ptolemäerreich, Klio,* supplementary volume XVIII (Leipzig 1925) 66-67, 85.[4]

Harwoj — brother of Pasan (*infra* s.v. *Pasan*) and like him "a great ambassador of Rome," F. Ll. Griffith, *Catalogue of Demotic Graffiti,* Philae no. 416.

Hôros — a native of Philae, born in Egypt, mentioned in an agreement for sale of land, considered to be an Ethiopian, 115-108 B.C., F. Ll. Griffith, *Catalogue of the Demotic Papyri in the John Rylands Library, Manchester* III (Manchester and London 1909) no. XXIII.

Khensthoüt — a Blemmys, born in Egypt, from Pathyris, 152

B.C., son of Harpaêsis and Tshenpuêr, F. Ll. Griffith, *Demotic Papyri, Manchester* III no. XVI.

Malêwitar — "chief envoy of Rome," known from a stele at Faras, F. Ll. Griffith, *Meroitic Inscriptions* pt. II [Napata to Philae and Miscellaneous] (London 1912) 54-55, no. 129.

Moses — a black Ethiopian Father of the desert of Scetis, who died at the end of the fourth or in the first years of the fifth century; for sources on the life of Father Moses, see Chapter IX.

Pasan — son of Paêse, an ambassador sent by Teqērideamani, perhaps a Meroïtic king, to Roman authorities, 253 A.D. F. Ll. Griffith, *Catalogue of Demotic Graffiti*, Philae no. 416.

Sales — designated as a Trogodyte[5] in a papyrus account of records and expenditures, 257 B.C., W. L. Westermann and E. S. Hasenoehrl, ed., *Zenon Papyri: Business Papers of the Third Century B.C. Dealing with Palestine and Egypt*, Columbia Papyri, Greek Series, no. 3, I (New York 1934) no. 5.

Sarapion — a Trogodyte, an assistant of a prefect, ca. 146 A.D., A. S. Hunt, ed., *The Oxyrhynchus Papyri* VIII (London 1911) no. 1102, 24-25.

Silko — "basiliskos of the Nobades and all the Ethiopians," a Christian who defeated the Blemmyes about 545 A.D., *CIG* III 5072, W. Dittenberger, ed., *Orientis Graeci Inscriptiones Selectae* (Leipzig 1903) I, no. 201; see Chapter V.

Sophonias — whose name, designated as Νουβα(ῖος), appears in the temple of Philae, from the Christian Period, J. Kraus, *Die Anfänge* 117.

Greek or Latin names.

Amyntas — preference for a dark Amyntas (*fuscus*) is explained by noting that violets and hyacinths are black, Vergil *Eclogues* 10.37-39.

Antonius — designated in a papyrus as a Trogodyte, F. Preisigke, *Sammelb.* I (Strasbourg 1915) no. 282.

Aphrodite — designated as ἡ Αἰθιόπισσα in an ostracon from Upper Egypt of uncertain Ptolemaic date, P. Viereck, ed., *Ostraca aus Brüssel und Berlin* (Berlin and Leipzig 1922) no. 16, p. 12.

Apollonios — one appearing in a list of soldiers (second century B.C.) found in Egypt (Dimê) in which two soldiers of the same name are mentioned, one designated as μέλας and the other as λευκός, B. P. Grenfell and A. S. Hunt, ed., *The Amherst Papyri*, pt. II (London 1901) no. LXII, 6-7; another — an interpreter of the Trogodytes, of the Roman period from Thebes, 134 A.D., U. Wilcken, *Urkunden der Ptolemäerzeit* (*Ältere Funde*) II (Berlin 1957) 296-297, no. 227.

Atalous, also called Eutychia — a twelve-year-old slave girl described as Μαύρα sold by Ethiopian slave-dealers, sixth century A.D., F. Preisigke, "Ein Sklavenkauf des 6. Jahrhunderts," *Archiv für Papyrusforschung* III (Leipzig 1906) 415-424, esp. 419, 11.36-38.

Cypassis — fusca Cypassis, a slave girl and rival of Ovid's Corinna, Ovid *Amores* 2.8.

Didyme — whose black beauty is praised by Asclepiades in *Anthologia Palatina* 5.210 (I.232 Loeb).

Epitynchanon — a black (χροιὴν . . . μελάντερος) slave from the land of Ethiopia, whose epitaph appears in a Greek inscription from Antinoë in Egypt, third century A.D., C. Schmidt, "Eine griechische Grabinschrift aus Antinoë," *Aegyptiaca: Festschrift für Georg Ebers* (Leipzig 1897) 100, J. Geffcken, *Griechische Epigramme* (Heidelberg 1916) no. 371; W. Peek, *Griechische Grabgedichte* (Berlin 1960) no. 420.

Eurybates — the herald of Odysseus, described as black-skinned (μελανόχροος) and woolly-haired (οὐλοκάρηνος), two physical characteristics of importance in identifying the Ethiopian or Negroid type, Homer *Odyssey* 19.246-248.[6]

Glycon — a *tragoedus* of Nero's time, three of whose racial characteristics — dark color, lower lip, and height — suggest Ethiopian or Negroid extraction: "staturae longae, corporis fusci, labio inferiore demisso," *Scholia ad Persium* 5.9, ed. E. Kurz (Burgdoff 1889).

Helenos — designated as Αἰθίοψ and mentioned three times in Zenon collection from 257-249 B.C. *Sammelb.* III 6783, 4; *Papiri greci e latini* (*Pubblicazioni della Società Italiana per la Ricerca dei Papiri Greci e Latini in Egitto* V (Florence 1917) 503, 3; C. C. Edgar, *Zenon Papyri* in (*Catalogue général des antiquités égyptiennes du Musée du Caire*) I (Cairo 1925) 59087, 3-4, and III (Cairo 1928) 59326, 173-174; *id.* IV (Cairo 1931) 59782 (a), 69, described as a lamp-bearer.

Helix — designated as Αἰθίοψ in a papyrus of the Roman

period (268 A.D.) from Hermopolis Magna, G. Vitelli, ed., *Papiri fiorentini, documenti pubblici e privati dell'età romana e bizantina* I (Milan 1905) no. 50, 94 [hereafter abbreviated *PFlor*].

Lycoris — Lycoris, who is described as blacker (*nigrior*) than a falling mulberry, Martial 1.72.5.

Memnon — a very appropriate name for an Ethiopian particularly since Memnon in Roman times was considered black and Ethiopian: a bust of a Negro (Fig. 73) has been regarded as that of Memnon, a pupil of Herodes Atticus; P. Graindor, "Tête de nègre du Musée de Berlin," *Bulletin de correspondance hellénique* XXXIX (1915) 402-412 and *Un milliardaire antique: Hérode Atticus et sa famille* (Cairo 1930) 114-116 = *Université égyptienne, Recueil de travaux publiés par la Faculté des Lettres*, fasc. 5. Recent confirmation of Herodes Atticus and his favorites came to light in discoveries at the estate of Atticus in Kephissia, where busts of Atticus himself and of another favorite, Polydeukes, were found together with an arm in black marble, undoubtedly a part of a statue of Memnon; see E. Vanderpool, "News Letter from Greece," *AJA* LXV (1961) 299.

Menalcas — a black (*niger*) Menalcas is contrasted with a white (*candidus*) Alexis, with the warning that the white Alexis should not have too much faith in his color because white privets fall but black hyacinths are picked, Vergil *Eclogues* 2.15-18.

Nepheron — designated as Αἰθίοψ in a papyrus of the Roman period (268 A.D.) from Hermopolis Magna, *PFlor* I (Milan 1905) no. 50, 62.

Nicaeus — a boxer from Byzantium whose grandfather was Ethiopian, Pliny *Historia naturalis* 7.12.51.

Olympius — a celebrated *venator* from Egypt, whose exploits in the amphitheater and Carthage are praised, with several references to his black color, *Anthologia Latina* (ed. Riese) I (Leipzig 1894) nos. 353-354.

Pancrates — a temple-scribe from Memphis; although his color is not mentioned, four of his physical characteristics (height, nose, lips, and legs) noted in classical descriptions of the Negro type are included: "ἐπιμήκη, σιμόν, πρόχειλον, ὑπόλεπτον τὰ σκέλη" (tall, flat nosed, lips protruding, and with thin legs) Lucian *Philopseudes* 34.

Pannichus — a wrestler, whose flat nose and puffy lips ("sima nare, turgidis labris") suggest Ethiopian extraction, Martial 6.39.8-9.

Philaenion — Philodemus sings of the beauty of a Philaenion who is black (μελανεῦσα) and whose hair is more curled (οὐλοτέρη) than parsley, *Anthologia Palatina* 5.121 (Loeb 1.184).

Santra — a cook described by Martial as a Moor with tightly curled hair, Martial 6.39.6-7.

Scybale — a Scybale, her Negroid traits more fully described than those of any other single Ethiopian in Greek or Roman literature, the sole companion of Simylus, *Moretum* 31-35.

Theodosios — whose name, designated as Νουβα(ῖος), appears in the temple of Isis of Philae, from the Christian period, *CIG* IV 8948a; J. Kraus, *Die Anfänge* 117.

Thespesion — the president of the Gymnosophists, who blushed visibly in spite of the blackness of his complexion, reportedly visited by Apollonius of Tyana, Philostratus, *Vita Apollonii* 6.10, 12.

II. The Physical Characteristics of Ethiopians – the Archaeological Evidence

Complementing and confirming in a most vivid manner what the texts have to say about the physical characteristics of certain Ethiopians, classical art provides a century-by-century commentary on the meaning of Ethiopian. Art is in some respects more valuable than literature as a source of information for anthropological data because it tells us much that the texts do not about the amount of prognathism or its total absence, the extent of platyrrhiny and of lip-eversion, facial proportions, and form of hair. Though the numerous likenesses of Negroes are the work of artists and not of photographers, there can be little doubt that the Greeks and Romans were well acquainted with types we today call Negroes and that their artists have left us a rather accurate picture of the Negroid Ethiopians whom they saw in their daily life.

The extensive art corpus of Negroes from classical antiquity corroborates the accuracy of ancient commentators not only as to features frequently noted but as to details mentioned by only a few authors. Stone figures of the sixth century B.C. depicting Negroes with contracted waists (Fig. 1) may be early examples of a later type represented by a Negro woman described in the *Moretum* as "compressior alvo," (with belly somewhat pinched.)[1] The pendulous breasts of a Negro dancer (Fig. 2) in a scene painted on an Apulian askos (ca. 380-360 B.C.) throw light on the meaning of two extant observations on the breasts of Ethiopian women.[2] Petronius is the only classical author who mentioned cicatrices on the foreheads of Ethiopians. Worthy of note in this connection are the cicatrices in the form of three vertical incisions on each cheek appearing on a Roman terra-cotta head of a Sudanese woman (Fig. 3).[3] Details not mentioned in the texts are observable in art. The painter of a fifth-century B.C. red-figured pelike from Boeotia, contrasting, feature by feature, Heracles and the Negroid attendants of King Busiris, is obviously calling attention to the uncircumcised Heracles and the circumcised, macrophallic Ethiopians (Fig. 4).[4] Three rather steatopygic Negro women are among the participants depicted in a ceremony which has been associated with the festivals of Isis and Serapis (Figs. 5a–b, 105).[5] One Kabeiric vase depicts a pygmy with a fat stomach (Fig. 6), perhaps calling attention to a characteristic noted by modern anthropologists who describe the abdomen of African pygmies as protuberant.[6]

Long ago E. Babelon observed that a comparison of different classical monuments depicting the Negro would demonstrate that the ancients were portraying no uniform type. He believed that a comparative study would be interesting from an anthropological view and would result in the identification of different groups of Ethiopians and subdivisions of these groups.[7] Hence, the long history of the Negro in classical art must be examined for the light that it throws on certain physical types which the Greeks and Romans had in mind whenever they used the word "Ethiopian," and for a record of many Negroes seen at different periods on the streets of Alexandria, Athens, Rome, and elsewhere. The significance of the word "Ethiopian," unless supplemented by archaeological evidence, cannot be fully understood.

Although blacks appeared in Mediterranean art outside of Africa as early as Minoan times,[8] for a detailed study of the physical characteristics of certain types of Ethiopians as seen by Greek artists a beginning should be made in the sixth century B.C. Starting with this century we have sufficient representations of Negroes in enough detail to permit an accurate analysis of racial features. From the sixth century onwards until late in the Empire, for a period covering a span of nearly one thousand years, artists, using the Negro as a model in almost every medium and as a favorite in many, have bequeathed us a valuable anthropological gallery.

It was a pronounced Negro type which was most frequently represented in the art of the three centuries beginning with the sixth B.C. From this period there are only a few examples which would not be classified as the "true" or "purest" type of African

Negro. Black skin; tightly curled or woolly hair; broad, flattened noses; lips thick, often puffy and everted; prognathism, often marked in the subnasal region — these are the characteristics of most Negroes from the sixth century B.C. to Hellenistic times.

Cypriote stone figures found at Ayia Irini, dated about 560 B.C., represent Negroes with broad flat noses, full protruding lips, prominent chests, and somewhat contracted waists.[9] The following excerpt from a modern classification of the "true" Negro aptly describes certain aspects of these figures: "short and stocky, strongly built and heavily muscled, with triangular torso, broad shoulders and narrow waist."[10] A late sixth- or early fifth-century B.C. terra-cotta mask of a Negro (Figs. 7a–b), found at Agrigento, though its artist was following the canons of the archaic style, adumbrated the Negroid type depicted by artists from the sixth to the fourth centuries. The fidelity with which the artist of the Sicilian mask portrayed the extremely broad, flat nose, thick lips, pronounced subnasal prognathism, and short, tightly curled hair reveals a careful study of his model. Laver-handles decorated with heads of Negroes (Fig. 8) from Centuripe furnish another example of Negroid types with which Sicilian Greeks of the sixth century B.C. were acquainted.[11]

Vivid testimony of the Ethiopian known to the Greeks of the late sixth and early fifth centuries B.C. is provided by numerous plastic vases in the form of Negro heads. The physical characteristics of this group are markedly alike — deep black skin-color; tightly curled hair depicted by small, raised dots; receding foreheads; strong subnasal facial protrusion; and thick, puffy, and everted lips. Illustrative of the racial type depicted on the vases of this period is an Attic head-vase (Fig. 9) with cylindrical mouth attached to the head by two vertical handles.[12] A comparison of these heads with types designated today as Negro reveals an amazing similarity as to features. Among the Negro types included in Hooton's plates illustrating racial types is an American Negro who resembles these Negroes as to color, hair, receding forehead, nose, subnasal prognathism, lips, and type of chin.[13] A Shilluk from the Sudan, whom Carleton Coon provides as an example of the Congoid subspecies, also bears a striking resemblance to these Negroes of early Greek art.[14] A fifth-century B.C. terra-cotta head from Salamis (Fig. 10), shaped like a mask, is another interesting study of the physical features of a pronounced Negroid type.[15]

The first anthropological contrast of blacks and whites — Thracians and Ethiopians — is found in Xenophanes, a contrast that was later to appear frequently in a Scythian-Ethiopian commonplace and in the environment theory of the origin of racial differences.[16] It is not surprising, therefore, that a similar black-white contrast had a counterpart in early Greek art. By combining in Janiform vases the heads of whites and Negroes, the artists contrasted whites and blacks, feature by feature, and thus brought out effectively the physical differences as to color, hair, nose, lips, prognathism and the absence thereof. One of the earliest of these conjoined heads is a tiny faience ointment vase (late seventh century B.C.) made in Naucratis and found in Cyprus (Fig. 11). The vase juxtaposes a bearded barbarian and a Negro with flat nose, thick lips, and woolly hair represented by lozenge-shaped incisions, with a dot in the center of each.[17] Other Janiform heads are represented by a white-ground kantharos (ca. 510 B.C.) from Tarquinia (Figs. 12a–c); another head-vase, an aryballos (end of the sixth century B.C.) from Greece (Fig. 13); and a kantharos (ca. 480-470 B.C.) with conjoined heads of Heracles and a Negro (Fig. 14).[18]

Racial contrast was not limited to Janiform vases. The mysterious and romantic clash of color, which later fascinated Shakespeare in his portrayal of the Venetian girl and the dusky Moor, apparently appealed also to the Greek artist. Though the artist evidently saw the aesthetic value of racial contrast, he no doubt, like Xenophanes and the environmentalists, had a scientific interest in a "newly discovered" racial type. The artist who painted a woolly-haired, snub-nosed, prognathous archer between two Amazons (Figs. 15a–b) on a mid-sixth century B.C. black-figured neck-amphora, was certainly interested in a dramatic composition, but also in the racial traits of his subjects.[19] Much of anthropological significance can be derived from such compositions. A fifth-century B.C. alabastron, with a Negro warrior on one side and an armed Amazon on the other, contrasts the short, tightly curled hair of the Negro, represented by small black dots, and the long hair of the Amazon; the short, snub nose and thick lips of the one and the long, straight nose and thin lips of the other

(Figs. 16a–b).[20] Mention has been made above of a scene depicting Heracles and the Negroid attendants of Busiris.

Though their techniques differed from those employed by the producers of plastic vases, the early vase painters were also showing the "true" Negro. The painters at times very successfully give the effect of a mass of soft, woolly hair as in the case of the Negro in the scene with two Amazons mentioned above and of the kneeling Negro warrior, with a lance in his right hand and a shield in his left, depicted on the interior of a red-figured kylix of the period 520-500 B.C. (Fig. 17);[21] at times they represent the hair by painting black dots on white, especially on fifth-century B.C. alabastra (Figs. 16a, 80, 81); and, in the treatment of figures in profile, by separated tufts projected slightly from the head, a technique applied, for example, to the attendants of Memnon on two late sixth-century B.C. black-figured neck-amphorae (Figs. 18, 19).[22] The short, snub nose common in portrayals of Negroes in profile is obviously the artist's attempt to depict the broad, flat nose of the "true" Negro. Pronounced prognathism is noticeable in many of these vases. Illustrations of "true" Negroes in vase paintings of this period are numerous. Suffice it to mention further only the lively Negroes of the black-figured Caeretan hydria rushing to assist the captured Busiris (Fig. 20);[23] a heavily armed warrior raising his shield from the ground, appearing on a lekythos from Cumae painted in the so-called Six's Technique (Fig. 21);[24] a trumpeter employed in a shield design on a fifth-century B.C. red-figured amphora from Vulci (Fig. 22).[25] It was the "true" Negro also who was the subject, though less frequent, depicted on gems, pendants, coins, and tesserae of the fifth century B.C. Illustrative of such Negroes in miniature are a delicately wrought Negro woman on a fifth-century B.C. sard scarab (Fig. 23) and a pendant in the form of a Negro head hanging from a gold necklace from Canusium (Fig. 24). Even when working with Negroes on such a small scale, the artists were scrupulously faithful to the Negroes' racial features.[26]

In two vase paintings the hair of certain figures (a woman appearing in a grave scene on a fifth-century B.C. white-ground lekythos from Eretria (Figs. 25a–b), and the Ethiopians in an Andromeda scene on a fifth-century B.C. hydria from Vulci (Figs. 26a–b) with snub noses and thick lips differs from the usual woolly mass, dots, or tufts which characterize the Negroes of late sixth- and early fifth-century art.[27] The hair is longer than that usually found in Negroes of the period and may have resulted from the artist's intent to represent so-called frizzly hair, which, according to Hooton, is longer than woolly hair with its tightly coiled spirals. Hence, the artist's model may have resembled the Nilotic type of Negro, whose hair is less tightly curled, or a racial type in which there is a generous admixture of Negro.[28]

The late fifth and fourth centuries B.C. continue vivid studies of a pronounced Negro type. Plastic drinking cups in the form of Negro heads emphasize the physical characteristics in much the same manner as earlier vases, the chief difference being that the hair is now represented by raised spirals, somewhat similar in appearance to snail shells (Figs. 27a–b, 28).[29] To the fourth century B.C. belong several terra-cotta vases, some from Etruria, in which the platyrrhiny and prognathism are reduced, but the blackness of color, thickness of the lips, and hair in the form of raised spirals resemble somewhat these same features in the plastic cups just mentioned (Figs. 29–32).[30] In one south Italian (Apulian) plastic group of a Negro boy seized by a crocodile, the hair is suggested by black dots on a white background (Fig. 33).[31] An Apulian head-vase of a Negro from the second half of the fourth century B.C. or possibly later is a masterpiece of work in terra cotta (Figs. 34a–b).[32] A south Italian lekythos has preserved a charming profile head of a Negro whose tightly curled hair is represented by dots of black paint (Fig. 35).[33]

A group of vases — a few, products of the late fifth and fourth centuries B.C. — includes Negroes in scenes which have been interpreted as caricatures. In a skyphos, found in the sanctuary of the Kabeiroi near Thebes, Circe is depicted offering a cup to Odysseus (Fig. 36). The snub nose, subnasal prognathism, and thick lips of Circe are clearly Negroid. Similar physical features characterize other figures in Kabeiric skyphoi.[34] An interesting fourth-century study of a Negro from Boeotia is an askos in the form of a boy bent over to the ground (Fig. 37).[35] Another askos, in the form of a Negro seizing a goose, is also an example of the fourth-century concept of the Negro (Fig. 38).[36] Three concentric rows of Negro heads, increasing in size toward the rim, decorate a gold phiale of the late fourth century B.C., discovered in Bulgaria (Figs. 39a–b). Like the other artists of the fourth century, the craftsman who designed these heads portrayed a pronounced

Negroid type resembling peoples designated today as "true" Negroes.[37]

From the third century B.C. onwards, the artists portrayed a greater variety of Negroid types than had their predecessors. The less Negroid type appears frequently along with the "true" Negro. Negro terra cottas from Greco-Roman Egypt illustrate the variety of types that appealed to the artist (Figs. 40a–b). From an examination of the Negro terra cottas in the museum at Alexandria, for example, one receives a vivid impression of the wide variety of Negroid types who inhabited Alexandria, the Fayum, and Upper Egypt from the third century B.C. to the early centuries of the Christian era.[38] Such a variety derives in large part from the deepened interest of the Hellenistic artist in realism and the influence of this realism on the art of later periods. The question arises, however, whether the prominence of Negroid traits in their most pronounced form and the almost complete absence of the less Negroid types in the art of the earlier centuries mean that the types appearing in later art were less familiar to earlier Greeks. On the other hand, the earlier emphasis upon the extreme Negro type may have been the result of deliberate choice by artists of the sixth and fifth centuries, who, fascinated by a "newly discovered" race, ignored less Negroid types and established a vogue continued in the fourth century.

Although certain artistic conventions make precise racial classification difficult, the blacks of these later periods may be divided into at least three groups: (1) a type, like the so-called true or pure Negro, with Negroid traits in their most marked forms (Figs. 41a–59); (2) a type with less pronounced Negroid features explicable perhaps as resembling either the Nilotic Negro or a Negroid type with Caucasoid admixture (Figs. 60a–75); and (3) the pygmy (Figs. 76–77). The illustrations give examples of these three Negroid types and demonstrate vividly the wide variety within these types. These Negroes were obviously no stereotypes but individuals who were, if not actual models, at least common types known to the artist of the period. As to those whom I have classified in the first two groups, not all will agree. In practically every case, however, I have studied the original and I am convinced, on the basis of this study, that at least a dual classification is justified. Those who wish to make a more precise classification may compare the classical representations of Negroes with

L. Oschinsky's photographs of the Baganda and other East African tribes. Such a comparison shows in some instances marked similarities between the ancient Negroes and types which Oschinsky classifies as Bantomorph, Nilotomorph, Hamitomorph, Nilohamitomorph, Mulattomorph, Congomorph, Congomorph-Bantomorph, and Bambutomorph.[39]

Illustrations 1-77

1. Stone figures of Negroes from Ayia Irini, Cyprus, ca. 560 B.C.

2. A Negro participant in a dancing scene from an Apulian askos, ca. 380-360 B.C.

3. Terra-cotta head of woman with cicatrices, probably from the Fayum, Roman period.

4. Heracles and Negroid attendants of King Busiris, from a scene on a red-figured pelike, fifth century B.C.

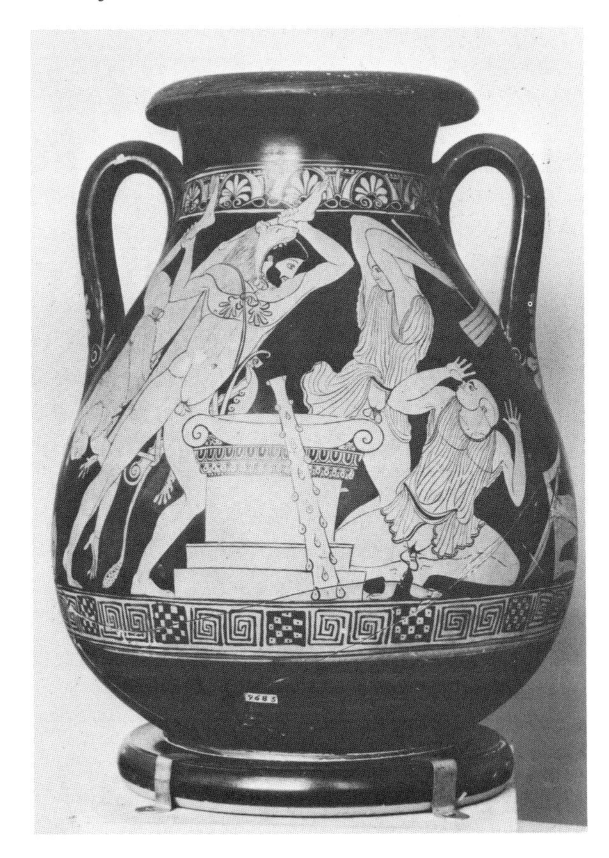

5. Steatopygic women on marble relief from tomb near Ariccia, early second century A.D.

6. Pygmy with protuberant stomach on Kabeiric skyphos.

7. Front and side views of a terra-cotta mask from Agrigento, late sixth century or early fifth B.C.

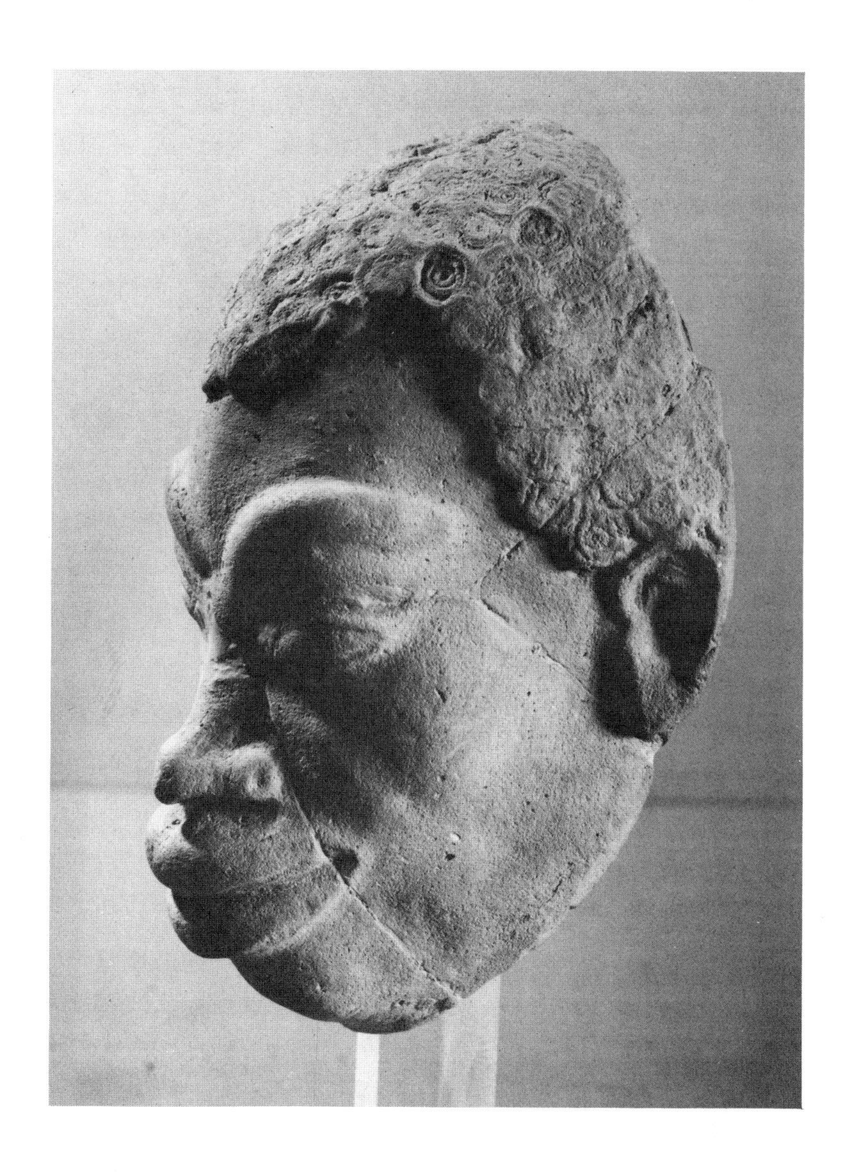

8. Laver-handles decorated with Negroes, from Centuripe, Sicily, sixth century B.C.

9. Attic head-vase, 6th-5th century B.C.

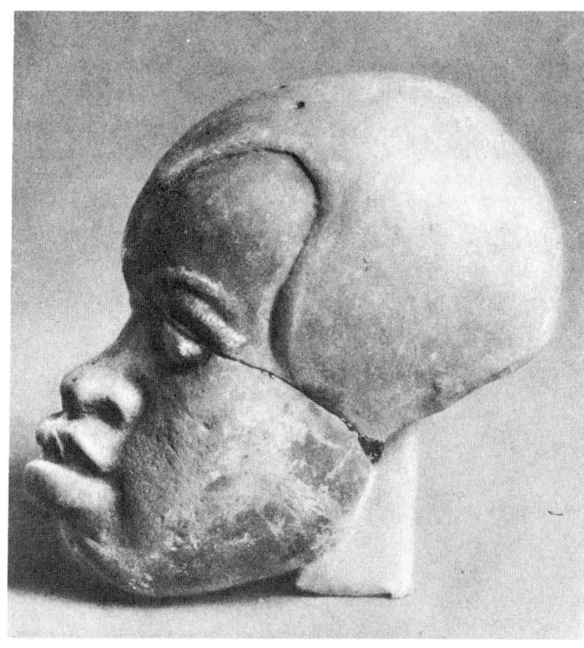

10. Mask-like terra-cotta head of a Negro from Salamis, fifth century B.C.

11. A faience vase in shape of Janiform heads of Negro and bearded barbarian from Cyprus, late seventh century B.C.

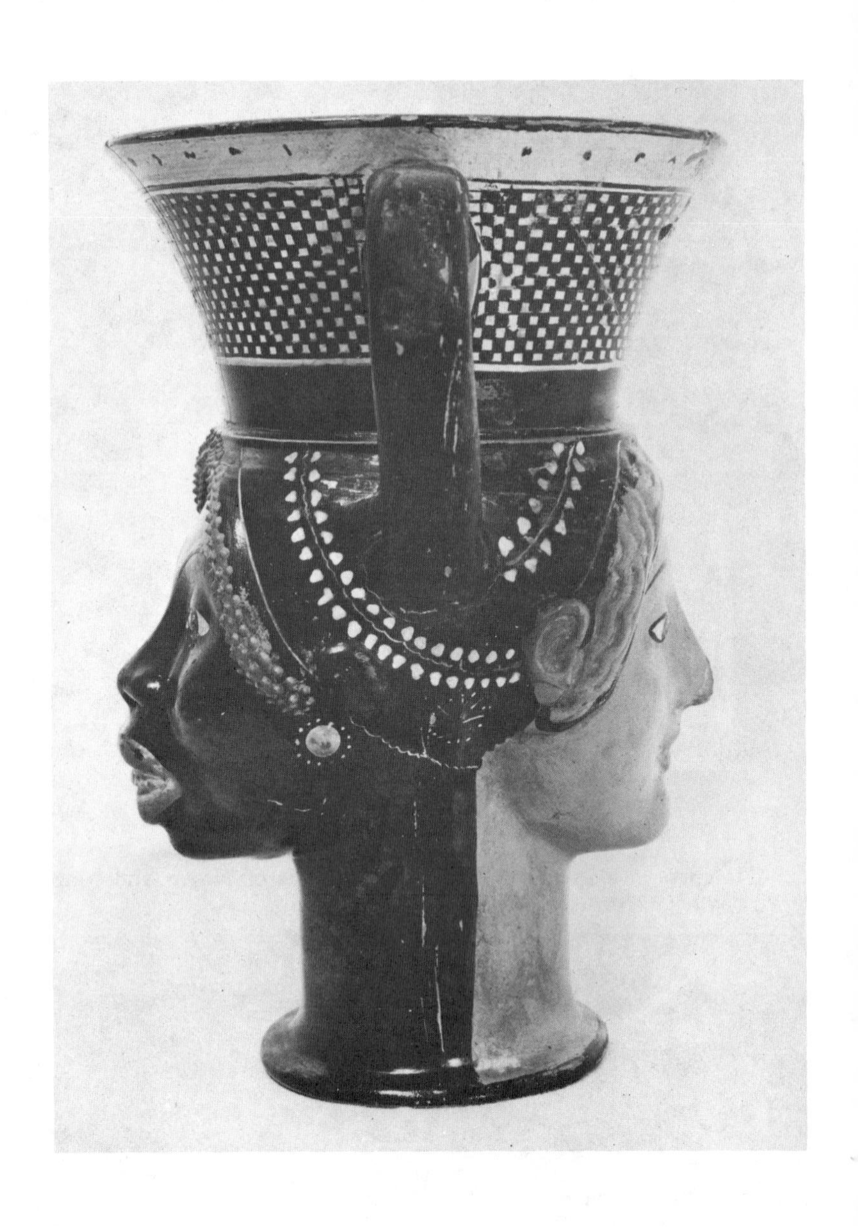

12. Side and front views of white-ground kantharos in shape of Janiform heads of a Negro and a white from Tarquinia, ca. 510 B.C.

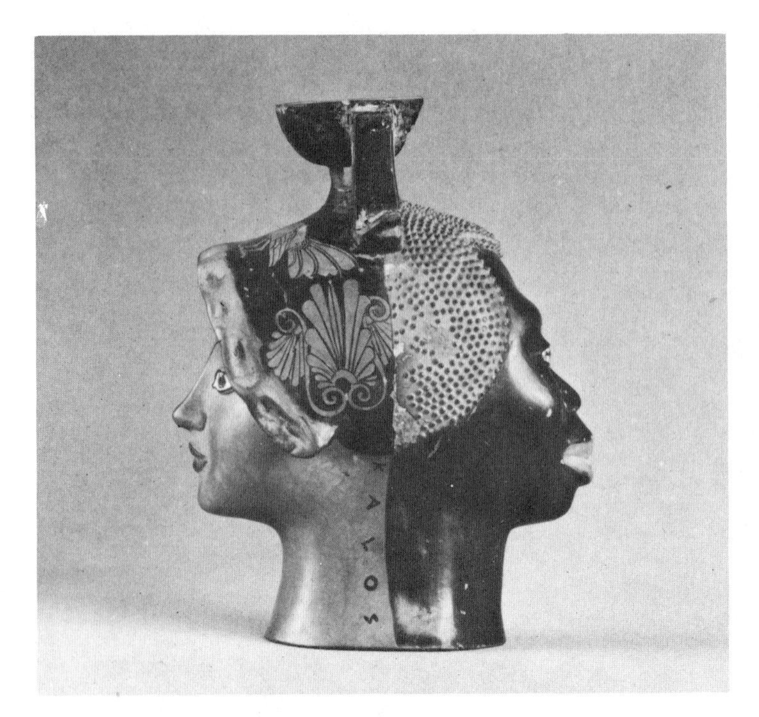

13. Aryballos in form of conjoined heads of a Negro and a white, end of sixth century B.C.

14. Front view of kantharos in form of conjoined heads of Heracles and a Negro, ca. 480-470 B.C.

15. Negro (Memnon?) and two Amazons in scene, black-figured neck-amphora and detail of the Negro, ca. mid-sixth century B.C.

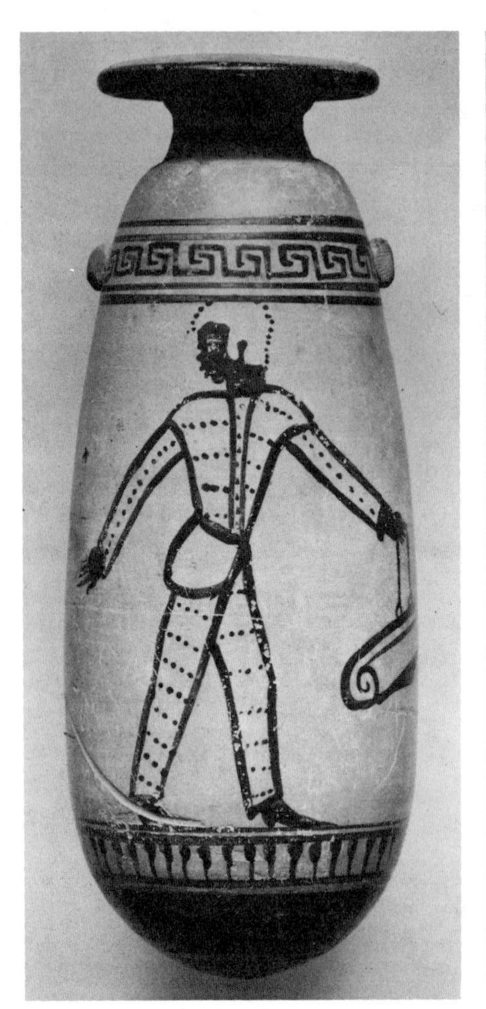

16. Negro and Amazon depicted on fifth-century B.C. alabastron.

17. Warrior on interior of red-figured kylix, from Poggio Sommavilla, ca. 520-500 B.C.

18. Detail of heads of Memnon and Negroes from black-figured neck-amphora, ca. 530 B.C.

19. Detail of one of Memnon's Negro companions from black-figured neck-amphora, ca. 540-530 B.C.

20. Soldiers coming to the assistance of King Busiris, scene from Caeretan hydria, ca. 530 B.C.

21. Warrior lifting shield from ground, from a polychrome lekythos in Six's style from Cumae.

22. Negroid trumpeter on shield of warrior from fifth-century B.C. red-figured amphora from Vulci.

23. Woman on sard scarab, fifth century B.C.

24. Gold ornament in form of a Negro head hanging from gold necklace from Canusium, ca. fifth century B.C.

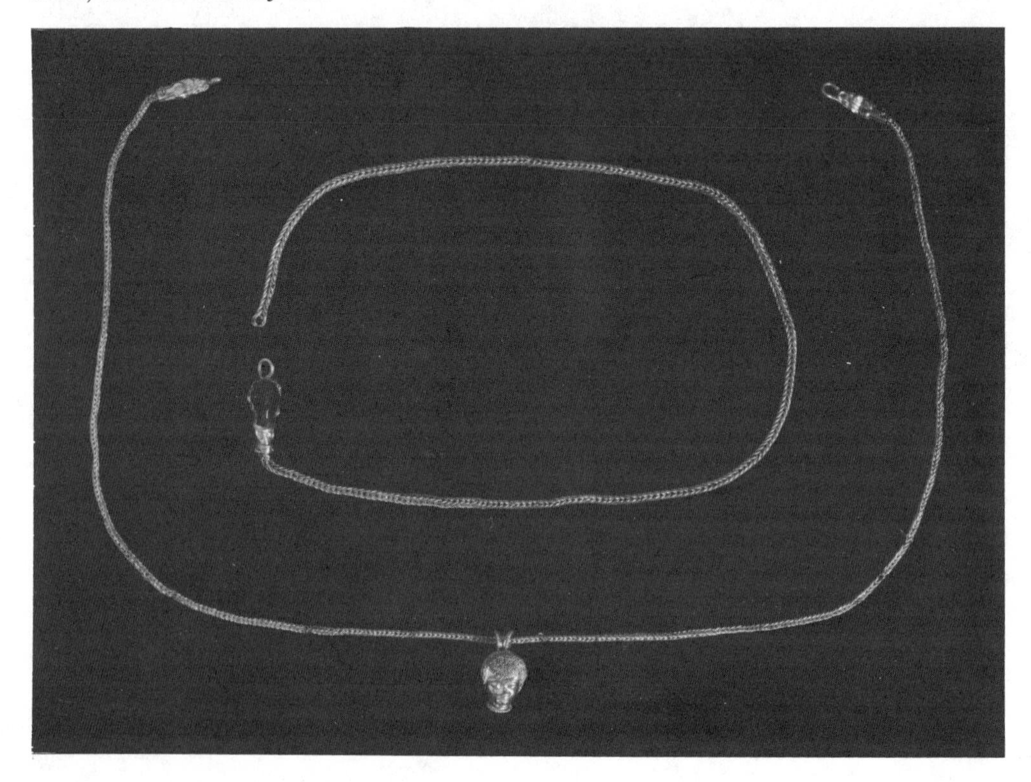

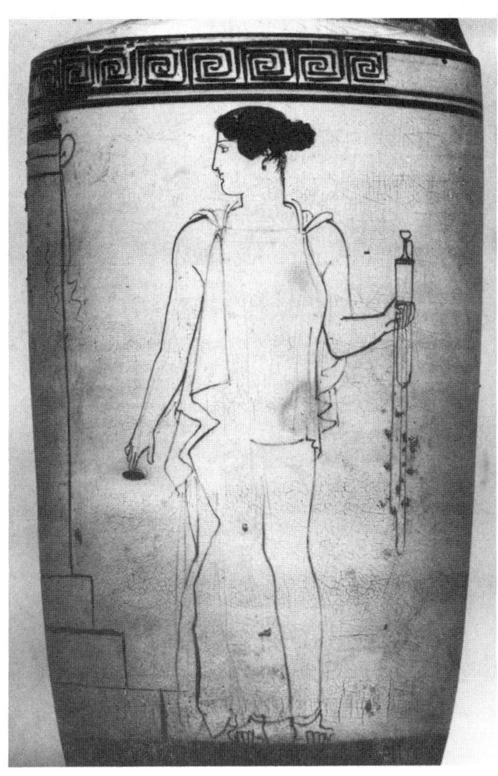

25. Negroid diphrophoros contrasted with white figure in a grave scene from a white-ground lekythos from Eretria, fifth century B.C.

26. Ethiopians in scene from Andromeda myth and detail of one of the Ethiopians on a red-figured hydria from Vulci, fifth century B.C.

27. Front and profile views of a vase in form of Negro's head from Vulci, fifth-fourth century B.C.

28. Vase in form of Negro's head, fifth-fourth century B.C.

29. Negro-head oinochoe, from near Viterbo(?), fourth century B.C.

30. Etruscan Negro-head mug, fourth century B.C.

31. Plastic Etruscan vase in form of Negro head, second half of fourth century B.C.

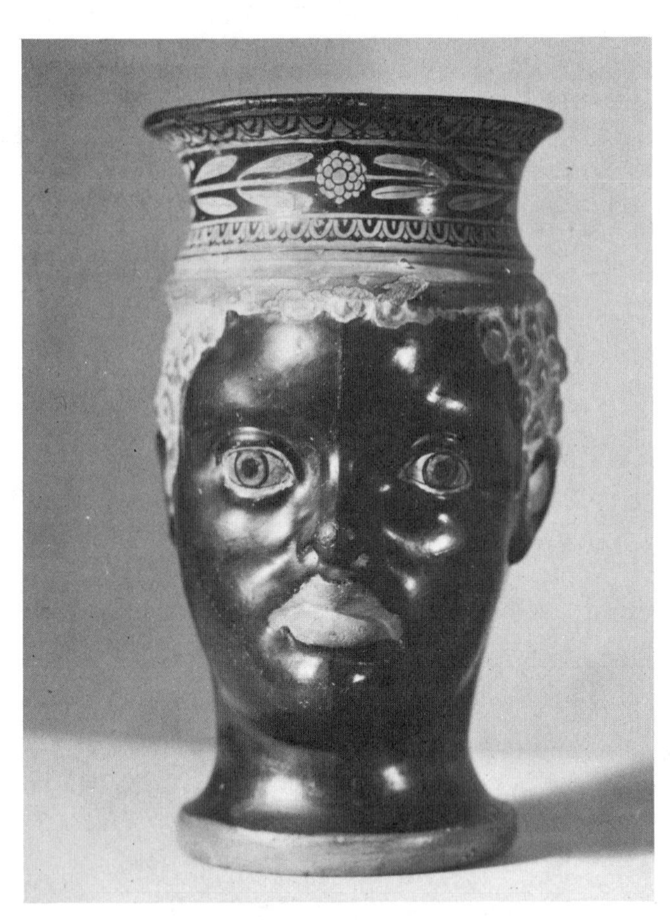

32. Etruscan vase in form of Negro's head, fourth century B.C.

33. Negro and crocodile, south Italian (Apulian).

34. Front and side views of Apulian head-vase, second half of the fourth century B.C. or later.

35. South Italian lekythos with profile of Negro head, fourth century B.C.

36. Negroid Circe and Odysseus on Kabeiric skyphos.

37. Askos in form of a boy bent over to the ground from Boeotia, fourth century B.C.

38. Askos in form of a boy seizing a goose from south Italy, fourth century B.C.

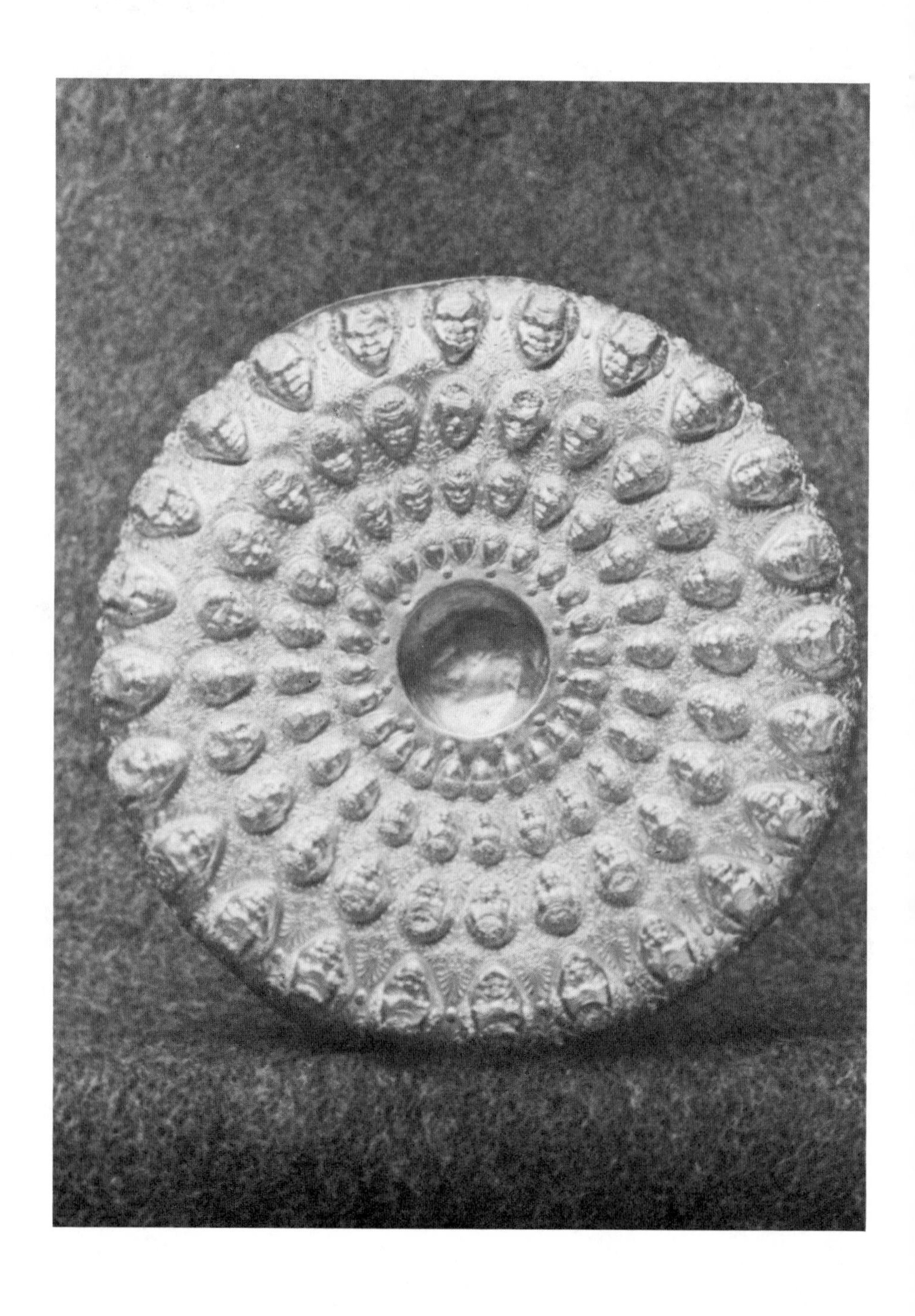

39. Gold phiale with concentric circles of Negro heads and detail from Panagurishte, middle of fourth century B.C.

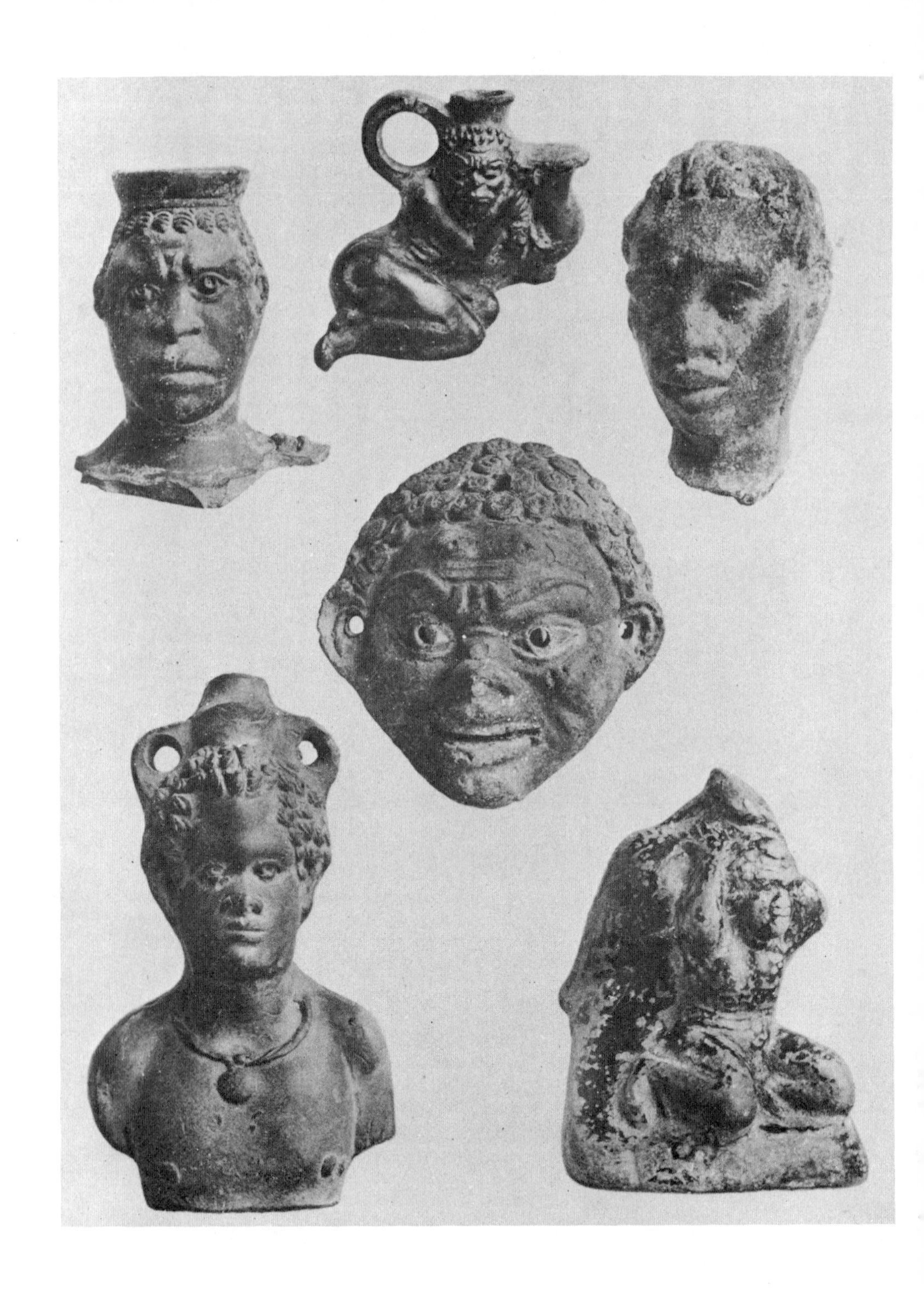

40. Terra cottas of Negroes from Egypt, largely Greco-Roman.

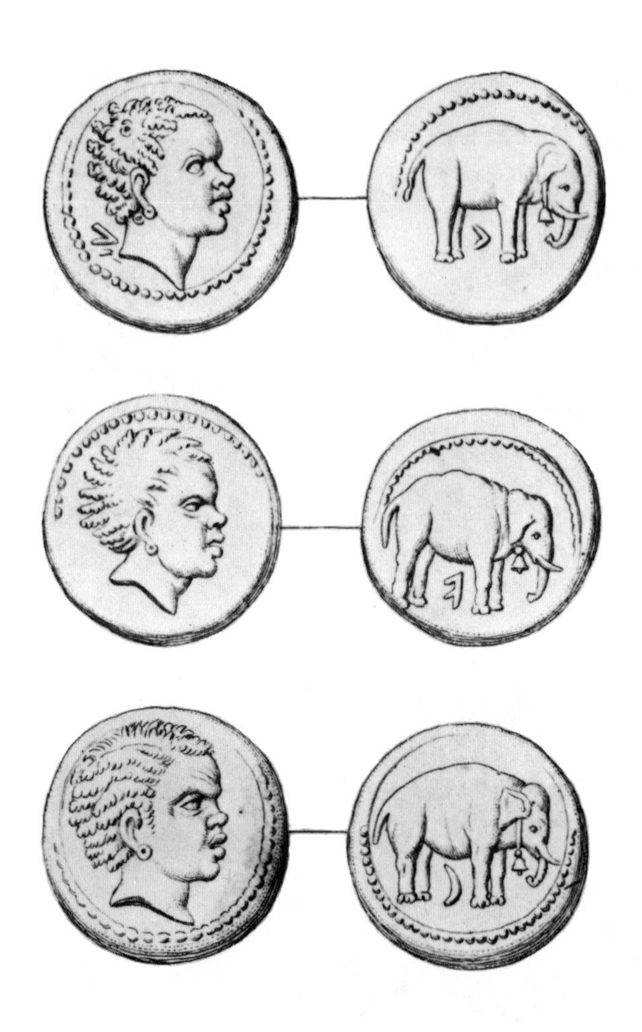

41. Bronze coinage from central Italy depicting some of Hannibal's mahouts—profile, hair frizzly, broad nose, thick, everted lips; C. T. Seltman, *Greek Coins: A History of Metallic Currency and Coinage down to the Fall of the Hellenistic Kingdoms* (London 1933) 250 and my chapter V.

42. Black steatite statuette of a crouched boy, perhaps a captive, Alexandrian — hair in rows of tight curls radiating from center of head, broad nose, high cheekbones, subnasal prognathism, thick lips.

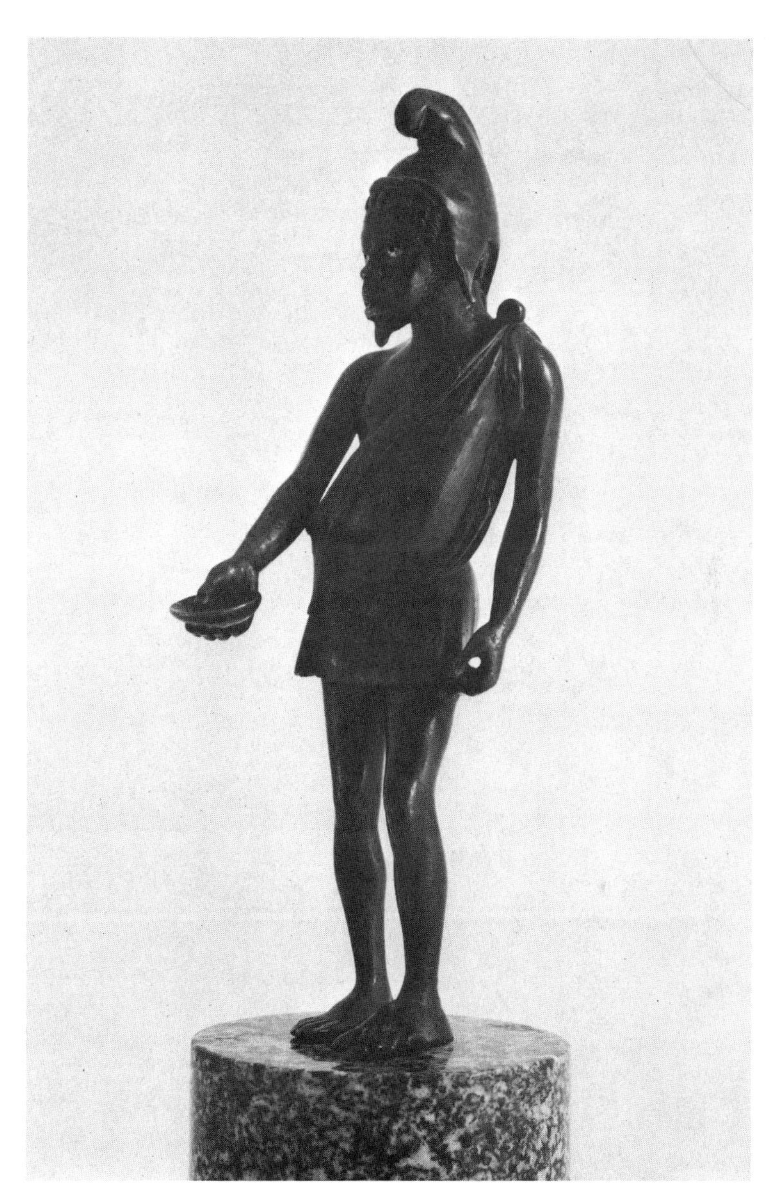

43. Bronze statuette of a beggar, Egypt, Alexandria (?) first century B.C.

44. Bronze statuette of a boy, Hellenistic — hair in long spiral curls close to head, very broad nose, rather thick lips. G. M. A. Richter, *Handbook of the Greek Collection,* The Metropolitan Museum of Art (Cambridge, Mass. 1953) 125, plate 104f.

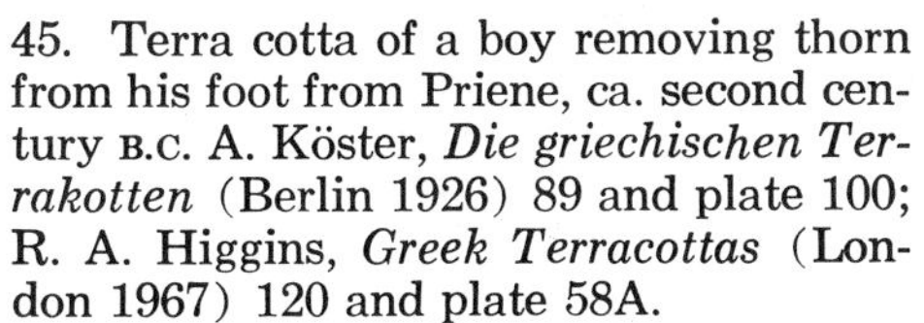

45. Terra cotta of a boy removing thorn from his foot from Priene, ca. second century B.C. A. Köster, *Die griechischen Terrakotten* (Berlin 1926) 89 and plate 100; R. A. Higgins, *Greek Terracottas* (London 1967) 120 and plate 58A.

46. Hellenistic terra cotta in the form of a Negro boy sleeping beside an amphora. *Ashmolean Museum Summary Guide Department of Antiquities*[4] (Oxford 1931) 90.

47. Limestone figure from Ptolemaic times. O. Koefoed-Petersen, *Egyptian Sculpture in the Ny Carlsberg Glyptothek*[2] (Copenhagen 1962) 36 and plate 52; cf. terra-cotta figurine representing a squatting, sleeping Negro boy (a rattle from a baby's grave in Corinth from time of Nero) — black clay varnished to produce glossy appearance of skin, tightly curled hair in a series of rows, broad nose, thick lips, T. L. Shear, "Excavations in the North Cemetery at Corinth in 1930," *AJA* XXXIV (1930) 429 and figure 19.

48. Bronze figure of a sleeping boy, perhaps a Hellenistic original. F. Poulsen, *Catalogue of Ancient Sculpture in the Ny Carlsberg Glyptotek* (Copenhagen 1951) 609, no. 16. For a study of this type of subject, see U. Hausmann, "Hellenistische Neger," *AthMitth* LXXVII (1962) 266-269 and figures 76-79.

49. Terra-cotta statuettes of boxers, late Hellenistic—tightly curled hair close to head, broad nose, thick lips. H. B. Walters, *Catalogue of the Terracottas in the Department of Greek and Roman Antiquities, British Museum* (London 1903) D-84 and D-85.

50. Marble relief of a charioteer from Herculaneum, ca. first century A.D. — profile, tightly curled hair close to head, broad, flat nose, thick lips, subnasal prognathism. A. Ruesch, *Museo Nazionale di Napoli* (Naples 1908) 167-168, no. 570; S. Reinach, *Répertoire de reliefs grecs et romains* III (Paris 1912) 94, no. 1.

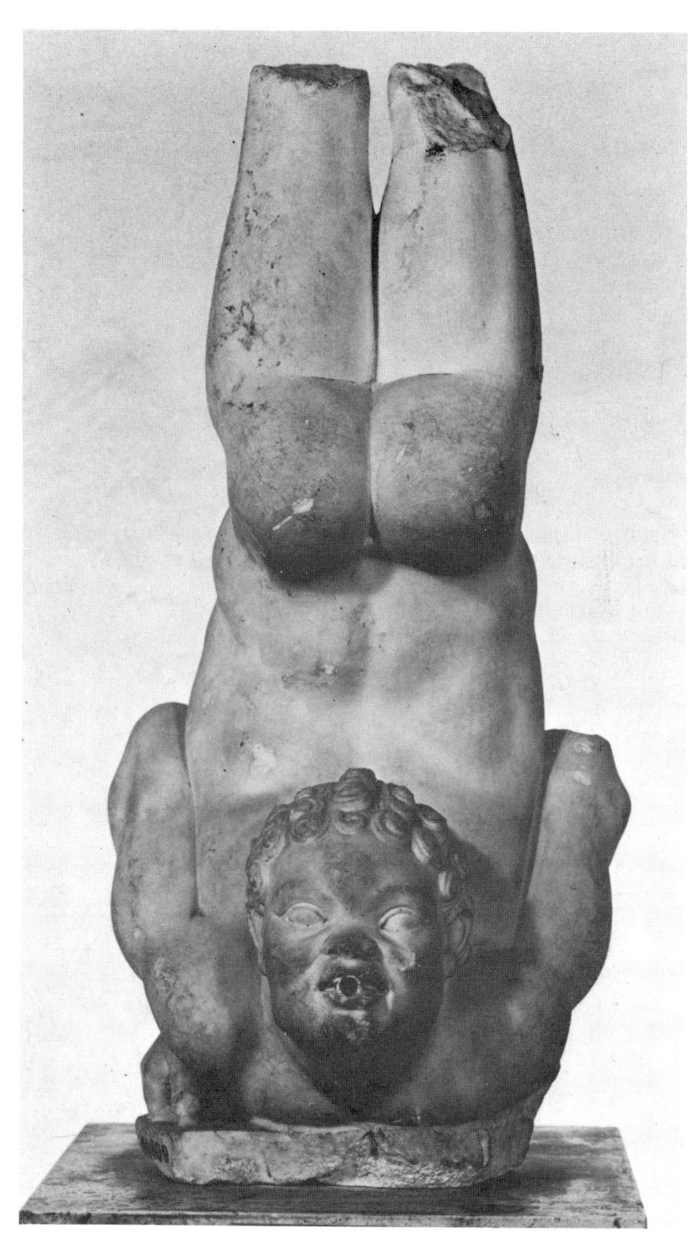

51. Marble statue of an acrobat, Roman work in Hellenistic style — hair in corkscrew curls, broad, flat nose, high cheekbones, thick lips. S. Aurigemma, *Le Terme di Diocleziano e il Museo Nazionale Romano* (Rome 1946) 72, no. 184.

52. Bronze upper bust of a diver, Roman — hair arranged in rows of thick curls, broad nose, thick lips. H. B. Walters, *Catalogue of the Bronzes, Greek, Roman, and Etruscan, in the Department of Greek and Roman Antiquities, British Museum* (London 1899) 269, no. 1674.

53. Small bronze bust of Negro, Roman—hair in form of thick mass of short curls, broad nose, thick lips. G. Calza, "Expressions of Art in a Roman Commercial City: Ostia," *Journal of Roman Studies* V (1915) 165-167 and figure 41; A. de Ridder, "Bulletin archéologique," *Revue des études grecques* XXX (1917) 199 suggests that the bust was made at least in Italy, if not in Rome itself; and R. Calza, *Museo Ostiense* (Rome 1947) 17.

54. Bronze head, Roman — hair arranged in long rows of tight curls, broad nose, high cheekbones, subnasal prognathism, thick lips. E. Babelon, "Tête de nègre de la collection de Janzé au Cabinet des Médailles," *Gazette archéologique* IX (1884) 204-206 and plate 27; E. Babelon and J.-Adrien Blanchet, *Catalogue des bronzes antiques de la Bibliothèque Nationale* (Paris 1895) 443-444, no. 1018.

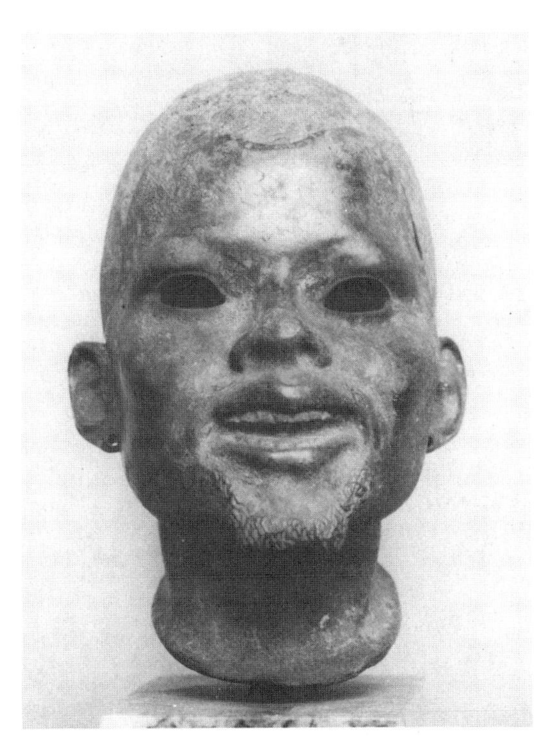

55. Bronze vase (hollow) in the form of a goateed Negro — markedly prognathous, head sloped strongly backwards. [W. Froehner] *Collection Auguste Dutuit: Bronzes antiques* (Paris 1897) 34, no. 60 and plate LVI describes the bronze as Alexandrian work. F. Poulsen, however, ("Aux musées d'antiques parisiens," in *From the Collections of the Ny Carlsberg Glyptothek 1942* III [Copenhagen 1942] 158-160 and figures 14 [p. 162], 15-16 [p. 163]) states that the piece added to the top of the head does not seem to be ancient, compares the head to the hollow bronze described above (Figure 54), and considers this bronze, which was used as a lamp, a fine example of Roman industrial art.

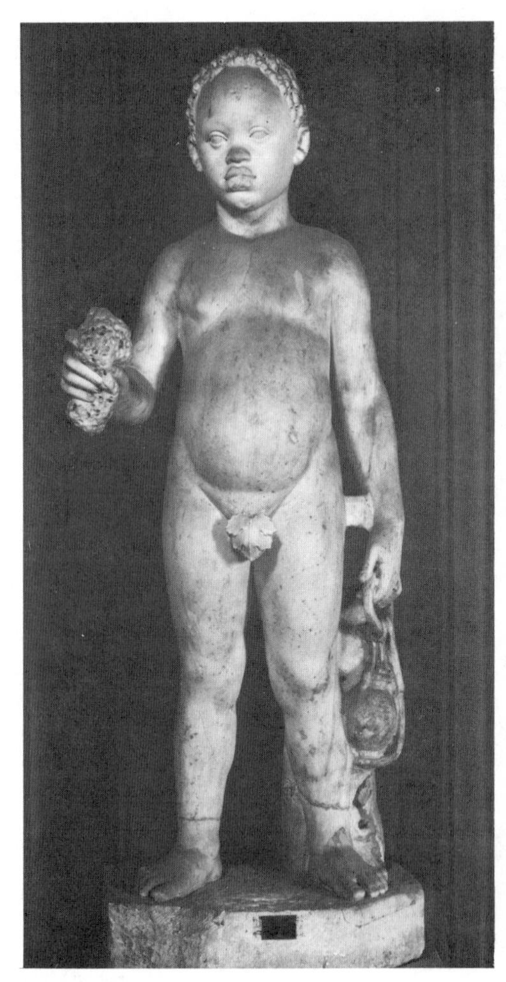

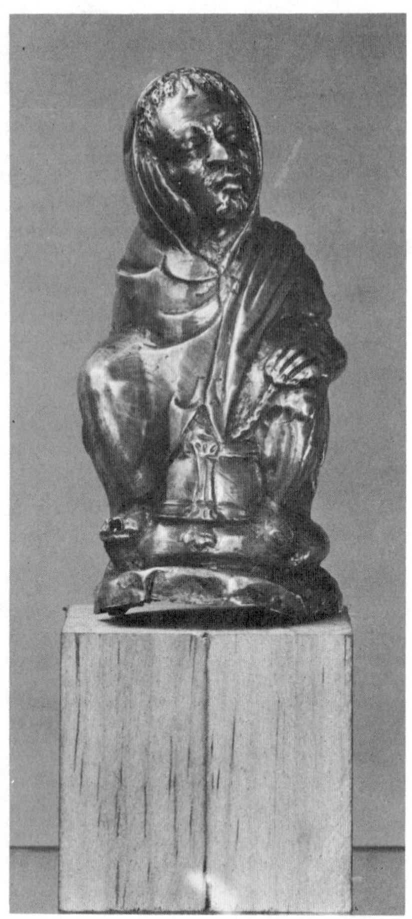

56. (left) Marble statuette of a youthful bath attendant, Trajanic-Antonine period, carrying a lekythos — short tightly curled hair, short broad nose, very thick lips, head and body of different periods. G. Lippold, *Die Skulpturen des Vaticanischen Museums* III2 text (Berlin 1956) 394-395 and III2 plates (Berlin 1956) plate 168, no. 32 and plate 169, no. 32; W. Helbig, *Führer durch die öffentlichen Sammlungen klassischer Altertümer in Rom*[4], revised by H. Speier (Tübingen 1963) 444, no. 563.

57. (right) Silver pepper caster in form of sleeping old man, second century A.D., Roman, from near Montcornet, a part of the Chaource Treasure — hair frizzly, broad nose, thick lips. H. B. Walters, *Catalogue of the Silver Plate (Greek, Etruscan, and Roman) in the British Museum* (London 1921) 38-39, no. 145, and plate XXIII.

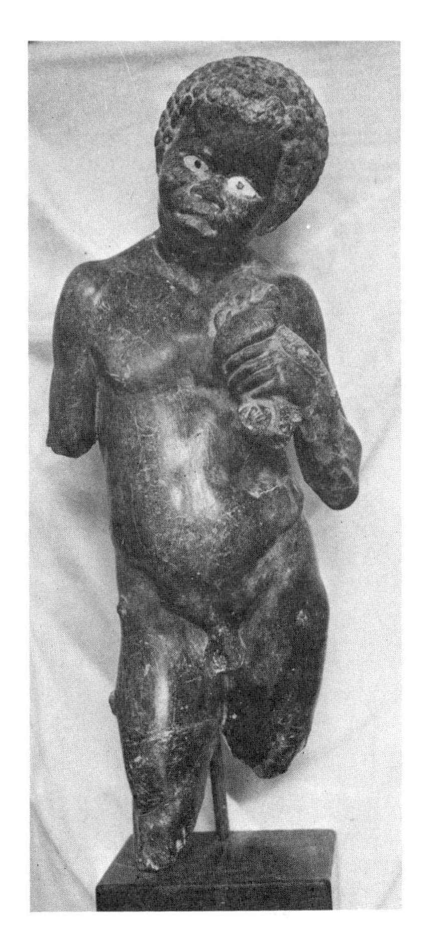

58. (left) Black marble statue of a Negro boy, second century A.D. — mass of short, thick, woolly hair, flat nose, and thick lips, part of a group in relief from Hadrumetum (Sousse). P. Gauckler, E. Gouvet, and G. Hannezo, *Musées de Sousse,* Musées et collections archéologiques de l'Algérie et de la Tunisie (Paris 1902) plate XIII, no. 2. J. W. Salomonson, *Mosaïques romaines de Tunisie: Catalogue* (Brussels 1964) 43, no. 43; L. Foucher, *Hadrumetum:* Publications de l'Université de Tunis, Faculté des Lettres — 1ère série: *Archéologie. Histoire* — vol. X (Paris 1964) 170-171 and plate XIId. The boy wore only one earring, a custom, according to Gauckler et al. (39), observed by the indigenous population of Tunisia at the time of their writing.

59. (right) Glass cup molded in form of a head, Roman, first to fourth centuries A.D. — frizzly hair close to head, broad nose, thick lips; cf. similar head from Pompeii, Museo Nazionale, Naples, no. 199404.

60. Bronze statuette perhaps of a street singer, Hellenistic — hair somewhat similar to that of bust described below (Figure 61), which it also resembles with respect to nose, though the lips are a little thicker. E. Babelon and J. A. Blanchet, *Catalogue des bronzes antiques de la Bibliothèque Nationale* (Paris 1895) no. 1009; J. Babelon, *Choix de bronzes de la Collection Caylus* (Paris and Brussels 1928) 55-56 and plates XXIII and XXIV. M. Bieber, *The Sculpture of the Hellenistic Age,* rev. ed. (New York 1961) 96, gives a date of about 200 B.C. for the figure.

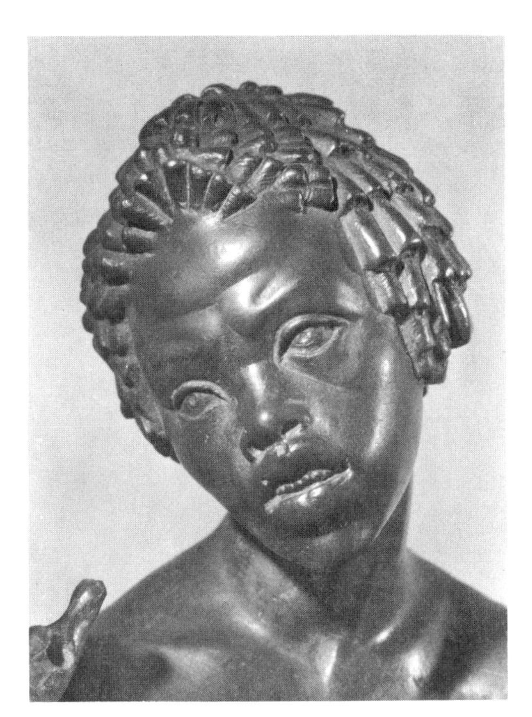

61. Small bronze bust of a young child, Hellenistic—hair arranged in irregular rows of small, corkscrew curls, nose broad, and lips thick but not to the extent of more pronounced Negroid types. *The Illustrated London News,* no. 6079, vol. CCXXVII (Oct. 22, 1955) 681. The fashion of the hair resembles that of certain African tribes who arrange the hair similarly and use mud as a fixative (cf. the arrangement of hair of a Shilluk from the Sudan in C. S. Coon, *The Origin of Races* [New York 1963] plate IV); D. E. L. Haynes, "Bronze Bust of a Young Negress," *The British Museum Quarterly* XXI (1957) 19-20, plate IV, considers the style Hellenistic and similar to a marble head from Smyrna of about 100 B.C. This type of Negro resembles a tribe designated "Hamitomorph" by L. Oschinsky (*The Racial Affinities of the Baganda and other Bantu Tribes of British East Africa* [Cambridge, Eng. 1954], no. 34-36 in appendix C) with respect to nose, lips, and general shape of face. Other examples very similar to the British Museum figure as to features and arrangement of hair are a bronze of the Fouquet Collection from Tell Moqdam (Leontopolis), P. Perdrizet, *Bronzes grecs d'Egypte de la Collection Fouquet* (Paris 1911) plate XXV, and p. 57, no. 94 and the bust which follows (Figure 62). The British Museum head suggests to one observer that the model may have belonged to one of the half-Hamitic tribes of East Africa (M. A. Bennet-Clark quoted in n. 2, p. 19 by Haynes).

62. Small bronze bust of a young child of Nilotic type, Hellenistic. Printed as the frontispiece in H. Read, *A Coat of Many Colours: Occasional Essays* (London 1945).

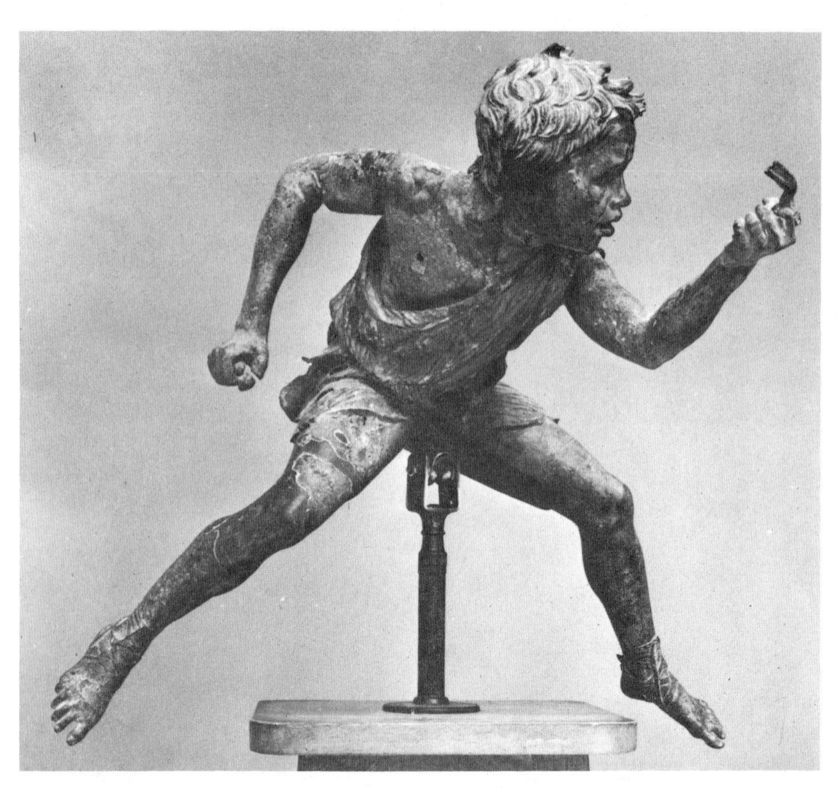

63. Bronze jockey, Hellenistic — hair curly and resembling that of several other Negroid figures. D. K. Hill, *Catalogue of Classical Bronze Sculpture in the Walters Art Gallery* (Baltimore 1949) xvi-xvii dates this figure found off Cape Artemisium as second or possibly first century B.C. and considers the figure Negroid; and G. M. A. Richter (*A Handbook of Greek Art*[5] [London 1967] 166), photograph on same page, dates it as ca. 240-200 B.C. and G. M. A. Hanfmann, *Classical Sculpture* (Greenwich, Conn. 1967) 329 and plates 232 and 233 as 230-200 B.C. Many descendants of Negro and white racial mixture resemble this boy. In light of our knowledge of Negroes in the ancient world as charioteers or grooms, it is reasonable to consider the boy as a black-white cross who adopted an occupation of his father.

64. Bronze statuette of boyish orator, Hellenistic-Alexandrian—rather long, tightly curled hair, nose and lips Negroid but not extreme. C. C. Vermeule, "Greek, Etruscan and Roman Bronzes Acquired by the Museum of Fine Arts, Boston," *CJ* LV (1960) 199-200 and figure 7. For a study of several bronze statuettes of mantled Negro youths, see R. Steiger, "Drei römische Bronzen aus Augst," in *Gestalt und Geschichte: Festschrift Karl Schefold,* supplementary vol. IV, *Antike Kunst* (Bern 1967) 192-195 and plates 62-63.

65. Bronze statue of boy, perhaps also an orator, Hellenistic — tightly curled short hair, round face, neither lips nor nose extreme, some subnasal prognathism, stomach somewhat protruding, second or first century B.C. Discovered in 1963 in Bodrum by fishermen diving for sponge, *Art Treasures of Turkey,* circulated by the Smithsonian Institution 1966-1968 (Washington, D. C. 1966) 93 and no. 145.

66. Bronze statuette of a boy of slender proportions on a pedestal, found at Perugia, late Republican or early Imperial Rome — hair curly, nose and lips Negroid. H. B. Walters, *Select Bronzes, Greek, Roman, and Etruscan, in the Department of Antiquities* [British Museum] (London 1915) plate LXVIII.

67. Marble statue of a Negroid woman interpreted as a personification of Africa, first century A.D. or little earlier from lower Egypt — features are clearly Negroid with respect to rather broad nose and thick lips, although the hair is long, rather smooth, and loosely waved. S. Reinach, *Répertoire de la statuaire grecque et romaine*[2], IV (Paris 1913) 552, no. 1; M. Collignon, "L'Afrique personifiée: Statuette, provenant d'Egypte acquise par Jean Maspero," *MonPiot* XXII (1916) 163-173 and plate XVI. Collignon (165) states that the artist clearly wanted to depict the characteristics of the black race (flat nose, thick fleshy lips, and with the lower part of the face protruding), and adds (172-173) that the long, smooth hair is evidence that the sculptor did not want to represent a pure Negro but a racial type resembling certain populations of Abyssinia and south Ethiopia. The charming Negro woman, in my judgment, resembles descendants of black-white mixture.

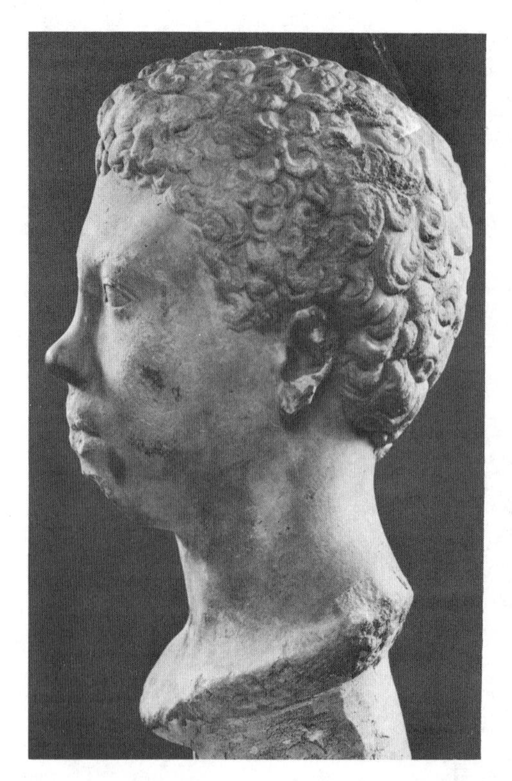

68. Marble bust of a man of African origin, Augustan or Julio-Claudian period — the closely cropped hair, subnasal region, and lips suggest Negroid admixture. C. C. Vermeule, "Greek, Etruscan, and Roman Sculptures in the Museum of Fine Arts, Boston," *AJA* LXVIII (1964) 336, plate 107, figure 29 states that the face differs greatly from that of a "true" Ethiopian and that the African is a mixture of the aristocratic Negro and Arabian or African desert types.

69. Yellow limestone head of a Negro from Meroë — originally painted black, contrasted with white eyes and scarlet lips, considered a gift of a Roman official to a Meroïtic king or the work of an itinerant Roman sculptor in Nubia, about 100 A.D. O. Koefoed-Petersen, *Egyptian Sculpture in the Ny Carlsberg Glyptothek*[2] (Copenhagen 1962) 38 and plate 53.

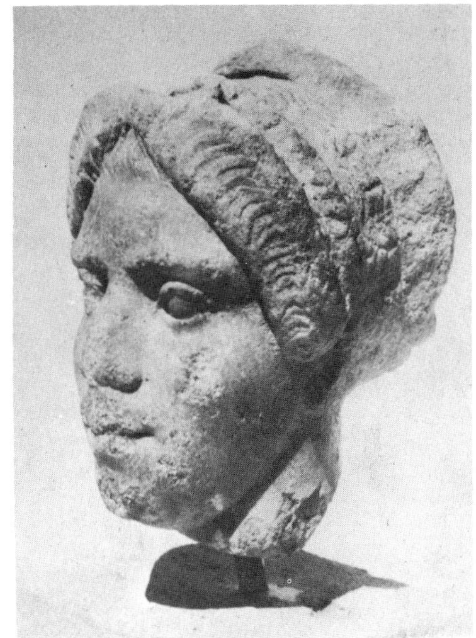

70. Small marble head of a woman, found in the Agora, Trajanic period — hair long and arranged in a coiffure rolled in such a way as to frame the face, with the ends twisted into a ropelike strand, somewhat broad nose, and rather thick lips. H. A. Thompson, "The Excavation of the Athenian Agora Twelfth Season: 1947," *Hesperia* XVII (1948) 178 and plate LV says that the features mark the woman as of Negro origin; E. B. Harrison, *The Athenian Agora, Results of Excavations Conducted by the American School of Classical Studies at Athens,* vol. I: *Portrait Sculpture* (Princeton 1953) 32 and plate 15 states that "the broad nose, the high cheekbones and the projecting, seemingly thick lips suggest that the subject may be a negress." My examination of the marble convinces me that there is no doubt of Negroid admixture.

71. Over-life-sized basalt head of a man from Egypt, perhaps the Fayum — tightly curled hair, somewhat similar to that of Memnon, the pupil of Herodes Atticus (Figure 73 below), nose broken, but lips rather thick. P. Graindor, *Bustes et statues-portraits d'Egypte romaine*, Recueil de travaux publiés par la Faculté des Lettres (Cairo n.d.) 141-142 (photograph on plate LXVIIb) considers the head that of a person of the same race as Memnon, and suggests a Trajanic date. B. von Bothmer et al., *Egyptian Sculpture of the Late Period: 700 B.C. to A.D. 100* (Brooklyn 1960) 170-171 dates the figure as belonging to the period 80-50 B.C., considers the subject a warrior, perhaps a general in the Ptolemaic army, and denies that the figure is "Ethiopian," "Nubian," or Negro. The frizziness of the hair von Bothmer explains as a result of the stylization met in other sculptures of the period in non-Negroid figures. The frizzly hair (markedly similar to that in Figure 73 below) and the thick lips suggest Negroid admixture; hence, Graindor's view as to the race of the subject is more convincing.

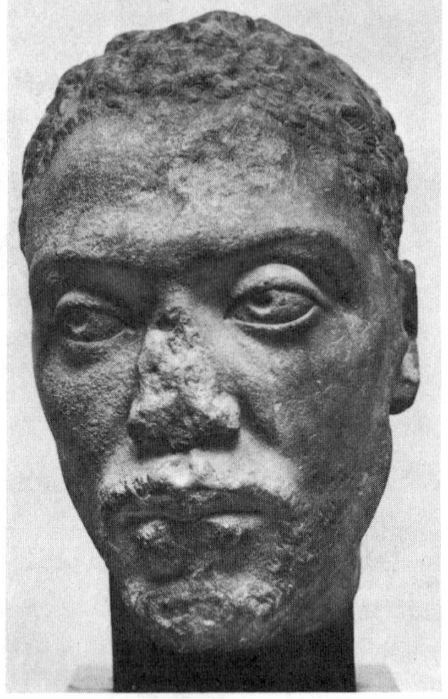

72. (left) Marble head of a Negroid woman, Roman, probably Hadrianic period — hair in mass of tight curls, nose slightly broad, and rather thick lips. R. Paribeni, "Monumenti d'arte alessandrina nel Museo Nazionale Romano," in *Saggi di storia antica e di archeologia a Giulio Beloch* (Rome 1910) 203-209 (photographs in figures 4 and 5) considers the hair, nose, and lips indicative of Negro origin, not of the "true" Negro, however, but of the more regular features characteristic of certain populations of North Africa or East Africa along the Red Sea.

73. (right) Pentelic marble head of a Negroid male, perhaps Memnon, a pupil of Herodes Atticus, found in Thyreatis, ca. 160-170 A.D. — hair short and tightly curled (woolly effect), nose, though broken, obviously broad, and thick lips. P. Graindor, "Tête de nègre du Musée de Berlin," *Bulletin de correspondance hellénique* XXXIX (1915) 402-412 considers the subject of mixed race but with predominance of Negro type of North Africa, Nubia, or Abyssinia; C. Picard, *La Sculpture antique de Phidias à l'ère byzantine* (Paris 1926) 444 describes the head as that of a Negro or mulatto; G. Sena Chiesa, s.v. *Memnone* — 2º *Enciclopedia dell'arte antica* IV (Rome 1961) 1001.

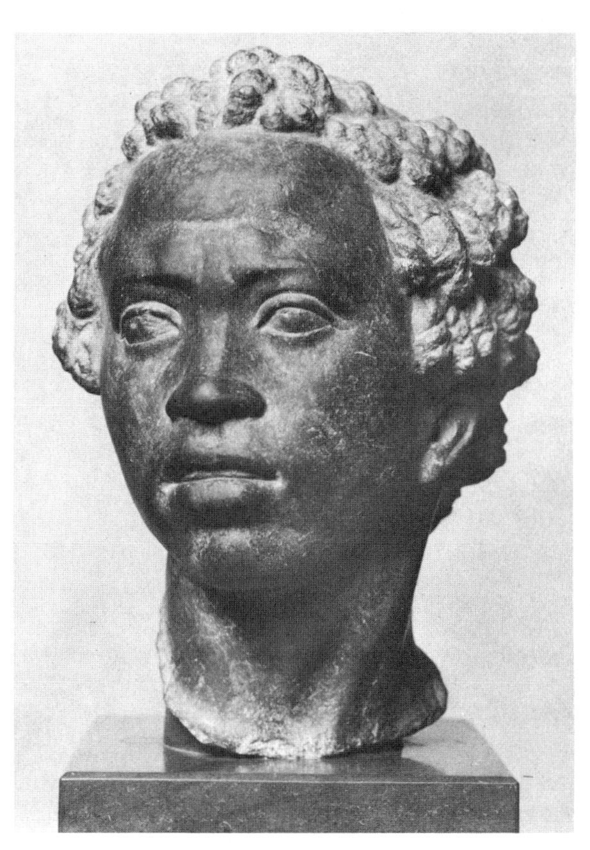
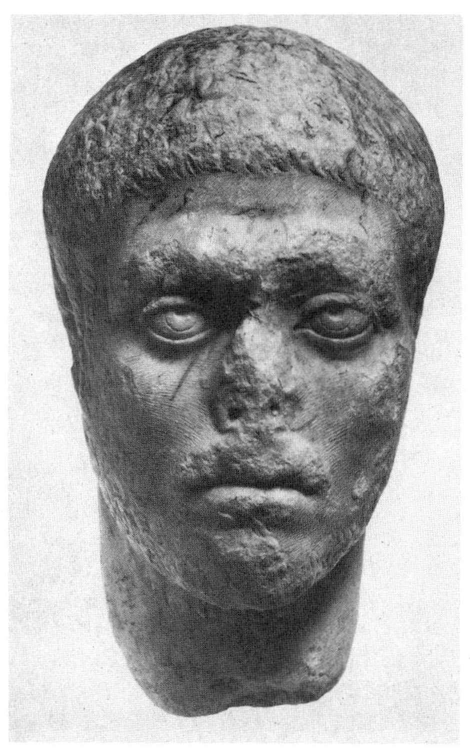

74. (left) Black marble head of a youth from Asia Minor, second century A.D. — hair in thick mass of curls, slight broadness in nose and thickness in lips. *Stephanos: Theodor Wiegand* (Berlin 1924) plate XIII and p. 16.

75. (right) Pentelic marble head of a young man, found in Agora, ca. 250-260 A.D. — close-cropped hair, nose broken, lips slightly thick. E. B. Harrison, *The Athenian Agora* 59-60 speaks of "seemingly Negroid features" and of a "distinctly Negroid look" in describing the statue, but notes that the hair is not unusually curly, no. 45, plate 29.

76. Pygmy fighting with crane, a scene from the top of a two-handled red-figured rhyton, fifth century B.C. J. C. Hoppin, *A Handbook of Attic Red-Figured Vases,* I (Cambridge, Mass. 1919) 138, no. 90; and J. D. Beazley, *Attic Red-Figure Vase-Painters*², I (London 1963) 382, no. 188 attributes the vase to the Brygos Painter. See also pygmy with large head, thick hair, and protruding abdomen on Kabeiric vase in Museum of Fine Arts, Boston, no. 99.534, reproduced in Figure 6 and cited in note 6 Chapter II, and Kabeiric vases in Athens, National Museum, nos. 10425, 12547.

77. Pygmies engaged in capturing a crocodile depicted in a Pompeiian fresco. For a reproduction in color of a detail from this hunt, see *Roman Painting,* text by A. Maiuri (Editions Albert Skira, Geneva 1953) 111. For a terra-cotta pygmy from Egypt, see Perdrizet, *Les Terres cuites grecques d'Egypte,* Series I, plate CVI, lower right, and no. 290; and for pygmies in trouble with crane and hippopotamus in a mosaic from north African Roman baths of third century A.D. at Uàdi Ez-Zgàia, see S. Aurigemma, *L'Italia in Africa: Le scoperte archeologiche (a.1911–a.1943), Tripolitania,* vol. I — *I monumenti d'arte decorativa, parte prima — I mosaici* (Rome 1960) 44-45 and plates 71-73; see Chap. I, n. 72, for a discussion of pygmies; cf. L. Foucher, "Les Mosaïques nilotiques africaines," in *La Mosaïque gréco-romaine,* Colloques internationaux du Centre National de la Recherche Scientifique (Paris 1965) 138-141 and figure 22.

III. Greco-Roman Acquaintance with African Ethiopians

The purpose of this chapter is to trace the manner in which Greeks and Romans widened their knowledge of African Ethiopians and to indicate the regions of Africa in which they located Ethiopians. The chapter concludes with a brief consideration of the Ethiopians who lived south of Egypt because these Ethiopians, more than those of other regions of Africa, figured most prominently in Greco-Roman records and contributed significantly to the classical image of Ethiopians.

The earliest Greek poets mentioned Ethiopians. Their observations, however, as to the physical characteristics and provenience of these peoples were either sparse or vague. Beginning with the fifth century B.C., the Greek writers were more generous in providing anthropological and geographical details concerning African Ethiopians. Although as early as Herodotus Ethiopia was believed to be in the south and India in the farthest east, subsequently India and Ethiopia were at times confused in the minds of some, despite increased geographical knowledge. Yet it is often possible to determine whether a writer was referring to Ethiopians or Indians.[1]

The first Greek poet had heard of Ethiopians. Not only does Homer mention Ethiopians but he describes a well-known herald of Odysseus as black-skinned and woolly-haired. It is uncertain whether Homer's Ethiopians were African and whether Odysseus' herald was Ethiopian. According to the evidence, however, the former may have been African, and the latter, Ethiopian.

Homer's Ethiopians are remote peoples, sundered in twain, the farthermost men, some dwelling where the sun rises and others where it sets. Their home is by the streams of Ocean. Menelaus, having wandered over Cyprus, Phoenicia, and Egypt, visited other peoples, the first mentioned being the Ethiopians,[2] and the routes by which he reached Ethiopia were discussed seriously by later writers.[3] Although Homer says nothing of the physical characteristics of his Ethiopians, there is substantial reason to believe that by Homer's day the Greeks had heard of blacks, by direct or indirect accounts, and that the Ethiopians of his epics were black. Eurybates, the herald of Odysseus, who had accompanied him from Ithaca to Troy, was black-skinned and woolly-haired. A black-skinned, woolly-haired individual, we have seen, was to the Greeks an Ethiopian. The only person so described in Homer, Eurybates was apparently well known. For it was in reply to Penelope's request for a description of the comrades accompanying her husband that the disguised Odysseus mentioned Eurybates. The mention of Eurybates was one of the sure tokens which Penelope recognized as proof of her husband.[4] Nor should it be overlooked that one of the Ithacan lords was named Aegyptius.[5]

Although the onomastic significance of Aegyptius should not be overemphasized in this case, it is perhaps not stretching the evidence too much to suggest, in the light of both Eurybates and Aegyptius, that the Ithacans had some special experience with or specific knowledge of both Ethiopians and Egyptians. After all, Homer had heard of pygmies, who also dwelt by the streams of Ocean, and before Homer's time black men — depicted in Minoan and Pylos frescoes — were known outside of Africa. Furthermore, among the names of individuals mentioned several times in the Pylos tablets was that of ai-ti-jo-qo (Aithiops). On the basis of the total evidence from this early period it is not possible to determine the precise meaning of ai-ti-jo-qo in the Pylos texts. Whether this personal name indicates a Negroid type from Africa or merely an individual of dark color, perhaps from Asia, is uncertain. At any rate, the possibility that the name indicated a Negro or Negroid type cannot be excluded and has been noted by Dihle.[6]

As to the location of the Homeric Ethiopians, the ancient evidence is not precise; and modern scholars differ. One view holds that the Homeric Ethiopians dwelling near the rising sun were Negroes who inhabited the regions near Egypt, while those in the vicinity of the setting sun dwelt near the Pillars of Hercules. Other scholars identify the eastern branch as Negroes of the Somali coast and the westerners as occupants of the Sudan whose land stretched westward ad infinitum from the Nile valley. Still another view places Homer's eastern Ethiopians near the Red

Sea and the western branch not far west of the upper Nile.[7]

Hesiod is the first to group Scythians with Ethiopians, peoples who later came to be cited frequently as examples of racial and geographical extremes — northerners and southerners.[8] In this instance Hesiod does not describe his Ethiopians, but elsewhere he mentions a people and city of dark men.[9] Though Eos and Tithonus, the parents of Memnon, according to early Greek poets, dwelt, like Homer's Ethiopians, by the streams of Ocean at the ends of the earth, there is no precision in these poets as to where Memnon lived.[10] It should be noted that, according to Athenaeus, Archilochus mentioned an Aethiops of Corinth, who participated in the founding of Syracuse. Even if an Aethiops actually lived in Corinth at the period of the establishment of Syracuse (ca. 734 B.C.), we do not have sufficient evidence to know precisely what the word Aethiops meant at that time. We can say, however, that the physical characteristics of Eurybates as recorded by Homer and Hesiod's mention of dark men give some indications as to the possible meaning of Aethiops in the time of Archilochus. Whether Aethiops of Corinth was from the east or the west we do not know.[11] Mimnermus locates his Ethiopians in the east, when he describes the sun as being carried from the country of the Hesperians to the land of the Ethiopians.[12]

Aeschylus is the first Greek to locate Ethiopians definitely in Africa. Io, according to the prophecy of Prometheus, was to visit a distant country, and a black people, who lived by the waters of the sun, where the Ethiopian river flowed, and was to go to the cataract where the Nile sent forth its stream from the Bybline Mountains.[13] It is not at all surprising that Aeschylus places Ethiopians in Africa. Ionian and Carian mercenaries served under Psammetichus (Psamtik) I (663–609 B.C.).[14] By the sixth century B.C. Greeks were well established in Naucratis. Greek residents of this community were in a position to acquire a sound knowledge of the country and its peoples, and it was no doubt through Naucratis that the Greeks developed the interest in the Negro reflected in the art of the sixth century. Further, if a mold of a Negro found at Naucratis (Figs. 78a–b) dating from the fifth century B.C. is representative, Greeks in Egypt at that time were well acquainted with the pronounced Negroid type. It has also been suggested that the Busiris legend came into being in the sixth century, perhaps at Naucratis, and was transmitted by

Greek traders or travelers. Amasis, according to J. Boardman, was perhaps a dusky-skinned metic, born in Egypt of a mother herself Egyptian and grew up in all likelihood at Naucratis. He may have been Negroid, as I have argued above. Greek mercenaries, perhaps Egyptian-born and children of the mercenaries who had served under the earlier Psammetichus, had been employed by Psammetichus II (594–588 B.C.) in his Nubian campaign; inscriptions at Abu Simbel record the participation of Greek mercenaries in the campaign; and, according to one modern view, Psammetichus II reached the Fourth Cataract.[15] By the time of Aeschylus, therefore, sufficient time had elapsed to allow for reports based on recently acquired Greek knowledge of Ethiopians to circulate in Greece. Further, Aeschylus himself had fought in the Persian wars. Perhaps his interest in Ethiopia may have derived from experiences with Ethiopians in the army of Xerxes.

Xenophanes, when he described Ethiopians as black-faced and flat-nosed, was the first to apply to an Ethiopian a physical characteristic other than color.[16] In this connection it is interesting to note that one of the Greek mercenaries in the army of Psammetichus II who left his name at Abu Simbel was, like Xenophanes, a Colophonian.[17] A likely source, therefore, for Xenophanes' anthropological details was the account of some Colophonian mercenary who, upon his return to Ionia, entertained his friends with stories of the black, flat-nosed Ethiopians whom he had encountered.[18]

The anthropological characteristics mentioned by Xenophanes and the geographical details provided by Aeschylus were apparently reflections of an increased knowledge of Ethiopia and Ethiopians. Fifth-century dramatists, for example, wrote plays involving Ethiopian myths, made references to Ethiopians, and included intriguing geographical details such as snows in the Upper Nile which fed the waters of the Nile.[19] It is obvious that from the fifth century onwards Ethiopians were without question an African reality. For example, it is reasonable to assume that the dramatists had not only received reports from Greeks with Egyptian and Ethiopian experience but had perhaps seen Ethiopians in Athens, including some captives taken after the defeat of Xerxes.

Of the Greek writers who visited Africa Herodotus is the first to whom we can turn for a substantial account of Ethiopians. He ascended the Nile as far as Elephantine and supplemented his personal observations by interviews with others who knew Ethiopia. His geographical knowledge, like that of many writers who followed him, leaves much to be desired. His picture, however, of black peoples living in various parts of Africa was important for its influence in molding the Greek image of Ethiopians not only in his day but later.

Although Herodotus makes brief mention of Asiatic Ethiopians, it is clear that he was writing primarily about African Ethiopians, the most woolly-haired of all men,[20] whom, together with the Libyans of the north, he classified as aboriginals of Libya.[21] Herodotus wrote most fully of the Ethiopians who lived south and southeast of Elephantine, where the area, he noted, began to be occupied by Ethiopians.[22] The information which Herodotus gave concerning the Ethiopians south of Elephantine includes the following: (1) The capital of all Ethiopia was the great city of Meroë, situated at a distance of approximately two months' journey from Elephantine, the center of an established religion, which despatched its armies in obedience to its gods; (2) Along the Nile about a two months' journey southwest of Meroë lived Ethiopians influenced by the customs and manners of the 240,000 Egyptian deserters, called Asmach, who had migrated and settled in the region in the reign of Psammetichus I; (3) The Macrobian Ethiopians, the tallest and most handsome men on earth who chose the tallest as kings, against whom Cambyses made an expedition, dwelt on the sea to the south and lived at the extremity of the world; and (4) Cave-dwelling Ethiopians, the swiftest of men, whose diet included snakes and lizards and whose language resembled the squeaking of bats and was unlike any other in the world, lived south of the Garamantes.[23]

Herodotus reported the presence of Ethiopians elsewhere in Africa. Although the precise area is by no means clear, his account of small black men visited by the Nasamones refers to a region across the desert in central Africa, in the judgment of some.[24] The little men who covered themselves with palm-leaf raiment, reported by Herodotus as seen by the Persian Sataspes (ca. 485–464 B.C.) during a voyage down the west coast of Africa, have been interpreted as Negro tribes living in Senegal or perhaps Guinea.[25]

In short, Herodotus, in spite of an annoying geographical imprecision, preserves accounts of Ethiopians living in various regions south of Egypt and perhaps in central and even west Africa. In one instance he refers to the Ethiopian's woolly hair; in another, to his blackness. He located the Macrobian Ethiopians further south than later writers, and their Table of the Sun recalls the divine feastings of the Homeric gods. Yet it is clear that as early as the fifth century B.C., Ethiopians south of Egypt were no longer the rather vague, shadowy peoples of the earlier poets but an African reality.

Although Herodotus provided more details about these southern Ethiopians than any other single source of the fifth century, he recorded little about western Ethiopians. His account of the circumnavigation of Africa reportedly undertaken in the reign of the Pharaoh Necho (the Necos of Herodotus, 609–594 B.C.), made no mention of peoples seen, and his description of the west African peoples encountered by Sataspes is meagre.[26] A translation of an inquisitive Greek has preserved an account of the country and Ethiopian peoples whom Hanno the Carthaginian reportedly encountered during his voyage about 500(?) B.C. down the west coast of Africa. Modern scholars differ as to the exact location of the coastal regions which Hanno visited and as to the southernmost point which he reached. In spite of uncertainty as to geography, however, the Greek translation of Hanno's voyage described some of the peoples seen: a wild tribe who inhabited a mountainous area swarming with wild beasts; Troglodytes of strange appearance able to run faster than horses; mountain-dwelling savages who prevented the Carthaginians from landing by hurling stones; a tribe who spoke a language unintelligible to the interpreters provided by the Lixitae and who fled at the sight of ships; and another people whose pipes, drums, and cymbals terrified the explorers.[27]

The island of Cerne,[28] mentioned by Hanno, was frequently referred to in the fourth century B.C. and later as a landmark of Ethiopians in the west. The *Periplus* of Scylax (fourth century B.C.), for example, describes Cerne as a market of a trade between Carthaginians and Ethiopians of the opposite coast who bartered skins of deer, lions, leopards, the hides and tusks of elephants, and wine for perfume, Egyptian stones, and Athenian pottery. These Ethiopians used ivory for cups and bracelets, and in ornaments for houses. When Scylax described these western Ethiopians as the tallest and most handsome of men who chose the tallest as rulers, he was no doubt following the tradition of Herodotus.[29] Palaephatus, writing also in the fourth century, informs us that the inhabitants of Cerne were Ethiopians who inhabited an island outside the Pillars of Hercules.[30] Ephorus reported that Ethiopians overran Libya as far as the Atlas Mountains and that some remained in this region, while others occupied a substantial portion of the seaboard.[31]

Knowledge of Ethiopians in west Africa, therefore, had reached the Greeks, if not in the fifth, certainly in the fourth century B.C. The record, though not so detailed as that of eastern Ethiopians, represented most of them as wild but some as knowledgeable traders. From the fifth century B.C. onwards, as a result of increased contacts with Ethiopians, the Greeks and later the Romans deepened their knowledge of African reality. Since details of most of these later contacts are given elsewhere in this book, it will suffice here to indicate only briefly how the Greeks and Romans furthered their acquaintance with African Ethiopians.

Although Herodotus did not travel beyond Elephantine, some later writers visited Ethiopia itself. The widely traveled Democritus, for example, is said to have visited Ethiopia.[32] Pliny states that Simonides the Younger resided in Meroë for five years while engaged in a work on Ethiopia and that a certain Dalion sailed, perhaps in the reign of Ptolemy II, far south of Meroë.[33] Unfortunately, we know little of their findings except for a few references primarily in Pliny the Elder. Nor are there extant the works entitled *Aethiopica,* which Charon of Lampsacus (469–400 B.C.), Bion of Soli (first half of the third century B.C.), Philo (290 or 200 B.C.), and Marcellus (the Empire?) are said to have written. Of these Bion is less shadowy, in that he was known not only to Pliny but also to Varro, Athenaeus, and Diogenes Laertius.[34] Actual visits of travelers to Ethiopia, therefore, contributed to an extension of Greco-Roman acquaintance with Ethiopia and Ethiopians. Others, in the tradition of Herodotus, used sources available in Egypt. Agatharchides, for example, lived at Alexandria; Diodorus interviewed Ethiopian ambassadors resident in Egypt; Strabo accompanied Aelius Gallus, when prefect of Egypt, up the Nile as far as Syene and the frontier of Ethiopia; and Athenaeus was from Naucratis. Ethiopians such as King Ergamenes, who, according to Diodorus, received a Greek education and studied Greek philosophy, were also undoubtedly important sources of information concerning Ethiopia.[35]

The Ptolemies, as a result of their commercial interests and military activity, extended their acquaintance with Ethiopia and Ethiopians living south of Egypt and in regions of east Africa along the Red Sea coast. Eratosthenes (ca. 275–194 B.C.), for example, head of the Alexandrian Library under Ptolemy Euergetes I, reflected an enlargement of geographical knowledge by his description of the so-called island of Meroë as formed by the junction of the Astaboras and the Astapus and by his mention of the Megabari, Blemmyes, Troglodytes, and Nubae.[36] Eudoxus of Cyzicus, who had been sent on an honorary mission to Ptolemy VIII (Euergetes II 170–163 and 145–116 B.C.) is reported to have made visits not only to east but also to west Africa. During a voyage which took him, according to Posidonius as cited by Strabo, to the coastal regions of Ethiopia below Egypt, Eudoxus made a list of words spoken by the inhabitants. On a later voyage in which he hoped to circumnavigate Africa from west to east, Eudoxus is said to have discovered that the western Ethiopians spoke the same language as the eastern Ethiopians whose language he had written down during his earlier visit in the east.[37]

An indication of the kind of information acquired during the Ptolemaic period appears in the geographical writings of Agatharchides, who served as a guardian of a young Ptolemy, perhaps Soter II. Extracts from the *De Mari Erythraeo*, preserved in Photius, comment on elephant hunting conducted by the Ptolemies, and on gold mines situated on the borders of Egypt and in Ethiopia near the Red Sea, still in operation when Agatharchides wrote. Among those whom this second-century B.C. geographer mentioned were the Ichthyophagi who inhabited the western shores of the Red Sea and several tribes who lived inland beyond the regions of Meroë and south of Egypt. Although Agatharchides was vague as to the geographical location of the Ethiopian peoples he described, he had obviously acquired new information concerning the physical characteristics of the people and their customs. Some were so markedly flat-nosed as to be called Simi; others, the Acridophagi, were so much blacker than the majority as to deserve special reference to their color. Agatharchides described the diet of the Ethiopians, reflected in the names which the Greeks gave to certain tribes, such as Rhizophagi, Hylophagi, and Struthophagi; commented on the cave- and tree-dwelling habits of some, the skill of others in archery, and their method of elephant hunting; and mentioned customs, such as nudity and the possession of wives in common, characteristic of some Ethiopians.[38]

For a complete image of the Ethiopian in Ptolemaic times we must supplement the Agatharchides account with that of Diodorus. Although Diodorus cites three main sources for his description of Ethiopians — Agatharchides, Artemidorus, and interviews with Ethiopian ambassadors — an examination of similarities shows that he followed Agatharchides rather closely whenever they discussed the same peoples. It is likely, therefore, that in his account of the Ethiopians dwelling in Napata, the island of Meroë, and the regions adjoining Egypt Diodorus was also drawing in large part from Agatharchides and was reflecting Ptolemaic knowledge. At any rate, Diodorus makes a clear distinction between savage, squalid Ethiopians and civilized Ethiopians not described in Agatharchides. Of the former, Diodorus says, some wore no clothing at all, some covered only their loins, and others their bodies up to the waist; still others kept their nails long like wild beasts, and in general differed strikingly from the Greeks in their behavior. The civilized Ethiopians, however, according to Diodorus, were the first to honor the gods whose favor their enjoyed, as evidenced by the fact that they had been free from foreign invasion. These Ethiopians were not only pioneers in religion, Diodorus informs us, but also originators of many customs practiced in Egypt, for the Egyptians were colonists of the Ethiopians. From these Ethiopians the Egyptians derived, for example, beliefs concerning their kings, burial practices, shapes of statues, and forms of letters. Further, if Diodorus' account of Ethiopians who lived near the Nile is derived from Agatharchides, he may be recording a Ptolemaic description of the "pure" Negro. The majority of Nile-dwelling Ethiopians, according to Diodorus, were black, flat-nosed, and ulotrichous.[39]

Military experiences brought the Romans in contact with Ethiopians in various parts of Africa and at different periods of their history. Like the Greeks, the Romans came to know the Ethiopians south of Egypt very well. From the time of Augustus until the sixth century A.D. the exigencies of frontier defense resulted in military operations and diplomatic relations involving the Romans' black and dark neighbors to the south of Egypt. Information concerning Ethiopians would have reached Rome from the soldiers stationed at military posts in the Dodekaschoinos, which the Romans occupied after the settlement of Augustus with the Ethiopian Candace. In the reign of Nero a group of praetorian troops reached the sudd. Seneca had spoken with two centurions upon their return to Rome from this mission. With respect to Roman knowledge of sub-Egyptian Ethiopians the distribution of Roman coins in this region is relevant. Of the dependable finds studied by M. P. Charlesworth and T. V. Buttrey three coins have been found on the east coast, two in the Sudan, one in the (Belgian) Congo, one in Kenya, and one in Uganda. The earliest of these is a silver denarius of Trajan from the Congo, one is a sestertius of Severus Alexander, and the others belong to the late third or early fourth century A.D. The majority of these coins, in the judgment of Charlesworth, seems to provide evidence that citizens of the Empire occasionally traveled south of the equator during the late third and early fourth centuries A.D. As to a Diocletianic coin found in the Sudan, Diocletian's military and diplomatic activities with the Blemmyes and Nobades should be kept in mind. Constantius II's missionary zeal among the Axumites may account for the presence of one of this Emperor's coins in Ethiopia.[40]

The Romans, however, as a result of their activity in various parts of North Africa, developed a more intimate acquaintance than the Greeks with Ethiopians living in Africa west of Egypt. There is considerable evidence from the Roman period for the presence of Negroes in cities along or near the north African coast. The racial characteristics of some of these Negroes are vividly preserved in several artistic media from cities such as Lepcis Magna, Hadrumetum, Thysdrus, Carthage, Hippo, Thuburbo Maius, and Thamugadi.[41] That Roman acquaintance with Ethiopians in northwestern Africa, however, was not limited in the first century A.D. to those living in the coastal areas is demonstrated by the evidence of two expeditions of the Romans into the interior. Toward the end of the first century Septimius Flaccus, a legate of Augustus, advanced into Ethiopian territory, a distance of three months' journey beyond the country of the Garamantes. A second expedition against Ethiopians, under the leadership of a certain Julius Maternus, setting out from Lepcis Magna a short time thereafter, went first to Garama, and then penetrated inner Africa as far as the region of Agisymba. Although the extent of Roman penetration of inner Africa in these two instances is not certain, some scholars suggest that the second expedition reached the Sudanese steppe.[42] Further, the several Ethiopian peoples located by Pliny and Ptolemy in various parts of northwest Africa are additional testimony that the Romans had more contacts than the Greeks with Ethiopians in this part of Africa.[43] Hence, whereas most of the Ethiopians who reached the Greek world originated in Egypt or various regions south thereof, Ethiopians in the Roman world came not only from these regions but also from various parts of north Africa.

Reports of African Ethiopians, we have seen, may have reached even the Homeric world. There is no doubt, however, that by the time of Herodotus and several other writers of the fifth century B.C. the Greeks had become acquainted, either directly or by hearsay, with African Ethiopians. Further, from the fourth century onwards Ethiopians of both east and west Africa continued to receive notice in the literature, first of the Greeks, and, later, of the Romans. It should be emphasized, in connection with Greco-Roman knowledge of the Ethiopian, that the contemporary renderings of Negroes by sensitive artists have not received adequate attention. The numerous depictions of Negroes from the sixth century B.C. onwards demonstrate more convincingly than the often inadequate literary evidence and the scanty anthropological remains the physical characteristics of Ethiopians who came from various parts of Africa to the classical world.

Although increased contacts with Africa widened the horizons of the classical world with respect to the Ethiopians, the authors, even in Roman times, were not sufficiently specific to enable us always to draw precise anthropological and geographical conclusions. J. Desanges's useful study of African tribes west of the Nile, for example, demonstrates the many difficulties involved in determining what the ancients believed to be the exact physical characteristics and geographical location of the several Ethiopian populations of which they had received reports.[44] Conflicting accounts, often of the same people, are part of a confused picture and leave scholars divided on many points. The detailed catalogue of tribes which Desanges has classified, however, gives a general idea of the regions of Africa considered as inhabited by Ethiopians in classical antiquity. Ultimately Ethiopians were located in certain areas bounded on the east by the Red Sea and on the west by the Atlantic, perhaps as far south along the western coast as Cameroon. The major areas in which Ethiopians were located may be classified as follows: (1) regions in western Africa south of Tingis, Caesarea, Africa, Cyrenaica, and to the southwest of Darnis; and (2) areas southeast of Darnis, south of Marmarica, Libya, and Egypt.[45]

With respect to certain populations situated in the northwestern part of Africa the records seem to describe mixed Negro-white populations. The Garamantes, for example, were designated by some authors as Ethiopians; by others they were distinguished from Ethiopians.[46] They were at times described as dark (*perusti, furvi, nigri*).[47] On the question of the race of the Garamantes modern scholars differ. S. Gsell says that they were certainly very dark-skinned and places them among the Ethiopians.[48] Others maintain that the Garamantes were not Ethiopians.[49] Anthropological researchers have classified the skeletal remains of the populations of the Fezzan contemporary with the Roman period as a mixture of "eurafricani" and "eurafricani negriformi."[50] Desanges believes that the Garamantes, like certain other peoples in northwest Africa, were probably mixed.[51] Descriptive names such as Leucaethiopes and Melanogaetuli, according to O. Bates, demonstrate the classical contrast of whites and blacks in the Sahara and their fusion. These and similar phrases like "Libyans resembling Ethiopians" may indicate, as Bates has pointed out, a vague acquaintance with Negroid Libyans.[52] Noting Gsell's suggestions that the Melanogaetuli may refer to a people who had black as an emblem, and the Leucaethiopes to Ethiopians who painted themselves white, Desanges inclines to a view that both peoples were mixed populations.[53] The Melanogaetuli, according to this interpretation, would represent a mixture of Gaetuli and Ethiopians, and the Leucaethiopes an amalgam of Ethiopians and an unnamed Libyan people.

Since my primary focus is on the Ethiopian in the classical world, it is outside the province of this book to detail the history of the Ethiopian peoples located in Africa by the Greeks and Romans. The Ethiopians inhabiting the regions south of Egypt, however, have a special relevance for this book and, hence, merit a fuller treatment. In the first place, it was the Ethiopians south of Egypt with whom Greeks and Romans had contacts extending over the longest period of time. Secondly, it is certain that Greco-Roman experience with these Ethiopians and the records thereof, providing more details than of any other Ethiopian peoples, molded to a great extent the classical image of Ethiopia and Ethiopians and influenced attitudes toward dark or black Africans, regardless of the part of Africa from which they came. Furthermore, it was to the kingdoms of Napata and Meroë (frequently mentioned by classical authors) that a large portion of Greco-Roman observations on Ethiopia referred.

Classical scholars, in their interpretation of what the Greeks and Romans had to say about the Ethiopians below Egypt, have in too many instances overlooked the history of these peoples as reconstructed by Egyptologists and other Africanists. Such an approach has often resulted in a failure to appreciate properly the full significance of classical references to Ethiopians and to understand the role of these southern Ethiopians in shaping the general Greco-Roman image of Ethiopians. A brief consideration, therefore, of some aspects of these peoples in their native country is pertinent at this point.

The history of the independent Ethiopian kingdom south of Egypt (Kush in the terminology of many Africanists and Egyptologists) is divided usually into three periods — the Napatan (751–542 B.C.), the Meroïtic (542-B.C.–339/350 A.D.), and the X-group period (339/350–550 A.D.).[54] Although Greek reports pertaining to the first period are much more meagre than the records relating to the last two, even these are by no means without value.

Prior to the emergence of the independent kingdom of Kush, with its capital at Napata, near the Fourth Cataract, the southern neighbors of Egypt had experienced various kinds of Egyptian domination for centuries and in the New Kingdom (1570–1085 B.C.) occupation as far south as the Fourth Cataract. Egyptian-Nubian relations are shrouded in obscurity for the period from the eleventh to the middle of the eighth century B.C. In the course of their extended contacts with Egypt, however, the southerners had acquired considerable experience as soldiers, having been recruited by the Pharaohs for their armies and having been employed as police.[55] With the reign of Kashta in the eighth century B.C. a new day began to dawn for the Ethiopian kingdom of Kush in its relations with Egypt. Under the leadership of Kashta's successors, Piankhi (751–716 B.C.) and Shabako (the Sabacôn of Manetho, 716–701 B.C.) the Ethiopians marched north, Piankhi completing his conquests of Egypt about 730 B.C., occupied Egypt, and gave Egypt the Twenty-Fifth Dynasty.

Shabako was succeeded by Shebitku (the Sebichôs of Manetho, 701–690 B.C.), who was followed by Taharqa (the Tarcos or Taracos of Manetho, 690–664 B.C.). During the reign of Taharqa Ethiopian rule was threatened and finally broken by Assyrian campaigns in Egypt. Having been driven south by Esarhaddon (680–669 B.C.), who sacked Memphis in 671 B.C., Taharqa recaptured Memphis and occupied it until he was driven out again in 667 B.C. by Ashurbanipal, Esarhaddon's successor. The last king of the Ethiopian Dynasty, Tanwetamani (664–653 B.C.), reoccupied Memphis but under the pressure of a second campaign by Ashurbanipal abandoned Memphis first and then Thebes.

Almost seventy years had elapsed between the conquests of Piankhi about 730 B.C. and the withdrawal of the Ethiopians to Napata in 663 B.C. when they were beaten back by the Assyrians.[56] The Ethiopian Dynasty had eventually ruled an empire that extended from the shores of the Mediterranean to the far south. The temples, pottery, hieroglyphic texts, and other artifacts dating from the Napatan period when the Ethiopians ruled Egypt are testimony to the vigorous energy which they, with the aid of Egyptian artisans, applied to the development of their kingdom.

As to the racial origins of the Twenty-Fifth Dynasty, scholars differ. Some have maintained that these Ethiopians (Kushites) were of Libyan origin; others, that they arose from the ranks of Egyptian priests; and still others, that they were natives of the area itself. The outlandish and non-Egyptian names and vigorous energy, according to another opinion, suggest fresh blood from somewhere else. One view holds that after the capital was moved to Meroë, the Dynasty ruled over a mixed population of Caucasians and Negroes, with Negroes predominating.[57] The only known representation of Kashta has been described as "un type à demi negroïde." Taharqa, the fifth Ethiopian ruler of the

Twenty-Fifth Dynasty, is depicted with Negroid features in some representations (Fig. 79). The kneeling figure appearing in a stele erected at Zinjirli in north Syria by Esarhaddon, the victorious conqueror of Taharqa after his successful expedition against the Ethiopians, is unmistakably Negroid. Whether this stele depicts Taharqa, as some have argued, or one of the soldiers in his army, it is an important commentary on the Ethiopian population of the period. Commenting on the difficult question of the physical appearance of the inhabitants of Meroë, P. L. Shinnie concludes that the ethnic composition of ancient Nubia was no different from what it is today — a predominantly brown-skinned people of aquiline features possessing in varying degrees Negro admixture.[58]

At some time in the sixth century B.C. the Ethiopians transferred the seat of their government from Napata further south to Meroë, situated between the Fifth and Sixth Cataracts, about 120 miles north of Khartoum. Meroë had several advantages which the Ethiopians could exploit in the continuance and development of their power: the fertility of the area known as the "Island of Meroë," its location with respect to trade routes, and its importance as a center of iron works. Although the Greeks had received some reports of the Napatan Twenty-Fifth Ethiopian Dynasty, it was the Ethiopians of the second or Meroïtic period (542 B.C.–339/350 A.D.) with whom the Greeks, and later the Romans, were most familiar. It was the Ethiopian people and civilization of this period that evoked the attention of classical writers and attracted Greek and Roman visitors. It was to a large extent Ethiopians from this period who formed a part of the Greco-Roman world — the subject of this book.

Like the earlier Ethiopians who founded the Twenty-Fifth Dynasty and conquered Egypt, the Meroïtic Ethiopians used their military skill to further territorial expansion and for many years occupied an area that extended southward from Lower Nubia to Sennar and Kosti and westward to Kordofan and perhaps beyond. Another manifestation of the military nature of these peoples appears in their military and diplomatic relations, first, with the Ptolemies and, later, with the Romans, who at various periods from the time of Augustus until late in the Empire were concerned in disputes involving their southern frontiers in Egypt.[59]

Meroë under Ergamenes, a contemporary of Philadelphus, in the words of Rostovtzeff, was a Nubian Alexandria. A renaissance of temple building at Meroë paralleled the outburst of temple building in Ptolemaic and Roman Egypt. Ethiopian cities like Kerma, Karanòg, and Faras flourished during the first two centuries of the Christian Era. Meroïtic decorated pottery, reflecting Egyptian and Greco-Roman influence, but thoroughly Meroïtic in inspiration and execution, surpassed anything made in Egypt at the time. The pottery, in the opinion of Shinnie, ranks among the finest in the ancient world and is the major contribution of Nubia to the art of the Nile Valley.[60] Graffiti and ostraca in Meroïtic script, developed during the period, are evidence of a literacy more widespread than previously. A recent evaluation regards the Meroïtic culture as a homogeneous blend of native and imported Egyptian and Greco-Roman elements; its accomplishments in the material and artistic fields more fully the work of local artisans and superior to those of the earlier eras; and its achievements in political and religious fields as nearly the equals of the Napatan of the Twenty-Fifth Dynasty.[61]

The third and last group of sub-Egyptian peoples contemporary with classical sources has been described by Africanists and Egyptologists as that of the so-called X-group culture, which flourished in Lower Nubia between the fourth and sixth centuries after Christ. Several peoples from regions below Egypt intermittently during this period disturbed Roman frontiers, and the ensuing disputes constituted an important part of Roman military activity in the late Empire. The puzzle of the X-group population, however, has presented knotty problems as to the identification of the peoples involved. It is generally agreed that after the collapse of Meroë one or more new ethnic groups moved into the area. Differing in their views as to the identifications of the migrants, scholars have suggested the Blemmyes, Nobatae, and Nobades.[62] According to one interpretation, however, the ethnological evidence is too inadequate and the cultural manifestations of the X-group culture too widespread and generalized to warrant a definite association with a single tribe. Hence, this view concludes that the X-group peoples and culture were an amalgam not only of Blemmyes, Nobatae, and Nobades but also of other groups whose names are not extant and of the numerically dominant Meroïtic population.[63]

As to the Blemmyes, Nobatae, and Nobades, classical sources present conflicting reports. Although the Blemmyes (Blemyes) were mentioned as early as the third century B.C. in Theocritus,[64] they received, as it will be pointed out in Chapter V, particular notice during the late Empire. They are described by a scholiast on Theocritus as a black-skinned Ethiopian race, by Dionysius "Periegetes" as burnt-colored, and by Avienus as black-skinned.[65] Nonnus referred to woolly-haired Blemmyes.[66] Some modern scholars have identified the Blemmyes with the Beja tribes of today.[67]

Classical authors differ as to the location of the Blemmyes. According to Theocritus, they lived far to the south near the source of the Nile.[68] Eratosthenes, cited by Strabo, located them on either side of Meroë along the Nile in the direction of the Red Sea and said that, like the Megabari, they were subject to the Ethiopians bordering on Egypt.[69] Elsewhere, however, Strabo refers to "Troglodytes, Blemmyes, Nubae, and Megabari, those Ethiopians who live above Syene."[70] Even though these authors place the Megabari and Blemmyes in the south, Ptolemaic documents suggest that at least some of these Ethiopians had migrated to Egypt as far north as Apollinopolis Magna as early as the third century B.C. These Megabari and Blemmyes who had migrated northward were descendants of mercenaries who had served in the Egyptian army.[71] Pomponius Mela noted their nomadic nature when he described the Blemmyes as a people who wandered about without established abode.[72] An examination of the sources just cited and of the notices in later geographers has led to the view that the Blemmyes, frequently mentioned in the Roman period, were a collection of nomadic peoples who moved about the eastern desert between Abyssinia, Egypt, and the Red Sea in the manner of the modern Beja who occupy approximately the same area.[73]

The use of different names at different periods adds to the difficulty of untangling the conflicting and imprecise reports concerning the Nubae, Nobatae, and Nobades.[74] Eratosthenes, as reported by Strabo, describes the Nubae as a large tribe, not subject to the Ethiopians, living on the left bank of the Nile between Meroë and the great bend of the Nile.[75] Strabo himself, however, includes the Nubae, as already stated, among those Ethiopians who live above Syene.[76] Nubaei Aethiopes are located by Pliny at a distance of an eight days' journey from an (unlocated) island of the Sembritae on the Nile.[77] The Nubae are described as *exusti* by Silius Italicus.[78] The ancient evidence has been interpreted as indicating two divisions of Nubae, one in the western desert between Meroë and Dongola and another to the south of Meroë.[79] Ptolemy's mention of Nubae not only south of Egypt but also in inner Libya has also given rise to a view that the Nubae were Libyan in origin.[80] With the exception of Claudian's notice that Nubae were among the troops of Gildo, the term Nubae disappears in the third century and is later replaced by the Nobatae, who came, according to Procopius, from Oasis (Kharga), and the Nobades. The Nobades or the Nobatae, although it is a disputed matter, have been taken as the same people as the Nubae. The Nobatae, in the opinion of A. J. Arkell, may have been unrelated to Nubae, and the word may have been derived from Napata.[81]

The late Meroïtic and X-group peoples, according to some authorities, were markedly Negroid. One study of the skeletons of the late Meroïtic period (first, second, and part of the third centuries A.D.) concludes that the racial characteristics were diverse, with a prevalence of a Negroid element. The X-group peoples, according to another view, were composed mainly of two pronouncedly Negroid types and hybrids resulting from interbreeding. A recent study points out, however, that there are some doubts as to the earlier hypothesis of a strong Negroid admixture in the X-group peoples.[82] In summary, scholarly opinion is divided as to the physical characteristics of the inhabitants south of Egypt from the fourth to the sixth centuries. At any rate as far as some Greeks and Romans were concerned, the Blemmyes and Nubae were both Ethiopians and dark or black.

The significance of Greco-Roman observations on the Ethiopians south of Egypt becomes clearer when considered in light of the history of the peoples of that region. Although other sections of this book illustrate in more detail the significance of the knowledge of the Ethiopian peoples to whom the Greeks and Romans referred, a few comments are appropriate at this point.

Certain populations of the Napatan, Meroïtic, and X-group periods, regardless of the races to which they actually belonged, or of what modern scholars believe them to have been, were designated as Ethiopians by some Greek and Roman authors. Peoples from sub-Egyptian Ethiopia, we have seen, developed military skill; some acquired experience in government; the

Meroïtic kingdom covered an extensive area; their cities at various times were rich in temples, palaces, and necropoleis; at periods Egyptian influence was apparent in their religion and their art; and a Negroid element was present at times in the population.

To regard, therefore, classical references to Ethiopians in Egypt and below as valueless or the Greco-Roman image of Ethiopians as a glorification of a distant, unknown, mysterious people is to miss the mark. There is in many instances a remarkable coincidence between certain classical observations on sub-Egyptian Ethiopia and the facts as reconstructed by Africanists.[83] As early as Herodotus Meroë was described as a great city, reported to be the capital of all Ethiopia.[84] The Greeks had received accounts of the Twenty-Fifth Ethiopian Dynasty. Herodotus mentions one of the kings of that Dynasty — Sabacos (Shabako); Manetho lists three — Sabacôn (Shabako), Sebichôs (Shebitku), and Tarcus/Taracus (Taharqa); and Diodorus, two — Actisanes and Sabaco, although it has been argued that Actisanes is a double of the latter.[85] The statement — attributed by Strabo to Megasthenes — that Tearco the Ethiopian advanced as far as Europe perhaps echoes reports of the power of an Ethiopian people who conquered Egypt.[86] Diodorus is not correct, of course, when he says that the Ethiopians never experienced the rule of foreign invaders, but, like Megasthenes, he reflects some acquaintance with the scope of the Ethiopian military.[87] Both of these men, however, writing at periods far removed from the events described, recorded an awareness of the profound upheaval that had taken place and involved Ethiopians in Egypt.

The long tradition of Ethiopians as soldiers explains to some extent the prolonged difficulties of the Romans with Meroïtic Ethiopians and later with the Blemmyes and the Nobades. Here also may lie a partial explanation for Augustus' conceding to an Ethiopian queen everything she requested, including remission of tribute, and for Diocletian's payment of an annual subsidy to both Blemmyes and Nobades.[88]

Egyptian influence in Napatan and Meroïtic Ethiopia has been noted above. Herodotus, when he says that Ethiopians learned Egyptian customs and acquired milder manners from Egyptians who settled among them, was apparently following sources which attributed similarity in Ethiopian and Egyptian culture to Egyptian influence. Diodorus, also noting similarities between certain Egyptian and Ethiopian practices, recorded a tradition which regarded most Egyptian institutions as derivatives of Ethiopian civilization — a view resembling that of some scholars who believe that several Egyptian customs originated south of Egypt.[89]

As to the much debated question of the Negroid element in the populations south of Egypt both classical art and literature provide some evidence. The evidence of art is perhaps more valuable than the texts on this point, because for a period extending from the sixth century B.C. to the third century A.D. there exists, we have seen, a rather extensive century-by-century gallery of Negroid types.[90] A very large number of these representations obviously depicted individuals who had come from the region south of Egypt or were descendants of these peoples. Even when the artist depicted Negroes residing in Greece or Italy, they had often reached Greece and Italy via Egypt. It is not possible, of course, to know the extent to which the Negro types depicted — whether "true" Negro or mixed — by Greek and Roman artists represented the total population of the region below Egypt. Diodorus, however, tells us that the majority of Ethiopians who dwelt among the Nile was black-skinned, flat-nosed, and woolly-haired, and Ptolemy states that the people in the vicinity of Meroë were black and pure Ethiopians.[91]

The above illustrations are only a few of the instances in which Greco-Roman observations appear to reflect an acquaintance with African reality. Further, there was a remarkable lack of bias in the classical commentaries. The Greeks expressed no astonishment that Ethiopians, a people whom they at times described as black or dark and as having several so-called Negroid physical traits, had conquered Egypt or had constructed great temples. Westerners, it has been pointed out, have traditionally regarded the civilization of the Napatan and Meroïtic periods as Egypt "running downhill to an inglorious and too long protracted conclusion."[92] No such view existed among the Greeks and the Romans. The Ethiopia of this period, according to one modern view, when considered from the perspective of African history, was ancient Egypt moving closer to black Africa at a time when a portion of black Africa possessed a capacity, greater than ever before in its history, of experiencing influences from an urban civilization.[93] The Greco-Roman view of the Ethiopia of this period, it will be seen, had more in common with the latter approach.

IV. Greek Encounters with Ethiopian Warriors

Discussions of the Ethiopian warriors whom the Greeks and Romans encountered have failed to take into consideration the long history of earlier contacts between inhabitants of Egypt and black or dark soldiers from the south. This failure has often resulted in a lack of the perspective necessary to assess properly classical references to Ethiopian warriors. An evaluation, for example, of the Ethiopian contingent in the Persian army as a "humble and almost grotesque auxiliary"[1] is not justified by the substantial evidence relating to the use of Ethiopian troops made elsewhere by Aegean and Mediterranean peoples.

As a part of their policy in holding the shifting Nubian frontiers, Egyptians reinforced their own troops by using black or dark troops from the south. Since the time of the old Kingdom, southerners who apparently enjoyed considerable prestige among the Egyptians had been recruited by the Pharaohs. A career in the Egyptian army and police offered southerners an opportunity for achieving positions of importance and of security. Among the eighty wooden models of soldiers found beside the coffin of a military prince of Assiut were forty archers whose skin is almost black. Egyptian tomb paintings have preserved other vivid representations of Nubians who served at various times under Egyptians.[2] The story of King Sesostris in Europe and of some of his soldiers who settled by the Phasis River has been related to Herodotus' report of black, woolly-haired Colchians and has been interpreted as evidence of a classical tradition that there were Ethiopians among the troops of the Egyptian Sesostris.[3] From the south also had come Ethiopians (Kushites) who had overrun Egypt and ruled it for more than half a century.[4] It was perhaps via Egypt that the blacks, depicted on a Minoan fresco, had come to Crete to serve as auxiliaries.[5] In light of a long tradition of black warriors south of Egypt it is not surprising, therefore, that the Greeks and, later, the Romans had encounters with Ethiopian soldiers emanating from Egypt and regions to the south.

If the black-skinned, woolly-haired Eurybates was Ethiopian or Negroid, and such a possibility cannot be excluded, the Homeric mention of an Ethiopian outside Africa refers to a herald from Ithaca who served among the Greeks at Troy. It was Eurybates who accompanied Odysseus on the embassy to Achilles, the companion whom Odysseus esteemed more highly than his other companions because he had a mind like his own. Under what circumstances Eurybates may have come to Ithaca is not known, but, as suggested above, it was perhaps via Egypt.[6] Although Memnon was known to Homer, the Homeric epics provide no information concerning the role of Memnon and Ethiopians in the Trojan War.[7]

It was perhaps in Egypt that Greeks first met Ethiopian soldiers and first received reports of their activities. Psammetichus I, a king of the XXVIth dynasty, recruited Ionian and Carian mercenaries in his efforts to re-establish himself in Egypt after the period of Ethiopian domination. The extent to which these mercenaries encountered Ethiopians in the course of their assistance to the Egyptian king is not certain. These mercenaries, however, in all probability received reports of Ethiopian soldiers, for, as Herodotus believed, it was from these settlers in Egypt that Greeks gained exact knowledge of Egyptian history from the reign of Psammetichus onwards.[8] There were also Greeks among the foreign mercenaries who accompanied Psammetichus II (594–588 B.C.) on his expedition into Ethiopia. An inscription on the leg of a statue of Ramesses II at Abu Simbel records the participation of several Greeks. One was a Psammetichus, the son of Theocles, perhaps a Greek mercenary who had served under the first Psammetichus, another was from Teos, another from Colophon, and still another from Ialysos. Scholars are not agreed as to how far into Nubia the second Psammetichus penetrated, although a recent suggestion has conjectured a major Nubian operation as far as the Fourth Cataract.[9]

The most convincing explanation of Negroid stone figures found in Cyprus is that the sculptures were portraits of Ethiopians in the civil and military service of the Egyptians during Egyptian occupation of the island under Amasis (568–525 B.C.). The sculptures in question were discovered in Ayia Irini and, according to

E. Gjerstad, on the basis of style cannot be dated later than 560 B.C. One figure is dressed in a short tunic which leaves the legs free; a long, plain chiton covers entirely the body of the other; and both wear conical caps (Fig. 1). A striking piece of corroborative evidence for the presence of Ethiopians in Cyprus is the traditional opinion of the Cyprians themselves, recorded by Herodotus, that one component of their population was Ethiopian. The combined literary and archaeological evidence, together with the fact that Egyptians had a long history of recruiting Ethiopians, tends to confirm the view that the figures depicted Negroes present during the military occupation of Cyprus in the sixth century. It is not possible to determine the size of the Negroid contingents among the Egyptian forces, but it does not seem likely that the Cyprians would have included Ethiopians in a statement of population statistics — the others mentioned being Salaminians, Athenians, Arcadians, Cythnians, and Phoenicians — had the numbers been negligible.[10]

Herodotus notes that there were Greeks in the army of Cambyses (525–522 B.C.) at the time the Persian king planned his expedition against the Ethiopians. Since Cambyses left the Greeks behind before he set out on his ill-fated Ethiopian mission, it is doubtful that the Greeks encountered Ethiopian soldiers. The Greeks, however, were certainly aware of the reports which reached Cambyses via the Ichthyophagi concerning the defiant Macrobians and which must have been an important source in the creation of the Greek image of the Ethiopian warrior whom the Greeks later encountered in the Persian wars.[11]

The Herodotean account of the Persian wars included Ethiopian contingents from Africa as a part of Xerxes' army. These Ethiopians from above Egypt, the most ulotrichous men on earth, fought with the Arabians under the command of Arsames. They were dressed in lion and leopard skins and were equipped with bows of palmwood, short arrows tipped with stone, spears pointed with gazelle-horn, and clubs. When they marched into battle, they painted their bodies with gypsum and vermilion. The Ethiopians, according to one interpretation, not only fought at Marathon but may also have been among those whom the Greeks encountered in the earlier Ionian conflict with the Persians.[12]

Since Aeschylus fought at Marathon and perhaps at Salamis,

certain passages in the *Persians* have relevance for African participation in the Persian wars. Among the leaders of the Persian fleet listed by Aeschylus was one Arcteus, who lived by the waters of the Nile, perhaps, according to one interpretation, from Upper Egypt, if not from Nubia itself, and whose name, according to another suggestion, was the equivalent of the Ethiopian Taharqa.[13] The thirty thousand "Black Horse," mentioned in the report of the messenger on the Persian leaders who perished at Salamis, appear to be a reference to men, not to the type of horse mounted.[14] Hence, even if we do not interpret Aeschylus literally in these two instances, we cannot overlook the possibility that the references to a Persian leader from the region of the Nile and to black horsemen contain a nucleus of fact and reflect the poet's contemporary experience with and knowledge of Ethiopian contingents among Persian troops.

A series of alabastra from the fifth century B.C. depicting a Negroid type has been frequently interpreted as the work of Athenian potters inspired by the defeat of the Persians and impressed by the blacks whom they saw for the first time in large numbers in Greece. The hair in these figures is represented by dots, the method chosen by the artist to represent the kinky hair of the Negroes that always fascinated the Greeks. This group of alabastra repeats with variations a black figure, dressed in a short, loose, parti-colored tunic and trousers, usually holding in the right hand an axe, with the right arm covered by what appears to be a folded cloth or skin, often fringed. Sometimes there is a quiver attached to his back and at times a mantle surrounding the arms and hanging over the shoulders. The Negro stands most frequently with his feet to the spectator's right and his head to the left. Nearby there is usually a palm tree, close to the foot of which stands a small quadrangular object (Figs. 80, 81). Although Athenian pride may have been a source of inspiration for the selection of Negroes as symbolic of the defeated Persians, the contemporary curiosity about foreigners, reflected in the literature of the period, was perhaps a contributing factor. In some vases of the same type the profile of the central figure is white and not Negro, but the other details of dress and equipment are almost identical to those of the Negro vases; in one instance, a Negro and the white figure, generally interpreted as an Amazon, appear on the same vase (Figs. 16a–b).[15]

Pride in Greek victory over the Persians may have also provided motivation for the Ethiopians depicted on a phiale (Figs. 39a–b) described by Pausanias. In describing a sanctuary of Nemesis at Rhamnus, not far from Marathon, Pausanias mentioned a statue of Nemesis carved from a block of abandoned Parian marble which the Persians had brought to Marathon in the hope that they would construct a trophy to commemorate a victory. The statue held in its right hand a phiale on which Ethiopians were carved. These Ethiopians, like the blacks on the above-mentioned alabastra, have been interpreted as an allusion to the black troops in Xerxes' army and as symbols of the vanquished Orientals.[16] A gold phiale from the late fourth century B.C., found at Panagurishte (in Bulgaria) featuring Negroes as a chief motif, has been considered a replica of the well-known Rhamnus original. Even though such an identification is not at all certain, the artist of a fourth-century phiale may have at least looked to the earlier work for inspiration.[17]

One final bit of evidence should be mentioned with respect to Ethiopian participation in the Persian wars. Some light on the physical characteristics of types of black troops in the Persian army is provided by reliefs on the stairway of the Apadana or Audience Hall at Persepolis, begun by Darius. Among the tribute-bearing delegations depicted, two attendants with Negroid features and hair bear gifts — a vessel with a lid, an elephant tusk, and an okapi.[18] Instead of tribute, the Ethiopians nearest Egypt whom Cambyses conquered on his way to the Macrobian Ethiopians and those in Upper Nubia brought gifts, among which Herodotus listed gold and elephant tusks. Perhaps the vessel carried by the tribute-bearer at Persepolis contained gold. At any rate, the Persepolis depiction is a striking confirmation of the Herodotean statement and gives an artist's conception of Ethiopians known to the Persians, and perhaps of one Ethiopian type serving in Xerxes' army.[19]

Whether Sicilian Greeks also encountered Negro warriors in the fifth century B.C. is not at all certain. According to Frontinus, Gelon (ca. 540–478 B.C.), the tyrant of Syracuse, in a war against the Carthaginians captured many prisoners, among whom were very black auxiliaries. Although a Roman notice of the first century A.D. concerning the participation of blacks in a Carthaginian expedition of a much earlier period may very well point only to a legend, the report is worthy of note in a discussion of Ethiopian warriors.[20] A fourth-century Sicilian tyrant of Syracuse, Agathocles (361–289 B.C.), may also have been responsible for Greek contact with Ethiopians. In his conflict with Carthage Agathocles resolved to attack his opponents in north Africa. One of his commanders, Eumachus, made an expedition into the inland regions of Libya, marched across a high mountain range, came to one region where there were many apes, conquered one city, won two others by diplomacy, and went no further after he heard that the neighboring barbarians were assembling great forces against him. There is obviously a problem of identification of the region which Eumachus reached, but the mention of apes suggests that it was some part of inner black Africa.[21] An interesting fourth-century record of an Ethiopian warrior is preserved on the bezel of a bronze ring representing a youthful soldier with Negroid features who defends himself in a crouching position with a sword in one hand and a round shield in the other.[22]

The Ethiopian warrior was well known to Ptolemaic Egypt. The Ptolemies conducted operations in Ethiopia, motivated, in the opinion of M. I. Rostovtzeff, to a large extent by commercial interests and by a desire to have access especially to the gold and elephants in Ethiopian territory. There was gold in the Nubian desert south of Egypt and in the eastern desert between roads leading from Coptos and Apollinopolis to Berenice on the Red Sea. Meroë was important not only for some gold and iron but also as a center through which products from central Africa passed. Eastern Africa and especially the area of Somaliland were sources of elephants, which the rival Seleucids were able to obtain from India. The military efforts of the Ptolemies against the Ethiopians, Rostovtzeff suggests, were in support of commercial and diplomatic interests, of securing the Egyptian southern frontier, of ensuring a Meroïtic supply of gold, and of providing protection for elephant-hunting parties.[23]

Diodorus states that until Ptolemy II (Philadelphus 283–246 B.C.) no Greek had penetrated Ethiopia, none even as far as the boundaries of Egypt, and that he was the first Greek to lead an army into Ethiopia.[24] Greeks, however, as mentioned above, had served in the army of Psammetichus II which invaded Ethiopia.[25] Diodorus' notice of Ptolemy II's Ethiopian expedition mentions neither the itinerary nor the purpose of the expedition. The commercial motives noted above, however, may have had some relevance. One of the purposes of the expedition, it has been argued, was the restoration of communications between Egypt and Ethiopia which had been seriously disrupted between the end of Ethiopian rule in Egypt and the accession of the Ptolemies, a conclusion strengthened by the fact that Diodorus seems to have lost memory of what had happened prior to the undertakings of Philadelphus.[26]

The names of Pasimenes and Iason, both from Cyrene, engraved on a temple at Buhen, below the Second Cataract, go back, according to one interpretation, to the third century B.C. and represent the names of mercenaries of Philadelphus, one of whose coins has been found also at Buhen.[27] It has been suggested that a military communiqué from the garrison commander at Elephantine addressed to a Ptolemy also belongs to the reign of Philadelphus. The fragments of a third-century papyrus include the statements that "Ethiopians came down and besieged" and ". . . by constructing a stockade, I and my two brothers . . . as reinforcements . . ." Apparently Ethiopians had taken the initiative by laying siege to a city, the name of which has been lost. The incident doubtlessly represents action taken by Ethiopians who opposed aspects of Ptolemaic military, diplomatic, or commercial policy.[28]

Zoological interests and requirements of elephants for the military also provided motives for Ptolemaic involvements in Ethiopia, especially east Africa. Ptolemy II explored the coast of the Red Sea, established stations for hunting elephants, and founded harbors for shipping them to Egypt, where they were trained for military purposes.[29] Several Greeks are known to have visited Ethiopia during the reign of Philadelphus, some perhaps out of curiosity and others in search of information for the Ptolemy. Timosthenes, who was in charge of Philadelphus' navy, had traveled from Syene to Meroë in sixty days. Dalion, who was said to have been the first Greek to penetrate Ethiopia beyond Meroë, made his journey probably early in the reign of Ptolemy II.[30]

A festival of Dionysus celebrated by Ptolemy II included a great procession which took all day to pass through the stadium at Alexandria. Among those who paraded were many Ethiopians bearing ivory, ebony, gold, and silver.[31] And, according to Theocritus, Philadelphus took a portion of the country of the black

Ethiopians. Theocritus, the first Greek author to mention the Ethiopian Blemmyes, may be reflecting his knowledge of the results of the explorations along the Upper Nile undertaken in the reign of Ptolemy Philadelphus.[32] Since our records are meagre in this instance, it is neither clear why the Ethiopian giftbearers were present in the parade at Alexandria nor what is meant by the Theocritean reference to Ptolemy's taking a region of Ethiopia. At any rate, we are poorly informed as to the extent of Philadelphus' operations in Ethiopia and as to how much he obtained by diplomatic negotiations. Reference has been made to the military opposition of Ethiopians to Ptolemaic intrusion. But since the interests of Philadelphus in Ethiopia seem to have been largely commercial, diplomacy rather than arms would have been to his advantage. A mutually satisfactory arrangement, for example, would have been beneficial to Ptolemy's plans for elephant hunting and to his avid enthusiasm for collecting animals. The men in Ptolemy's hunting parties, anxious to profit from the huge sums of money spent for such purposes, had much to gain from the friendly cooperation of the indigenous population.[33]

Some of the later Ptolemies continued elephant hunting in Ethiopia. The third Ptolemy (Euergetes I, 246–221 B.C.), shared his predecessor's interest in hunting elephants and sent a friend, Simmias, to explore the territory along the coast of the Red Sea.[34] Under Ptolemy IV (Philopator 221–205 B.C.), Lichas, son of Pyrrhus, an Acarnanian, was sent to take command of the forces conducting operations in elephant country along the Somaliland coast. Another record of officers and soldiers of a Ptolemaic commander, Charimortus, who conducted operations in elephant country, appears in the form of a prayer to Ares, the god who grants victory and good hunting.[35]

In some of the Egyptian rebellions which plagued the later Ptolemies, especially in Upper Egypt, Ethiopians played a role. An important factor inspiring their revolts, it has been suggested, was the maintenance of a continued Pharaonic tradition in the region south of Egypt which, unlike Egypt, had not been subjugated by the Greek conquerors. The existence of an old tradition and an independent Nubia, just beyond their southern frontier, was a source of hope to nationalists who remembered legends of Egyptians who had taken refuge in Ethiopia and had returned to recover what had been lost. Ethiopians, witnessing the success of the Ptolemies in Ethiopia, would readily see the advantages of military cooperation with their neighbors in Upper Egypt and would be willing to lend military assistance.[36]

A fragment of Agatharchides, without mentioning the Ptolemy intended, refers perhaps to the reign of the fifth Ptolemy (Epiphanes 205–180 B.C.). The passage states that Ptolemy formed a corps of five hundred horsemen from Greece for his war against the Ethiopians.[37] Nubians may have been among the insurgents in a revolt directed against Epiphanes in the south by two natives, Harmachis and Anchmachis.[38] The policy of Ptolemy VI (Philometor 180–145 B.C.) and Euergetes II appears to have been directed at strengthening the Ptolemaic position in the south and to have resulted in ending the struggle between the Ptolemies and Nubia.[39]

The Pharaohs had drawn on their southern neighbors for police and soldiers. In employing southerners as mercenaries, therefore, the Ptolemies were continuing an old tradition. It is not possible to determine precisely the extent to which the Ptolemies used soldiers from the south of Egypt. M. Launey, though noting that black Africans were included among contingents in Hellenistic armies, believes that the Ptolemies were circumspect in their use of peoples of the African desert and the black races, because they could not expect great profit, either military or economic, from undisciplined peoples. However, the tradition of black warriors as auxiliaries in the Mediterranean suggests that Launey has underestimated the use of black troops by the Ptolemies, and that there is no reason to believe that the Ptolemies developed a policy of eschewing black or dark southerners.[40]

V. Roman Encounters with Ethiopian Warriors

Ethiopians and Nubae burnt by the sun's fierce fury, according to Silius Italicus, were among the troops mustered by Hannibal.[1] That this notice, coming from an author of the first century A.D., was based on a well-established tradition as to blacks in Hannibal's army is indicated by evidence contemporary with the Carthaginian's Italian campaign. A bronze coinage associated with Hannibal's invasion of Italy preserves on the obverse the head of a Negro, whose race is vividly delineated by his broad nose, thick lips, and kinky hair (Figs. 41a–c). E. Babelon suggested that these coins, which carry an elephant on the reverse, were inspired by the role which Hannibal's elephants played in the Italian campaign and by the impression which these elephants and their Negro mahouts made upon the population of north Italy — an impression similar to that made at an earlier date by Pyrrhus and his elephants.[2] C. T. Seltman follows Babelon in the opinion that the coins may have been among those which Hannibal's allies in Italy added to the Carthaginian's war chest.[3] H. H. Scullard also believes that the usual attribution to Hannibal may stand and that the Negro, if he depicts the driver, shows that natives had replaced Indians as mahouts.[4]

There is no reason to doubt that Hannibal employed Negro mahouts. Although neither Livy nor Polybius makes specific reference to Hannibal's use of Negroes as mahouts, references to the skill and experience of Ethiopians in handling elephants are numerous.[5] Arrian states that Indian and Ethiopian armies used war elephants before the Macedonians and that the Carthaginians employed them for military purposes.[6] War elephants, one being led by a rope, have been represented at Musawwarat-es Sofra, about 125 kilometers northeast of Khartoum and about 30 kilometers from the Nile, in reliefs on a Meroïtic temple built in the last quarter of the third century B.C. In fact, the frequent presence of the elephant in Meroïtic sculpture may mean that the Ethiopians not only used the elephant for military purposes but also attached a ceremonial importance to the animal. Among the remains of a "Great Enclosure" at Musawwarat-es Sofra are a series of ramps and corridors and a unique wall terminating in the figure of an elephant. It is likely that this complex of enclosures and ramps was a center for the training of elephants and that African elephants used for military purposes in the Ptolemaic and Roman periods were almost certainly trained by Meroïtes.[7] Further, Plautus, whose *floruit* included the period of the Second Punic War, writes as if African blacks were on Roman soil in his day. A reference in the *Poenulus* to those blacker than the *Aegyptini* who carry buckets around at the circus suggests Ethiopians and has been so interpreted, and the specific mention of circus points to the presence of Ethiopians in Italy.[8]

The evidence as a whole, then, seems to indicate that the Negro depicted on the coinage was one of the black mahouts who survived the rigors of the Alps; that the Plautine reference to *Aegyptini* was contemporary testimony of Roman knowledge of blacks in Hannibal's army; that Silius Italicus was following a well-authenticated tradition in listing Ethiopians and Nubae in the Carthaginian army; and that a Pompeiian terra cotta of a tower-bearing elephant with a Negro driver (Figs. 82a–b)[9] may have been inspired by the artist's acquaintance with the role of Ethiopian mahouts in the Second Punic War. It is not necessary, however, to conclude that Hannibal employed blacks only as mahouts, because the use of other types of Negro auxiliaries in the Mediterranean is well attested. As far as the coinage and the Pompeiian terra cotta were concerned, it was the black mahouts who made the most lasting impression.

The Romans were involved with peoples south of Egypt in military and diplomatic relations from the time of Augustus until late in the Empire.[10] Although the exigencies of frontier defense required some military action against those Ethiopians of inner Africa who were a source of annoyance to the Romans in north Africa in the first and, perhaps, the second century A.D., it was the Ethiopians of the so-called Meroïtic period south of Egypt with whom the Romans were most concerned for several centuries. Roman involvement with the Ethiopians south of Egypt resulted from considerations similar to those which had involved the

Ptolemies. During their occupation of Egypt the Romans were required to evolve a policy which would ensure the security of their southern boundary and would protect trade with the kingdom of Meroë and routes to the eastern desert and to central Africa.[11]

Cornelius Gallus, the first governor of Egypt, was confronted with a revolt in the Thebaid, where the Ptolemies had encountered difficulties from their southern neighbors. Strabo, who provides a rather full account of Roman-Ethiopian friction during the rule of Augustus, informs us that the sedition had arisen because of dissatisfaction with the tribute imposed and that the revolt was suppressed within a short time.[12] Conferring with Ethiopian ambassadors at Philae, the governor effected a settlement which received the Ethiopian king under Roman protection and installed a prince over a district known as the Triakontaschoinos, an area of the Nile Valley south of Egypt between the First and the Second Cataract. Gallus' vainglorious record of his military success is recorded in an inscription dating from 29 B.C. at Philae, which boasts that he had led his army to a region never penetrated by the armies of the Roman people or the kings of Egypt.[13]

The agreement which the Ethiopians made with Cornelius Gallus was of brief duration. Sometime thereafter the Ethiopians, while a portion of the Roman garrison had been withdrawn to provide troops for Aelius Gallus' campaign in Arabia, crossed the Roman frontier, attacked the Thebaid, took Syene, Elephantine, and Philae, enslaved the inhabitants, and tore down the statues of Caesar. The Roman counteraction that followed involved C. Petronius, prefect of Egypt, in two Ethiopian campaigns — one not later than 24 B.C., and a second, which was perhaps terminated in 22 B.C. Petronius forced the Ethiopians back to Pselchis and sent ambassadors for an explanation of their actions. Upon learning that the Ethiopians had considered themselves wronged by the nomarchs, Petronius explained that Caesar, not the nomarchs, was their ruler and granted their request for a three-day moratorium for deliberations. Dissatisfied with their inaction Petronius quickly routed them, captured Candace's[14] generals, and sent them to Alexandria. He then captured Pselchis, seized more captives, went from there to Premnis, which he also took, and finally captured Napata, although the Ethiopian Queen offered to return the captives and statues taken at Syene. Believing that deeper penetration into Nubia would be too difficult, Petronius returned, strengthened Premnis, where he left a garrison, and departed for Alexandria. He sold some of the captives and sent one thousand to Augustus, who had recently returned to Rome from Cantabria. Candace marched against the Premnis garrison with many thousands of men, but Petronius arrived first. Ethiopian ambassadors conferred with Petronius, who instructed them in turn to confer with Augustus at Samos. And, concludes Strabo, the essentials of whose account of the episode have been summarized above, "when the ambassadors had obtained everything they pleaded for, he [Augustus] even remitted the tributes which he had imposed upon them."[15]

The concessions of a Roman emperor to the Ethiopian Candace must have resulted from a different set of circumstances than those described by Strabo, who was apparently exaggerating the successes of Petronius. There appear to be inconsistencies in the Strabo account.[16] Pliny in his account of the Petronius campaign and the sacking of Napata states that it was not Roman arms which made Ethiopia a desert but that Ethiopia had been exhausted by a series of wars with Egypt.[17] It is unfortunate that an inscription, considered to be an Ethiopian version of the Petronius campaign and of a victory for the Meroïtic queen, is still largely untranslatable. Both Strabo and the *Monumentum Ancyranum* may have overdrawn Roman successes.[18] At any rate, reliefs on the temple of the sun at Meroë depicting bound prisoners under the feet of a conquering king are perhaps a record of some of the Roman captives taken by the Ethiopians.[19] It is likely that Candace did not return all the statues of Caesar which the Ethiopians had torn down, for a splendid head of Augustus (Fig. 83), apparently buried ceremonially as an important trophy, was discovered in excavations at Meroë.[20] In light of difficulties which the Romans later experienced in the same area and of the type of settlement which Diocletian made with the hope of securing the peace, the concessions of Augustus at Samos probably reflected wisdom.

Some of the Ethiopians whom Petronius took as prisoners of war, having been sold, reached various parts of the Roman world. Strabo described the protective equipment of the Ethiopian soldier as consisting of large, oblong shields, made of raw oxhide, and his weapons as axes, pikes, or swords.[21] Several terra-cotta figurines of Negro warriors in full military equipment provide additional evidence as to physical type and equipment of these Ethiopian adversaries of the early Roman Empire. Rostovtzeff has pointed out that one of these Negroid figurines, dressed in a heavy cloak with fringes and equipped with an axe and shield, even if of Roman times and representing an actor in a mime, gives a good idea of the southern enemies of Ptolemaic and Roman Egypt.[22] The terra-cotta collection of the Greco-Roman museum in Alexandria contains other vivid examples of Negroid warriors showing types known to Romans of the early Empire: one of the largest in the collection shows a figure garbed in a short dress, perhaps of leather, a short chlamys hooked on the shoulder, a double axe held by the handle in the right hand and supported on the right shoulder; another, with an oval shield in the left hand and a double axe in the right; and a third, described as a gladiator or soldier, dressed in a tunic with long sleeves, armed with breastplate, short broad-bladed sword or dagger, and a rectangular shield.[23] A pair of bronzes in Berlin (Fig. 84), according to K. A. Neugebauer, was inspired by the Petronius campaign. If this identification is correct, the statuettes may represent Ethiopian prisoners taken in the encounter.[24]

The maintenance of the peace which followed Augustus' treaty with the Ethiopian queen apparently owed no little to the establishment of diplomatic relations between the two peoples. A precedent for mutual understanding through ambassadors had been set at Samos. A Greek inscription of 13 B.C. records a Meroïtic mission of a certain Harpocras, who passed through Pselchis on his way up-country.[25] Other inscriptions, not always datable, provide additional evidence of traffic and some diplomatic exchange between Ethiopians and Romans. A sepulchral stele at Karanòg mentions an ambassador to Rome (literally "of Rome").[26] A Malêwitar, "chief envoy of Rome," is known from a stele at Faras.[27] A demotic inscription of 253 A.D. records the presence of Pasan, son of Paêse, in Philae at a time when the Blemmyes were in conflict with the Romans. Bearer of the title, "the great ambassador of Rome," like his brother Harwoj, Pasan had been sent by his king, Teqērideamani, to Roman authorities. Pasan's mission, however, was not limited to diplomatic matters, because a part of his assignment was to import objects for his king.[28] A Greek graffito from Philae records a visit in 260 A.D. by Abratoi, the son of the Ethiopian king, on behalf of his father.[29] It has been suggested that the several embassies to Philae and the frequency of the use of the important-sounding ambassadorial title point to long-range negotiations between Roman authorities and Teqērideamani concerning boundary problems and peace. Further, annual Meroïtic pilgrimages to the temple of Isis at Philae provided occasions for contacts between Romans and southerners.[30]

Nor were envoys to Meroë lacking. Among those posted to Ethiopia was a Cladon(s) who, without telling his purpose, left a record of his Ethiopian mission and that of companions at the tomb of Ramesses V as he passed through Egypt.[31] On a pyramid in Meroë is a reference to a mission which brought gifts from "the Pharaoh of the west."[32] An inscription from Musawwarat, the southernmost of Latin inscriptions in the Sudan, preserves the record of a passerby who, according to one view, was a visitor from Rome on a pilgrimage to commune with Isis, but, according to another view, a delegate of a Meroïtic queen to Rome.[33]

Roman contacts with the Ethiopians in the reign of Nero receive notice in Pliny and Seneca.[34] The former states that Nero sent a party of praetorian troops under the command of a tribune into Ethiopia to explore the country at a time when he was planning an attack on Ethiopia. Seneca, who says that the purpose of the expedition was to discover the sources of the Nile, had spoken with two centurions upon their return to Rome. The king of the Ethiopians assisted the exploratory party, perhaps with guides and a military escort, and provided it with letters recommending to neighboring tribes beyond Meroë that safe conduct be granted to the Romans. The expedition reached the sudd, the southernmost limit of Roman penetration recorded in this region of Africa.

Some scholars accept the statement of Seneca concerning the scientific aspects of the expedition, whereas others, following the testimony of Pliny that Nero was planning an attack on Ethiopia, suggest that the emperor envisioned military measures which he perhaps considered necessary in support of Imperial commercial interests. Protagonists of a military interpretation relate the mustering of German troops at Alexandria to the Ethiopian project. Those who favor a commercial motive point out that the increasing power of Axum was considered a threat to Roman commercial interests. By moving into the Upper Nile region the Axumites were displacing the Meroïtes who had been on friendly terms with the Romans since the peace of Augustus. An aim, therefore, of Nero in Ethiopia may have been to support Meroë against Axum and to secure control of trade routes over which products, especially ivory, came from the south.[35]

A record of a military engagement between Romans and Ethiopians has been preserved in a fragmentary papyrus, which has been dated not later than the early second century, perhaps between 60 and 94 A.D. The papyrus mentions a conflict in the desert between Romans, who employed a cavalry *ala*, and Troglodytes and Ethiopians.[36] One interpretation suggests that the encounter may be related to the Nero expedition which may have had as one of its aims the discovery of routes leading from the Nile to the Red Sea, south of Coptos.[37] Another view holds that "Troglodytes" in the papyrus are the equivalent of "Blemmyes" and that the episode concerned the activity of a Roman cavalry unit stationed at one of the Roman positions along the Nile.[38]

The history of the prolonged Roman difficulties with the Blemmyes from the middle of the third century until late in the sixth century A.D. demonstrates the wisdom of Augustus in recognizing the hazards associated with the protection of Egypt's southern boundaries. Diodorus mentioned the problems involved in conducting military operations in Ethiopia.[39] After sacking Napata, Petronius had decided not to go further south because of difficulties which deeper penetration would entail.[40] At any rate, during the three-hundred-year period beginning about 250 A.D., the Blemmyes invaded Egypt again and again and, in spite of Roman repulses and victories, were able to return; they took advantage of Rome's difficulties with others and allied themselves with Rome's enemies; for a considerable period they occupied Egypt as far north as Ptolemaïs. Their successes led Diocletian to a decision, in the interest of keeping the peace, to abandon the old Roman frontier and to make a settlement in which he ceded Roman territory to the Nobades, neighbors of the Blemmyes, and made an annual payment to both peoples; they attacked Christian communities and were a constant threat to Roman lives; at times they even allied themselves with the Nobades, although it was the Nobades who finally dealt the blow from which the Blemmyes never recovered.[41]

During the reign of the Emperor Decius (249–251 A.D.) the Blemmyes attacked the southern frontier of Egypt.[42] About ten years later Aemilianus, one of the so-called Thirty Tyrants, met their threat by driving them back as best he could.[43] At a time when Roman rule was being threatened in several directions, the Blemmyes invaded Egypt and occupied Coptos and Ptolemaïs. A demotic inscription of 273 A.D., which mentions a certain Jeho, perhaps admiral of a fleet operating for or against the Blemmyes, has been interpreted as evidence of an expedition sent to punish the Blemmyes for their incursions into Egyptian territory.[44] Aurelian (270–275 A.D.) seems to have subdued the Blemmyes and in his triumphal procession exhibited Blemmyes, together with other prisoners.[45] Yet they were undaunted by Aurelian's victory and again invaded Upper Egypt. Probus (276–282 A.D.) rescued Coptos and Ptolemaïs, the latter allied with the Blemmyes, and sent captives back to Rome, where they created a sensation among the amazed Roman people. He celebrated a triumph over the Blemmyes and presented them among the gladiators who fought in the amphitheater.[46]

That the Roman victory of Probus had little permanent effect on the military strategy and power of the Blemmyes is apparent from the arrangement which Diocletian (284–305 A.D.) made toward the close of the third century. The Emperor's settlement had several aspects. In the first place, he abandoned Lower Nubia and withdrew the Roman frontier to the First Cataract. Secondly, he invited the Nobades, a people who lived in the vicinity of Oasis (Kharga) and had been ravaging neighboring territory, to occupy the Roman settlements and land on both sides of the Nile beyond the city of Elephantine. His hope was that the Nobades, by settling in this area, would serve as a buffer state between his new frontier and the troublesome Blemmyes. In the third place, Diocletian gave an annual grant of money to both the Nobades and the Blemmyes with the stipulation that they were no longer to plunder Roman territory — a sum which Procopius said they were still receiving more than 200 years later, in his day. And, finally, in a spirit of friendship the Emperor instituted an intercultural and interreligious venture whereby he set up certain temples and altars and settled priests from among the Romans, Blemmyes, and Nobades. He hoped that the experience of common worship would result in friendship between the Romans and their southern neighbors and in the solution of persistent difficulties.[47] Diocletian's arrangement was worth the effort, for the agreement seems to have been respected for a considerable period after his death. Although there may have been minor raids during the period, there is no record of any serious violation of Roman territory.

In the fourth and fifth centuries A.D. the Blemmyes consolidated their power in Lower Nubia and ousted the Nobades from portions of the Dodekaschoinos ceded by Diocletian. Within the same period the development of Christianity in Egypt and the introduction of Christianity into Axum had an effect upon the Blemmyes, who, it appears, felt isolated and hemmed in by Christianity. They were the champions of dying paganism. In this connection, they gave a sympathetic audience to the pagan historian Olympiodorus, who visited the Blemmyes in the first quarter of the fifth century when they were established as far north as Talmis.[48]

Theodosius II (408–450 A.D.), believing that the southern frontier needed to be strengthened, divided the Thebaid into two provinces, upper and lower, perhaps in the latter half of his reign, and assigned the civil and military administration of the upper province to the same individual. In a papyrus mentioning the governor of the province reference is made to the barbarian menace of both Blemmyes and Nobades.[49]

In the reigns of perhaps both Theodosius II and Marcian (450–457 A.D.) the Blemmyes raided Christian communities, and sometime during this period they attacked the Christian settlement at Kharga, where their captives included the exiled Nestorius, who had been patriarch of Constantinople from 428–431 A.D. In a letter to the governor of the Thebaid Nestorius wrote that Oasis, having been reduced to utter destruction, had fallen into the hands of the barbarians.[50] In the latter part of the reign of Theodosius II, Appion, Bishop of Syene and Elephantine, sent an appeal to the Emperor for military assistance, for both the Blemmyes and the Nobades had formed an alliance in opposition to the growing influence of Christianity. Churches built on the island of Philae near the temples involved in Diocletian's international project were being threatened.[51]

The seriousness of the situation in Egypt led the Emperor Marcian to the conclusion that decisive Roman action was essential. His general of the east, Maximin, conducted a successful campaign against the combined forces of the Blemmyes and Nobades, who sent ambassadors to Maximin to request an armistice for the purpose of making peace. The determination of the Romans to put an end to the menace of the Blemmyes by this campaign is evident from the terms of the peace upon which Maximin insisted. The Blemmyes were to restore, without ransom, Roman captives taken previously, to return captured booty, to refund expenditures incurred, and to give nobles, rulers or children of rulers, as hostages for the maintenance of the peace, a condition to which the Blemmyes had never before submitted. Maximin made one concession — the southerners were permitted to make their annual pilgrimage to the temple of Isis at Philae. In this Maximin followed the precedent established by Diocletian, as he did also in his agreement to pay an annual subsidy to the vanquished. Although the Blemmyes during the negotiations first proposed that the armistice should last as long as Maximin remained in the Thebaid and, when this proposal was refused, suggested a truce for the period of his lifetime, Maximin would agree only to a hundred-year truce. Maximin, aware of the respect which the southerners had for the temples at Philae, had the treaty ratified there by representatives of the Romans, Nobades, and Blemmyes. He no doubt had in mind not only the appeal Diocletian had made to religion but also the Ethiopian practice of making an annual pilgrimage to Philae to bring a statue of Isis from the island to their own land, of using it for religious purposes, and of returning it to Philae. In spite of Maximin's care in the matter of religious sanction of the treaty, the southerners, upon hearing of the death of Maximin, invaded Egypt again and seized the hostages whom they had been required to offer against their will.[52] Florus, the prefect of Alexandria, repelled the invaders, but made no issue over the recaptured hostages.[53]

It was in the reign of Justin I (518–527 A.D.) that Upper Egypt was again exposed to incursions from the south if the date of 522 A.D. (?), assigned to two papyri, is correct. According to one papyrus, Flavius Marianus, *dux* of the Thebaid at the time, received a petition from officials of the city of Omboi in which they sought protection against a certain Kollouthos, apparently a pagan who had stirred up the Blemmyes against them and had pillaged the city with the aid of barbarians.[54] In another petition addressed to the *dux* of the Thebaid the inhabitants of Antaiopolis described their city as devastated by the Blemmyes since the time of their ancestors and as burdened by the exactions of a certain Florentius, who, it seems, had summoned the Blemmyes to plunder their city.[55]

Fragments of a heroic poem, the so-called Blemyomachia, have been interpreted as referring to the Blemmyan danger of the fifth century, perhaps during the reign of Marcian or Justin I. The very fragmentary condition of the poem, however, makes it difficult to determine to what, if any, historical event the poem refers. The use of fictitious names and the lack of definiteness in the fragments have led to a view that the poem has no more historical flavor than the *Dionysiaca* of Nonnus, who described the victory of Dionysus over a Blemys, an eponymous founder of the Blemmyes. Even though the poem may not refer to a particular episode in the Roman conflicts with the Blemmyes, the poet may have been to some extent motivated by the protracted Roman troubles with the Blemmyes. The Blemmyan danger was real; the southern enemies of the Romans were not inglorious warriors. The menace was worthy of the attention of a poet laureate.[56]

The extent of penetration of the Blemmyes into the Thebaid and the danger of their presence in this area are evident from a letter written perhaps in the sixth century A.D. The document, written in Greek by a scribe for Charachen, the basiliskos of the Blemmyes, indicates that the Blemmyes were rather firmly established as far north as the island of Tanare, probably to be identified with an island just south of Gebelein, where the letter was found. In instructions to his sons not to permit the Romans to infringe upon the rights of the Blemmyes in the administration of the island, the basiliskos may have been referring to the tribute granted, according to Procopius, by Diocletian and paid until Justinian's era.[57]

When Christianity spread among the Nobades, about the middle of the sixth century (ca. 540 A.D.), as a result of the competing missionary efforts of Justinian and Theodora,[58] this people inclined more and more to the Romans and began gradually to fulfill more effectively the role which Diocletian had envisioned at the end of the third century. Taking advantage of the conversion of the Nobades, Justinian (527–565 A.D.) concerned himself with the lingering paganism at Philae. He sent Narses, the commander of the Roman troops in southern Egypt, to Philae, where he closed the Isiac shrines, imprisoned the priests, and had the images of the goddess sent to Constantinople.[59] The military triumphs of Justinian over the Blemmyes were celebrated by Dioscorus, son of Apollôs, a mediocre Egyptian poet of the sixth century A.D., who expressed his joy that neither the Blemmyes nor the Saracens and their plundering robbers were any longer to be feared as a result of the divine peace which flourished everywhere.[60] Silko, who called himself basiliskos of the Nobades and all the Ethiopians, perhaps in conjunction with the troops commanded by Narses, defeated the Blemmyes, who took refuge in the eastern desert. The Christian Silko's triumphal stele, set up at Talmis about 545 A.D., recorded in Greek his victory over the Blemmyes.[61] With the exception of minor episodes, there is no record of further serious attacks from the south in the sixth century and later.

The frontiers of Roman provinces in north Africa were also threatened by Ethiopians who lived to the south of Roman territory. Conflicts with Ethiopians in this area, however, were apparently much less severe than those posed by the prolonged difficulties with the Blemmyes. At any rate, the few notices of Roman conflicts with Ethiopians in this region point to Roman encounters in the first and perhaps second centuries. Sometime in the last years of the first century (ca. 86 A.D.) Septimius Flaccus, *legatus Augusti pro praetore* in command of the third legion, setting out from Libya, advanced into Ethiopian territory, "three months" beyond the country of the Garamantes. The exact extent of Flaccus' penetration into inner Africa is uncertain because neither the rate of his march nor the duration of his rests in the oases is known. Ptolemy, who cites Marinus of Tyre as his source for this military expedition, is equally vague in describing a second mission directed a few years later by Julius Maternus, perhaps a merchant, who left Lepcis Magna and went to Garama, where he was met by the king of the Garamantes for a joint march toward the Ethiopians. Bearing continuously southward they came within four months to Agisymba, the country of the Ethiopians, a region in which there were many rhinoceroses. Desanges has suggested that as a result of the military success of Septimius Flaccus Roman relationships with the Garamantes were improved and Julius Maternus, a civilian, was enabled, a short time thereafter with the assistance of the king of the Garamantes, to conduct his Ethiopian mission probably for commercial purposes. From Agisymba, according to Desanges, Julius Maternus brought back wild beasts, among which were two-horned rhinoceroses exhibited in games by Domitian, whose coins carried an African rhinoceros of the two-horned type.[62]

The vagueness and sparseness of these accounts provide little as to the nature of the relations between the Romans in north Africa and the Ethiopians to the south. Apparently the Roman expeditions were directed against raids upon Roman territory or interference with caravan routes.[63] At any rate, the Ethiopian menace was serious enough to require two expeditions deep into Ethiopian territory. Julius Maternus may have reached the Sudanese steppe, near Lake Chad. A Negro herm in black limestone, found in the thermae of Antoninus at Carthage, possibly belonged to a monument of a triumphal nature. The Negro herm and another of a Libyan (Fig. 85), dating from the middle of the second century A.D., have been regarded as representing prisoners captured by the Romans in the north of the Oran Sahara.[64] Some of the other Negroes depicted in north African mosaics may also represent Ethiopians captured in similar campaigns. It has been suggested, for example, that representations of Negroes were in vogue in Roman Africa during the Antonine period as a result of the victories over the rebellious populations of the Sahara which included Negroes.[65]

Lepcis Magna was the point of departure for Julius Maternus' expedition into inner Africa. Interesting in this connection is the fact that our records preserve notice of an Ethiopian in the army of Septimius Severus, a native of Lepcis Magna.[66] This Ethiopian soldier, stationed among the troops of Septimius in Britain, famous as a jester, belonged to the *numeri*, units of infantry or cavalry recruited from provinces recently conquered or slightly romanized and normally assigned in areas distant from the region in which they had been recruited.[67] Were other Ethiopians recruited for the *numeri* by Septimius Severus? Worthy of note in this respect are the features of one of the soldiers on the Emperor's arch in the Roman Forum (Fig. 86). The broad, rather flat nose and thick lips of the warrior are not unlike these features as depicted in other Roman representations of Ethiopians.[68] Even if the soldier on the arch was not intended as an Ethiopian, the literary mention of an Ethiopian among the troops of Septimius

Severus raises the question of the extent to which the Romans recruited *numeri* from Ethiopians such as the Blemmyes, Nobades, and dark Africans whom they had encountered in various parts of Africa. Lusius Quietus, either a Moor or full-blooded black Ethiopian,[69] *praefectus alae Maurorum* under Domitian, had achieved success in Trajan's Dacian and Parthian campaigns.

Certain auxiliaries, appearing in scenes from the siege of Verona and the battle of the Milvian bridge depicted on the Arch of Constantine, according to H. P. L'Orange, are to be identified as those Ethiopians whose special mode of fighting is mentioned by several classical authors.[70] The unusual equipment — arrows bound in a circle to the head — of some soldiers on the frieze of the arch, L'Orange has noted, points to a practice of peoples from the interior of Africa: Ethiopians, Blemmyes, and Troglodytes as described by Lucian, Heliodorus, Claudian, and in the *Panegyricus Genethliacus* to Maximian.[71] Heliodorus, who gives the fullest account, records that the Ethiopians, following this method of fighting, stuck their arrows in a circle in a round band placed on their heads, with the feathered ends toward the head and the points sticking out. Plucking the arrows from the band as from a quiver, Heliodorus continues, the Ethiopians approached their enemies with twists and contortions, a point noted by Lucian in his observation that the Ethiopians did not release the arrows, taken from their heads, until they had first danced and terrified the enemy by their prancing. The similarity between the martial headdress as represented on the arch and that of warriors unanimously defined as Ethiopians in the literary sources led L'Orange to conclude that Constantine employed Moorish auxiliaries in the siege of Verona and the battle of the Milvian bridge and, further, that Ethiopians and Mauri fought in the great imperial armies on all fronts and far from their homelands in the same manner as black soldiers of colonial countries formed a part of later European armies.[72] Apropos of L'Orange's conclusion, it should not be overlooked that the arrangements which Diocletian had made for the settlement of his difficulties with the Blemmyes and Nobades would have been favorable for the recruitment of Ethiopians in a region that had been a source of great trouble to the Romans. Nor would such recruitment have been inconsistent with the long tradition of Ethiopian auxiliaries in the Mediterranean.

VI. Ethiopians in Classical Mythology

Homer tells us that the Olympians were fond of visiting the Ethiopians. Zeus, followed by all the gods, went to feast with the blameless Ethiopians, where he remained for twelve days.[1] Poseidon also visited the distant Ethiopians to receive a hecatomb of bulls and rams.[2] At the end of the *Iliad* Iris informs the winds that it is not possible for her to remain but that she must return to the streams of Ocean in order to participate in a sacred feast offered by the Ethiopians. Hence, the goddess makes a special trip alone.[3]

The Homeric precedent of these Olympian-Ethiopian consortia[4] and an image of pious, just Ethiopians became so imbedded in Greco-Roman tradition that echoes are heard throughout classical literature. Is there anything in Ethiopian annals that could have been the basis for such a classical image? Pertinent in this connection is the remarkable stele of the Ethiopian King Piankhi (ca. 751–716 B.C.). This record of Piankhi's conquest of Egypt, found at Gebel Barkal, shows the Ethiopian king scrupulously attentive to religious ritual, respectful of the temples and gods of Egypt, unwilling to deal with conquered princes who were ceremonially unclean, chivalrous in battle, and moderate in his relations with the vanquished.[5] Official documents, of course, must always be regarded with caution, but, as A. Gardiner has observed, the "moral and intellectual atmosphere" of Piankhi's sentiments is vastly different, and "behind the verbal expression we cannot fail to discern . . . a temperament which had also as ingredients a fanatical piety and a real generosity."[6]

There is sufficient substance in the stele to have given rise to talk about Ethiopian piety and devotion to the gods. Piankhi's dates are rather late for reports of Ethiopian piety to have reached Homer[7] unless there was such a tradition antedating Piankhi.

Sufficient time, however, had passed after Piankhi's death to allow Herodotus to receive accounts of the Ethiopian's achievements. And in fact Herodotus is the first Greek author in whom we find somewhat detailed references to Ethiopian piety and justice.

Herodotus wrote that Sabacos, of the Ethiopian dynasty, when king of Egypt never put to death Egyptian wrong-doers but instead required them, according to the severity of their offence, to contribute to civic improvement by raising the embankments of their cities. Concerned lest he commit sacrilege, Sabacos, in the Herodotean account, voluntarily retired from Egypt after he had been terrified by a dream that he would assemble all the Egyptian priests and put them to death.[8]

At the time of the Persian expedition into Ethiopia, the Macrobian king of the Ethiopians, discerning the deception of the Ichthyophagi dispatched by Cambyses, remarked that the king of the Persians was not a just man, for no just man would covet a land not his own. Stirred to anger by the reply of the Ethiopian king, Cambyses marched against the Ethiopians and, Herodotus notes, by failing to admit his wrong and to lead his army back when supplies failed, lost vast numbers by cannibalism among his own men.[9] The spirit of both Sabacos and the Macrobian king was in the tradition of Piankhi's piety and generosity.

The Sabaco(s) of Diodorus resembles very closely the account of the same king given by Herodotus, with one exception. Diodorus adds that in piety and uprightness Sabaco(s) far surpassed his predecessors. He abolished the death penalty and required malefactors to perform forced labor on public works. Distressed by a dream similar to that recorded by Herodotus, Sabaco(s), preferring to depart free of defilement, returned rule to the Egyptians and retired to Ethiopia.[10] This account is also reminiscent of the Piankhi stele. Actisanes, an Ethiopian king of Egypt, according to Diodorus, carried his good fortune as a man should and was kindly toward his subjects. Diodorus contrasts the justice of Actisanes with the harshness, injustice, and arrogance of the Egyptian Amasis.[11]

An interpretation of the Homeric references to the Olympian visits among the Ethiopians appears in Diodorus and is of such significance for the question of the classical image of Ethiopian piety and justice that it should be cited in large part:

> And they say that they [Ethiopians] were the first to be taught to honour the gods and to hold sacrifices and festivals and processions and festivals and the other rites by which men honour the deity; and that in consequence their piety has been published abroad among all men, and it is generally held that the sacrifices practised among the Ethiopians are those which are the most pleasing to heaven. As witness to this they call upon the poet who is perhaps the oldest and certainly the most venerated among the Greeks; for in the *Iliad* he represents both Zeus and the rest of the gods with him as absent on a visit to Ethiopia to share in the sacrifices and the banquet which were given annually by the Ethiopians for all the gods together. . . . And they state that by reason of their piety towards the deity, they manifestly enjoy the favour of the gods, inasmuch as they have never experienced the rule of an invader from abroad; for from all time they have enjoyed a state of freedom and of peace one with another, and although many and powerful rulers have made war upon them, not one of these has succeeded in his undertaking.[12]

Diodorus concludes this observation by pointing out that Cambyses lost all his army and exposed himself to great peril by his expedition, that Semiramis gave up her venture into Ethiopia, and that Heracles and Dionysus in their visitation of the entire world failed to subdue only the Ethiopians above Egypt, not only because these peoples were pious but because the enterprise involved insuperable obstacles.

Several points in the Diodorus commentary should be noted: (1) the obviously widespread reputation of the Ethiopians for piety; (2) the apparently frequent citation of the Homeric passages by commentators in explanations of the unusual delight the gods took in Ethiopian sacrifices; (3) two observations which appear for the first time: (a) the Ethiopians were the first to be taught to honor the gods and to perform religious rites in their honor, (b) by reason of their piety the Ethiopians enjoyed divine goodwill and, as a result of this favor, were blessed with internal security and freedom from invasion. Both Cambyses and Semiramis had failed in their Ethiopian expeditions. The exegesis of Diodorus marks a new stage in the transmission of the Homeric observation, for Diodorus has apparently related the Homeric view to certain materials in his sources and to reports gathered from Egyptian priests and Ethiopian ambassadors whom he consulted in Egypt.[13] He calls upon the authority of Homer to support what his research has found, and interprets the history of the Ethiopians in such a light.

The image of just Ethiopians, beloved of the gods, persists in the Empire. The contempt of the Macrobian Ethiopians for Cambyses and his spies evoked Seneca's admiration. The freedom-loving Ethiopians, Seneca writes, rejected Cambyses' threat of slavery and "instead of embracing servitude with outstretched arms sent envoys and made reply in the independent words which kings call insults."[14] In connection with the campaign of C. Petronius against the Ethiopians, Strabo recorded that the ambassadors of the Ethiopian queen received from Augustus everything they pleaded for, including a remission of the tribute which Augustus had imposed.[15] Perhaps contemporaries acquainted with the tradition of Ethiopian justice saw in the Ethiopian queen a revival of pristine, just Ethiopian rulers.

Statius refers to the inhabitants of heaven who are said "to burst forth from their secret portals whenever they wish the pleasure of visiting the homes and shores and lesser banquets of the red Ethiopians."[16] Lucian evokes on several occasions divine visits to the Ethiopians. Obviously echoing Homer, he says the gods are away from home across the Ocean no doubt visiting the blameless Ethiopians; the gods are accustomed to feasting with the Ethiopians continually, at times even self-invited;[17] and, in commenting on the gods' practice of selling their blessings, Lucian notes that the Ethiopians are to be considered fortunate if Zeus is really compensating them for the hospitality which he and the other gods received when they enjoyed a twelve-day Ethiopian feast.[18]

The most just Ethiopians, according to Pausanias, inhabit the city of Meroë and the so-called Ethiopian plain.[19] Thespesion, the president of the Ethiopian Gymnosophists, expresses his view on justice to Apollonius of Tyana in part with these words: "It is not the man who refrains from injustice that is just but the man who himself does what is just and also influences others not to be unjust."[20] Aelian does not overlook the fact that Ethiopia is the place where the gods bathe.[21]

Heliodorus continues the Homeric tradition and also echoes other early records of Ethiopian piety and justice. His Ethiopian king Hydaspes is a model of wisdom and righteousness, resembling in some respects the Ethiopian kings described by Herodotus and Diodorus. Hydaspes does not like to put men to death; he sends messengers to instruct his warriors to refrain from slaughter and to take as many of the enemy alive as possible.[22] In this same tradition is the decision of the Ethiopian priest to abolish human sacrifice forever.[23] Determined to save life wherever possible, Hydaspes proclaimed, as he glanced at the bleeding Oroondates, in words reminiscent of Anchises' "spare the humbled and subdue the proud": "A noble thing it is to surpass an enemy in battle when he is standing but in generosity when he has fallen."[24] Reminiscent of the Macrobian king, who does not covet what is not his own, and of Sabacos, who withdrew from Egypt at the sight of a terrifying vision, Hydaspes does not wish to expand his kingdom by conquests, is content with natural boundaries, the Cataracts, and, having obtained his objectives, retires again to Ethiopia because of his reverence for justice.[25]

To Dionysius "Periegetes" the Ethiopians were godlike and blameless.[26] Arnobius says that the gods are to be everywhere, to pervade all things with their power, not to feast with the Ethiopians and to return to Olympus after twelve days.[27] The Ethiopians, according to Stobaeus, practice piety and justice; their houses are without doors and no one steals the many things left in the streets.[28] Ethiopians, as Diodorus had said earlier, were the first to honor the gods.[29]

An appropriate summary of the classical tradition of divine love for the Ethiopians and of the ancient records on Ethiopian justice appears in the words of a sixth-century A.D.(?) grammarian, Lactantius Placidus: "Certainly they [the Ethiopians] are loved by the gods because of justice. This even Homer indicates in the first book by the fact that Jupiter frequently leaves heaven and feasts with them because of their justice and the equity of their customs. For the Ethiopians are said to be the justest men and for that reason the gods leave their abode frequently to visit them."[30]

Negroes appearing as a primary motif on phialai may be related to the tradition of just and blameless Ethiopians whom the Olympians were fond of visiting because they were the first to honor the gods and their sacrifices were most pleasing to the gods. Why Ethiopians on phialai? A most frequent rite among the Greeks was the libation. Bowls of and for the gods, phialai were made of precious metals — silver and less often gold. From Attic inventories Ethiopian phialai are known among gold offerings to Athene.[31] A gold phiale of the late fourth century B.C., found at Panagurishte (Bulgaria), as has been mentioned earlier, features Negroes as a chief motif (Figs. 39a–b).[32] The phiale has five concentric rows of decoration in relief on the outside. The row closest to the center has twelve rosettes; the second, a row of twenty-four acorns; and the next three rows are composed of twenty-four heads of Negroes, increasing in size as they reach the rim. Negro heads, in combination with rows of acorns and bees, appear also on a terra-cotta phiale of unknown date found in a temple deposit at Locri in south Italy.[33]

The blessings of Hesiod's just city, it has been suggested,[34] inspired the artists of these phialai, the acorns and bees recalling Hesiod's vision: "The earth brings forth for them a bounteous life and on the mountains the oak bears acorns on top and in the middle bees."[35] If such an interpretation is correct and justice is the artist's theme, most appropriate would be the inclusion of Ethiopians, blameless and just, whose sacrifices are most pleasing to the gods. It would be in keeping with the Greek image that a rite involving a dedication to the gods should include Ethiopians as a major motif.[36] Nor should it be overlooked that a Hesiodic fragment includes high-souled Ethiopians among the descendants of the almighty son of Kronos and that Zeus himself, according to Tzetzes, was given the appellation of Αἰθίοψ by the inhabitants of Chios.[37] Of the several explanations of this appellation, one — that of Eustathius — illustrates the persistence of the Homeric tradition by pointing out that the epithet had its origin in the fact that Zeus was particularly fond of visiting the Ethiopians.[38]

The triumph of Bacchus depicted on a marble sarcophagus from the second century A.D., one of several belonging to the family cemetery of the Calpurnii Pisones, includes two Negro boys astride a pair of panthers who draw Bacchus' triumphal chariot (Fig. 87). The young postillions, clad in the panther skin of the god, have been interpreted as initiates in the service of Bacchus and as symbols of innocent youth.[39] Why did the artist select Negro boys for such a role in the triumph of the god? According to Diodorus, Dionysus during his victorious campaign punished the faithless and the impious but imparted the secrets of his rites to all the pious who had cultivated a just life and initiated them into his mysteries.[40] Further, as noted above, Ethiopian piety was one of the reasons given for the failure of Dionysus to subdue the Ethiopians. The Negroes on the sarcophagus, therefore, may have been inspired by the artist's knowledge of the tradition of Ethiopian piety and justice. The small barbarian children, as K. Lehmann-Hartleben and E. C. Olsen have pointed out, are in marked contrast to the "old sinners" on the sarcophagus, who are bound together with spoils on an elephant. Hence, it is reasonable to suggest that the sculptor of the sarcophagus, because, like others, he regarded the Ethiopians as symbols of piety and justice, accorded them a special place of honor in the god's triumphal return to Europe from a journey that had taken him to the southernmost limit of the world.

Homer's original depiction of Ethiopians as blameless may have derived from vague reports of a distant people. Later descriptions of Ethiopians as blameless and just may have been due in part to an idealization of dark-skinned inhabitants of sub-Egyptian Africa.[41] It is not improbable, however, that even the original image was based to some extent on reports of piety and justice reminiscent of the Piankhi stele.

In light of references to Ethiopians in the *Iliad* and the *Odyssey* and of the persistence of the Homeric tradition, it is not surprising that Ethiopians appear elsewhere in Greek and Roman mythology. Delphos, the eponymous founder of Delphi, according to one version, was the son of Poseidon and Melantho or Melaena.[42] According to another tradition, his parents were Apollo and a woman whose name is variously given — Celaeno, Melaena, Melanis and Thyia — in all cases, except the last, derivatives of words meaning black.[43] The arguments which have been advanced that the name of Delphos' mother points to a Negroid origin, are, of course, not in themselves sufficient to establish such an identification. Earlier discussions of this problem, however, have overlooked the evidence showing the extent to which μέλας and similar words were used by classical peoples as equivalents of Αἰθίοψ.[44] Particularly relevant is the tradition ascribed to Musaeus and recorded by Philodemus that Argos begot four Ethiopians by Celaeno, the daughter of Atlas.[45] If a Celaeno, daughter of Atlas, was the mother of Ethiopians, there is no reason to doubt that the mother of Delphos, bearing the name Celaeno or its equivalent, was in the course of time believed to have given birth to an Ethiopian offspring. Nothing, therefore, in Greek, loose, mythological usage excludes the possibility that Ethiopian was indicated by the variants for the name of Delphos' mother. Hence, Delphos is as strong a candidate as any of the others who have been suggested as the Negro appearing on certain fifth-century coins of Athens and Delphi.[46]

A legendary character of divine descent who came to be regarded as Ethiopian and black during the transmission of a myth is Memnon, son of Tithonus and Eos. Though associated with the east and Asia in certain, particularly early, accounts, Memnon was eventually localized unmistakably in Egypt and Ethiopia also. King of the Ethiopians as early as Hesiod[47] but perhaps even before, in the *Aethiopis* of Arctinus, Memnon went to the aid of Priam at Troy, where he distinguished himself by his nobility and his bravery, killed Antilochus but spared his father, and finally met death at the hands of Achilles.

As to an eastern origin it was Susa with which Memnon was frequently associated.[48] In the course of time Memnon acquired both an Asian and an African provenience. Diodorus, for example, was acquainted with Asian and African versions. For in one instance Memnon, the son of Tithonus, according to Diodorus, was sent by Teutamus, the king of Assyria to Priam with a force of twenty thousand troops, one half Ethiopian and the other half from Susa. In this version Memnon had built a palace in the upper city of Susa called Memnonium in his honor. This attribution, however, was disputed, Diodorus reminds us, by the Ethiopians bordering upon Egypt, who maintained that Memnon was a native of their country and, in support of their claim, pointed to a place which bore his name.[49] Strabo also knew two traditions — Susa was founded by Tithonus, the father of Memnon, and its acropolis was called Memnonium; but he also mentions Memnon in Abydos and Thebes.[50]

In other versions of the Memnon story Africa or Ethiopia is frequently Memnon's country. The curious Alexander wanted to see Ethiopia, Q. Curtius Rufus informs us, because it had been Memnon's kingdom.[51] Memnon, according to Dio Chrysostom, came from Ethiopia to assist the Trojans.[52] Athenaeus relates a story that the Ethiopians, upon learning of the death of Memnon, who had been dispatched to Troy by Tithonus, placed wreaths on the acacia trees in the region of Abydos.[53] The Ethiopians, according to Heliodorus, included Memnon together with Perseus and Andromeda among the founders of their race.[54] That by the time of the Empire Memnon was definitely located in Africa is also apparent from the numerous references to the "vocal" Memnon — one of two colossi at Thebes[55] which attracted tourists because of the legend that the statue "sang" at dawn. The statue was placed in Ethiopia itself by Callistratus, who regarded it as a miracle differing from a human being only in its body but guided by a kind of soul; it was a work of the Ethiopians surpassing in skill even the masterpieces of Daedalus.[56] Around Meroë and Memphis Ethiopians and Egyptians sacrificed to Memnon at sunrise when his statue greeted worshippers.[57]

No Negro figures in scenes from the Trojan War appearing on Greek vases can be definitely identified as Memnon, although it might be argued that two vase paintings depict Memnon: one of a Negro standing between two Amazons (Figs. 15a–b), and another representing a slightly bearded Negro, wearing a helmet, cuirass, and chiton, with both hands lifting his shield from the ground (Fig. 21).[58] Hence, the evidence of extant vases suggests that early paintings were for the most part following the tradition of an Asiatic provenience by presenting Memnon as white. A painting by Polygnotus representing a scene from the Trojan War depicts a naked Ethiopian boy beside Memnon. The presence of the boy, according to Pausanias, is explained by the fact that Memnon was king of the Ethiopians. Apparently Memnon in the painting was depicted as white (as he had been frequently in vase paintings); this is perhaps the reason Pausanias in his description includes the statement that Memnon came to Troy *not* from Ethiopia but from Susa in Persia.[59] In other words, Polygnotus had followed the Asiatic version of Memnon's provenience, which Pausanias was attempting to explain by his comments. Philostratus, however, mentions a picture in which Memnon was obviously depicted as black. Having come from Ethiopia, runs the Philostratus description of the painting, Memnon slew Antilochus and seemed to strike terror among the Achaeans, for "before Memnon's time black men were only a myth."[60] In a description of another scene of the Trojan War Philostratus notes that the pure black of Memnon's face shows a certain ruddiness, and adds that in Ethiopia Memnon was transformed into a statue of black marble.[61] Further, in earlier accounts Memnon had been referred to as king of the Ethiopians or as leading Ethiopians to Troy, and no mention was made of his color. In the Roman period, however, Memnon was considered at times definitely black and Ethiopian. He is described by Catullus[62] as Ethiopian, as black by Vergil,[63] Seneca,[64] and Ovid, who refers to a black lover of Aurora.[65]

In its later transmission the Memnon legend acquired an African locale, although some writers, still faithful to the memories of earlier tradition, did not lose sight of an Asiatic Memnon. Attempts to reconcile the two Memnons persisted. Memnon, according to Philostratus, was not killed in Troy, where he never went, but died in Ethiopia after he had ruled for five generations. It was not Memnon, the Ethiopian, but another Memnon, a Trojan, who was killed by Achilles and placed upon the funeral pyre of Antilochus.[66] As Nilotic Ethiopia became better known through merchants, mercenaries, and travelers, Memnon, who had earlier been located in the east, was moved to a more familiar Ethiopia. Memnon became black and Ethiopian. Aeneas, as he gazed at the story of Troy depicted on the temple to Juno being built in Carthage, recognized himself and the arms of his black ally, Memnon.[67] Formerly, palaces in Susa had been attributed to Memnon; now structures in Egypt became associated with him.[68]

Accounts of Andromeda, Cepheus, and Perseus experienced a history of transmission somewhat similar to that of the Memnon story. Each legend has both Asiatic and African settings; both Memnon and Andromeda, though conceived of at first as white, undergo a change in color; and vase-paintings and the theater as well as the literature draw from both legends. Some Roman writers attempted to reconcile Ethiopian and Asiatic versions, Pliny, for example, saying that Syria was a part of Cepheus' kingdom, and Tacitus maintaining that a group of Ethiopians who fled the tyranny of Cepheus founded Jerusalem.[69]

Jope or Joppa, a seaport of Phoenicia, according to one version, was the place where Andromeda was exposed upon a rock to a sea monster.[70] Inhabitants of Joppa pointed out the marks made by the chains with which Andromeda was fettered,[71] and rocks on the shore from which Perseus rescued Andromeda were still shown in Jerome's day.[72] Others, however, followed a tradition in which Cepheus, the father of Andromeda, was the king of the Ethiopians. Greek artists depicted Andromeda and her father as whites; the people of the country in which they lived, as Negroes.[73] In the Empire the locale of Andromeda's exposure is often Ethiopian. Pliny in his observations on the power of Ethiopia in earlier days cites the stories about Andromeda as proof that Ethiopia dominated Syria and the Mediterranean shores at the time of Cepheus. In other words, Pliny believes that the story had African and Asiatic associations because Cepheus, the king of the Ethiopians, had extended his power from Africa to the Asiatic coast.[74] Propertius speaks of Cephean Meroë and its dark realms.[75] Perseus finds Andromeda bound to a cliff after he has reached the Ethiopians and the kingdom of Cepheus.[76] Apollodorus locates the scene in Ethiopia, where Cepheus is king.[77] In fact, variants or derivatives of Cepheus became synonyms of Ethiopian.[78]

Andromeda, like Memnon, also experienced a change in color, with two differences however: (1) Andromeda became dark (*fusca*), whereas Memnon had become black, *niger;* (2) Memnon, once his color changed, retained his new hue more consistently than Andromeda. Ovid, for example, seems definitely to regard her as dark. Dark with the hue of her native land, Andromeda, the daughter of Cepheus, according to Ovid, captivated Perseus by her exquisite beauty.[79] When Ovid says that Perseus brought Andromeda from the black Indians, he was apparently referring also to Ethiopians and was using *Indi* poetically.[80] Philostratus, on the other hand, is as definite about the setting of Andromeda's rescue as he was about her color. In a description of a painting of the legend he emphasizes that it is not the Red Sea nor the inhabitants of India depicted but Ethiopians. It is a case of a Greek man as well as of a white Andromeda in Ethiopia.[81] Achilles Tatius mentions a painting of Andromeda whose arms are spotlessly white.[82] The *Aethiopica* of Heliodorus follows a tradition that Andromeda was white, as is evident from the explanation given when Queen Persinna discovered that she had given birth to a daughter with a white complexion, a color alien to her native Ethiopian hue.[83]

A few other myths involved Ethiopians, but records do not

preserve as many details as are available for the legends already discussed. It was Aethiops, a son of Vulcan, from whom Pliny says the Ethiopians derived their name.[84] An Ethiopian woman was the mother of seven of Danaüs' fifty daughters, and in this connection my discussion of the dark- or black-skinned Danaïdes should be noted.[85] A Negroid Nike is known from a late fifth- or early fourth-century B.C. oinochoe (Fig. 88).[86] Circe appears as a Negro in Kabeiric vases (Fig. 36).[87] A Negroid follower of Theseus is depicted on a vase.[88] And finally, a scene depicting a Negroid woman has been interpreted as the Libyan queen Lamia beloved of Zeus or as the foreign woman tortured by satyrs (Fig. 89).[89]

VII. Ethiopians in the Theater and Amphitheater

It is not surprising that Ethiopians were among the foreigners who interested the tragic poets of the fifth century B.C.[1] Reports of Ethiopia and Ethiopians had for some time been reaching Greece from Naucratic traders, settlers in Egypt, and mercenaries who had served in the army of Psammetichus II. Ethiopians, if Herodotus is correct, had fought in the army of Xerxes, perhaps in Greece itself. Some Ethiopian soldiers may have served as models for contemporary ceramicists. *Aethiopica*, therefore, provided an opportunity for the dramatists to play to a curiosity about "a far-off country of a black race who lived by the fountains of the sun,"[2] a distant people brought close to home by recent experience.

Unfortunately the plays involving Ethiopian themes or topics have been lost and are known only through fragments, titles, and the depictions of vase painters. The fragmentary evidence is sufficient, however, to indicate that as early as Aeschylus Ethiopians were presented as black, as speaking a different tongue, and as living in Africa.[3] And if Ethiopians appearing in scenes from vases on the Andromeda theme are accurate reflections of the tragic poets, we have further suggestions as to how the fifth-century dramatists presented the Ethiopians in their plays. In some vases Ethiopians were unmistakably Negroid with respect to their black color, woolly hair, and flat noses. The river of their country was the mysterious, snow-fed Nile. Aeschylus' and Euripides' references to the phenomenon of a river in a torrid country whose rising waters were due to melting snows[4] must have provoked fascinating discussions following the productions. It would be interesting to know what Aeschylus had to say to postperformance symposiasts about the "thirty-thousand black horsemen" in his *Persians* and the Ethiopian tongue and black-skinned race mentioned in his lost plays.[5]

The *Suppliants* of Aeschylus, though not treating an Ethiopian subject, should be mentioned because of its presentation of black-skinned Africans. The fifty sons of Aegyptus were described as black. If Danaüs was able to see the black limbs of his nephews show out from their white robes,[6] it is likely that Aeschylus did not fail to make the most of the dramatic possibilities of the Danaïdes. For Aeschylus emphasizes their "un-Greekness" and their "Africanness" to an extent not observable in his description of the sons of Aegyptus. The Danaïdes described themselves as "black and smitten by the sun"[7] and thus remind us of the proverbial Ethiopian blackness. To King Pelasgus they have the appearance of Libyans, or inhabitants of the Nile, or Cyprians, or nomadic camel-riding neighbors of the Ethiopians, or flesh-devouring Amazons.[8] The precise physiognomonical intent of this multiple comparison is not clear, although the image is illuminated somewhat by a tradition of Ethiopians in Cyprus and of African Amazons who lived near western Ethiopians.[9] Aeschylus also says, however, that the Danaïdes differed from the Greeks not only as to *color* but also as to *form*,[10] and, hence, apparently conceived of the Danaïdes as physically different from their black cousins. Since Aeschylus never describes the Danaïdes as Ethiopians but as blacks resembling several African peoples, neighbors of Ethiopians, perhaps he had in mind a people descendant of a black-white racial mixture. Interesting in this connection is a later reference to seven of Danaüs' daughters born of an Ethiopian woman.[11] Regardless of Aeschylus' exact anthropological concept of the Danaïdes, however, one point is certain. There is no antipathy because of their color. Most un-Greek in appearance, these black refugees received asylum in Greece.[12]

Aeschylus' treatment of the Danaïdes suggests that he exploited the possibilities offered by plays such as his *Memnon* and *Psychostasia*, which, like the *Aethiopes* of Sophocles, probably introduced Ethiopians.[13] Both Sophocles and Euripides composed an *Andromeda*.[14] Hence, the theater may have been the inspiration for those vase painters who treated the Andromeda theme. In a scene from a fifth-century B.C. hydria depicting the chaining of Andromeda in the presence of Perseus, eight Negroid figures (Figs. 26a–b) appear, some of whom prepare the spot where Andromeda is to be sacrificed; others bring offerings — a diphros, a pyxis, and a mirror; and an elderly Negro directs their activity. Of the three white figures in the scene, two are dressed in Oriental costume, in contrast with the Negroes who wear short, elaborately decorated, sleeveless chitons. One of these, a central figure supported by two Negroes, is Andromeda; the other, Cepheus. A third figure is Perseus, recognizable by his traditional winged cap, chlamys, and sandals.[15] Negroes appear in another vase painting depicting the Andromeda myth — on a red-figured pelike from the workshop of the Niobid painter (Fig. 90). Three figures, whose Negroid characteristics are strikingly outlined in white, are beautifully contrasted with two white figures, Andromeda and her father. One of the Negroes ties Andromeda to a stake, another carries a diphros, and a third serves as an attendant of Cepheus.[16]

The general setting of the *Andromeda* of Euripides, if M. Bieber is correct, can be judged from the Andromeda krater in Berlin. The grouping of the actors and the reproduction of an altar on this vase, in the opinion of Bieber, so strongly suggest the influence of an actual performance that the scene must have been painted when the artist was freshly inspired by what he had seen in the theater. Ethiopia and its people are represented by a member of the chorus attired in a tight jersey and a richly designed chiton. This figure whose mask is Negroid represents the country of the Ethiopians where the scene of the play was laid, while the actors have Greek features.[17]

The evidence of the vase paintings — Andromeda and her companions as white, their apparel as Oriental, and the presence of Negroes — suggests that the dramatists of the fifth century B.C. were following a version of the Andromeda myth which conceived of Andromeda as a white princess among Negroid peoples in Ethiopia. Similarly, the craftsmen portraying the Memnon story in the sixth and fifth centuries B.C., with perhaps two exceptions as pointed out above, depicted Memnon as white and his soldiers as Negroes. Hence, the plays on the Andromeda and no doubt the Memnon themes demanded Ethiopian roles only for the chorus, to represent the Negroid population of the country in which Andromeda was captured or as the black soldiers whom Memnon commanded. It is tempting to believe that the dramatists made the most of the scenic and dramatic possibilities afforded by a story involving blacks and whites. The mask of the Berlin krater and the Negroes of the vase paintings, obviously based on models, illustrate the possibilities open to the playwright. It is not unlikely that the stage managers, like the vase painters, developed dramatically racial contrasts exploited by the ceramicists in the sixth- and fifth-century Janiform Negro-white vases. The painter of the British Museum Andromeda hydria — with a central white figure, supported by two Negroes, around whom he skillfully grouped the remaining eight figures — made an effective composition of contrasting racial groups, even if he did not, as has been suggested, actually contrast the energy of the Ethiopians and the languor of the central figure whom they support. An imaginative choregus in planning the dances could have given a touch of Ethiopian reality by including dances observed among Ethiopians resident in Athens.

The story of the Egyptian king Busiris, who, to bring prosperity to his land, sacrificed strangers to Zeus but was finally killed by Heracles, inspired comedies by Epicharmus, Ephippus, and Mnesimachus, and a satyr-play by Euripides. Several vase paintings, including the well-known sixth-century B.C. Caeretan hydria (Fig. 20), provide some suggestions as to the treatment which the playwrights may have given to the Negro auxiliaries of the Egyptian king who were killed together with Busiris. The comic note of some of these paintings, especially the Caeretan hydria, is what would be expected in a comic or satyric piece. Heracles throws black- and yellow-faced priests into utter confusion, and five hefty Negroes, equipped with sticks, arrive too late, in spite of their quickened pace, to assist their Egyptian king.[18] The moment at which Heracles, held prisoner by two Ethiopians, breaks his chains and lifts his club to kill Busiris is the subject of a scene preserved on a fragment of a red-figured vase.[19] Participation of Negroes in the Busiris story can be further illustrated by another scene on a red-figured stamnos representing the episode (Figs. 91a–b). Here Heracles, garbed in a chiton and a lion skin, seizes a Negro by the throat and forces him down upon an altar. If Heracles' victim is Busiris, as J. D. Beazley has suggested, the artist conceived of Busiris as Negro rather than Egyptian. As the central figure pleads with Heracles in supplication, other Negroes, dressed in either waistcloths or chitons rush about in fear, some in flight. Of these one bears an unlighted torch and another a sacrificial tray. The artist seemingly had in mind two Negroid types, since the hair of four of his figures is represented by a mass of black and that of the other four by detached dots. Negro attendants of Busiris also appear in a scene painted on a fifth-century B.C. column-krater (Fig. 92).[20]

Negro roles in other satyric plays are suggested by the evidence of vase paintings. Satyrs often resemble Negroes with respect to thickness of the lips and snubness of nose. In a plastic vase of the fourth century B.C. two heads, one of a Negro and the other of a satyr (Fig. 93), were actually made from the same mold. In this instance the head serving as a Negro is painted black with frizzled hair; otherwise the features of both heads are identical.[21] An episode from a satyr-play is one explanation that has been given of a scene on a fifth-century B.C. lekythos depicting a Negroid woman tied to a tree and tortured by five satyrs (Fig. 89). The woman may be the foreign woman whom, according to Pausanias, fearful sailors were forced to sacrifice after the women on their ship had been assaulted by the Sileni.[22] A nude Negro woman, strikingly reminiscent of the Negroid Scybale of the *Moretum*, is among the participants in a dance (Figs. 2, 94), others being a phlyax, a maenad, and a satyr, painted on an askos from Ruvo.[23] It is perhaps a scene from a satyr-play depicted on a fourth-century B.C. calyx-krater involving two Sileni and two actors, one actor an old, baldish, beardless Negro, wearing a skin fastened to his shoulder, who supports himself with a staff in his right hand and holds a flaming torch in his left; the other actor, a taller, bearded figure, draped in a long, sleeveless dress. The arrangement of the figures and the secrecy of the Sileni have suggested that the Sileni are conspiring for some reason against the two actors by furtively lighting their torches from that of the Negro slave, who is apparently unconscious of what is taking place.[24]

A Nike of a pronounced Negro type — flat nose, protruding jaw, and thick lips — is the subject of a scene on an oinochoe found in Cyrenaica (Fig. 88). Driving Heracles in a two-wheeled chariot drawn by four centaurs, the Nike is preceded by a whiffler. Although the reason for the appearance of a Negro victory is not clear, perhaps the painter represented a scene from a satyr-drama or comedy. It has also been suggested that the artist mixed mythology and reality by including on a vase destined for Cyrenaica a Negro who would recall an element of the local population.[25]

Negroes appear in several scenes preserved on a group of vases, usually skyphoi, dated by some in the second half of the fifth century and by others in the fourth century B.C., which have been found in the sanctuary of the Kabeiroi near Thebes.[26] Part of the ceremony connected with the worship was perhaps dramatic, and it may be a dramatic element to which Pausanias refers by his use of δρώμενα in his description of Kabeiric ritual.[27] The subject matter of these vases is often mysterious, but most agree that there is an element of caricature and burlesque in the scenes which derive their fundamental inspiration from mythology and sacred legends. Two of these vases depict Odysseus and a Negro Circe — in one, Odysseus receives the magic draught from the black enchantress, one of whose victims, already a swine, stands by her loom. In the second, Odysseus, wearing a phallus and with a chlamys over his arm, seems to recoil in terror as he holds his sword in one hand and the sheath in the other, while a Negroid Circe, dressed in a long chiton, mixes her potion in a two-handled cup (Fig. 36).[28]

Why Greek artists chose to depict Negroes and Negroid pygmies in Kabeiric scenes is not clear. Although it is difficult to determine the extent to which artists intended figures in Kabeiric vases as Negroes, such an intent is apparent in several instances (Figs. 95a–c). E. Romagnoli in his study of Kabeiric scenes called attention to the appearance of Negroes, especially women, in these scenes. In one vase, at the left, Mitos embraces Krateia, while a child, Pratolaos, looks on with a startled expression; to the right, a boy stands before an amphora pouring something into it, and beyond is a seated Kabeiros holding a cup (Fig. 96). According to Romagnoli, Mitos and Pratolaos are Negroes; the others, white.[29] The flat noses of Pratolaos and Mitos and the thick lips of Pratolaos contrast sharply with the non-Negroid features of the other figures. The hair of these two figures is portrayed in a manner similar to that used by the artist of the vase depicting the Negroid woman tortured by the satyrs. The artists in both cases perhaps had adopted the same method of representing the hair of certain Negroid types. The artist apparently intended to contrast strongly two distinctly different racial types. Figures with Negroid traits appearing in other Kabeiric vases include Aphrodite, Hera, Cephalus, initiates, and pygmies (Figs. 97a–b).[30]

Terra-cotta masks from both the Greek and the Roman periods

point to roles involving Ethiopians in various types of performances, dramatic or religious. A vivid example of such masks is that of a pronouncedly Negroid type from the late sixth or early fifth century B.C., found in Agrigento (Figs. 7a–b), along with representations of Demeter, Persephone, and their worshippers.[31] Another terra-cotta mask of unknown provenience but perhaps Sicilian from the middle of the fourth century B.C. seems to be a faithful copy of a comic mask. This life-sized mask, with the mouth, nostrils, and eyes pierced in such a way that it could be worn, depicts a Negro whose hair falls in clusters of curls over his forehead and ears and whose grin makes it possible to see his upper row of teeth (Fig. 98).[32] Among several terra-cotta masks of about 350 B.C., found in a tomb at Lipari, was that of an old Negro woman, whose racial characteristics are vividly portrayed. The group has been interpreted as representations of characters from the Euripidean tragedies of the Trojan cycle, with the suggestion that the Negro woman was the nurse of Astyanax.[33] A scene on a krater of about 350 B.C., attributed to Assteas, includes two women wearing masks of distinctly Negroid features who look down from windows as Dionysus and two phlyakes watch a tumbler.[34] A small terra-cotta Roman mask from the first century B.C. is a realistic depiction of a Negro (Fig. 99).[35] From the Agora comes another mask of the first or second century A.D., which preserves the features of a Negro with black skin, broad nose, and teeth visible through his grinning mouth.[36] Professor K. T. Erim has kindly called to my attention an almost life-sized terra-cotta mask of a Negro of the first or second century A.D. found in recent excavations behind the Odeon at Aphrodisias.[37]

Striking evidence of a Negro actor seen by audiences in the area of Taranto has been preserved in a Hellenistic terra cotta. The woolly-haired, flat-nosed, thick-lipped actor, whose head is covered with a conical cap, dressed in a himation, stands with his hands uplifted, and with his left foot raised as if to begin a lively dance (Fig. 100). This Negro actor has been considered one of the phlyakes, common in south Italy, and perhaps a forerunner of the Neapolitan "pazzariello."[38] A later illustration of an actor comes from the third century A.D. in the form of a dwarf with Negroid features and is interpreted as part of a market group from a mime. Wearing a conical cap and dressed in a short-sleeved tunic, the dwarf, depicted on a clay lamp from Athens, stands behind a basket and looks intently on a cup or funnel which he holds over the mouth of a jar set in a basket.[39]

A very black, charming nurse, Giddenis, appears in the *Poenulus* of Plautus.[40] In the *Eunuchus* of Terence an Ethiopian slave girl is one of two valuable gifts which Phaedria buys for Thais.[41] Although it is not always easy to classify the Roman elements in Plautine and Terentian comedy, Roman experience with Ethiopians in the Hannibalic war may have occasioned the introduction of the black nurse and the Ethiopian slave girl.[42]

Ethiopians appeared in dramatic performances of various types in the Empire. A nocturnal performance in which scenes from the lower world were enacted by Egyptians and Ethiopians is pertinent evidence from the end of Caligula's reign.[43] Glycon, a tragic actor in the time of Nero, a tall, dark man with a hanging lower lip, was the joint property of Vergilius, also a tragic actor, and of some other person. Glycon attained great popularity and was manumitted by Nero, who paid Vergilius 300,000 sesterces for his share in the actor.[44]

An interesting note concerning Nero's entertainment of Tiridates records that Nero in 66 A.D. gave a gladiatorial exhibit at Puteoli for the visiting easterner from Armenia. Nero's freedman Patrobius, who was the manager of the Puteoli affair, made it a most brilliant and expensive spectacle, as may be seen by the fact, Dio Cassius says, that "on one of the days no one but Ethiopians — men, women, and children — appeared in the theater."[45] It is not surprising to find Ethiopians in the Campanian area, since Puteoli was a thriving harbor and docked a steady succession of ships from Alexandria. Furthermore, Nero had such an interest in Ethiopia that he sent an expedition which penetrated, as has been noted earlier, deeply into Ethiopia. Hence, if Nero had some special interest in exhibiting Ethiopians to Tiridates, he certainly would have had easy access to them.

Entertainment not requiring masks eventually became very popular among the Romans. By its mimicry, buffoonery, and treatment of everyday life the mime made a strong appeal to the man in the street. The popularity of the mime has been attested by clay statuettes of performers in this medium, and, in this connection, many of the so-called "grotesque" bronzes and terra cottas have been explained not as examples of realism or charms against the evil eye but as representations of *mimologi*.[46] For certain roles in an art that relied heavily upon facial expressions without the use of masks, the Ethiopian's color had obvious advantages. A clever Ethiopian *mimologus* would be capable of turning in a creditable performance when the mime-theme called for the utterance of outlandish tongues. A favorite subject in Roman mimes was adultery. Ovid speaks of the popularity of the mime in which the stupid husband is duped by an artful wife and her lover. Another mime-theme developed the faithless wife's attempt to seduce her slave.[47] Since crossings between whites and blacks received notice from the satirists, and white mothers of dark or black children, accused of adultery, pleaded "maternal impression,"[48] a very fertile imagination would not be required to produce a hilarious mime on the adultery theme involving Ethiopians. Scenes from the homeland of Ethiopian residents, whether North Africa, Egypt, or Ethiopia itself, would certainly enjoy a vogue in the cosmopolitan centers of the Roman Empire and in cities like Puteoli and other regions of that area so close to an important terminus of the Egyptian-Italian commercial route. *Isiaci* who had seen dances such as those depicted on the Ariccia marble or in the Herculaneum wall paintings or those whose interest in Egypt or Ethiopia had been aroused by stories about Africa would want to see African dances and to hear African rhythms.[49]

In addition to playing roles in which their color was an advantage, Ethiopian *mimologi*, of course, exhibited their histrionic talents in the same way as their fellow artists. A Negro juggler, a performer associated with mimes, for example, has been preserved in terra cotta. Jugglers were held in high esteem, Athenaeus tells us, and statues were erected in their honor.[50] A figurine, coming from Thebes, shows a Negro juggler skillfully managing three balls at a time — with his head, hand, and knee (Fig. 101).[51]

The ballet of the mime called for musicians and dancers. In Hellenistic or Roman art we have an opportunity to study several Negro singers and dancers. Among some Ethiopians the dance was so popular that, according to Lucian, even in waging war the warriors did not shoot their arrows until they had first danced.[52] Their war dances, according to Heliodorus, involved abandoned vaults and satyrlike leaps.[53] The contortions of a Hellenistic Negro in bronze from Carnuntum (Fig. 102) have something in common with the violent leaps of the Ethiopians just described.[54]

In marked contrast to such violent poses are the charming stance of a bronze dancer of Hellenistic conception from Egypt (Fig. 103)[55] and the slow movement executed by a bronze Negro from Herculaneum, who gracefully balances himself on his left foot, with right foot skillfully poised in the air behind him (Fig. 104).[56] Although the tomb-relief found on the Appian Way near Ariccia is probably to be associated with the Isiac worship, the Negro women depicted thereon, whose violent dance involves bending the knees and tossing back the head, were executing movements no doubt common in mimes (Fig. 105).[57] A Hellenistic terra cotta from Taranto has preserved a Negro wearing a loin cloth and holding castanets in his hand.[58] Like the dark-skinned dancer in a Herculaneum fresco (Fig. 119),[59] this terra cotta may be a record of African tribal dancers popular in Italy.

The much-admired Hellenistic boy, found at Chalon-sur-Saône, portrays a slender Negro youth whose body is bent gracefully at the waist. The statuette has been interpreted as a singing musician since his left arm seems to have held some object, perhaps a trigonon, and his facial expression resembles that of a singer (Figs. 60a–c). A Negro playing what appears to be a long reed instrument and another making an expressive gesture with his left hand as if directing the music of the participants who include two nymphs clashing cymbals are depicted in a second-century A.D. Nilotic scene in a mosaic from near Lepcis Magna.[60] A bronze of an emaciated Negro playing a lyre recalls the spirit of the series of skeletons on the Boscoreale cups. The Negro resembling a skeleton because of his emaciation was perhaps intended, in the manner of the Boscoreale skeletons, as an exhortation to enjoy life.[61]

The Ethiopian Nicaeus, a boxer born in Byzantium, was well-known in the Roman world, perhaps to the same extent as the celebrated bronze boxer in the Museo delle Terme. Pliny the Elder was acquainted with the reputation of this pugilist.[62] Although we do not have a statue that can be identified as Nicaeus, some idea of how other Negro boxers looked and what pugilistic postures they assumed can be formed from a pair of late Hellenistic terra cottas in the British Museum (Fig. 49). One of these stands with legs straight and body thrown back, with his hand, protected by the caestus, raised in front as if to ward off the blow which his opponent is about to deal. The other, a more youthful figure, advances on his left foot, with his right arm raised and drawn back, and his left arm advanced in a defensive attitude.[63] Worthy of note in this connection is another unknown Negro whose fine athletic body has been preserved in a Hellenistic terra cotta (Fig. 106). Although it has been suggested that he too was a boxer, it is not at all certain what type of athlete the full-length, nude terra cotta represented. A flat-nosed, puffy-lipped wrestler, Pannichus, was apparently well known in Martial's day.[64]

Negroes were among those who performed as acrobats in the ancient world. Roman marble statuettes of Hellenistic style show Negroes balancing themselves on their hands and chests, with feet in the air. We learn from Pliny that the Tentyritae, men of small stature, had a reputation for pursuing crocodiles and actually dove into the river and mounted their backs.[65] In light of the archaeological evidence associating both pygmies and Negroes with the crocodile, it is easy to understand why a sculptor chose as his subject a Negro acrobat poised upon the back of a crocodile (Figs. 51, 107).[66] Further, when crocodiles were brought to Rome for exhibition, Strabo informs us, they were attended by Tentyritae from near Coptos who dragged them in a net to a basking-place where the spectators could see them.[67] A Pompeiian fresco depicting pygmies capturing crocodiles has been interpreted as a genuine representation of a real method of hunting crocodiles used by the Tentyritae and, perhaps also, by those pygmies inhabiting, according to classical tradition, the crocodile regions of Africa.[68] It is tempting to suggest, therefore, that some Negro attendants, like the Negro acrobat poised on the back of a crocodile, were present in Rome when Marcus Scaurus exhibited five crocodiles and a hippopotamus at Rome for the first time in 58 B.C. at the games he provided as aedile[69] and at the games of 2 B.C. when thirty-six crocodiles were killed in a pool in the Circus Maximus.[70]

One hundred Ethiopian huntsmen, together with the same number of Numidian bears, were presented in the circus by Domitius Ahenobarbus as curule aedile in 61 B.C.[71] The role of Ethiopians as mahouts in Hannibal's army has been presented above. The Roman also had an opportunity to witness in peacetime the Ethiopian's skill in handling elephants. Seneca, in a discussion of expert animal trainers, mentions a diminutive Ethiopian whose art consisted in training an elephant to sink on his knees and to walk a rope. The tiny Ethiopian is cited as an example of flawless, unerring trainers able to subdue and to tame savage, ferocious animals.[72] Martial also attests the skill of a black trainer in perfecting pachydermatous ballerinas; the elephant bidden to dance lightly, does not dare say "no" to his black master.[73] An Ethiopian, described as a type of elephant-horseman, was said to be feared by his elephant which fawned on him, attended to his voice, and submitted to prodding from his master's iron goad.[74] Such skill is what would be expected in light of the Ethiopian's experience and traditional association with elephants. A Hellenistic painting of the late third or early second century B.C. from Marissa (Palestine) includes in an animal frieze an elephant and a Negro attendant, a sort of personification of inner Africa. The Negro, above whom the word Αἰθιοπία appears, stretches one arm toward the elephant's tusks and carries a long-handled axe over his shoulder.[75]

A black huntsman, Olympius, a winner of innumerable victories, a Hercules in strength, admired for his courage, speed, and spirit, won the plaudits of the people of Carthage.[76] His epitaph concluded with these words: "The fame of thy renown will live for many years after thee and Carthage will ever speak thy name." A Negro, relaxing with four of his companions at a drinking bout, perhaps on the eve of their appearance in the amphitheater, has been preserved in a third-century A.D. mosaic from the north African city of Thysdrus. Dressed in a green tunic with black bands, his forehead adorned with a wreath, the Negro gladiator enables us to reconstruct the spirit of the occasion by his words "we have come to drink."[77] Romans had an opportunity to witness an exhibition by Ethiopian gladiators when Probus presented three hundred pairs of gladiators, including many of the Blemmyes who had been led in his triumph.[78]

The distinction of being preserved in bronze or marble fell to the lot of Negroes engaged in the equestrian art. A bronze jockey from Artemisium of ca. 240–200 B.C. (Fig. 63) is in the National Museum in Athens.[79] A recently discovered stele of perhaps the second half of the third century B.C. depicts a Negro, whose body was painted in black, offering something to a spirited horse.[80] A Herculaneum marble portrays a Negro driving a *biga*, with a warrior walking in front of the horses. The driver leans eagerly forward as he holds the reins in his hands (Fig. 50).[81] A Negro groom bidding farewell to his mounted master is painted on an Egyptian funeral stele from the second century B.C.[82] An undefeated black charioteer received the following tribute in a poem of the *Anthologia Latina:* "Memnon, though a son of Dawn, fell at the hands of the son of Peleus. But thee, offspring of mother Night, Aeolus, if I mistake not, begat and, as a child thou wast born in the caves of Zephyrus. Never will there be born an Achilles who will surpass thee. Memnon thou art in appearance, but in fate thou art not."[83]

VIII. Greco-Roman Attitude toward Ethiopians – Theory and Practice

The absence of color prejudice in the Greco-Roman world has been noted by numerous classicists, anthropologists, and sociologists. Observations on this social phenomenon, however, have usually been made only in the most general terms, unaccompanied by detailed, specific discussion of the etiology of a racial outlook differing substantially from many later western attitudes which attached great importance to the color of the skin.

Theory

J. Bryce[1] observed that in the Roman Empire we hear little of any repugnance to the dark-skinned Africans; E. Baring,[2] that color antipathy, considered by itself, formed no bar to social intercourse in antiquity; E. E. Sikes,[3] that the ancients were apparently quite free from the antipathy of the color bar; A. Zimmern,[4] that the Greeks showed no trace of color prejudice; W. L. Westermann,[5] that Greek society had no color line; T. J. Haarhoff,[6] that there never has been any color prejudice in Italy; Kluckhohn,[7] that the Greeks did not fall into the error of biological racism, that color was no stigma, that men were classified not as black or white but as free or servile; and H. C. Baldry,[8] that the Greeks were spared the modern curse of color prejudice.

Although this is not the place to trace in detail the development of classical concepts of non-Greek and non-Roman peoples, brief mention of certain aspects of this development is necessary to present the framework within which classical and early Christian observations on the Ethiopian should be discussed.

The history of the Greco-Roman image of other peoples reveals instances of conflicting attitudes, often in the same author. Certain general views, however, are rather common. The well-known distinction between Greek and non-Greek appears in the history of the word "barbarian," and of the division of the world into Greeks and barbarians.[9] Mythology, on the other hand, in marked contrast to a distinction between Greek and barbarian, introduced several foreigners among the ancestors and the legends of the Greeks.[10]

As contacts increased with non-Greek peoples, the Hellenes developed an awareness of their own similarity as contrasted with the diversity of non-Greek peoples apparent in obvious physical and cultural differences. These and other variations, according to one school of thought in the latter part of the fifth century B.C., were to be attributed to the effects of environment — the results of geographical and climatic accident.[11] In spite of obvious physical and cultural differences and an increased Greek self-consciousness after the Persian wars, whereas there were Greeks who looked down with contempt on barbarians because of a belief in the superiority of their own culture and institutions, there were others who admired non-Greek peoples and even idolized these peoples and certain aspects of their culture.[12]

Although there were Sophists who argued for the elimination of the common division between Greeks and non-Greeks and for a community of all men despite racial and cultural differences, Plato continued a bipartite distinction in his sanction of war against the barbarian, for against the barbarian, Plato says, there is a war that exists by nature.[13] Isocrates seemed to point the way to a differentiation less racial and more cultural when he spoke of the name of Hellenes as suggesting no longer race but intellect and as a designation to be applied to those sharing in the culture rather than in the ancestry of the Greeks.[14] Departing from the approach of Aristotle, who had justified slavery on the basis of the innate differences and capacities of individuals,[15] the cosmopolitanism of the Hellenistic world emphasized a cultural rather than a racial differentiation. Eratosthenes, after withholding praise from those who divided mankind into two groups, Greeks and barbarians, added that it would be better to make such distinctions according to virtue and vice; for not only were many of the Greeks bad but many of the barbarians were refined.[16]

The Romans continued a distinction between peoples in which they recognized Romans, Greeks, and barbarians. They offered, however, no counterpart of the Greek explanation of the origin of slavery based upon the theoretical consideration of the inferiority of certain peoples as natural objects of enslavement.[17] Among the Romans "barbarian" was applied to those outside the world of Greco-Roman culture; the term was sometimes used by the early Christians of those outside the Church.[18] In the Empire the concept of a community of men was furthered by the spiritual egalitarianism of Stoicism as, for example, in Seneca's formulation of the doctrine of the equality of all men and his application of this doctrine to slaves,[19] and in Epictetus' statement that all men derive their descent from God.[20] Slavery is not a question of descent from servile parentage or of races, but a matter of character and excellence.[21] Finally, the Christians like Paul, who had recognized the traditional Greek division of mankind in his statement that he was "under obligation both to Greeks and to barbarians," proclaimed the spiritual unity of men, with their emphasis on the equality of all men and on a brotherhood of believers — slave or free, Greek or Jew, barbarian, or Scythian — once baptized as Christians.[22]

Greek observations on races of other physique and other cultures often took the form of antitheses involving racial extremes unlike the Greeks. A similar practice is reflected in some of the numerous Janiform art objects which contrasted white and Negroid types. One of the earliest of these, a faience vase of the seventh century B.C., made in Naucratis, juxtaposed a bearded barbarian and a Negro, with flat nose, thick lips, and woolly hair.[23] Among detailed anthropological antitheses of the type mentioned above, one of the earliest is found in Xenophanes, who stated that the Ethiopians represented their gods as black-faced and flat-nosed, whereas the Thracians showed their gods to be blue-eyed and red-haired.[24] Although it is the Thracian in this first instance, it is most frequently the Scythian whom the Greek, and later the Roman, cited, together with the Ethiopian, in numerous examples of distinctly un-Greek and un-Roman physical types. This Scythian-Ethiopian contrast, when examined, reveals an interesting history which provides an important addition to our knowledge of the Greco-Roman image of other peoples.

Ethiopians are first grouped with Scythians in Hesiod, in a line which lists no anthropological characteristics of the people but reads only: "The Ethiopians, the Ligurians and also the Scythians, Hippemolgi."[25] As the Ethiopian-Scythian τόποι became more numerous, the antitheses became more detailed and were employed (1) as examples of anthropological or geographical opposites or extremes differing from the Greek; (2) in explanations of the diversity of racial types; (3) in statements of conviction that (a) race is of no consequence in evaluating men and (b) all whom God created He created equal and alike.

As pointed out above, the first detailed anthropological contrast of non-Greek types — Thracians and Ethiopians — appears in Xenophanes in the sixth century B.C.[26] The rather extensive accounts of Scythia and Ethiopia in Herodotus provided specifics about the countries and the peoples which must have played a large role in shaping later concepts of these two peoples. In recording explanations of the rising of the Nile, Herodotus mentions an Ethiopia-Scythia geographical contrast and associates skin-color with heat — features that were to appear frequently in the environment theory of anthropological differences.[27] Prometheus, in his prophecy to Io, foretold that she would visit the Scythian Nomads[28] as well as a remote country of a black race which dwells by the waters of the sun, where the river Aethiops is.[29]

The Hippocratic Corpus appears to be the *fons et origo* of the belief that the flora, fauna, and the human inhabitants of a region and their manner of life are determined to a large extent by the diversity of climatic, topographical, and hydrographical conditions prevailing there. The author of *On Airs, Waters, and Places* points out that physical characteristics and character of men follow the nature of a country — soil, water, climate, and exposure — and illustrates this theory by describing the effect of these factors upon the physique, character, and institutions of the Egyptians and the Scythians.[30] Similarly, *On Regimen* observes (1) that southern countries, being very near the sun, are hotter and drier than the northern; and (2) that the races of men and plants in southern countries must therefore be drier, hotter, and stronger than those in the opposite countries; and suggests a comparison of the Libyan and the Pontic, and also the races nearest each.[31]

An interesting application of the environment theory in Polybius[32] is pertinent because it illustrates an important Greek approach in racial matters. Polybius has occasion to mention the Cynaetheans who, although unquestionably of Arcadian stock, not only differed from other Arcadians (who had a high reputation for virtue, hospitable character, and piety to the gods) but at one time surpassed all Greeks in wickedness. The Cynaetheans, according to Polybius, grew into savagery because they had neglected entirely certain civilizing institutions developed by primitive Arcadians as part of an assimilation to the cold, rugged, inclement atmospheric conditions prevailing in Arcadia — conditions to which all men by their very nature must necessarily adapt themselves. Difference in environmental conditions not only accounts for the great divergence in character, features, and color of peoples living in widely separated regions but also explains to a great extent different modes of life.[33] Greeks, then, just as the northern Scythians or the southern Ethiopians of a different color, are subject to the same laws of nature.

A. J. Toynbee states that favorite Hellenic illustrations of the environment theory were taken from the diversity among the Egyptians and Scythians.[34] This statement, however, overlooks a Greco-Roman practice, as demonstrated in this study, of citing rather Ethiopians and Scythians in this environment context. While it is true that *On Airs, Waters, and Places* specifically mentions Egyptians, *On Regimen* cites the Libyan and Pontic. Although Ethiopians could possibly be included in "Libyan-Pontic," they are certainly to be comprehended in "the races nearest each."

Later illustrations of the environment theory and adaptations thereof demonstrate the prominence given to the Ethiopian and to the Ethiopian-Scythian antithesis. Ephorus, in his division of the world into four regions inhabited by Indians, Celts, Scythians, and Ethiopians, states that Ethiopia in the south and Scythia in the north are the larger of the four regions.[35] Aristotle attributes the straight hair of the Scythians and Thracians to a fluid, moist atmosphere and the woolly hair of the Ethiopians to their dry environment.[36] Posidonius notes differences between the Ethiopians of Libya and Indians resulting from the fact that the latter are less parched by the dryness of the atmosphere.[37]

Strabo points out that the differences between the remote confines of Scythia and Celtica to the north and the remote regions of Ethiopia are very great;[38] that, in the opinion of the ancient Greeks, the inhabitants of the known countries of the north were embraced under the single designation of "Scythians" or "Nomads" and those of all countries in the south which lie on

Ocean were comprehended by the designation of Ethiopians.[39] Diodorus, in a discussion of the distance between Lake Maeotis (near which certain Scythians dwell in frost and excessive cold) and Ethiopia, comments that the sailing distance from the cold to the warmest parts of the inhabited world does not exceed twenty-four days. He concludes that, in light of the great difference in climate in such a slight space, it is to be expected that not only the regimen and manner of life but also the bodies of the inhabitants should be very different from what one finds among the Greeks.[40]

The Ethiopians are obviously, in Pliny's view, burnt by the heat of the sun near them and are born with scorched complexions and frizzly hair, whereas the races in the opposite regions of the world have straight, yellow hair and white, frosty skins.[41] Pliny, like Posidonius and Manilius, calls attention to differences between Ethiopians and Indians. In this connection Pliny observes that in the area to the south of the Ganges the people are embrowned by the sun so that they are colored but not burned as black as Ethiopians and that the color of Indians becomes darker as they approach the Indus.[42] Vitruvius attributes the small stature, dark complexion, curly hair, strong legs, and thinness of blood in southern peoples to the nearness of the sun and a concomitant removal of moisture; and the tall stature, fair complexion, straight red hair, blue eyes, and fullness of blood of northerners to the cool climate and abundance of moisture.[43]

Although Pliny mentions only the Ethiopians specifically and leaves the northerners unnamed and Vitruvius omits specific names altogether in his north-south contrast, it is highly probable that both had in mind the familiar Scythian-Ethiopian formula, in much the same way as does Strabo in the passage cited above[44] and as Ptolemy in an antithesis in which he describes Ethiopians and Scythians in language somewhat similar to that of Vitruvius. According to Ptolemy, the inhabitants of the region from the equator to the summer tropic, known by the general name of Ethiopians, have black skins and thick woolly hair, are shrunken in stature and sanguine in nature because they are burnt by the sun which is over their heads. Those in more northern parallels, on the other hand — designated by the general name of Scythians — are white-complexioned, straight-haired, tall and well nourished, have a more abundant share of moisture, and are somewhat cold by nature, since they are far removed from the zodiac and the sun. Climate also explains the habits of the population of Scythia and Ethiopia, for, according to Ptolemy, the Ethiopians are for the most part savage because their homes are oppressed by the heat and the Scythians are savage because their dwelling places are continually cold.[45]

The usual formula is varied by Sextus Empiricus in a contrast of Ethiopians and Persians.[46] A Briton-Ethiopian variation is preserved in a statement that Ethiopians age early and the Britons, later (in the one hundred and twentieth year); the former because their bodies are burned by the raging sun and the latter because their natural heat is maintained longer.[47] Seneca tells us that the color of the Ethiopian among his own people is not notable and that among the Germans red hair gathered into a knot is not unbecoming a man. And, Seneca adds, you are to consider nothing in a man odd or disgraceful which is characteristic of his nation.[48] Other variations of the Ethiopian-Scythian antithesis include Germans (*candidi*), Thracians (*rubei*), Ethiopians (*nigri*),[49] Gauls (*candidi*), and very black Ethiopians (*nigerrimi*).[50] Paulus Orosius knew the traditional formula,[51] as did the Emperor Julian, who, in his observations on the extent to which Germans and Scythians differ from Libyans and Ethiopians, asks whether such a difference can be due to a bare ordinance and whether climate or the country does not have a joint influence with the gods in determining different types of complexions.[52]

It would seem, therefore, that for a considerable period of classical antiquity Scythians (and to a lesser extent Thracians) and Ethiopians were cited as easily identifiable examples of racial extremes differing from the Greeks and the Romans. Gauls and Germans were substituted for Scythians or added to the traditional contrast, especially in later periods.

The Greeks and Romans, in explanation of the physical differences which they recognized between themselves and other races, the evidence has shown, accounted for the characteristics of the Ethiopian by an environment theory in the same way as they explained the characteristics of the Scythians, Thracians, or any other people who were unlike themselves. The Greeks recognized Greeks and non-Greeks, frequent examples of the latter being Scythians and Ethiopians, a practice which the Romans continued as illustrations of racial extremes differing from themselves. The Greeks and Romans attached no special stigma to color, regarding yellow hair or blue eyes a mere geographical accident, and developed no special racial theory about the inferiority of darker peoples qua darker peoples. H. L. Shapiro notes that "modern man is race conscious in a way and to a degree certainly not characteristic previously," and points out that in earlier societies the ability to see obvious physical differences did not result in "an elaborate orientation of human relations within a rigid frame of reference."[53]

Racial diversity, then, was explained in a uniform manner that applied as well to the Ethiopian as to any other people, and any special racial theory about darker peoples was completely absent.[54] Yet, just as views of other non-Greek and non-Roman peoples were modified in one way or another by various influences, so also the attitude toward the Ethiopian underwent similar modifications.[55] A change in attitude toward the white, straight-haired, blue-eyed Scythian of the north was accompanied by a corresponding modification of the image of the black, woolly-haired, platyrrhine Ethiopian of the south. Our records preserve striking testimony that the Ethiopian was included in the various views of the community of all men as recorded by protagonists of these views. The evidence demonstrates further that the inclusion of the Ethiopian was not reflecting the rejection of a special racial theory as to the inferiority of the Ethiopian qua Ethiopian but was merely perpetuating a modification in the Ethiopian-Scythian tradition described above.

Although classical statements on the community and equality of men are often couched in general terms without specific references to racial groups, a striking illustration in the Ethiopian-Scythian tradition is found in Menander, who says that persons of no account attempt to compensate for worthlessness by reciting pedigrees; but Menander records the view that pedigree is unimportant, for

> The man whose natural bent is good,
> He, mother, he, though Aethiop, is nobly born.
> "A Scyth," you say? Pest! Anacharsis was a Scyth![56]

In other words, it is unimportant whether one is as racially different from a Greek as the Ethiopian or Scythian cited by our experts on environment, says Menander; it is natural bent, not race, that determines nobility.

Antiphon the Sophist had insisted that the Greek practice of honoring those of good birth and of looking down upon those of humble family was barbarous, since by nature all — both barbarians and Greeks — are born alike in all things. Menander's pronouncement seems to be a development of the Sophist's view.[57] That Menander would have included Ethiopians in Antiphon's *all* is clear. Menander's successful rival, Philemon, was commenting on the natural equality of master and slave: "Even though a man is a slave, he is made of the same flesh (as you). For no one was ever made a slave by nature . . . but chance has enslaved a man's body."[58] Menander, by his Ethiopian-Scythian antithesis, was expressing a version of the sentiment of the earlier Sophists and his contemporary Philemon in language which, he intended, should have unequivocal clarity as to its inclusiveness. For the Ethiopian-Scythian formula had appeared as early as Hesiod and had become a frequent, if not the favorite, Hellenic illustration of the boundaries of the north and south as well as of the environment theory, that is, the effects of Ethiopian and Scythian environment upon the inhabitants and their institutions.

Greeks know, said Agatharchides, that color is inconsequential. He notes that Ethiopians would inspire fear in the Greeks not because of their blackness or the difference of their external features; such a fear ceases at childhood, for it is known that questions are decided in battle not by external appearance or color but by courage and military science.[59] Generals are not occupied with racial purity, for they know that it is personal quality that counts, not race or origin.[60] To the Roman, circumstances, not color, excited contempt. Soldiers, whether white or black, when captured and stripped, according to Frontinus, are worthy of contempt.[61] In the amphitheater at Carthage the strength and skill of Olympius, the black huntsman, not his color or his looks, were the important factors.[62]

Two later observations on the Ethiopian are somewhat reminiscent of the earlier Greeks and in particular of Menander, but at the same time closely resemble in terminology and in spirit the early Christian use of the Ethiopian's blackness. Candace, in the Alexander Romance, cautioned the world conqueror about drawing conclusions from the Ethiopian's color for, she said, "we are whiter and brighter in our souls than the whitest of you."[63] Similarly, a Greek metrical epitaph, from Antinoë in Egypt dated in the third century A.D., in memory of a male Ethiopian slave reads in part: "Among the living I was very black, darkened by the rays of the sun but my soul, ever blooming with white flowers, won my prudent master's good will, for beauty is second to a noble soul and it is this which covered well my black body."[64] Westermann, in commenting on the absence among the ancients of distinctions in status strongly founded in recognized differences of race or color, considers this inscription "a remarkable example of the lack of race feeling based upon distinctions of color."[65] Remarkable though the sentiment may be for certain later ideologies, it is not surprising from the Greco-Roman point of view but is, rather, just what would be expected in light of the classical outlook — the initial environmental approach to racial differences and the various views of the community of man as conceived by Sophists, Hellenistic theorists, Stoics, and Christians.

As to the color of the skin and the Greco-Roman concept of beauty, attitudes apparently varied with individuals. Sextus Empiricus said that although men agree on the existence of beauty, they disagree on what constitutes the beautiful woman — the Persians preferring the whitest and most hook-nosed, the Ethiopians, the blackest and the most flat-nosed, and others considering the one who is intermediate in features and color the most beautiful.[66] Herodotus did not hesitate to call Ethiopians the most handsome people on earth.[67] Philostratus speaks of charming Ethiopians with their strange color.[68] Pseudo-Callisthenes declared the black Queen of Meroë, whom Alexander reportedly visited, to be of wondrous beauty.[69] With respect to persons described by adjectives for "black" or "dark" and "white" or "fair," some preferred the former, and some the latter. In view of the usage of μέλας and *niger* as the equivalent of Ethiopian, the preferences indicated are worthy of note in several instances. A poem to a certain Philaenion, short, black, with hair more curled than parsley and skin more tender than down, concludes: "May I love such a Philaenion, golden Cypris, until I find another more perfect."[70] Asclepiades praises the beauty of a Didyme of whom he writes: "Gazing at her beauty I melt like wax before the fire. And if she is black, what difference to me? So are coals but when we light them, they shine like rose-buds."[71]

Although *candidus* is frequently used to denote fair and *niger*, dark complexion, and may be at times the equivalents of "blonde" and "brunette" types, such an interpretation is doubtful in certain contexts. Hence, the graffito (portions of which appear several times) from a Pompeiian "grand *lupanar*" should perhaps be rendered: "A white girl has taught me to spurn black girls. I will if I can but I shall not love unwillingly." In this case P. Gusman translates *nigras* as *noires*.[72] Ovid wonders how Corinna heard of his affair with dark (*fusca*) Cypassis and asks what wrong is there in love for a slave girl.[73] Martial did not hesitate to write that though he was sought by a girl whiter than a washed swan, than silver, snow, a lily, and privet, he sought a "super-black" girl.[74] A writer of a poem in the *Anthologia Latina*, on the other hand, though commenting on the beauty of "blackness," seems to point clearly to a preference among some for "whiteness."[75] On the whole, however, the number of expressed preferences for blackness and whiteness in classical literature is approximately equal.[76] The evidence, then, shows that, as in several modern societies with white and black peoples, the matter was one of individual preference and that those with preference for blacks had no reluctance in saying so. In short, as Propertius observed, a tender beauty, whether white or dark, attracts.[77]

The swarthy — Egyptians and Ethiopians — as well as the woolly-haired, were cowardly, according to certain physiognomonical interpretations. The excessively fair, however, were also considered cowardly.[78] There was a belief in certain circles that the color of the Ethiopian's skin was ominous, related no doubt to the association of the color black with death, the underworld, and evil. It was noted, for example, among omens presaging disaster that ill-starred persons were known to have seen an Ethiopian before their misfortune. An Ethiopian who met the troops of Cassius and Brutus as they were proceeding to battle was considered an omen of disaster.[79] Among the events listed as foreshadowing the death of Septimius Severus was his encounter with an Ethiopian. On one occasion in Britain, upon his victorious return to his quarters, as Septimius was wondering what omen would be presented, he saw an Ethiopian soldier. Enraged by the ominous color of the soldier and the portentous nature of a garland of cypress boughs which he was carrying, the Emperor, it is reported, ordered the Ethiopian to be removed from his presence.[80] The author of a poem in the *Anthologia Latina* attributes the fall of Troy to Priam's acceptance of ill-omened assistance from Memnon and his black troops.[81]

In spite of a superstition in the minds of some with respect to the Ethiopian's color, the classical evidence as a whole supports Agatharchides' observation that such a fear ceased at childhood and indicates that serious evaluations of dark- or black-skinned persons were not affected by beliefs that the Ethiopian's skin was ominous or that black was a symbol of death or evil.[82]

Observations on the Ethiopians in their native land are in the tradition of the Ethiopian-Scythian explanation of differences among mankind and are characterized by a lack of color antipathy. The Greeks, for example, were acquainted with two types of Ethiopians and Scythians. Ptolemy, we have seen, attributed the savage habits of primitive Ethiopians and Scythians to the oppressive heat in the one case and to the continual cold in the other.[83] A knowledge of primitive Scythians who even ate human beings did not close the eyes of the Greeks to those Scythians who excelled all men in justice. Ephorus, for example, says that others write only about the savage Scythians because they know that the terrible and the marvelous are startling, but insists that the opposite facts should be noted also.[84] Similarly, the Greeks were acquainted with primitive Ethiopians living beyond Napata and Meroë who — resembling wild beasts in their way of living and cultivating none of the practices of life as found among the rest of mankind — presented a striking contrast to Greek customs.[85] A knowledge of these Ethiopians, however, did not cause the Greeks to overlook more developed Ethiopians, or to generalize and to classify all Ethiopians as primitive because some were savage. Diodorus spoke highly of the Ethiopians who inhabited Meroë and the land adjoining Egypt. He regarded the Ethiopians as the first people to worship the gods and most Egyptian institutions as derivatives of Ethiopian civilization.[86] Lucian informs us that Ethiopians gave the doctrines of astrology to men and that their reputation for wisdom was great, "being in all else wiser than other men."[87] Pliny records a similar view of Ethiopians when he attributes the wisdom of Ethiopians to the mobility of their climate and the fierceness of northerners to the rigidity of their region.[88]

A high esteem for Ethiopians appears as early as Homer, whose black, woolly-haired Eurybates won the high respect of Odysseus.[89] Color did not prevent Ethiopians from becoming favorites of the gods. Ethiopian piety and justice are the subjects of many comments and receive words of praise from numerous authors throughout classical literature.[90] As late as Heliodorus, an Ethiopian king was a model of wisdom, righteousness, and magnanimity.[91]

A discussion of the Greco-Roman attitude toward Negroes would be incomplete without a consideration of the archaeological evidence. Conclusions as to ancient attitudes toward Ethiopians which have been drawn from representations of the Negro in art have often been too simplistic. Interpretations have varied from those which have seen in portrayals of the Negro, nobility and intelligence or the sympathetic treatment of a racial type to those which have suggested that the selection of the Negro appealed to the comic instinct of the artist or stemmed from an interest in the grotesque and a desire to avert the evil eye.[92] Interpretations have in many cases explained all Negroes by a single theory, and at times have assigned modern attitudes to the ancients, which are not supported by the evidence. Further, there are those who have overlooked the fact that although artists may be influenced by their times, they are also *artists* motivated by aesthetic considerations. By tracing the entire history of the Negro in classical art, G. Becatti has demonstrated the importance of a comprehensive consideration of the treatment of this motif for what it reveals about Greco-Roman attitudes toward the Negro.[93]

Of the various foreign populations in the ancient world, the Negro attracted the artist over a longer period of time than any other foreign type. The popularity of the Negro in the sixth and fifth centuries B.C. was a reflection of an interest in a newly discovered people, which had its counterpart in anthropological observations of the period. One of the basic reasons, however, for the selection of the Negro was that the racial type appealed to the artist. As J. D. Beazley has properly observed, "the black man gets in not because he has strong prophylactic properties, nor because he is more addicted to wine, or perfume, than the white man nor because there were both perfumes and black men in Egypt, but because it seemed a crime not to make negroes when you had that magnificent black glaze."[94] Other artists saw in the juxtaposition or combination of black and white racial types an opportunity to create effective contrasts. The artists of different periods found in the Negro's distinctive features a challenge to their skill to represent by texture and paint the black man and especially his woolly hair.

At times contemporary events were responsible for the selection of the Negro. If an artist was inspired by mythology, he included the Negro when he was part of the myths. Delphos, or some unknown Negro, appeared on the coinage of Athens and Delphi in the fifth century B.C.[95] In Kabeiric burlesques the Negro and the pygmy, like others represented in these scenes, were caricatured in humorous situations. Some artists depicted ithyphallic Negroes who, like hunchbacks, have been interpreted as evidence of a belief in the black man's prophylactic powers. A similar explanation has been given for the use of Negro heads on pendants, earrings, and necklaces. When the Hellenistic artist turned to realistic portrayals of everyday life, he expanded his range of Negroid types to include the mulatto and Nilotic types in a wide variety of activities. The Roman world continued this tradition and selected Negroes from different social classes. A marble statue of a Negroid woman from Lower Egypt from the beginning of the Imperial period or a little earlier has been interpreted as a personification of Africa (Fig. 67);[96] a head (part of a statue) of approximately the same period from the vicinity of Rome, described as the idealized portrait of a young quadroon or mulatto from Cyrene, has been regarded as a personification of Libya.[97]

In short, after the initial excitement and curiosity about a new racial element in the population had abated, the Negro continued to appeal to generations of artists for much the same reasons as other subjects selected for artistic media.

Practice

In light of the Greco-Roman racial outlook as recorded in classical literature and of an insistence, such as that of Ephorus, on looking at both sides of the question in racial matters, it is understandable that social intercourse did not give rise among the Greeks and Romans to the color prejudice of certain later western societies. The Greeks and Romans developed no doctrines of white superiority unsupported by facts or theoretical justifications for a color bar.

The presence of large numbers of Negroes in a white society, according to some modern views, gives rise to anti-Negro feeling. Ethiopians were far from rare sights in the Greco-Roman, particularly the Roman, world. Yet the intense color prejudice of the modern world was lacking. Although it is impossible to estimate the Negro element in the classical world in terms of precise statistics, it is obvious that the black population in Greece and Italy was larger than has been generally realized.[98] Negro and Negroid peoples had lived in Egypt long before the Greeks and Romans arrived. Hence, Negroes were no strangers to the many Greek and Roman residents of Egypt or visitors to that country. References to Ethiopians in classical and early Christian literature and representations of Negroes in Greek and Roman art demonstrate clearly that the physical type denoted by *Ethiopian* was well known in widely scattered areas of the Greco-Roman world. The Ethiopian appeared frequently in illustrations of geographical and environmental theories, in explanations of racial types, in proverbs, and in statements of conviction that race is of no consequence in evaluating men. The Greeks and Romans knew the Ethiopians as military opponents at home and abroad. Further, the monumental evidence of classical art points to the presence of the Negro in sizeable numbers over a long period of time in various parts of the ancient world. Even when the artist was treating mythological subjects, he was portraying not mythical Ethiopians but those whom he had seen in the agora or the forum, in the household or the theater.

The few instances, if sources are accurate, which attest rather large numbers are of some value in suggesting estimates of the Ethiopian element in the numerous cases where figures are not mentioned. In the reign of Ptolemy II, for example, if Athenaeus is accurate, Ethiopians were present in sufficient numbers to carry two thousand ebony logs, six hundred tusks of ivory, and sixty bowls of gold and silver, at the time of Ptolemy's great procession.[99] One thousand prisoners from Petronius' campaign against the Ethiopians were sent to Augustus; others were sold — and though Strabo was probably exaggerating, he described the Ethiopian forces once as consisting of thirty thousand and at another time of many thousands.[100] One hundred Ethiopian huntsmen were presented in the circus in 61 B.C.[101] Only Ethiopians — men, women, and children — entered the theater when Nero was entertaining Tiridates at Puteoli.[102] Kinky-haired Ethiopians were present at the opening of the Colosseum in sufficient numbers to attract Martial's attention.[103] It would be hazardous to generalize on the basis of these few cases. But when one considers the long residence of Greeks and Romans in Egypt, the scope of the Persian invasion in which Ethiopians fought, the probable participation of Negroes in Hannibal's efforts, and the extensive military contacts the Romans had with the Ethiopians and Blemmyes in incessant frontier disputes, the few figures available take on greater significance. The exact number of Ethiopians who entered the Greco-Roman world as a result of varied military, diplomatic, and commercial activity is difficult to determine, but all the evidence suggests a sizeable Ethiopian element, especially in the population of the Roman world.

Allusions to Ethiopians in Greek literature pointing to actual residence of Ethiopians in Greece proper are few. The Herodotean mention of Ethiopians in Xerxes' army and the Negroes on Athenian vases of the fifth century B.C. have led to the conjecture that it was at this time that blacks were seen for the first time in Greece in large numbers. Aristotle's several notes on Ethiopians, the geographical commentary of Ephorus, and the cosmopolitan observations of Menander seem to imply a physical type well known by the average Greek of the period. Aristotle's mention of a woman from Elis whose child had an Ethiopian father points to Ethiopians resident in Greece. It is reasonable to assume, therefore, that a number of Ethiopians who accompanied Xerxes remained in Greece. As captives, many of them would have become slaves of various sorts. In addition, Ethiopians as other non-Greeks and non-Romans, would have reached the Greco-Roman world through the slave market. Adulis was a large trading center of the Troglodytes and the Ethiopians, from which slaves reached Egypt. Ethiopian slave dealers are mentioned in a sixth-century A.D. papyrus.[104] The Aristotle reference to race mixture between a Greek woman and an Ethiopian, the first of several in classical literature, indicates that the descendants of such unions were mulattoes, and, in the course of time, if such race mixture continued, would no longer be physically "Ethiopians." The concomitant racial assimilation and disappearance of Negroid physical characteristics would account for a failure of many writers to refer to Ethiopians unless the individuals in question were Ethiopians of a pronounced physical type, recent arrivals easily recognizable as Negroes, or mulattoes who received occasional notice in classical texts.

The founding of Alexandria substantially increased contacts between Greeks and, later, Romans with Ethiopians. The subsequent history of Alexandria as a melting pot of a motley conglomeration of peoples brought Greeks and Romans into contact with the numerous Ethiopians who participated in the polyglot life of that busy seaport. And from Alexandria Ethiopians were to reach Italy and Greece in the steady succession of ships that left the harbor for the various ports of the Mediterranean world. Greco-Roman and Roman terra cottas (Figs. 40a–b) graphically illustrate the role of the Ethiopian in the life of Alexandria, the Fayum, and neighboring regions. The terra cottas in the Graeco-Roman Museum in Alexandria which formerly decorated the houses and the tombs of the ancient seaport give a vivid idea of the life of that city in Roman times. The rather large number of statuettes depicting Negroes in this collection is a significant commentary on the Negro element in the population of that seaport. The collection preserves a variety of Negro types — two of the largest in the entire museum being Negroes, a soldier and a lamp-bearer (Fig. 113); the smaller figurines representing soldiers, gladiators, a slave carrying a child, another with an amphora, a little child sleeping in a crouched position, lantern-bearers, and several unidentified heads.[105]

Allusions to Ethiopians, few in the Roman Republic, were more numerous in the Empire. The Romans saw Ethiopians in numbers in Italy itself for the first time perhaps when Hannibal invaded the peninsula. Varro mentions Ethiopians in racial contrasts.[106] The *Rhetorica ad Herennium* is one of several indices attesting the popularity of Ethiopians as bath attendants.[107] The numerous references to the Ethiopian in the Empire have been cited elsewhere in this book and need not be repeated here. The fact that the Ethiopian appears much more frequently in Imperial than in Republican literature can be explained as a result of later Roman activity in Egypt and various regions of north Africa. Scybale was certainly a type with which the author of the *Moretum* was well acquainted.[108] Increased interest in the Ethiopian, obviously because he was beginning to appear in Italy in greater numbers, also accounts for the fact that the most detailed anthropological descriptions date from the early Empire — *Moretum*, Diodorus, Pliny the Elder, and Petronius.[109]

Even though we cannot state, in the manner of modern sociologists and historians, the ratio of blacks to whites in either Greece or Italy, we can say that Ethiopians were by no means few or rare sights and that their presence, whatever their numbers, constituted no color problem.

Modern racial experts, in evaluating the position of blacks in a predominantly white society, consider certain criteria essential. Although evidence with respect to the Ethiopian in the ancient world is not available for the application of all the criteria used by scholars today, we are able to see how the Ethiopian fared in certain crucial areas: occupations, religion, social acceptance, and race mixture. An examination of these areas demonstrates that Greco-Roman practice conformed with Greek and Roman beliefs as to the origins of racial diversity and their utterances as to the insignificance of racial differences in judging men.

A large, doubtlessly the largest, portion of the Ethiopians in Greece and Italy arrived as prisoners of war or as slaves. Others, however, came on diplomatic and commercial missions. Among the ambassadors in attendance at the palace of Constantine were Blemmyes and Ethiopians. The noblest of these received offices of such dignity from the Emperor that many preferred to continue residence in Italy, with no desire to revisit the countries of their origin.[110] Still others, particularly those who had been successful in Egypt, were attracted to Athens or Rome in the same way as other foreigners. Some, for example, sent their children to Alexandria and other cultural centers to be educated. Ergamenes, the Ethiopian who began to rule during the reign of Philadelphus, it will be recalled, had a Greek education and studied philosophy.[111] The disciples of Aristippus of Cyrene were his daughter Arete, Antipater of Cyrene, and Aethiops of Ptolemaïs, otherwise unknown.[112] A charming Hellenistic bronze of a Negro boy making a speech has been interpreted as a princely lad from Upper Egypt or beyond sent to study among the philosophers and teachers of rhetoric in Alexandria (Fig. 64).[113] A similar explanation is appropriate for a bronze recently discovered at Bodrum (Figs. 65a–b).[114]

What did the Ethiopians do after arrival in Greece or Italy? What were their activities? How did they fare in their new homes? That they succeeded in their daily occupations no differently than others of foreign extraction is clear from much that has been said in preceding chapters. The evidence of the terra cottas from the Graeco-Roman Museum in Alexandria illustrates the occupations of Negroes in one cosmopolitan center. In the entertainment world Negroes found opportunities for employment as actors, *mimologi*, dancers, jugglers, boxers, acrobats, animal tamers, *venatores*, gladiators, and charioteers. Negroes also served as bath attendants, bootblacks (Fig. 108), cooks, courtesans, divers (Fig. 52), laborers pulling cables (Fig. 109) or working Archimedean screws (Fig. 110), lamp-bearers (Figs. 66, 111, 112, 113), and personal attendants of their masters (Fig. 114).[115]

To a large extent it is the life of the humbler classes that is depicted in terra cottas. For a commentary on other social classes we must look to other media, particularly marble and bronze. A basalt head of a bearded and mustachioed figure with Negroid features from Egypt, perhaps from the region of the Fayum, is part of an over-life-sized statue (Figs. 71a–c). Although authorities disagree on the date (80–50 B.C. or the Trajanic period), the figure gives some idea of a Negroid officer or ambassador of his time. One suggestion is that he was a warrior, perhaps a general in the Ptolemaic army. A Roman bronze in the Bibliothèque Nationale represents an unknown Negro dignitary with elaborate mustache and whiskers (Fig. 54).[116] A life-sized bust, with a draped cloth over the left shoulder, assigned to the Flavian period, has been interpreted as that of a Negro who came to Rome as an ambassador or hostage and during his stay had his portrait made (Fig. 115).[117] It has been suggested that a Negro, whose life-sized statue of white marble was found near Naples, was a singer or actor of the second century A.D. (Fig. 116). The figure draped in a short, sleeveless tunic hanging from the left shoulder leaving the chest and right shoulder bare, stands with his left leg against the trunk of a tree.[118] Memnon, whose head has been preserved in Pentelic marble (Fig. 73), was treated as a son by Herodes Atticus, a most influential member of the international aristocracy of the second century after Christ. The famous sophist and patron of learning mourned Memnon's death and that of two other of his foster children as if they had been his own because they were noble-minded, honorable youths, fond of learning, and worthy of their upbringing in his household.[119] The sympathetically executed marble head of a Negro woman from Athens of the Trajanic era has been regarded as that of a lady of at least wealth, if not rank (Fig. 70). To a similar class of Negro ladies of distinction belongs the marble head of a woman from perhaps the Hadrianic period (Fig. 72). Another marble head of a Negro from Athens of 250–260 A.D. cannot be identified with certainty, but, like many other portraits of Athenians of this period, perhaps represented a gentleman of the upper social classes (Fig. 75).

If we knew more about the subjects of these portraits and other unidentified Negro marbles and bronzes, we could be more specific about the careers and positions of the blacks in classical antiquity. We know enough, however, to say that manumission and a "carrière ouverte aux talents" were equally available to Ethiopians as to others. Aesop, according to some accounts, was Ethiopian. Amasis, it has been suggested, was a dusky-skinned metic from Naucratis and perhaps Negroid. The dark- or black-skinned Terence arrived in Rome as a slave from Carthage and achieved fame as a comic poet. He was accepted in the literary and high social circles of the day, and his daughter is said to have married a Roman knight. Heliodorus, the author of the *Aethiopica,* it has been suggested, was a colored man.[120] An Ethiopian soldier served in the army of Septimius Severus in Britain. Lusius Quietus, whether Moor or Negro, attained positions of great power under Trajan. Although we can identify with some degree of certainty only one of the Negroes preserved in marble or bronze, we are justified in assuming that at least the busts of unidentified Negroes in marble and bronze depicted Negroes of the less humble social classes who had achieved some sort of renown. Further, with respect to the men, their distinction was due perhaps to their prominence in diplomacy, the military, or business. In commenting upon certain opportunities available to newcomers to Italy, O. Seel observes that there was no apartheid; whoever laid down arms after having fought only yesterday against Rome was welcome, whoever came to Rome was there, no one inquired after origins — all those with talent, industry, and good fortune had chances to forge ahead.[121]

Modern discussion of the origin and development of color

prejudice considers the attitude of religions toward the Negro as important. With respect to two religions, the Isiac and Christian, to be treated in the next chapter, we have substantial information from classical antiquity.

In the spread of Isiac worship during the Empire Ethiopians played a substantial role. In their native Ethiopia, Isis was one of four deities whom the people in the vicinity of Meroë worshipped because they believed that these particular divinities had been benefactors of the human race.[122] Egyptians, according to one tradition, were colonists sent out by the Ethiopians under the leadership of Osiris, who was worshipped in Ethiopia.[123] From the so-called temple of Isis at Meroë come two great columnar statues of an Ethiopian king and queen(?) done in sandstone.[124] Depicted on the wall of a Meroïtic pyramid is a seated Negroid king, in back of whose throne Isis stands; in front, a priest holds a censer of burning incense.[125] The prominence of Isis in Meroë of the third century A.D. is attested by the records of obeisance to the goddess at Philae. Among those southerners to leave testimonials of their devotion to Isis at Philae was Pasan, son of Paêse, who, when on a mission on behalf of his king, "the beloved son of Isis," left an offering for the goddess and prayed for a safe return to Meroë.[126] Among tribes in the vicinity of Philae the Isiac cult flourished after the spread of Christianity elsewhere in the region, and the temple of Isis at Philae continued in use until it was finally closed by order of Justinian.[127]

Since the worship of Isis was highly regarded by Ethiopians, whether in their native land or in Egypt, those who had settled elsewhere would tend to continue their interest in the cult. The head of a mulatto, discovered at Athens, has been interpreted as that of a native priest whom Egyptian metics demanded for their worship.[128] Whether a Hellenistic statuette of black diorite or marble from Aphrodisias (Fig. 117) is an *Isiacus*, as has been suggested, is not certain.[129] In two Herculaneum frescoes depicting Isiac ceremonials some of the participants are white and others dark-skinned. It is difficult to determine from the facial features alone, with one exception, the precise anthropological intent of the artist since he merely sketched the faces roughly. In one of these frescoes (Fig. 118), however, it is clear from the scene as a whole that some of the participants were intended as Negroid and perhaps some as Egyptian types. The dark-skinned figures

(Rostovtzeff called them the black attendants of the priests)[130] are dressed in robes extending from the armpits to the feet while the robes of the white worshippers extend from the shoulders. In this fresco a dark cultist, with his right arm outstretched, stands in the center of the congregation who, grouped in two rows in a court, make a gesture of adoration or hold the sistrum.

The companion piece presents as a central figure a dancing black on a platform who is the focus of attention (Fig. 119). This figure, whose head is crowned with a wreath of green water plants, is nude except for a kind of grass skirt. His body, arms, and forehead are covered with strokes of light paint applied in a pattern which suggests that the artist was well acquainted with one of the methods some Ethiopians used to paint their bodies. The dancer has been considered an Ethiopian; his dance, a mimetic attempt to interpret the Nile. The dark cultist below the platform at his right is the one figure whose features, in my opinion, are clear enough to suggest a Negroid type. Another dark worshipper to his left who plays a long reedlike instrument bears a striking resemblance to a Negroid figure, nude from the waist up, who holds a similar musical instrument, appearing in a ritualistic Nilotic scene on a mosaic of the second century A.D. from Lepcis Magna. A third dark-skinned figure claps enthusiastically in a kneeling position. The total impression is one of black Africa — an exotic dancer striped in paint, a practice noted by classical authors, African music, and rhythmical clapping. The entire fresco breathes the same spirit as the Ariccia relief in which Negroes and Egyptians appear and strongly suggests that the artist intended some, if not all, of the dark-skinned figures as Negroes.[131]

A nocturnal performance in which scenes from the lower world were enacted by Egyptians and Ethiopians is pertinent evidence from the end of Caligula's rule.[132] The scenes in question may have represented an episode such as the installation of Osiris as king in the underworld, or some related Isiac scene, for it was during the reign of Caligula that Isis was given her first public temple in Rome and that the dramatic festival of Osiris was established.[133]

A marble relief from a tomb on the Appian way near Ariccia depicts, according to R. Paribeni, a dance in which the dancers and spectators are undoubtedly Africans, that is, Egyptians and

Negroes (Figs. 5a–b, 105). The relief, Paribeni suggests, represents a ceremony or ritual associated with the worship of Isis and Serapis. In the right-hand corner of the scene is a small quadrangular podium from which six persons look toward the central figures in a transport of enthusiasm and accompany their dancing movement with a rhythmical clapping of their hands. These six figures, like the others in the relief, are subordinated to three central participants, rather steatopygic Negro women, dressed in long transparent tunics, whose violent dance involves bending the knees and tossing back the head. Two of these ladies hold crotala in their hands. Among the musician-dancers to the left of the Negro women moves a man of small proportions, with a decidedly Negroid head marked by considerable prognathism.[134]

Lucian mentions a thoughtful Negroid scribe, Pancrates, from Memphis, a clean-shaven scholar, dressed in white linen, who was well acquainted with the culture of the Egyptians and the magic of Isis.[135] Juvenal states that a noblewoman would make a pilgrimage to Meroë to obtain holy water for the temple of Isis in the Campus Martius.[136] Such a pilgrimage was no exaggeration if J. De Decker is correct in his interpretation that a Latin inscription found not far from Meroë is the *testimonium* of a pilgrim who had come from Rome to contemplate the Meroïtic goddess.[137] Though infrequent, pilgrimages from Rome or Alexandria to Meroë, undertaken by enthusiastic cultists, may have encouraged some native Meroïtic priests to return home with the inspired visitors.

A substantial Ethiopian influence on Isiac worship in Greece and Italy is strongly suggested, if not proved, by the tradition of Ethiopian association with the cult, by the Negroes depicted in Isiac ritual, and by other types of evidence cited above. Although many peoples in the ancient world worshipped Isis under a variety of names, it was the Ethiopians and the Egyptians who, as Apuleius points out, called the deity by her true name, *regina Isis*.[138] Just as temple administrators employed expert Egyptian priests to ensure that sacrifices and rites were performed properly,[139] Greeks and Romans who had been converted to the worship of Isis would likewise welcome the expert ritualistic knowledge of the Ethiopian. In a cult which attached importance to sacred dances or songs accompanied by the flute, initiates would respect the authenticity of dances such as that of the black in the Herculaneum fresco or of rhythms like those provided by the Negro women with their crotala as depicted in the Ariccia marble. Immigrants though Ethiopians may have been when they reached the shores of Greece or Italy, their devotion to Isis, already deeply rooted in Africa, and their acceptance by fellow Greek or Italian *Isiaci* gave them a spiritual security in their adopted country. A black man, far from his homeland, may have been like Apuleius' Lucius "a stranger to the temple but at home in the [Isiac] faith."[140]

One aspect of the Negro's role in the religion of Roman north Africa is suggested by scenes appearing in a fourth century A.D. mosaic from Carthage, which have been described and interpreted by G. Charles-Picard. The floor of the dining room of the so-called House of the Seasons depicts three religious scenes — the first, a nude man, representing Aion, who in the company of the seasons guarantees to the inhabitants of the house indefinite renewal of their prosperity. The second scene shows Venus, a symbol of the beneficent energy of nature, receiving offerings from two inhabitants of the house who seek the blessings of the goddess. In the third tableau a Negro, with frizzly hair and dark complexion, nude with the exception of a kind of scarf tied to his neck, stands full-front. On his left arm he holds his rolled-up tunic; he extends his right hand above an altar into which he throws incense. Above the altar are two stalks of millet. Nowhere else does a Negro appear in such a scene. The Negro, one of the numerous blacks in the area who were practitioners of magic, according to Charles-Picard, is performing an occult ceremony designed to invoke the powers of fertility. The ceremony is part of a religious triptych — to the classic powers of Aion and Venus the Negro adds the virtues of some strange ancient "voodoo."[141]

In the modern world the crucial test of the white man's acceptance of the Negro is the attitude toward miscegenation. Greek and Roman accounts of race mixture between Ethiopians and Mediterranean whites reveal no repugnance at the idea of racial crossings between whites and non-whites. Herodotus' report on the 240,000 rebellious Egyptians who settled in the reign of Psammetichus I among the Ethiopians and mixed with them is a case in point. The Egyptians, according to Herodotus, said that they would have no difficulty in finding wives wherever they went. Herodotus makes no comment on the episode other than that the Ethiopians learned Egyptian customs and became milder mannered by intermixture with the Egyptians. Nor does Plutarch, when citing the Herodotean account, have anything to say in condemnation of the Ethiopian-Egyptian racial mixture.[142] Similarly, the traditional opinion of the Cypriotes that Ethiopians were among those who composed the elements of their population is recorded without racial bias. No explanatory or apologetic note accompanies mention of Danaüs' seven daughters by an Ethiopian woman, or of the black lover of Aurora, the father of Memnon. Josephus records a legend which declared that Tharbis, the daughter of the king of the Ethiopians, fell madly in love with Moses when Ethiopia was invaded. Moses accepted her proposal of marriage and, after celebrating the nuptials, led the Egyptians back to their own land. Again, there is no comment on the interracial marriage.[143]

Both the literary and archaeological evidence points to a not infrequent crossing between blacks and whites. Nothing in the observations on such unions, whether marriage or concubinage, resembles certain modern strictures on racial mixture.

Our literary evidence for race mixture between blacks and whites is fuller for the Roman than for the Greek period. The humble rustic, Simylus, and his only helpmate, a woman of pronounced Negroid type, lived together and made the most of his meagre farm. Scybale carefully and devotedly assisted him in preparing their basic diet of bread and *insalata mista*.[144] A more well-to-do Roman perhaps demonstrated his affection by a memorial in the form of a head of a Negro woman from the second half of the second century A.D., whose fine features are delineated in black marble (Figs. 120a–b).[145] A similar motivation no doubt inspired two other heads of Negroid women from the Imperial period (Figs. 70, 72). Epigrams of affection and high praise for lovely black or dark ladies have been cited above.[146] A dark lady, Melaenis, was dear to the epigrammatist Marsus.[147] Mentioned also has been Martial's praise of a jet-black lady. Black courtesans were not unknown.[148] The appeal of black women was the subject of a graffito appearing on the wall of a villa at Boscotrecase, on the outskirts of Pompeii. The writer declared: "whoever loves Nigra burns as over black coals; when I see Nigra, I gladly eat blackberries." Black girls, as the other erotic Pompeiian graffito, mentioned previously, suggests, were the topic of frequent discussion at Pompeii.[149] And, as in slavery in other countries, the beloved were not forgotten in wills. Dion of Heraclea in his testament of 237–236 B.C. not only made provisions for his wife and son but left instructions that his slave Melaenis and his son by her should be set free and added "let no one lay hands on them."[150]

Racial mixture of white and Negroid types was frequent enough in the Empire for the satirists to find a source of amusement for the Roman public in references to miscegenation. Martial in an epigram on adultery mentions black children among the offspring.[151] Juvenal implies that mulattoes would be more common were it not for the practice of abortion.[152] Additional proof for the existence of intermixture between blacks and whites is found in Calpurnius Flaccus, a *rhetor* of the second century, whose declamation "Natus Aethiopus" considers this question: Is a white mother to whom a black child is born guilty of adultery?[153] St. Jerome mentions Quintilian's argument in a *controversia* that a matron, charged with adultery, had given birth to an Ethiopian as a result of "maternal impression."[154] Known also to Heliodorus was the apparently popular theory of "maternal impression." The black Ethiopian queen, Persinna, of the *Aethiopica,* upon discovering that she had given birth to a white daughter, recalled that at the time of conception she was looking at a picture depicting Perseus' rescue of Andromeda.[155] The mulatto offspring, therefore, was a subject for comment and discussion not only among satirists. Like Aristotle,[156] Plutarch and Pliny were interested in the transmission of the physical characteristics of descendants of black-white crosses. Pliny, for example, notes in this connection that the famous boxer Nicaeus, whose mother was the offspring of adultery with an Ethiopian but had a complexion not different from that of others, resembled his Ethiopian grandfather.[157] Plutarch relates a similar story about a Greek woman whose black baby caused her to be accused of adultery, although an investigation of her lineage revealed that she was the great-granddaughter of an Ethiopian.[158]

Mixture between blacks and whites is confirmed by the evidence of sculpture. In instances of physical types in which Negroid characteristics are not pronounced, as in the case of the "true" Negro, it is difficult to determine whether an artist is depicting a Nilotic type or the descendant of a black-white union

(Figs. 25a, 26a–b, 60–75). It is reasonable to assume, however, that in many cases it is a question of the latter, particularly in light of the literary references to black-white racial mixture and of the fact that many of the models probably were born outside of Africa. At any rate, few would doubt that certain figures manifesting some Negroid characteristics could be considered depictions of descendants of black-white crosses. Such an interpretation has been made in numerous instances.[159]

No laws in the Greco-Roman world prohibited unions of blacks and whites. Ethiopian blood was interfused with that of Greeks and Romans. No Greek or Roman author condemned such racial mixture. Martial and Juvenal condemned adultery when a mulatto child was evidence of illicit relations but said nothing of "racial purity." The scientists Aristotle and Pliny, like Plutarch, commented as scientists on the physical appearance of those born of black-white racial mixture but included nothing resembling certain modern strictures on miscegenation.[160] The statues of mulattoes and of mixed racial types are proof of the miscegenation noted in the texts. It is safe to assume, therefore, that in course of time many Ethiopians were assimilated into a predominantly white population. Completely random mating regardless of racial differences in the United States, it has been pointed out, would result in the virtual elimination of darker shades of Negroes and in the almost complete disappearance of Negroid physical traits.[161] Some such process was not unlikely in the Greco-Roman world in view of the evidence for racial mixture in a society which had no prohibition against miscegenation.

IX. Early Christian Attitude toward Ethiopians

Creed

The early Christian view of the Ethiopian was in the same tradition as the Greco-Roman outlook, adumbrated at first by the environmental approach of the Greeks to racial differences and developed in later ideas of the unity of mankind. Further, the early Christians adapted to their credo a frame of reference which had been employed frequently by Greeks and Romans to express their opinions on the equality of men. In fact, the early Christians used the Ethiopian as a prime motif in the language of conversion and as a means to emphasize their conviction that Christianity was to include all mankind. That the Ethiopian was so used was a natural development of classical tradition, for the Ethiopian was in many ways a convenient symbol for certain patterns of Christian thought. The Ethiopian's blackness and other physical characteristics conspicuously called him to the attention of a predominantly white society. The Ethiopian was the blackest and most remote of men. Yet his blackness gave rise neither to a theory of racial superiority nor to an inferior treatment. It was in such a climate that the early Christians made it clear that the Ethiopian's blackness was to be of no more consequence to them than it had been to the Greeks and Romans.

The Ethiopian-Scythian formula of classical writers appears in various forms in early Christian writings. Just as Menander had employed the traditional antithesis to express a Greek view of equality of men, Origen used it, with appropriate extensions, for the expression of the Christian outlook. A man, Origen declared, may be born among the Hebrews, with whom he finds instruction in divine law, or among the Greeks, men of no small learning, or among the Ethiopians, who eat human flesh, or among the Scythians, who practice parricide sanctioned by law, or among the Taurians, who sacrifice strangers. Yet all whom God created He created equal and alike. And, Origen continues, the diversity among rational creatures derives not from the will or judgment of the Creator but from the will of the individual, which in some instances incites to progress by imitation of God or reduces to failure through negligence.[1]

Origen, therefore, in adapting to Christian beliefs the Ethiopian-Scythian formula of Greco-Roman thought and in using language so full of meaning for the ancient world, left no doubt as to the comprehensiveness and direction of his concepts. In a somewhat similar usage, Paul, employing only the second part of the formula, had spoken earlier of a brotherhood of believers in which "there cannot be Greek and Jew, circumcised and uncircumcised, barbarian, Scythian, slave, free man, but Christ is all, and in all." In fact, the apostle Paul, it has been argued, was acquainted with Menander and, like some other early Christian writers, found in the Greek poets a source of insight into the human situation. If Paul was acquainted with Menander, and it does not seem unlikely, his celebrated pronouncement on oneness in Christ may have been an adaptation of Menander's statement of the inconsequence of race.[2]

Athanasius sees the pervasiveness of Christianity in the fact that none other than Christ through His disciples has been able to travel so far as to go among the Scythians and the Ethiopians, with the mention of whom he begins a catalogue of other peoples so visited.[3] Paul, by penetrating Scythian snows, broke the cold of that region with the warm glow of his teachings, and by his words Matthew tempered the Ethiopian heat and made living rivers to flow in the parched deserts of the south. Thus, by the use of familiar geographical extremes Venantius Fortunatus dramatized the successes of traditional apostolic endeavors.[4] The life of the Ethiopian Moses, a black father of the desert of Scetis, was adjudged clear proof that the Kingdom of Heaven is closed to neither slave nor evil-doer, to neither Scythian nor Ethiopian.[5]

The Ethiopian-Scythian formula was not the only pattern of classical thought reflected in Christian imagery. The Aesopian fable of the Ethiopian who was vigorously scrubbed and washed to no avail, illustrating the permanence of nature,[6] appears in Christian literature in variations of Jeremiah's "can the Ethiopian change his skin or the leopard his spots?"[7] The eunuch, prepared for baptism by the reading of the prophet, is to St. Jerome proof that though it is against nature, the Ethiopian does change his skin and the leopard his spots.[8] The Christians made somewhat similar use of the classical proverb Αἰθίοπα σμήχειν, to wash an Ethiopian white.[9] A tradition, for example, naming Thomas, rather than Matthew, as apostle to the Ethiopians, uses the figure as follows: "Thomas through baptism whitens Ethiopians."[10] The concept of cleansing to remove the blackness of sin and the image of washing appear frequently in the language of conversion. Christ came into the world to make blacks radiantly bright.[11] The black Father Moses illustrated by his exemplary life that the proverb can be reversed.[12]

The Ethiopians, the blackest men on earth living at the ends of the world, became a symbol of the peoples out of whom the Church was destined to grow.[13] They became integral parts of an imagery of spiritual blackness and whiteness.

A pioneer in exegesis and in textual criticism of the Bible, Origen declared that at first we are like Ethiopians in our souls but that we shall be cleansed in order that we may become brighter, in accordance with the verse from the Song of Solomon: "Who is she that cometh up having been made white?"[14] Elsewhere Origen contrasts the Ethiopian's natural blackness, caused by the sun's rays, with blackness of the soul, which, he says, is acquired not by birth but by neglect.[15] That Origen had in mind the traditional northern-southern, perhaps the Ethiopian-Scythian, contrast is apparent from his elaboration of the contrast between blackness of the skin and that of the soul. The visible sun, Origen continues, blackens and burns bodies near it but does not burn at all those bodies which are distant from it when it is at the zenith. The spiritual Sun of Justice, on the other hand, illuminates the upright in heart and those close to the zenith of His Glory but looks askance at those who walk contrary to Him.[16] The early Christian adaptation of the familiar classical references to the color of the Ethiopian's skin is obvious in the above-cited commentary of Origen.

The Ethiopian appears frequently in early Christian interpretations of a second passage from the Song of Solomon, the familiar "I am black but comely" of the King James Version. The early commentators, however, read "and," which appears in the Septuagint, not "but," as in the Vulgate:[17] "I am black, and beautiful, O daughters of Jerusalem, like the tents of Kedar, like the curtains of Solomon. Do not look at me because I am blackened, because the sun has looked upon me."[18] Origen's comments on these verses in part are as follows:

> Moreover we ask in what way is she black and in what way fair without whiteness. She has repented of her sins; conversion has bestowed beauty upon her and hence she is sung as "beautiful." But because she is not yet cleansed of all the uncleanness of her sins nor washed unto salvation, she is said to be "black" but she does not remain in her black color — she becomes white. Therefore when she rises to greater things and begins to climb from the lowly to the lofty, it is said of her "who is she that cometh up having been made white?" . . . If, moreover, you do not repent, take heed lest your soul be called "black" and disgraceful and lest you be stained by a double foulness — "black" on account of your past sins; disgraceful because you continue in the same faults. But if you repent, your soul will be "black" because of your former sins, but because of your penitence your soul will have something of what I may call an Ethiopian beauty.[19]

In further interpretation of the same passage from the Song of Solomon Origen makes, among others, these points which appear in similar or modified form in other writers commenting on the words of the Bride to the young maidens of Jerusalem: (1) the Bride who speaks represents the Church gathered from among the Gentiles; (2) her body, black externally, lacks neither natural beauty nor that acquired by practice; (3) the daughters of an earthly Jerusalem, upon seeing the Church of the Gentiles, despise her because she cannot boast the noble blood of Abraham, Isaac, and Jacob; (4) the Bride's reply is that she is black and that though she cannot point to descent from illustrious men, she is nevertheless beautiful, for in her is the image of God and she has received her beauty from the word of God; (5) she is black by reason of her lowly origin but is beautiful through penitence and faith; (6) the daughters of Jerusalem in reproaching her on account of her blackness should not forget what Mary suffered when she spoke against Moses because he had married a black Ethiopian woman.[20]

The "black and beautiful" of the Song of Solomon, in the judgment of Gregory of Nyssa,[21] explains a whole philosophy and knowledge of God. The exterior beauty of the tent of witness was not equal to its hidden inner beauty. Those who saw only the exterior were able to see nothing precious except the curtains, whereas the inside of the tent of witness was resplendent with gold, silver, and precious stones. When she was black with sin, says the Bride, the Bridegroom by transferring to Himself the uncleanness of her sin bestowed upon her His purity and made her share in His beauty. A similar usage, Gregory notes, appears in Paul's reference to God's love for us[22] because while we were sinners and black, he made us radiantly bright and resplendent with grace. Just as at night even that which is radiantly bright by nature becomes black because of darkness, so when a soul is led from error to truth, darkness is changed to bright grace. What the Bride of Christ said to the young maidens, declares Gregory, Paul also had in mind when he said to Timothy that God considered him worthy to become beautiful, although formerly he had blasphemed, persecuted, and insulted the Lord. Paul had become radiantly bright from black.[23] Christ came into the world to make blacks radiantly bright,[24] not summoning to Himself the just but calling to penitence sinners whom through baptism He made to shine like heavenly bodies. It was this, according to Gregory, that David saw in the heavenly city and this at which he marveled, for in the City of God "Gentiles become dwellers of the city; Babylonians, Jerusalemites; the prostitute; a virgin; Ethiopians, radiantly bright and Tyre the heavenly city."[25]

Variations of the imagery of spiritual blackness and whiteness appear in other early Christian writers. Cyril of Alexandria interprets Ethiopians as those whose dark minds are not yet illumined and are without divine light. They who kneel before the Son, however, are regarded by Cyril as those of whom it has been said: "before Him shall the Ethiopians fall down";[26] whereas those whose uncleanness is hard to wash out and who remain in their blackness will feast upon the heads of the dragon[27] and will be exposed to the sword.[28]

Jerome reminds us that at first we are black by nature and, even after repentance, until we have ascended virtue's height, we may say "I am black and beautiful." As soon, however, as we decide to heed the wisdom of the true Solomon, our color will be miraculously changed.[29] In commenting upon "ye also, O Ethiopians, shall be slain by the sword,"[30] Jerome notes that those deeply sunk in vices are called Ethiopian in accordance with the words of Jeremiah. If the Ethiopian changes his skin,[31] in the conversion of the Ethiopians there will be the hope that no one wishing to repent will be without salvation. This is why a soul stained with the sordidness of sin says "I am black," but when later washed and purged through penitence, the Song of Solomon can sing of the same soul: "who is she that cometh up having been made white?"[32] The words of God, then, according to Jerome, threaten those who cling to sin and, forgetful of the sordidness of their sins, do not wish to wash away the dark color and turn to better things.[33] Reflecting the same tradition, an account of the life of the Ethiopian Moses described him as a man whose body was black but whose soul was brighter than the splendor of the sun.[34] Similar was the response of Moses himself to the bishop who consecrated him, clad in white vestments. In reply to the bishop's observation that he had, upon consecration, become all white, the black man said, "outwardly, holy Father, would that I were inwardly too!"[35]

The frequent usage of the Ethiopian in such imagery explains to some extent why early Christian writers, when commenting on a given Scriptural passage involving Ethiopians, developed a type of exegesis which collated several familiar references to Ethiopians. This practice constitutes such a significant part of the early Christian observations on the Ethiopian that a few examples should be presented.

A discussion of the Church which comes of the Gentiles and calls herself black and beautiful requires, in the judgment of Origen, a collation of passages from the Scriptures which foreshadow the mystery. Origen says that several passages suggest themselves to him as being in accordance with "I am black and beautiful." In this connection Origen first cites with brief comment and then presents a detailed exegesis of the following:[36] (1) Moses' marriage to the Ethiopian woman;[37] (2) the visit of the Queen of Sheba to Solomon;[38] (3) "Ethiopia shall stretch out her hand to God";[39] (4) "from beyond the rivers of Ethiopia will I receive my dispersed ones; they shall bring me sacrifice";[40] (5) the Ethiopian eunuch Abdimelech.[41]

Origen in the passage in question first discussed the marriage of Moses to the Ethiopian woman[42] because of whom Mary and Aaron spoke against Moses in these words: "Has the Lord indeed spoken only through Moses? Has he not spoken through us also?" If their trouble had been indignation about the Ethiopian woman, says Origen, Mary and Aaron ought to have said, "Moses, you should not have taken an Ethiopian wife, and one descended from Ham; you should have married one of your own race." Since however they said nothing of this sort, continues Origen, they seem to have understood what Moses had done in terms of the mystery, that is, Moses, the Spiritual Law, had entered into union with the Church gathered from among the Gentiles. Mary, typifying the forsaken Synagogue and Aaron, the priesthood, saw their kingdom taken away from them and given to a nation bringing forth its fruits. And never did Moses, in spite of his many, splendid achievements, receive from God such high praise as when he married the Ethiopian woman. For in this connection the Lord said of Moses, "he is entrusted with all my house; with him I speak mouth to mouth, clearly, and not in dark speech; and he beholds the form of the Lord. Why then were you not afraid to speak against my servant Moses?"[43] The black and beautiful woman, concludes Origen, is the same as the dark or black Ethiopian whom Moses married, although the daughters of Jerusalem (the people and their priests) speak evil of Moses (the Spiritual Law, the Word of God, and the Christ) for his having wedded the Ethiopian woman.[44]

Parenthetically, to interrupt the Origen commentary, the wrath of the Lord that struck Moses' detractors and His praise of Moses were often noted by the commentators but rarely as antithetically as Origen in one of his homilies: "You see what punishment the detractors got for themselves, and what praise for him whom they criticized: Shame for them, honor for him; leprosy for them, glory for him; reproach for them; nobleness for him — this is what they got."[45]

The Queen of Sheba, according to Origen's interpretation of the passage from I Kings,[46] by her visit to Solomon provides an important parallel to the person of the Church, who comes to Christ from out of the Gentiles. In fulfillment of the type represented by the Queen of Sheba, an Ethiopian, the Church comes from the Gentiles to hear the wisdom of the true Solomon and the true lover of Peace. She came to Jerusalem with a great following, not with a single nation as the Synagogue before her with Hebrews only, but she was accompanied by the races of the whole world offering worthy gifts to Christ. When this black and beautiful Queen had seen all in the House of the King of Peace, she expressed her amazement. But, Origen concludes, when she comes to the heavenly Jerusalem, she will see wonders more numerous and splendid.

How does Origen, in his collation of passages relating to Ethiopians, interpret "princes shall come out of Egypt; Ethiopia shall stretch out her hands to God" and "from beyond the rivers of Ethiopia will I receive my dispersed ones"?[47] The hands of Ethiopia, that is, the people of the Gentiles, in approaching God outstripped those to whom God's oracles had first been given. Israel by its failure had opened the way for the success of the Gentiles. It was thus, then, that the prophecy of the Psalms was fulfilled and that the "black one" became beautiful, although the daughters of Jerusalem envied and reviled her.

"Those from beyond the rivers of Ethiopia"[48] whom the Lord receives are, according to Origen, those who, because darkened with many serious sins and stained with the dye of wickedness, have become black and dark. The Lord, however, in Origen's interpretation, accepts even these if they offer sacrifices to God humbly and in the spirit of confession and repentance. Since the rivers of Ethiopia are a figure for the Gentiles, says Origen, the prophecy may also denote those who will come after the fullness of the Gentiles has come in, for, in accordance with the words of Paul to the Romans: "a hardening has come upon part of Israel, until the full number of the Gentiles come in, and so all Israel will be saved."[49]

What significance does Origen's account attach to Abdimelech's lifting of Jeremiah from the cistern?[50] This Ethiopian is said to be a eunuch either because he had made himself a eunuch for the kingdom of heaven or because he had himself no seed of wickedness. He is a servant of kings, his name meaning "servant of kings," because a wise servant rules over foolish masters. Abdimelech, a foreigner of dark and ignoble race,[51] represents the people of the Gentiles. It is the people of this race who, Origen says, believe in the resurrection from the dead of Him whom the princes had given over to death and who by their faith recall and bring Him back from hell. It is the eunuch, then, Origen concludes, who can be said by his faith in the resurrection of Christ to have drawn Him from the cistern.

In observations on Scriptural references to the Ethiopian, St. Jerome employs a method similar to that used by Origen and Gregory and in his exegesis cites in general the same passages and makes similar points. The Jeremiah proverb of the Ethiopian changing his skin and the leopard his spots also receives several comments from St. Jerome.[52] The Christian poet Arator in a poem on the Ethiopian eunuch whom Philip baptized included within the compass of a few lines mention of the marriage of Moses and the Ethiopian woman, its significance, God's approval, the familiar "dark and beautiful," and the visit of the Ethiopian Queen to Solomon.[53]

The full significance of the Ethiopian in Christian usage is brought out in another manner in the following commentary of St. Augustine on this verse of the Psalms, "Thou didst break to pieces the head of the dragon; thou didst give him for meat to the Ethiopian peoples".[54]

> How do I understand "Ethiopian peoples"? How else than by them, all nations? And properly by black men (for Ethiopians are black). Those are called to the faith who were before black, just they, so that it may be said to them "Ye were sometimes darkness but now are ye light in the Lord."[55] They are indeed called black but let them not remain black, for out of these is made the Church to whom it is said: "Who is she that cometh up having been made white?" For what has been made out of the black maiden but what is said in "I am black and beautiful"?[56]

St. Augustine, interpreting another verse of the Psalms, stated that under the name "Ethiopians" all nations were signified — as by a part the whole — and that that nation which was at the ends of the earth was chosen to be mentioned by name.[57] Elsewhere in the same passage St. Augustine declared that "the Catholic Church has been foretold not to be in any particular quarter of the world, as certain schisms are, but in the whole universe, by bearing fruit and growing even unto the very Ethiopians, indeed the remotest and blackest of men."[58] The shaking of the tents of the Ethiopians and of the land of Midian described in

Habakkuk signified for Augustine that even races not living under Roman law will be deeply moved by the news of His wondrous deeds and will be counted among Christian peoples.[59]

Man's common descent and his common human nature were recognized by the early Christians in these words of Augustine: "whoever is born anywhere as a human being, that is, as a rational mortal creature, however strange he may appear to our senses in bodily form or colour or motion or utterance, or in any faculty, part or quality of his nature whatsoever, let no true believer have any doubt that such an individual is descended from the one man who was first created. Yet there is a clear distinction between what has by nature persisted in the majority, and what is marvelous by its very rarity."[60]

The early Christians in their view of the Ethiopian continued the Greco-Roman tradition not only in sentiment but also in language and imagery. For Christian writers of the first centuries after Christ, it made no difference whether one was as racially different as the Scythian or the Ethiopian; of no importance was the region of the world or the cultural group from which a man came. Color was inconsequential; in fact, we have seen that they regarded as black all men who had not been illumined by God's light and considered all men, regardless of the color of the skin, as potentially Christians. Ethiopians were by all means to be embraced, for the Church, in the words of Augustine, was to reach even the Ethiopians, the remotest and blackest of men. All who were Christians were the same kind of men. The protagonists of these views were no minor figures in the early history of Christianity, and included among them were Origen, Jerome, and Augustine.

Conversion

"Aethiopia credet Deo."[61] With these words of Augustine early Christians expressed a faith in a brotherhood of believers. Another expression of the same faith appears in Gregory of Nyssa, who had said that Christ came into the world to make blacks white and that in the Kingdom of Heaven Ethiopians become white.[62] The Christian credo was unequivocally clear. What about the practice — actual membership of Ethiopians in the early Christian brotherhood?

That membership in the early Church was actually to include Ethiopians was a cardinal principle from the very beginning, for one of the acts of the apostles, Philip's baptism of an Ethiopian eunuch,[63] foreshadowed what was to be the practice of the early Church. The Ethiopian eunuch, a minister of Candace and in charge of all her treasure, was said to have been the first of the Gentiles to receive from Philip the mysteries of the divine Word and to have returned to preach the Gospel in his native land.[64] By the reading of the Prophet, in the interpretation of Jerome, the eunuch of the Queen of Ethiopia was prepared for the baptism of Christ. Hence, though it is against nature, the Ethiopian does change his skin and the leopard his spots.[65] To Theodoret, as to many others, the eunuch was proof that "Ethiopia shall stretch out her hands to God."[66] In the exegesis of Scriptural passages involving Ethiopians the conversion of the eunuch as recorded in Acts is cited together with other references as evidence that Christianity was destined to spread throughout the whole world.[67] Modern commentators have interpreted the episode similarly. The baptism of the eunuch, like that of Cornelius by Peter, marked an important stage in the question of the admission of Gentiles to the Christian church.[68] By the baptism of the eunuch, Philip proclaimed that considerations of race and external conditions are of no significance in determining membership in the Church. All believers in Christ are eligible.[69]

The eunuch came to be admired as a model of the diligent reader of the Scriptures. Jerome noted that the eunuch's zeal for the Word of God was so great that he read while in his carriage.[70] The inattentive who neglected opportunities offered by their teachers were reminded of the eunuch. John Chrysostom, for example, pointed to the eunuch as one who, though a barbarian without advantages, read Scripture in spite of important matters which occupied his attention during a journey.[71] The faithful were exhorted, in order to prepare the way for true understanding, to read beforehand, in the manner of the eunuch, passages to be explained.[72] The site of the eunuch's baptism is noted in an ancient guidebook to the Holy Land as being sixteen miles from Jerusalem.[73] A tradition grew that the eunuch became an apostle not only to Ethiopia but also to Arabia Felix and Taprobane (Ceylon).[74] To Eusebius the eunuch's apostolate demonstrated the fulfillment of the frequently cited prophecy that "Ethiopia shall stretch out her hands to God."[75] Justin Martyr (ca. 100–165 A.D.) may have had in mind the baptism of the eunuch when he cited this verse from the Psalms: "The Ethiopian shall fall down before Him and His enemies shall lick the dust."[76]

At some time in the early centuries of Christianity a tradition arose that the twelve apostles had by lot parceled the known world among themselves. Matthew, in a common form of the tradition, was reported to have preached in Ethiopia.[77] In commenting on the prophecy of Matthew that the Gospel of the kingdom "will be preached throughout the whole world as a testimony to all nations," Origen indicates that by his time Christians had already made some contact in Ethiopia. The Gospel, Origen writes, has not yet been preached throughout the whole world, for it is not claimed that it has reached all Ethiopians, especially those who are beyond the river, to say nothing as to the peoples of Britain, Germany, Dacia, Sarmatia, and Scythia.[78] We do not know to what extent the several legends of apostleships in Ethiopia and Origen's reference to the spreading of the Gospel among some Ethiopians actually represented missionary efforts in Ethiopia in the first three centuries after Christ. The report of Frumentius' experience with Christian merchants in Axum, however, suggests that even before the fourth century A.D. commerce and trade may have brought some Christians to the Axumite coast and Nilotic trade routes.

The earliest record of the introduction of Christianity in Ethiopia is associated with Ethiopian Axum and the Ethiopian coasts of the Red Sea. The traditional story, preserved in several ecclesiastical writers, attributes the founding of the Church in Axum to Frumentius in the fourth century.[79] According to the story, Frumentius and his brother Adesius had accompanied a kinsman, Meropius, from Tyre on a voyage to "India."[80] Upon their return, they stopped at an Ethiopian port on the Red Sea, where the inhabitants murdered the ship's crew but spared Frumentius and his brother. They eventually attained considerable influence at the palace of the Axumite king. While there, Frumentius summoned the Christian merchants in the region and encouraged the erection of a house of prayer. On a visit to Alexandria to report on his Axumite experiences, Frumentius requested Athanasius to send a bishop to Axum. Frumentius, according to the ecclesiastical writers, was consecrated by Athanasius, who chose him to minister to the peoples of Axum.

If the essentials of this story are true, the introduction of Christianity in Axum may be attributed to Frumentius. At any rate, we know from contemporary evidence that the Ethiopian Axumites received the attention of the Emperor Constantius II (337–361 A.D.) about the middle of the fourth century. In a letter preserved by Athanasius, addressed from Constantius to the Ethiopian Axumites,[81] we learn something of Constantius' anti-Athanasianism and of his determination to disseminate his own beliefs among the Christians of Ethiopian Axum. In a letter to the princes of Axum, Aezanes and Sazanes, Constantius expressed his concern for the Axumites and his wishes for the withdrawal of Frumentius, bishop of Axum. It was always a matter of grave concern to him, the Emperor wrote, to extend the knowledge of God, and in this extension the whole race of mankind claimed from him equal regard. Since he considered the Axumites deserving of the same provident care as the Romans, Constantius continued, he desired to show equal interest in their welfare by commanding that the same doctrines be professed in Ethiopian as in Roman churches. Within this framework the Emperor expressed his fear that Frumentius, an appointee of Athanasius, might corrupt the Axumites by spreading impious statements, and hence he urged the withdrawal of Frumentius.

Also at the time of Constantius, according to Philostorgius, Theophilus, a native of the island of Divus, who had been sent as a young hostage to the Romans during the rule of Constantine, was active as a missionary among the Homeritae (Himyarites) and the Axumites. This Theophilus, designated by Philostorgius as Indian and by Gregory of Nyssa as Blemmys,[82] was particularly successful, in the account of Philostorgius, among the Homeritae, and upon his return received great honors from Constantius.[83] If Gregory of Nyssa's designation of Theophilus as Blemmys is correct, and if this missionary was born in Ethiopia,[84] his assignment is additional indication of what other evidence demonstrates — that Ethiopians were beginning to assume positions of responsibility in the Church. By the end of the fourth century pilgrims from Ethiopia and the neighboring country of Egypt had visited Palestine.[85] Jerome, writing at the beginning of the fifth century in a letter celebrating the triumphs of Christianity, noted that among the monks welcomed daily in Palestine were Ethiopians.[86]

Both Rufinus of Aquileia and Palladius in their accounts of monks in the Egyptian desert reported that they saw Ethiopians with the monks and that many of them excelled in virtue, thus fulfilling the words of the Scriptures that Ethiopia shall stretch out her hands to God.[87] One of the most outstanding Fathers of the Desert was a tall, black Ethiopian, Moses, whose fame spread far from the desert of Scetis, where he acquired a reputation as a model of Christian virtue.[88] Conscience-stricken at the thought of his earlier life as a brigand and, according to some, as a murderer, he joined a monastery in the desert of Scetis. A man of great strength and courage, he came to be known for his humility and wisdom and was a great inspiration to others. He later became a presbyter, leaving some seventy disciples when he died at the age of seventy-five, at the end of the fourth or in the first years of the fifth century.[89]

Several episodes given by Palladius in his account of Moses' life illustrate the respect and fame he acquired. Once, four of his former associates in brigandage broke into his cell; Moses, whose exploits had included swimming across the Nile with a sword in his teeth, put the robbers in a sack and carried them to his brothers. Remarking that he was unable to do harm to anyone, he sought advice as to what should be done with the robbers. The robbers confessed and, upon recognizing Moses, were so moved by his example that they renounced the world, joined the monastery, and became highly regarded monks.

During a period when Moses was being tempted by demons to return to his earlier immorality, he shut himself up in a cell, fasted, and for six years stood up all night and prayed for God's help in overcoming his unrestrained desire. Still unsuccessful, he undertook hard physical labor, which included drawing water for aged monks and carrying it great distances. While so engaged, he was clubbed at the well, where he was found half-dead. His spiritual adviser Isidore sought to comfort him by advising him to cease his struggle, but Moses replied that he would never desist until the demons disappeared.[90]

The advice of Moses to a brother seeking his counsel was "go, sit in thy cell, and thy cell will teach thee all."[91] Another anecdote illustrates his humility and fear of vainglory. Having learned of a governor's intentions to visit him, Moses was fleeing to a swamp but along the way met the governor. In reply to a question as to the location of Moses' cell, Moses asked the visitor why he wanted to see a man who was a fool and departed unrecognized. The governor later explained to Moses' fellow-monks the purpose of his mission but added that a man whom he had just met had told him that Moses was a fool. Upon hearing that his informant was an old, tall, black man wearing old clothes, they told the governor that he had already seen the Father. Whereupon the governor departed a wiser man.[92]

On one occasion the archbishop of Alexandria, wishing to test Moses, instructed the clergy to drive him out of the sanctuary and to observe him. As they rebuked him and exclaimed, "begone, Ethiopian," he was heard to say, "they have treated you rightly, sooty-skinned black man. You are not a man. Why did you enter among men?"[93] A similar spirit of humility appeared in the hesitancy of Moses to judge his fellows. With reluctance consenting to attend a meeting convened to consider the conduct of an errant brother, Moses arrived carrying a broken basket from which sand was falling. To his colleagues who asked the meaning of what he was doing, Moses replied, "my sins flow down behind me; I don't see them, and yet I have come to judge the sins of another." Whereupon the brothers were silent and pardoned the monk whose transgressions they had assembled to judge.[94]

Moses, who had forewarned his brothers about the coming of the barbarians, on the day of their approach was asked if he would not flee. His reply was that he had been looking forward to the day when the words of Christ would be fulfilled: "all who take the sword shall perish by the sword." Adding that he was not at all concerned, he instructed each to make his own decision. Moses and seven who remained with him were slain.[95]

The Moses whom Cassian describes as having lived in a place in the wilderness called Calamus seems to be the same as the Father of the desert of Scetis.[96] Driven to a monastery through fear of death that threatened him because of murder, Moses, according to Cassian, made such a use of his compulsory conversion that his zeal turned it into a voluntary one, and he climbed to the topmost heights of perfection.[97] The Church historian Sozomen noted these points about the life of Moses: (1) after committing murder and other crimes, he embraced a life of asceticism in which he attained the highest point of philosophical perfection; (2) neither such a sudden conversion from vice to virtue nor such a rapid attainment in monastic philosophy had even before been seen.[98]

The significance of Father Moses' life is epitomized in an anonymous Byzantine Menologium, the beginning of which reads in part: "Neither to slave nor to evil-doer is the Kingdom of Heaven closed but within are they who have repented as they should and who have chosen to live rightly and according to God. Neither is the Kingdom closed to Scythian or to Ethiopian . . . This can be seen in the case of very many others but especially in the case of Moses the Ethiopian . . . This man whose body was black had a soul more radiantly bright than the splendor of the sun." The Menologium continues by pointing out that Moses was as famous for his virtue after his repentance as he had been before for his wickedness. He was everything to all, a model of the monastic life, on the lips of all, an excellent teacher, a Father's Father. In the person of Moses the words of the proverb that it is impossible to wash an Ethiopian white seemed to be altered.[99]

To some extent the life of Moses as recorded in the Menologium represents a summary of early Christian attitudes toward the Ethiopian. Several images originating in pagan literature and later modified to become an integral part of Christian symbolism appear in the Menologium, all familiar — the Ethiopian-Scythian formula, the black body with a soul brighter than the sun, and the reversal of the proverbial "to wash an Ethiopian white." Father Moses, himself a black man, adapted one of these images in his remark to the archbishop that he was white only outwardly but still black inwardly.[100] In other words, Father Moses, an Ethiopian, applies to himself the well-known Christian symbolism of spiritual blackness and whiteness which had its roots in pagan writers. This usage is an interesting application of the Christian imagery and suggests that it was accepted by Ethiopians who found it inoffensive to their blackness.[101]

St. Menas (ca. third-fourth century A.D.), whose relics were revered in a monastery southwest of Lake Mareotis, the reputed birthplace of the Egyptian martyr, is sometimes represented as a Negro on *ampullae* or pottery flasks bearing his effigy. These *ampullae*, dated as early as the fourth century but mostly from the fifth to the seventh centuries A.D., enabled the visitors to bring back to their homes either holy oil from the shrine of St. Menas or water from a sacred spring near his tomb. The widespread distribution of the flasks, found not only in Egypt and coastal Africa but also in Asia Minor, Greece, Italy, and southern France, attests the popularity of the saint among the many pilgrims who sought his blessing. Although it may be hazardous to draw conclusions as to the precise racial origins of St. Menas from the effigies on the *ampullae*, these representations are significant for the history of the Negro in early Christianity.[102]

From the end of the fifth century A.D. we have evidence of the Church's concern for a young Ethiopian slave. In a letter to Fulgentius, Bishop of Ruspe, in the north African district of Byzacena, a deacon, Ferrandus, raised the problem of a catechumen, Ethiopian in color, from the most distant parts of a barbarous region where men are darkened by the dry heat of the fiery sun. This Ethiopian had been directed to the Church by his faithful masters. He had become a source of concern to the deacon because, although he had been baptized while suffering from disease and not in possession of his mind, he had died before receiving the Eucharist.[103] The correspondence records an interesting practical application of the principle enunciated by St. Augustine that the Church, as the Glory of God demanded, was to embrace the Ethiopians who lived at the ends of the earth. In fact, the language in the correspondence recalls certain phrases used by St. Augustine, and the description of the Ethiopian slave as "not yet whitened by the shining grace of Christ" resembles the terminology appearing in early Christian symbolism of spiritual blackness and whiteness.[104]

The sixth century A.D. witnessed increased Christian activity not only in Axum but also in Nubia. Christianity had become so established in Axum in the reign of Justin I (518–527) that the emperor supported Ela Atzbeha (Elesboas), a king of the Axumite Ethiopians, in his efforts to halt the persecution of the Christians in the country of the Homeritae (Himyarites) on the opposite mainland in south Arabia.[105] When Dhu Nuwas, a Himyarite leader of the Jewish faith who had proclaimed himself king, had massacred a large number of Christians in 523, an appeal for assistance was sent to Elesboas, who in turn sought help from Justin. The religious sympathies of the emperor with the Ethiopian Axumites were such that through Timothy, the Monophysite Patriarch of Alexandria, he urged Elesboas to make war on the Himyarites. Although Timothy, on behalf of Justin, promised to send Blemmyan and Nubian troops to assist Elesboas in his holy war against Dhu Nuwas, there is no record of the participation of such troops. With the assistance, however, of ships which Justin (no doubt prompted by political and commercial as well as religious interests) provided from his commercial fleet for the transportation of Axumite troops, Elesboas defeated Dhu Nuwas and set up in his stead as a tributary king a Himyarite Christian named Esimiphaios. Elesboas remained among the Himyarites for three years and occupied himself with restoring Christianity and rebuilding churches in various cities of the country.

Cosmas Indicopleustes, writing at the time of Justinian, noted that Ethiopians, Axumites, and Nobades were among those reached by the Gospel of Christ.[106] Nubia received the competing attention of Justinian and the Empress Theodora in their zealous efforts to disseminate their faith, the former interested in Orthodox and the latter sympathetic to Monophysite Christianity.[107] Concerned that the Nobades, friends of the Roman empire, were still pagans, Justinian and Theodora sent rival delegations at approximately the same time. Theodora's mission, however, headed by a representative of the Monophysite Patriarch of Alexandria, arrived first as a result of the Empress' shrewd and energetic planning. By the time the Orthodox mission, dispatched by the Emperor, arrived, Theodora's priest, Julian, who had long been concerned about the Nobades living on the southern boundary of the Thebaid, had so influenced the king of the Nobades and his nobles that Justinian's mission was rejected. In spite of great suffering from the extreme heat, Julian remained two years among the Nobades, offered instruction and baptized not only the king and nobles but many of the people as well.

Some twenty years later Longinus arrived as bishop in the country of the Nobades, where, continuing the work begun by Julian, he offered instruction, ordained a clergy, and built a church. So pleased were the Nobades with the ministration of Longinus that an ambassador to the Romans declared, "though we were Christians in name, yet we did not really know what Christianity was until Longinus came to us." When Longinus was about to depart on another mission, in an attempt to prevail upon him to remain, the Nobades wept and said, "again, as before your arrival, we shall be like orphans without a father." Longinus extended Christianity further into Nubia by proceeding quite some distance south of the Nobades and converted another Ethiopian people, the Alodaei. While there, he baptized the king and the nobles of the Alodaei, who wrote a letter to the Nobades in appreciation for their having permitted Longinus to come to them.

It was in the reign of Justinian also, it will be recalled, that steps were taken to uproot the lingering paganism at Philae. The Isiac temples were closed, the priests imprisoned, and the statues of Isis taken to Constantinople. Silko, the king of the Nobades and all the Ethiopians as he called himself, ascribed to God his defeat of the Blemmyes about 545.[108] Christian missionary efforts in Nubia were meeting with success. A short time after Silko's rule the Isiac temple at Philae and other pagan shrines in the region as well were converted into Christian churches.[109]

As Augustine had said, Ethiopia was to believe in God. That the early Christians translated their creed into practice is demonstrated both by Christian efforts to convert the Ethiopian and by Ethiopian membership and activity in the Christian church at various times during the first six centuries after Christ. The baptism of the Ethiopian eunuch was a dramatic landmark — at the very beginning — indicative of what was to follow. Even if the tradition of Matthew's assignment to Ethiopia is a fiction, Origen's observations indicate that by his time the Christian faith had reached some Ethiopians. Axumite Ethiopians had received a bishop and the attention of the Emperor Constantius about the middle of the fourth century. By the end of the fourth century Father Moses was active in the desert of Scetis. In north Africa an Ethiopian slave was receiving instruction in the fifth century. The sixth century, we have seen, saw the firm establishment of Christianity in Nubia.

Interest in the Ethiopian's spiritual welfare was all-inclusive, varying from a concern for a humble catechumen, the subject of a correspondence between a bishop and one of his deacons, to vigorous, Imperial efforts like those of Constantius, Justinian, and Theodora to win the Ethiopians to their faith. There is no doubt that Ethiopians are to be counted among the nameless converts known to us only through the evidence of Christian burials. To the cause of furthering Christianity the Ethiopian also contributed his share, whether through the example of Father Moses, whose life was an inspiration to so many others, or through the expeditions which the Axumite king sent in support of his resolve to halt the persecution of fellow Christians — his neighbors across the sea.

Blacks in a White Society – a Summation

The first Ethiopians to appear in Greek literature were Homer's blameless Ethiopians. Dear to the gods and renowned for their piety and justice, Ethiopians enjoyed the favor of divine visits. High-souled Ethiopians, according to Hesiod, were among the descendants of the almighty son of Kronos. Xenophanes, the first European to contrast the physical characteristics of Negroes and whites, described Ethiopians and Thracians as he saw them and implied nothing as to the superiority or inferiority of either, whether physical, aesthetic, mental, or moral. Like Xenophanes, the artists who fashioned Janiform Negro-white heads depicted accurately what they saw. In short, those Greeks who first described and depicted dark or Negroid peoples did so without bias.

The early, unbiased approach toward colored peoples adumbrated what was to follow. Long after the Ethiopian was divested of any romanticization stemming from a mythological aura and long after he was well known to the Greeks and Romans, whether in Africa or in various parts of the classical world, antipathy because of color did not arise. The Greco-Roman view of blacks was no romantic idealization of distant, unknown peoples but a fundamental rejection of color as a criterion for evaluating men.

Scientists, in their environmental explanation of the origin of racial differences, developed no special theory as to inferior dark or black peoples and attached no stigma to color. The Thracian-Ethiopian contrast of Xenophanes became, in the hands of the environmentalists and other observers on racial differences, a Scythian-Ethiopian τόπος. This antithesis provided a medium for statements of conviction that race is of no consequence in judging man's worth. Though a man comes from faraway Scythia or distant Ethiopia, though a man is as physically different from the Greek or Roman as the blackest Ethiopian or the blondest Scythian, such distinctions are trifles. It is intrinsic merit, says

Menander, that counts. Similarly, the early Church embraced both Scythian and Ethiopian. It was the *Ethiopian*, the blackest and remotest of men, who was selected as an important symbol of Christianity's mission — by Ethiopians, all nations were signified; Christ came into the world to make blacks white.

That classical and early Christian views of Ethiopians were no theoretical pronouncements is amply demonstrated by the experience of Ethiopians in many regions of the Greco-Roman world. The Ethiopian was no rarity among classical peoples. Whether he came as slave, prisoner of war, ambassador, or adventurer, he experienced no exclusion because of his color. If Ethiopians were slaves, manumission and a career open to talent were available to them in the same way as to others of foreign extraction. If the Ethiopian excelled as charioteer, pugilist, or actor, he was celebrated by the poet or depicted by the artist. In fact, for centuries the black man appealed to artists who found in him an attractive model. Neither servile descent nor humble origin was a barrier to acceptance in artistic or literary circles. A former slave from Carthage, the dark- or black-skinned Terence received a social and literary recognition comparable to that later accorded Horace, whose father was a freedman, probably of Italian stock. References to race mixture of blacks and whites were not accompanied by strictures on miscegenation. Ethiopian blood was interfused with that of others. The Ethiopian worshipped Isis at the same shrine as other *Isiaci*. He was sought as a brother in Christ. Both the devotees of Isis and the converts of Christianity continued the tradition of Homer's gods, who knew no color line.

How much of the Greco-Roman attitude toward Ethiopians was a result of the original unprejudiced approach to colored peoples reflected in the environmental explanations of racial differences; how much is to be attributed to understandings developed through contacts between blacks and whites over many centuries; how much is to be explained by the fact that darker races were not the only or the largest part of enslaved peoples; or how much may have derived from the refusal of Christians to recognize color as a criterion for acceptance as a brother in Christ — all this is difficult to determine. There is nothing in the evidence, however, to suggest that the ancient Greek or Roman established color as an obstacle to integration into society.

The relationship of blacks and whites continues to be a critical problem of the twentieth century. Not without meaning for this vital question is the experience of the Ethiopian in classical antiquity — the first major encounter in European records of blacks in a predominantly white society. The Greeks and Romans counted black peoples in.

Illustrations 78-120

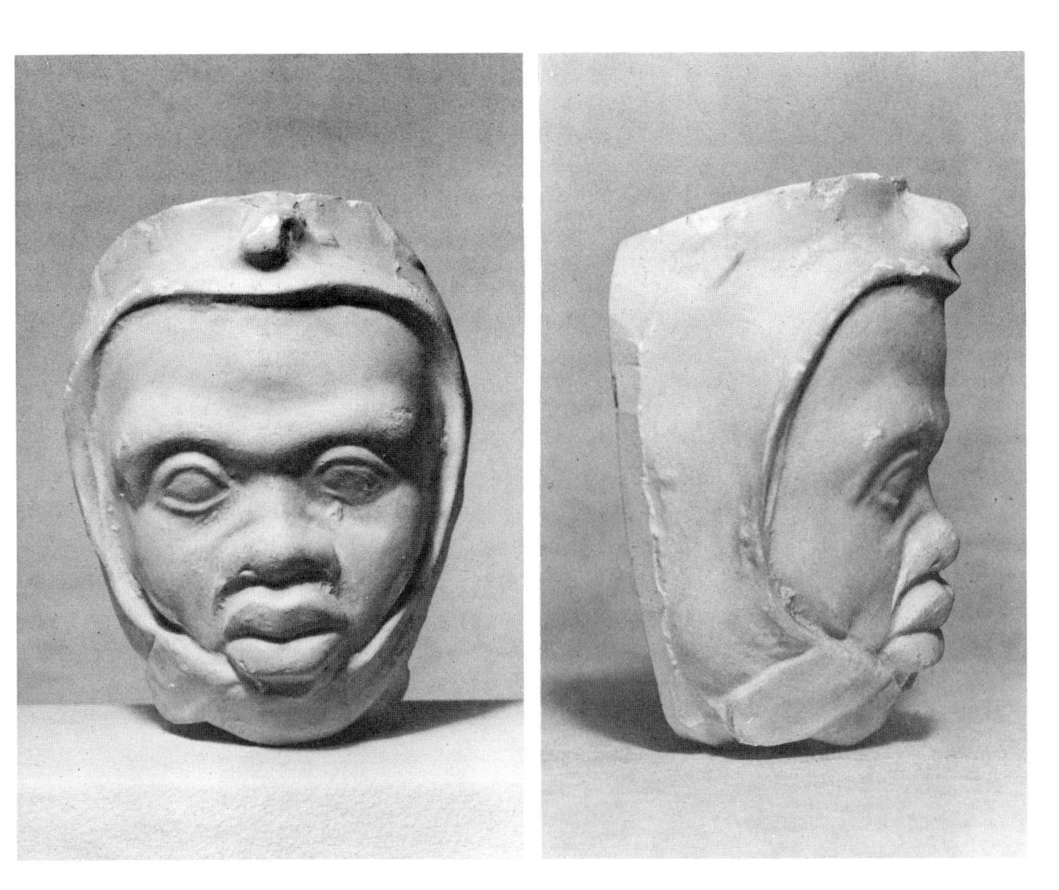

78. Cast from a mold found at Naucratis, fifth century B.C.

79. Black granite head of King Taharqa, Egyptian.

80. Plate with Negroid warrior from Taranto, fifth century B.C.

81. Alabastron with Negroid warrior crouching and reaching for his shield, fifth century B.C.

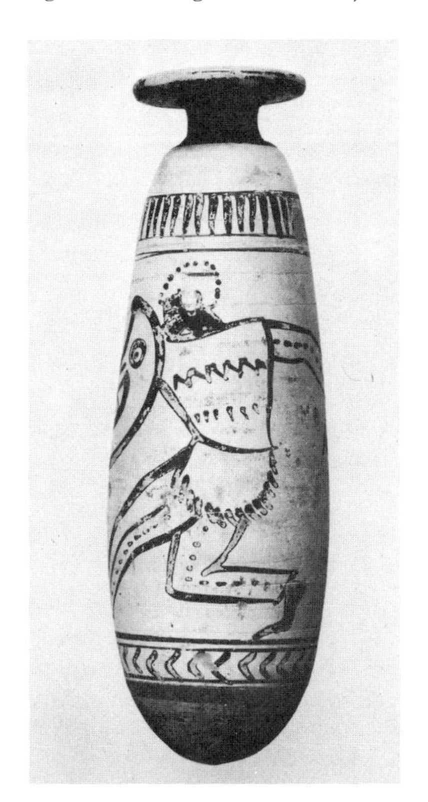

82. Negroid mahout and elephant and detail of the mahout, terra cotta from Pompeii.

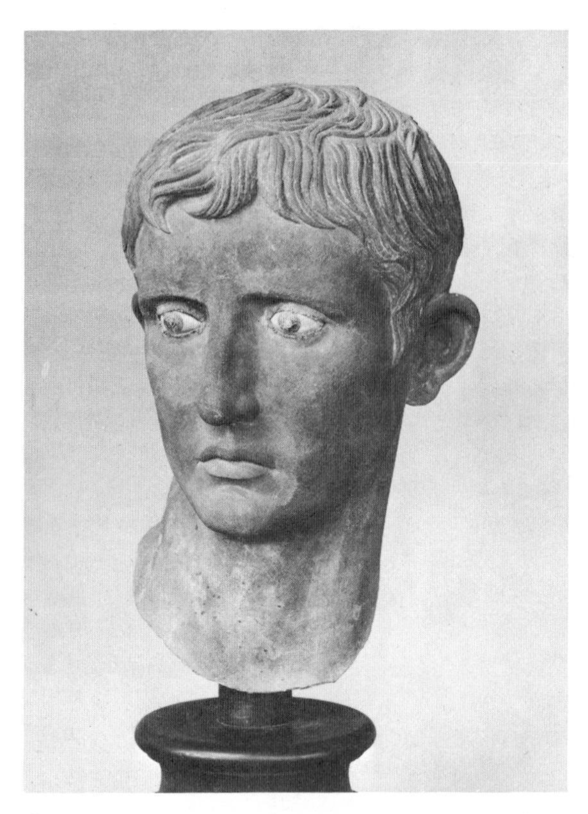

83. Bronze head of Augustus found at Meroë.

84. Bronzes of prisoners, early Empire.

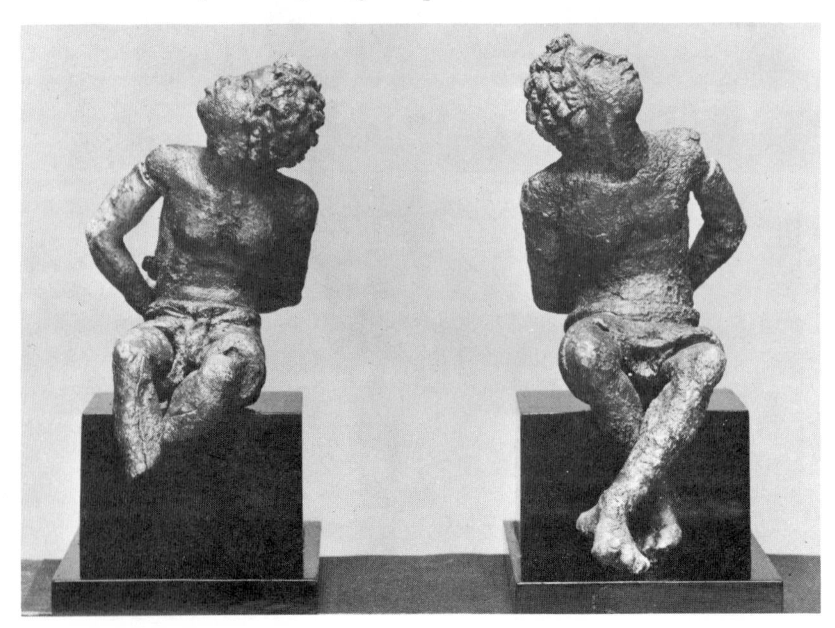

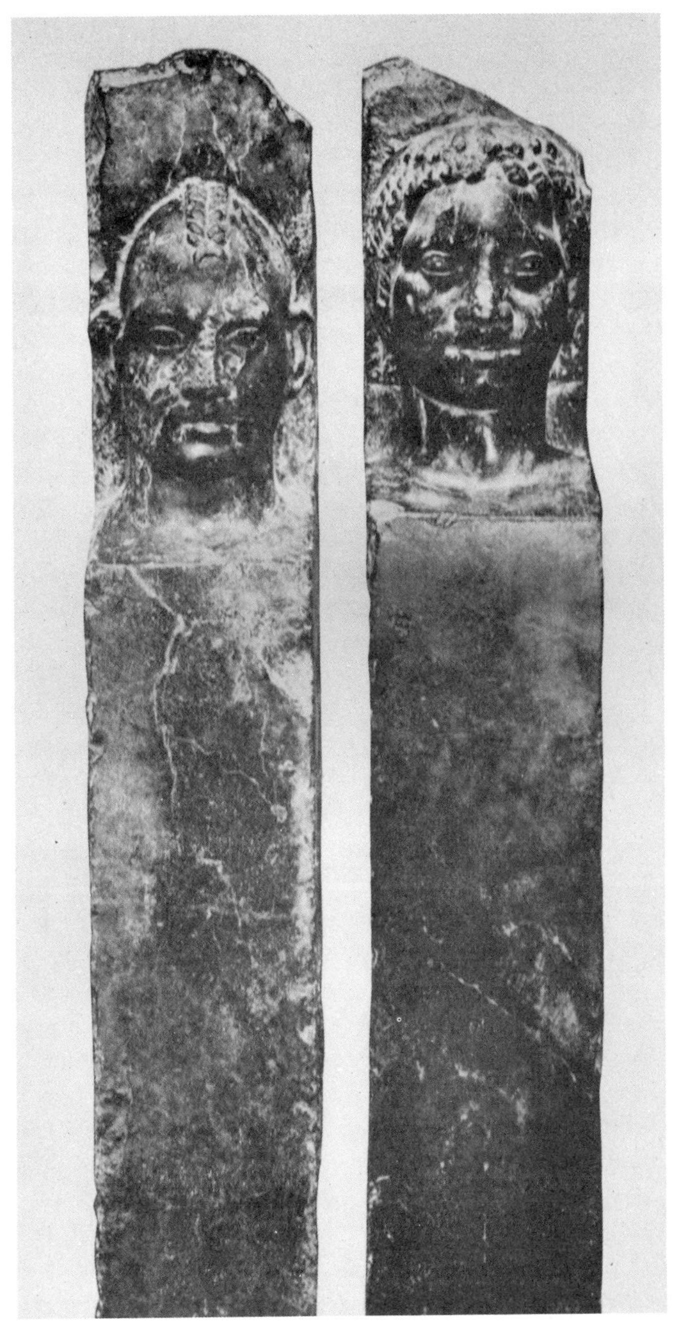

85. Negro and Libyan herms in black limestone from Carthage, middle of second century A.D.

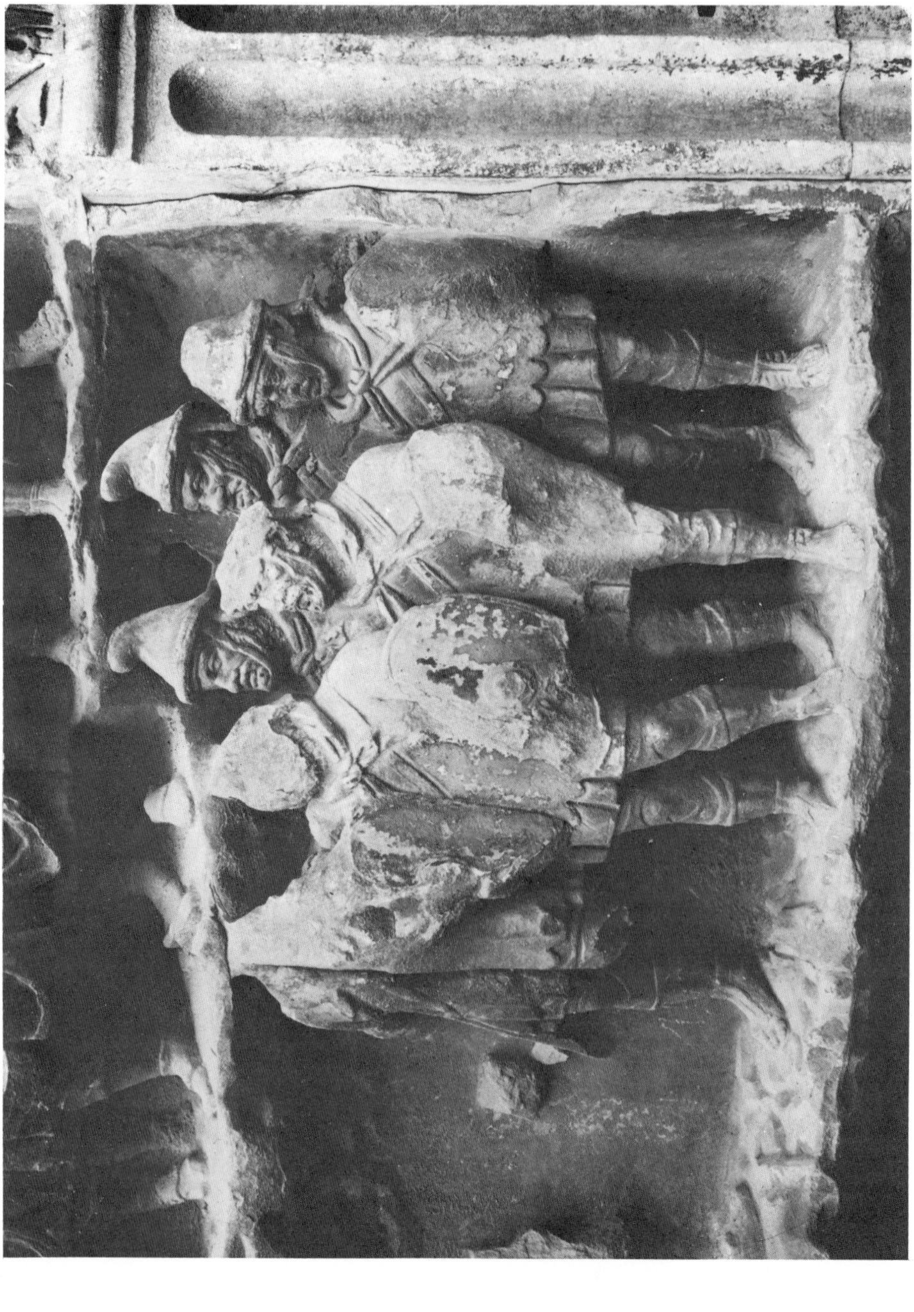

86. Negroid (?) soldier on Arch of Septimius Severus in Roman Forum.

87. Marble sarcophagus, ca. 180-200 A.D., depicting triumph of Bacchus, with two Negro boys astride a pair of panthers.

88. Negroid victory driving a chariot and a seated Heracles, scene on a red-figured oinochoe (from Cyrenaica) of the late fifth or early fourth century B.C.

89. Woman tortured by satyrs, scene from Attic, black-figured lekythos, fifth century B.C.

90. Ethiopians and the Andromeda myth in a scene from a red-figured pelike, ca. 560 B.C.

91. Heracles and Negroid Busiris and attendants of Busiris on red-figured stamnos, ca. 470 B.C.

92. Negroid attendants of King Busiris, on column-krater, ca. 470-460 B.C., from near Naples.

93. Plastic vase in form of conjoined heads of Negro and satyr from same mold, fourth century B.C.

94. Dancing Negro woman and satyr, participants in a dance with a phlyax and menads, a scene from an askos from Ruvo, Apulian, ca. 380-360 B.C.

95. Scenes from Kabeiric skyphoi.

96. Mitos, Krateia, and Pratolaos on Kabeiric skyphos.

97. Non-Greek, perhaps Negroid Aphrodite and Hera, from Kabeiric skyphos.

98. Life-sized terra-cotta mask, perhaps from Sicily, mid fourth century B.C.

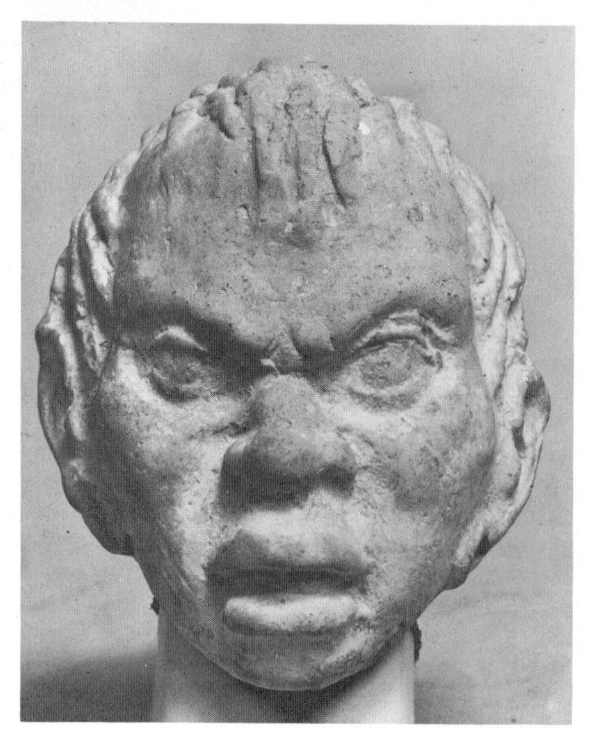

99. Small terra-cotta Roman mask, first century B.C.

100. Terra-cotta statuette of phlyax, Hellenistic, from Taranto.

101. Terra-cotta statuette of a juggler from Thebes.

102. Bronze of a dancer(?), Hellenistic, from Carnuntum.

103. Bronze statuette of a dancer, Hellenistic, from Erment, Egypt.

104. Bronze dancer from Herculaneum, Hellenistic.

105. Scene of dancing and clapping from a marble relief from Ariccia, early second century A.D.

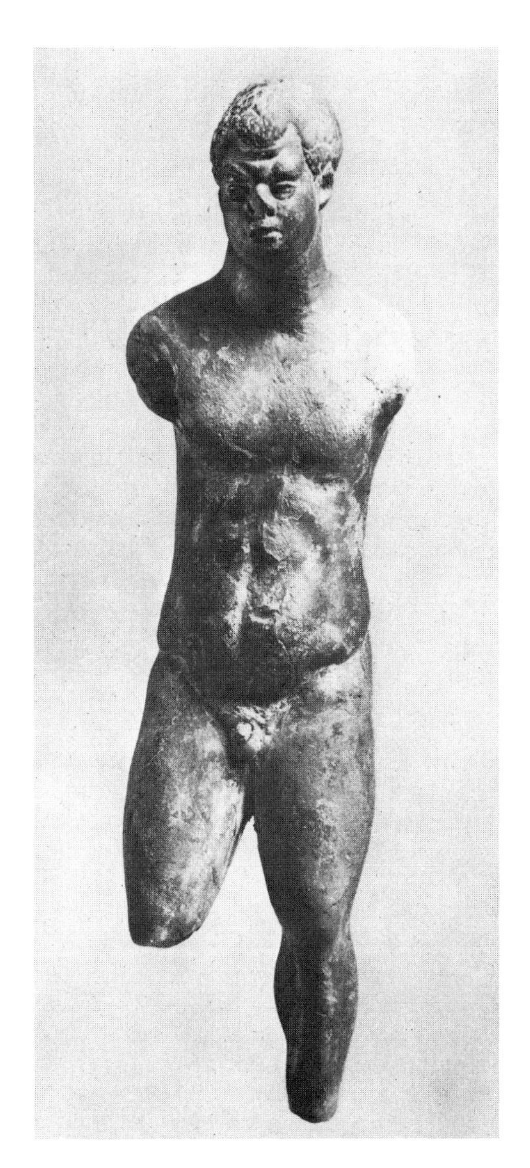

106. Hellenistic terra cotta of an athlete, perhaps a boxer.

107. Acrobat poised on crocodile, Roman after an Hellenistic original.

108. Bootblack in bronze, ca. 460 B.C.

109. Bronze of a worker pulling a cable(?) Alexandrian.

110. Laborer standing among vines and working an Archimedean screw with his feet, after 30 B.C.

111. Lamp-bearer in bronze, Roman.

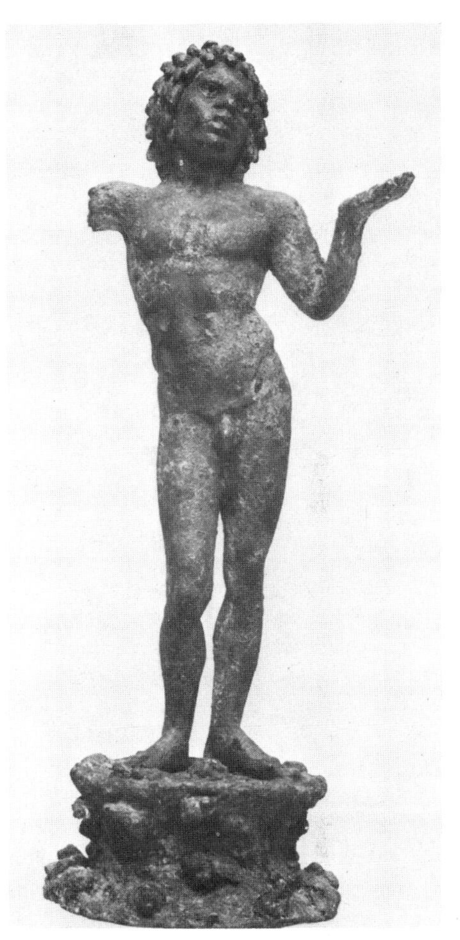

112. Standing bronze figure from Reims, Roman.

113. Terra-cotta lantern-bearer from Egypt, early Empire.

114. Young reveller attended by a slave carrying a lantern, from Alexandria, after 30 B.C.

115. Life-sized marble bust of an ambassador or hostage, Flavian period.

116. Life-sized white marble statue of an actor or singer of the second century A.D. from the vicinity of Naples.

117. Black diorite or marble statue of a bath attendant or *Isiacus*, Hellenistic, from Aphrodisias.

118. Dark Isiac cultists from Herculaneum wall painting, Neronian age.

119. Isiac scene from Herculaneum fresco.

120. Black marble head (bust modern) of a woman (front and profile) second half of second century A.D.

Notes and Indexes

Notes

I. The Physical Characteristics of the Ethiopians — the Textual Evidence

Note: It is especially in Chapters I and VIII that I have drawn on two of my articles: "The Negro in Classical Italy," *American Journal of Philology* LXVIII (1947) 266-292, and "The Negro in Ancient Greece," *American Anthropologist* 50 (1948) 31-44.

1. Sikes, *The Anthropology of the Greeks* (London 1914) 4, 10, 79, 81, 88; Kluckhohn, *Anthropology and the Classics* (Providence 1961) 24, 34; cf. J. L. Myres in R. R. Marett, ed., *Anthropology and the Classics: Six Lectures Delivered before the University of Oxford* (Oxford 1908) 133, 144; K. Trüdinger, *Studien zur Geschichte der griechisch-römischen Ethnographie* (Basel 1918) makes a few references to the Ethiopian (36, 113, 135-136).

2. The study is H. Schwabl et al., Fondation Hardt: Entretiens sur l'antiquité classique VIII, *Grecs et barbares:* [*Six exposés et discussions*] (Vandoeuvres - Genève 1962) H. Gallet de Santerre's review of this book in *Revue des études anciennes* LXVI (1964) 243 comments on a failure of the study to make use of the several disciplines. Dihle's observations on the Ethiopian appear in a chapter "Zur hellenistischen Ethnographie" 214-215. Den Boer's criticism of Dihle's views appears in his review of the book in *Mnemosyne,* fourth series, XVIII (1965) 212-213. The Agatharchides passage cited by Dihle is *De Mari Erythraeo* 16 *Geographi Graeci Minores* [hereafter abbreviated as *GGM*] I 118. Den Boer rightly observes that it is normal for a white child in a predominantly white society to notice the color of a black man, and that it is a completely innocent reaction and as harmless as the fact that Dutch children are frightened at a typically Dutch Christmas by the sight of black Peter, the servant of the good Bishop. The reaction of a black African child would be similar upon first encountering a white man and equally innocent. Only a retarded child would exhibit no such curiosity. For my interpretation of the Agatharchides passage and classical attitudes toward color, see Chap. VIII.

3. E.g., W. N. Bates, "Scenes from the Aethiopis on a Black-figured Amphora," *Transactions of the Department of Archaeology,* University of Pennsylvania Free Museum of Science and Art, I, pts. I and II (1904) 50 for the statement that as a rule the Negro is most absurdly drawn in Greek vases; C. T. Seltman, "Two Heads of

Negresses," *AJA* XXIV (1920) 14 for the opinion that the ugliness of the Negro seems to have appealed alike to sculptor, engraver, and painter; G. H. Beardsley, *The Negro in Greek and Roman Civilization: A Study of the Ethiopian Type* (Baltimore and London 1929) 37 who interprets the use of the Negro in certain crocodile vases as revealing "a keen sense of the comic interest of the Ethiopian"; M. Robertson, *Greek Painting* (Geneva 1959) 67 who explains a white Memnon as a result of a Greek aversion to Negroid features. For the Greco-Roman interest in the Negro as a model and for classical attitudes toward the Negro, see Chaps. II and VIII and for explanations of a white Memnon, Chap. VI.

4. Petronius *Satyricon* 34. W. D. Lowe, *Petronii Cena Trimalchionis* (Cambridge and London 1905) 25 and W. B. Sedgwick, *The Cena Trimalchionis of Petronius*[2] (Oxford, reprinted with corrections 1959) 94, explain *Aethiopes capillati* as ordinary slaves painted or dressed like Negroes.

5. H. W. Prescott's review of G. Norwood's *Plautus and Terence* in *CJ* XXVIII (1932) 215.

6. For Greco-Roman explanations of racial differences and the applicability of the environmental theory to Ethiopians, see Chap. VIII. For the effect of the sun on the color of the Ethiopian's skin, see Herodotus 2.22; [Aristotle] *Problemata* 10.66.898b; Lucretius 6.722, 1109; Vitruvius *De architectura* 6.1.3-4; Hyginus *Astronomica* 1.8 (p. 28, B. Bunte's edition); Manilius *Astronomica* 4.758-759; Strabo 15.1.24; Ovid *Metamorphoses* 2.235-236; Pliny *Naturalis historia* 2.80.189; Lucan 10.221-222; Seneca *Quaestiones naturales* 4a 2.18; Ptolmey *Tetrabiblos* 2.2.56; *Etymologicum Magnum* s.v. Αἰθίοψ.

7. [Aristotle] *Problemata* 10.66.898b.

8. 3.101; cf. Sidonius *Carmina* 11.106-107: *concolor Aethiopi . . . Indus* (an Indian like the Ethiopian in color).

9. Arrian *Anabasis* 5.4.4.

10. Pliny *Naturalis historia* 6.22.70; Arrian *Indica* 6.9 (comparing southern Indians and Ethiopians in several respects). The following adjectives were used to describe the color of Indians, some being applied likewise to Ethiopians: (a) μέλας, Herodotus 3.101; Arrian *Indica* 6.9, *Anabasis* 5.4.4; Philostratus *Vita Apollonii* 2.19, 3.11, 6.1; Achilles Tatius 3.9.2; (b) κυάνεοι or κυανόχροες, Nonnus *Dionysiaca* 17.390, 29.17, 31.275; (c) μελανόχροες, *ibid.* 16.121, 40.270-271; Oppian *Cynegetica* 3.259; (d) κελαινοί. Eustathius *Commentarii* 1153 *GGM* IV 404; (e) αἴθοπες, Nonnus *Dionysiaca* 16.254, 17.114; (f) *decolor* or *discolor,* Ovid *Metamorphoses* 4.21, *Tristia* 5.3.24, *Ars amatoria* 3.130; Propertius 4.3.10; Prudentius *Hamartigenia* 497. Indians and Ethiopians were at times intermixed as a result of an ancient confusion between south and east; cf. J. André, "Virgile et les Indiens." *Revue des études latines* XXVII (1949) 157-163; A. Lesky, "Aithiopika," *Hermes* LXXXVII (1959) 27-28. Vergil's reference to the

Nile as sweeping down from the swarthy Indians ("coloratis . . . Indis") *Georgics* 4.293 perhaps echoes such a confusion; cf. E. De Saint-Denis "Notes sur le livre IV des *Géorgiques*," *Revue des études latines* XXVIII (1950) 204-209. The black Indian from the Red Sea, "a rubris et niger Indus aquis" (Martial 7.30.4), is perhaps intended as an Ethiopian and has been so interpreted (cf. L. Friedlaender, *M. Valeri Martialis Epigrammaton Libri* I [Leipzig 1886] 489). Hence, *Indus* seems to have been used occasionally as a poetical equivalent of *Aethiops*. See Chap. III, n. 1 for confusion between India and Ethiopia.

11. Diodorus 20.57.5; for a discussion of Leucaethiopes and Melanogaetuli, see Chap. III and notes 51-53.

12. Achilles Tatius 4.5.2; Lucian *Bis accusatus* 6. Although it was the Ethiopian most frequently selected to illustrate blackness of color, the ancients recognized other peoples as colored. Indians, as n. 10 *supra* indicates, were regarded as colored peoples. Similarly, the color of the *Mauri* was at times noted: Manilius *Astronomica* 4.729-30; Lucan 4.678-679, noting the similarity of color in the Moor and the Indian ("concolor Indo Maurus"); *niger,* Silius Italicus *Punica* 2.439-441, Juvenal 5.53, Isidore 14.5.10 "Mauretania vocata a colore populorum; Graeci enim nigrum μαῦρον vocant" (Mauretania derives its name from the color of its people, for the Greeks render *nigrum* as μαῦρον); *fuscus,* Ausonius *Parentalia* 4.5.3-4. *Maurus* appears at times to have been a poetical equivalent of *Aethiops*. Martial's "retorto crine Maurus" (6.39.6) by its mention of the tightly curled hair associated with the Negro suggests that *Maurus* is a poetical substitute of *Aethiops,* cf. *Priapea* 45.3-5. For contrasts of blacks and whites and blackness as typical of the Ethiopian's color, see the following: Juvenal 2.23, 8.33; Jerome *Epistulae* 40.2; cf. Isidore *Origines* 1.37.24; Pliny *Naturalis historia* 22.2; Lucan 10.221-222; Ferrandus *Epistulae* 11.2, Migne *PL* 65.378; "in aspectu Ethiopissimam, neque Aegyptiam, sed totam nigram" (a woman most Ethiopian in appearance, not Egyptian but altogether black) *Actus Petri cum Simone* 22, in R. A. Lipsius and M. Bonnet, *Acta Apostolorum Apocrypha* I (Leipzig 1891) 70; cf. Boethius *In Porphyrium dialogus* II *PL* 64.69C-70B.

13. (a) μέλας: Xenophanes *Fragmenta* 16 (in H. Diels, *Die Fragmente der Vorsokratiker*[10] [Berlin 1961]); Herodotus 2.32 (Pygmies), 3.101; *Prooemium Vitae Aesopi* (Maximus Planudes) in B. E. Perry, *Aesopica* I (Urbana 1952) 215; Aristotle *Historia animalium* 3.9.517a, *Sophistici elenchi* 5.167a, 11.8-21; [Aristotle] *Problemata* 10.66. 898b, *Physiognomonica* 6.812a; Agatharchides *De Mari Erythraeo* 16, 58 *GGM* I 118, 148; Strabo 15.1.24; Diodorus 3.8.2, 3.29.1 (Acridophagi); Pausanias 9.21.6; Arrian *Indica* 6.9, *Anabasis* 5.4.4; Ptolemy *Geographia* 1.9.7 (here and elsewhere in C. Müller's edition, pt. 1 (Paris 1883) and pt. 2 (Paris 1901), *Tetrabiblos* 2.2.56; Sextus Empiricus *Adversus mathematicos* xi. 43; Ps.-Lucian *Philopatris* 4;

Philostratus *Vita Apollonii* 6.1, 6.2, *Imagines* 1.7 (Memnon); Heliodorus 2.30, 10.24, cf. 4.8, 8.16, and 10.14; Hesychius *De temperantia et virtute* 1.23, Migne *PG* 93.1488B, Eustathius *Commentarii* 285 *GGM* IV 266. (b) μελανόχροος: *Scholia in Theocritum Vetera* 7.114a (ed. C. Wendel [Leipzig 1914]) which explains the Blemmyes as ἔθνος Αἰθιοπικὸν μελανόχρουν (a black-skinned Ethiopian race); Quintus of Smyrna 2.642. (c) μελάμβροτος: Euripides *Fragmenta* (Nauck²) 228.3-4, 771.4; Quintus of Smyrna 2.32.

14. (a) αἰθαλοῦς: applied to Blemmyes, Dionysius "Periegetes" *Orbis Descriptio* 220 *GGM* III 114; Eustathius *Commentarii* 220 *GGM* IV 255. (b) κελαινός: Aeschylus *Prometheus Vinctus* 808; Theocritus 17.87; Dionysius "Periegetes" *Orbis Descriptio* 179 *GGM* III 112; Eustathius *Commentarii* 248 *GGM* IV 179. (c) κυάνεος: Quintus of Smyrna 2.101; Eustathius *Commentarii* 1153 *GGM* IV 404; perhaps Hesiod *Opera et dies* 527.

15. *Niger:* Lucretius 4.1160, 6.722, 1109 (inhabitants of regions south of Egypt); Manilius *Astronomica* 1.767 (Memnon); Lucan 10.303 (inhabitants of Meroë); Ovid *Metamorphoses* 2.236, *Amores* 1.8.3-4 (Memnon); Avienus 330 *GGM* III 180 (Blemmyes); Julius Firmicus Maternus *Mathesis* 1.2.1, 1.5.1; Claudian *Carmina minora* 28 (47) 16, *De consulatu Stilichonis* 1 (21) 265 (followers of Memnon); Macrobius *Commentarii in Somnium Scipionis* 2.10.11; Boethius *In librum Aristotelis* περὶ ἑρμηνείας *commentarii* 2.7, p. 169 (K. Meiser's edition² [Leipzig 1880]); Eugippius *Thesaurus* 73 (Migne *PL* 62.695A; *Corpus Glossariorum Latinorum* (ed. G. Goetz IV [Leipzig 1889] 65.47, 511.39; V (1894) 262.71, 291.6).

16. (a) *Ater:* Plautus *Poenulus* 1290-1291, where the adjective is applied to *Aegyptini,* which has been interpreted as *Aethiopes;* Pliny *Naturalis historia* 6.35.190 (describing a people he locates south of the Macrobii); Ovid *Amores* 1.13.33-34 (Memnon); Ausonius *Epigrammata* 41.9-10 (in a pun on Meroë). The contrast between a person having a black or dark skin (*ater*) and one with a white or fair skin (*albus*) became proverbial: Catullus 93.2 ("nec scire utrum sis albus an ater homo"); Cicero *Orationes Philippicae* 2.16.41; Phaedrus 3.15.10; Quintilian 11.1.38; Apuleius *Apologia* 16. The use of *Aethiops* in lieu of *ater* in a similar contrast (Varro *De lingua Latina* 8.21.41 "aut unus albus et alter Aethiops," 9.30.42 "si alter est Aethiops, alter albus," and Juvenal 2.23 "Aethiopem albus") indicates that *Aethiops* was the equivalent of *ater* in this variation of the usual phraseology and that by the *ater-albus* proverbial usage the Romans intended at times to contrast a black man or a Negro and a white man, and not merely a blond or brunet of the white race. (b) *Aquilus:* Plautus *Poenulus* 1112 (applied to a woman also described [1113] as "ore atque oculis pernigris"); cf. A. Ernout and A. Meillet, *Dictionnaire étymologique de la langue latine: histoire des mots,* I⁴ (Paris 1959) 74, who say on the basis of this passage that Plautus applies *aquilus*

to a Negress. (c) *Fuscus: Moretum* 33 (Negroid woman); Ovid *Ars amatoria* 3.191, *Heroides* 15.36 (Andromeda and people of Ethiopia); Propertius 4.6.78 (inhabitants of Meroë). *Fuscus* usually indicated to the Roman a lighter hue than *niger;* Sidonius *Epistulae* 2.10.4; Ovid *Ars amatoria* 2.657-658, *Remedia amoris* 327; Martial 4.62, 7.13. (d) *Ustus* (*adustus, exustus,* and *perustus*) — *ustus:* Lucan 10.131-132 (Cleopatra's attendants); *adustus:* Seneca *Quaestiones naturales* 4a 2.18; *exustus:* Pliny *Naturalis historia* 6.22.70; Silius Italicus *Punica* 3.269 (Nubae); *perustus:* Lucan 10.221-222; Hyginus *Astronomica* 1.8 (Bunte's edition 28). (e) *Percoctus:* Lucretius 6.722, 1109.

17. νυκτίχροος: Ps.-Callisthenes in W. Kroll, *Historia Alexandri Magni* (Pseudo-Callisthenes), I (Berlin 1926) 2.14.11 (p. 83, line 6); (b) *nocticolor:* Aulus Gellius 19.7.6 (Memnon); cf. Petronius *Frg.* 19 (Loeb 332) "Tinctus colore noctis/ . . . puer."

18. *Imagines* 1.29.

19. *Ibid.*, 1.7.

20. Statius *Thebais* 5.427-428; cf. J. H. Lewis, *The Biology of the Negro* (Chicago 1942) 27.

21. Agatharchides *De Mari Erythraeo* 58 *GGM* I 148 μέλανες δὲ ἐξαισίως; Diodorus 3.29.1: μέλανες δὲ καθ' ὑπερβολήν; cf. Heliodorus 2.30: τὴν χροιὰν δὲ ἀκριβῶς μέλας.

22. *Geographia* 1.9.7: κατακόρως . . . μέλανες τὰ χρώματα καὶ πρώτως Αἰθίοπες ἄκρατοι, cf. [Aristotle] *De coloribus* 5.795a: ἀκράτῳ τῷ μέλανι. The intensity of the black indicated by κατακόρως is suggested by Philo's description of the Ethiopian woman of unalterable and intense resolve wedded to Moses (*Legum allegoria* 2.67): τὴν Αἰθιόπισσαν, τὴν ἀμετάβλητον καὶ κατακορῆ γνώμην. Loeb (481) notes that κατακορῆ is probably used here with reference to the color of the Ethiopian woman.

23. Plautus *Poenulus* 1113: "ore atque oculis pernigris" and Lucretius 6.722, 6.1109: "percoctus."

24. 1.11.18. See Chap. IV.

25. 1.115.4-5: "nocte nigriorem/ formica pice graculo cicada." The intensity of blackness expressed in this comparison and the association with Ethiopians are suggested by the facts that (a) νυκτίχροος and *nocticolor* are used of Ethiopians (n. 17 *supra*) and (b) a poem in the Greek Anthology (7.196.4) refers to the sunburnt skin of the cicada as follows: αἰθίοπι . . . χρωτί; W. Pape, *Griechisch-deutsches Handwörterbuch*[3] (Graz 1954) s.v. Αἰθίοψ. "Blacker than darkness and pitch" was used of those who were extremely black (τῶν καθ' ὑπερβολὴν μεμελασμένων) *Appendix Proverbiorum* 3.84, p. 432 in E. L. von Leutsch and F. G. Schneidenwin, *Corpus Paroemiographorum Graecorum* I (Hildesheim 1958). For a similar series of images associated with Ethiopian, see *Anthologia Latina* no. 182 (ed. A. Riese [Leipzig 1894]) 155: "corvus carbo cinis concordant cuncta colori./ Quod legeris nomen, convenit: Aethiopis."

26. *Vita Apollonii* 6.2.

27. The Barberini mosaic, a late Hellenistic copy of an earlier Ptolemaic original. G. E. Rizzo, *La pittura ellenistico-romana* (Milan 1929) 81, plates 188-189, points out that the Negro hunters at the top represent the Ethiopians south of Egypt. G. Gullini, *I mosaici di Palestrina: Volumi di supplemento di archeologia classica,* I (Rome 1956), plates XX, XXIII, and XXV for the dark or black figures, and p. 43. G. Iacopi, *Il santuario della Fortuna Primigenia e il Museo Archeologico Prenestino*[2] (Rome 1963) 21-22 and fig. 57. See Pausanias 8.24.12 for images of the Nile made of black stone because the Nile descends to the sea through Ethiopia.

28. *Decolor:* Juvenal 6.600; *discolor:* Claudian *De Bello Gildonico* 1 (15) 192-193; cf. Achilles Tatius 3.9.2 for the color of a bastard Ethiopian. For *decolor* or *discolor* as applied to Indians and *Mauri,* see Ovid *Ars amatoria* 3.130, *Metamorphoses* 4.21; *Tristia* 5.3.24; Propertius 4.3.10; cf. Lucan 4.678-679.

29. Antigonus of Carystus *Mirabilia* 112 (122) in O. Keller's edition of *Rerum Naturalium Scriptores Graeci Minores* (Leipzig 1877); Aristophanes of Byzantium *Historiae animalium epitome* 2.272 in S. P. Lambros' edition, vol. 1, pt. 1, *Supplementum Aristotelicum* (Berlin 1885); Plutarch *De sera numinis vindicta* 21.563.

30. *Imagines* 2.7.

31. For black or Ethiopian Memnon, see Catullus 66.52: "Memnonis Aethiopis"; Manilius *Astronomica* 1.767: "Auroraeque nigrum partum" (Dawn's black offspring); Ovid *Amores* 1.8.3-4, and Vergil *Aeneid* 1.489: "nigri Memnonis"; Seneca *Agamemnon* 212: "Memnon niger"; cf. Ovid *Epistulae ex Ponto* 3.3.96 for an ironical reference to swans of Memnon's color: "Memnonio cycnos esse colore putem."

32. Ptolemy *Tetrabiblos* 2.2.56: black Ethiopians (μέλανες τὰ σώματα) and white Scythians (λευκοί τε τὰ χρώματα); Julius Firmicus Maternus *Mathesis* 1.2.1: black Ethiopians and white Germans "omnes in Aethiopia nigri, in Germania candidi"; Eugippius, *Thesaurus* 73 (Migne *PL* 62.695): black Ethiopians and white Gauls "nigros Aethiopes et . . . candidos Gallos"; Bede *In Samuelem Prophetam* 1.10 (J. A. Giles, *The Complete Works of Venerable Bede* VIII [London 1844] 29): black Ethiopian and white Saxon "niger Aethiops et Saxo candidus"; Eustathius *Commentarii* 285 *GGM* IV 266: white Germans (λευκὰ . . . φῦλα) and very black Ethiopians (μελάντατοι). Pliny *Naturalis historia* 2.80.189 contrasts Ethiopians and unnamed northerners of white and frosty skins "candida atque glaciali cute." Hence, Vitruvius 6.1.3-4 in contrasting unnamed dark-skinned southerners "colore fusco" and unnamed white northerners "candidis coloribus" is perhaps also referring to Ethiopians by his nameless southerners. See Chap. II for Negroes and whites in plastic vases.

33. *Scholia in Callimachi hymnos* 6.11a: τὼς μέλανας] τοὺς

Αἰθίοπας (R. Pfeiffer's edition [Oxford 1953] 77); *Scholia in Luciani dialogos marinos* 15.4 in H. Rabe's edition (Leipzig 1906) 268: μέλανας ἀνθρώπους ἑώρων] ὁ γὰρ Νότος ἀπὸ Λιβύης πνέει, ἔνθα οἰκοῦσι οἱ Αἰθίοπες; Zonaras *Lexicon* (ed. J. A. H. Tittmann I [Leipzig 1808]) 68: Αἰθίοψ] ὁ μέλας; *Scholia in Juvenalem Vetustiora* 15.49.1[d] (ed. P. Wessner [Leipzig 1941]) "nigro tibicine: Aethiope."

34. An adjective denoting color, without corroborative evidence, would of course not be sufficient to support identification as Ethiopian. Such adjectives were also used to designate not only the brown or blackish skin of various non-Greek or Roman peoples but also Greeks or Romans whose skin for any reason became brown or darkish. For Latin usage of this kind, see J. André, *Etude sur les termes de couleur dans la langue latine* (Paris 1949) 55, 123-127. The context leaves no doubt that Ethiopians were intended in cases such as Lucretius' description of black races thoroughly baked by the sun "inter nigra virum percocto saecla colore" and "usque ad nigra virum percocto saecla colore" (6.722, 1109); Lucan's mention of Meroë's black tillers of the soil, "nigris Meroe fecunda colonis" (10.303); and Claudian's reference to colored Memnon and his black troops "nigra coloratus produceret agmina Memnon" (*De consulatu Stilichonis* 1.265). The fact that the lord of the classical underworld had been described as "nigri Jovis" (Seneca *Hercules Oetaeus* 1705 and Statius *Thebais* 2.49), as "nigri Ditis" (Ovid *Metamorphoses* 4.438), as "nigro Diti" (Statius *Thebais* 4.291) and, because of his association with darkness, had been called the "black one" perhaps accounts in part for the early Christian practice of sometimes applying "Ethiopian" and "Egyptian" to the devil. For early Christian examples of such a usage, see F. J. Dölger, *Die Sonne der Gerechtigkeit und der Schwarze; Eine religionsgeschichtliche Studie zum Taufgelöbnis,* Liturgiegeschichtliche Forschungen II (Münster 1918) 51-57; E. C. Bucke, ed., *The Interpreter's Dictionary of the Bible: An Illustrated Encyclopaedia,* IV (Nashville, New York 1962) s.v. *Satan* 227.

35. 5.18.1.

36. *Adversus indoctum* 28. An epigram in the Palatine Anthology ascribed to Lucian (11.428) uses 'Ινδικόν instead of Αἰθιοπικόν in a variation of this proverb. The author of this variant, according to P. Perdrizet, *Les Terres cuites grecques d'Egypte de la Collection Fouquet,* I (Nancy, Paris, Strasbourg 1921) 139, is referring to Negroes.

37. *Corpus Paroemiographorum Graecorum,* vol. I, Zenobius 1.46 (p. 18); Diogenianus 1.45 (p. 187); vol. II, Diogenianus 1.19 (p. 4); cf. Macarius 5.50 (p. 184) and Apostolius 1.68 (p. 258).

38. *Corpus Fabularum Aesopicarum,* ed. A. Hausrath, H. Haas, and H. Hunger, I fasc. 2^2 (Leipzig 1959) 91-92, no. 274; cf. *Scholia ad Persium* 5.116, O. Jahn's edition (Leipzig 1843) 333 and Gregory the Great, *Epistulae* 3.67. Migne *PL* 77.668.

39. For the early Christian view that by conversion blacks can become whites and, though it is contrary to nature, the Ethiopian does change his color see Chap. IX. For applications of the proverb to Father Moses, see *Vita S. Moysis Aethiopis* 6, in V. Latyšev, *Menologii Anonymi Byzantini Saeculi X Quae Supersunt*, fasc. 2 (St. Petersburg 1912) 332.

40. *Frg.* 16 (Diels).

41. *De Mari Erythraeo* 16 *GGM* I 118.

42. Petronius *Satyricon* 102.

43. 3.8.2: οἱ παρὰ τὸν ποταμὸν οἰκοῦντες ταῖς μὲν χρόαις εἰσὶ μέλανες, ταῖς δὲ ἰδέαις σιμοί, τοῖς δὲ τριχώμασιν οὖλοι.

44. *Moretum* 31-35: "Erat unica custos/Afra genus, tota patriam testante figura,/torta comam labroque tumens et fusca colore,/pectore lata, iacens mammis, compressior alvo,/cruribus exilis, spatiosa prodiga planta." This description bears striking resemblance to the following passage from a modern anthropologist: "Narrow heads and wide noses, thick lips and thin legs, protruding jaws and receding chins, integument rich in pigment but poor in hairy growth, flat feet and round foreheads, tiny curls and big smiles — these are the outstanding features of the ancient and specialized Negro division of mankind." (E. A. Hooton, *Up from the Ape*, rev. [New York: The Macmillan Co. 1946] 662.)

45. *Prooemium Vitae Aesopi* (Maximus Planudes) in B. E. Perry, *Aesopica*, I 215: . . . ἦν, σιμὸς τὴν ῥῖνα . . . πρόχειλος, μέλας — ὅθεν καὶ τοῦ ὀνόματος ἔτυχε·ταὐτὸν γὰρ Αἴσωπος τῷ Αἰθίοπι . . . Though this account may be worthless as to the reliability of Aesop as "Ethiopian," it is valuable in corroborating the ancient view of Ethiopian physical characteristics. Aesop is described as black and flat-nosed in *Vitae* G, W (Perry 35, 81).

46. Ptolemy *Tetrabiblos* 2.2.56: τὰς τρίχας οὖλοί τε καὶ δασεῖς.

47. Herodotus 7.70.

48. Arrian *Indica* 6.9.

49. [Aristotle] *Problemata* 14.4.909a; cf. Aristotle *De generatione animalium* 5.3.782b.

50. Aristotle *De generatione animalium* 5.3.782b (Thracians, Scythians, and Ethiopians); Pliny *Naturalis historia* 2.80.189 (Ethiopians and northerners); Vitruvius *De architectura* 6.1.3-4 (southerners and northerners); Ptolemy *Tetrabiblos* 2.2.56 (Ethiopians and Scythians). For the woolly hair of an Ethiopian group, the Blemmyes, see Nonnus *Dionysiaca* 17.385 (Βλέμυς οὐλοκάρηνος) and 26.340-341 (οὐλοκόμων Βλεμύων).

51. 7.70.

52. Although various forms of οὖλος (often the superlative and an indication that Ethiopians were the most woolly-haired of all people) were used most frequently of Ethiopians, the "less than straight hair of other peoples" was also at times described as οὖλος, especially of Egyptians: Herodotus 2.104; [Aristotle] *Problemata* 14.4.909a.

53. *Moretum* 33.
54. Martial *Spectacula* 3.10.
55. Lucan 10.131-132.
56. Petronius *Satyricon* 102; cf. *Priapea*, no. 45.1-3 in L. Mueller's edition of Catullus, Tibullus, and Propertius (Leipzig 1897), 106.
57. *Naturalis historia* 2.80.189.
58. *Satyricon* 34. The accuracy of the ancient observers in describing the form of the Ethiopian's hair is obvious from a comparison of ancient and modern descriptions. Hooton, *Ape* 483 describes the Negro's hair, inappropriately called "woolly," as short, matted, wiry, and growing in tiny spirals; he notes that the so-called frizzly hair is longer than "woolly" hair with its tightly coiled spirals. The similarity of Hooton's observations and ancient descriptions is marked. It is interesting that although Hooton considers "woolly," applied to the hair of Negroes, as inappropriate, he (619), like other anthropologists, continues the practice of the Greeks in using "woolly" instead of the more accurate Roman "tightly curled." The ancients recognized the importance of the form of the hair in classifying Ethiopians. Hooton (483) points out that kinky or frizzly hair ordinarily appears in racial types in which there is at least a generous admixture of the Negro or Negrito. J. H. Lewis, *Biology* 61, in commenting on the hair of the Negro, like the ancients, makes a comparison with Indians — the hair of the Negro is more characteristic than is color of the skin; other races, e.g., east Indians, are as dark as Negroes; but no race other than the Negro or one intermixed therewith has woolly or kinky hair as a stable feature.
59. Diodorus 3.28.1; Quintus Curtius Rufus 4.7.19.
60. *Adversus mathematicos* xi.43.
61. *Indica* 6.9.
62. *Vita Aesopi*, cited in n. 45 *supra*.
63. *Moretum* 33 and Petronius *Satyricon* 102.
64. *Moretum* 35; *Vitae Aesopi*, n. 45 *supra;* [Aristotle] *Problemata* 14.4.909a; Petronius *Satyricon* 102.
65. *Moretum* 34 and Juvenal 13.163, who seems to write from what he had observed in Egypt. Lewis (*Biology* 77) notes that the pendulous breasts of multiparae are markedly accentuated in African women as compared to European women, probably a result of the lack of support provided by the clothing of the former.
66. M. J. Herskovits, *Encyclopaedia Britannica*, XVI (Chicago, London, Toronto 1960) s.v. *Negro* 193 explains the usage of "true" Negro; Hooton, *Ape* 622 uses the term "purest" type of African Negro. For a discussion of this and other subtypes of Negroes, see Herskovits 193-194, and Hooton 619-623. See Chap. II for examples in classical art of Negroid traits in their most marked form.
67. See L. Oschinsky, *The Racial Affinities of the Baganda and Other Bantu Tribes of British East Africa* (Cambridge, Eng. 1954),

Table LIX for the designations Hamitomorphs, Nilomorphs, and Nilohamitomorphs as applied to certain East African Negroes.

68. Herodotus 7.70; Pliny *Naturalis historia* 2.80.189; and Petronius *Satyricon* 34.

69. See Chap. II for examples of such individuals.

70. Herodotus 3.20.

71. Pliny *Naturalis historia* 7.2.31. Pliny cites Crates of Pergamum as his source for the statement that the Syrbotae were more than eight cubits in height.

72. See O. Waser and W. H. Roscher, *Ausführliches Lexikon der griechischen und römischen Mythologie* III, 2 (Leipzig 1902-1909) s.v. *Pygmaien* 3283-3317; E. Wüst, *RE* XXIII, 2 s. v. *Pygmaioi* 2064-2074; J. Desanges, *Catalogue des tribus africaines de l'antiquité classique à l'ouest du Nil,* Publications de la section d'histoire, no. 4, Université de Dakar, Faculté des Lettres et Sciences Humaines (Dakar 1962) 197-198. G. Becatti, *Enciclopedia dell'arte antica* II (Rome 1959) s.v. *Caricatura* 344-346, *ibid.,* VI (Rome 1965) s.v. *Pigmei* 167-169. Pygmies appear in Greek art for the first time in representations of the geranomachy — the oldest being the scene on the foot of the François vase in the first quarter of the sixth century B.C. Pygmies in the early paintings of their struggles with cranes are depicted as men of small proportions without deformities. In the burlesque scenes of the Kabeiric vases from the second half of the fifth and the early fourth centuries B.C., pygmies, like other figures in these vases, assume grotesque proportions. Here the artists present them with large heads, protuberant stomachs, as ithyphallic and, at times, steatopygic. In Nilotic scenes of Hellenistic origin pygmies are often the principal protagonists.

73. See notes 59-61 *supra.*

74. See notes 62-63 *supra.*

75. For a discussion of racial classification according to color, hair, and lips, see Hooton, *Ape* 455, 483-484, 523. For variation in the color of African Negroes, see Lewis, *Biology* 27.

76. Cf. Hooton, *Ape* 619, 623, and n. 64 *supra.*

77. *Moretum* 32.

78. S. Gsell, *Histoire ancienne de l'Afrique du nord*², VII (Paris: Hachette 1930) 2-8 and esp. 7, where Gsell points out that *Afri,* unlike Λίβυες, was at times used of all inhabitants of the African continent, whites as well as blacks; and M. Hammond, "Septimius Severus, Roman Bureaucrat," *Harvard Studies in Classical Philology* LI (1940) 146-147, where several usages of *Afer* are discussed. See n. 3, Appendix *infra,* for a discussion of Publius Terentius Afer and Helpis Afra in a Pompeiian graffito.

79. Vergil *Georgics* 4.293, and Ovid *Ars amatoria* 1.53. For the use of "Indians" instead of "Ethiopians" apparently as a designation for the southern neighbors of the Thebaid, see *Expositio Totius Mundi et*

Gentium 35, *GGM* V 520 (A. Riese, *Geographi Latini Minores* 113) and A. A. Vasiliev, "EXPOSITIO TOTIUS MUNDI: An Anonymous Treatise of the Fourth Century A.D.," *Seminarium Kondakovianum* VIII (1936) 32. See also discussion of this point in Chap. III, n. 1.

80. S. Weinstock, *RE* XIV s.v. *Mauretania,* esp. 2349.

81. *Astronomica* 4.729-730.

82. *Origines* 14.5.10. For the equivalence of *Niger* and *Maurus,* see *Poetae Latini Minores,* ed. E. Baehrens V (Leipzig 1883) no. LXIV, 11. 1-4.

83. 6.39.6.

84. 5.53-54.

85. *De consulatu Stilichonis* 1.248-263.

86. "Lusius Quietus, an Ethiopian," *Mnemosyne,* fourth series, III (1950) 263-265.

87. *Passio Bartholomaei* 7, in R. A. Lipsius and M. Bonnet, *Acta Apostolorum Apocrypha,* II, 146, line 23. For the proverb Αἰθίοπα σμήχειν see notes 36-39 *supra.* Den Boer, in a series of articles in *Mnemosyne* (fourth series) has demonstrated the need for reexamining the evidence with respect to *Maurus* and has argued that Lusius Quietus was μαῦρος, a black, full-blooded Ethiopian: "The Native Country of Lusius Quietus," I (1948) 327-337; "Lusius Quietus, an Ethiopian," III (1950) 263-267; "Lusius Quietus (III)," *ibid.* 339-343. A. G. Roos disputes Den Boer's conclusions as to the racial identity of Quietus: "Lusius Quietus Again," *Mnemosyne* III (1950) 158-165; "Lusius Quietus: A Reply," *ibid.*, 336-338.

88. F. Preisigke, "Ein Sklavenkauf des 6. Jahrhunderts," *Archiv für Papyrusforschung* III (Leipzig 1906) 415-424.

89. Cf. W. L. Westermann, *The Slave Systems of Greek and Roman Antiquity* (Philadelphia 1955) 96-97.

90. Cf. O. Seel, *Römertum und Latinität* (Stuttgart 1964) 318-319.

91. See Chap. VIII.

92. For United States sociological, rather than biological, designation of a person who may be blond and blue-eyed as a "Negro" because of distant Negro ancestry and for southern legal definitions of persons as Negroes if they possess any Negro ancestry regardless of number of white ancestors, see *Encyclopaedia Britannica,* XVI, (1960) s.v. *Negro* 193 and *Negro American* 194.

93. *Nigra* appears in a Pompeiian graffito (*CIL* IV 6892), a reading accepted by several commentators, G. Zottoli, M. Della Corte, and M. D'Avino; see Chap. VIII, n. 150. A stone discovered at Rusicade (modern Philippeville) preserves the bust of a woman whose kinky hair, broad nose, and thick lips are clearly Negroid. If Bertrand's interpretation of the woman's name, i.e., Julia Nigra, is correct, this evidence is significant, because the cognomen *Nigra*

in this instance would certainly denote Negroid extraction (*CIL* VIII 19888), L. Bertrand, *Bulletin de l'Académie d'Hippone: Comptes rendus des réunions* (Bône, Algeria 1892) p. L.

94. 7.29.8 The evidence which points to a usage of μέλας or *niger* (*fuscus*) in the sense of Ethiopian, especially when contrasted with λευκός and *candidus* in the sense of northerners, requires a re-examination of several passages in light of the anthropological significance of these words. Aeschylus *Persae* 315 refers to Black Horse (ἵππου μελαίνης) led by a Matallus of Chrysa. Since we know that Ethiopian contingents formed a part of Xerxes' army (Herodotus 7.69-70) Black Horse in this case was probably used by Aeschylus in lieu of Black Horsemen. H. J. Rose, *A Commentary on the Surviving Plays of Aeschylus* (Amsterdam 1957) 114 points out that the phrase may mean either that the horsemen were Africans or that the mounts were black chargers, but H. D. Broadhead, *The Persae of Aeschylus* (Cambridge, Eng. 1960) 110 prefers black horsemen because he considers a description of men more significant in the context than a designation of the type of horse mounted. The latter interpretation of this passage from the *Persae* is also that of P. Mazon (Paris 1920) 73; P. Groeneboom, I (Göttingen 1960) 79-80; L. Roussel (Montpelier 1960) 127. An interesting case for the use of μέλας in the sense of Αἰθίοψ appears in a list of soldiers found in Egypt. Two soldiers with the same name are designated as 'Απολλώνιος μέλας and 'Απολλώνιος λευκός, *The Amherst Papyri*, ed. B. P. Grenfell and A. S. Hunt, pt. II (London 1901) no. LXII, 6-7. In view of the evidence for the Negro's presence in Egypt and for his mercenary activities (see Chap. IV), it is likely that μέλας in this context is the equivalent of Αἰθίοψ or Negro; cf. F. Preisigke, *Wörterbuch der griechischen Papyrusurkunden,* II (Berlin 1925) s.v. μέλας. Although *candidus* and *niger* may mean "fair" or "blond" and "dark" or "brunet" as some have maintained (G. H. Beardsley, *The Negro* 118 and E. L. Highbarger, "Notes on Vergil's *Bucolics*," *CP* XL [1945] 45), the fact that *candidus* and *niger* (*fuscus*) or *Aethiops* were frequently contrasted anthropologically indicates that the anthropological interpretation of this contrast is as reasonable, if not more so in many instances, as the "fair-dark" interpretation. Further, *fuscus,* as R. Pichon, *De Sermone Amatorio apud Latinos Elegiarum Scriptores* (Paris 1902) 159 points out, seems never to refer to the color of the hair but always to that of the face. S. Gaselee (Loeb 573) considers the anthropological interpretation in his note (on Apuleius 11.20) to the effect that *servus candidus* may mean "my servant Candidus" or "my white servant." A poem beginning "Quadam nocte Niger dux nomine, Candidus alter/Forte subintrarunt unica tecta simul," replete with puns on *niger* and *candidus,* suggests a practice of *Niger* and *Candidus* as cognomina denoting physical characteristics, *Poetae Latini Minores,* ed. E. Baehrens V, 370 no. LXIV. Martial,

in describing two illegitimate daughters, refers to one as *nigra* and the other as *rufa,* the children of Crotus, the fluter, and of Carpus, the bailiff (6.39.18-19). "Ethiopian" or "Negro" and "red-haired" would certainly be more incongruous and pointed than "brunette" or "dark" and "red-haired." The anthropological significance of *candidus* and *niger,* therefore, should not be overlooked in instances such as these: "candida me docuit nigras odisse puellas/odero si potero, sed non invitus amabo" (an inscription in a Pompeiian *caupona-lupanar, CIL* IV 1520, "nigras puellas," interpreted as "les noires" by P. Gusman, *Pompéi, la ville, les mœurs, les arts* [Paris 1900] 67) but as "bionda" (blonde) and "bruna" (brunette) by M. Della Corte, *Amori e amanti di Pompei antica,* Antologia erotica pompeiana (Cava dei Tirreni n.d.) 59, see Chap. VIII, n. 72; "quamvis ille niger, quamvis tu candidus esses / o formose puer, nimium ne crede colori" (Vergil *Eclogues* 2. 16-17); "nigra melichrus est" (Lucretius 4.1160, trans. by W. H. D. Rouse (Loeb 331) as "The black girl is a nut-brown maid"; cf. Ovid *Ars amatoria* 2.657-658 and *Remedia amoris* 327); "vidistis pleno teneram candore puellam,/ vidistis fusco, ducit uterque color" (Propertius 2.25.41-42); "sic quae nigrior est cadente moro/ cerussata sibi placet Lycoris" (Martial 1.72.5-6); Digna tuo cur sis indignaque nomine, dicam/frigida es et nigra es: non es et es Chione" (*ibid.,* 3.34); "Et Maecenati, Maro cum cantaret Alexin,/ nota tamen Marsi fusca Melaenis erat" (*ibid.,* 7.29.7-8). Sidonius *Carmina* 5.460 speaks of Cleopatra's ships filled with pitch-black soldiers ("milite piceo"). The use of *piceus,* at times a poetical equivalent of *niger* (cf. J. André, *Etude* 61), and the inclusion of *pix* in Martial's description of a "super-black" woman "nocte nigriorem/ formica pice graculo cicada" (1.115.4-5) suggest that with "milite piceo" Sidonius was differentiating between Ethiopians and lighter Egyptians; cf. *Anthologia Latina* (ed. A. Riese) no. 183, p. 155: "et piceo gaudet corpore verna niger."

95. Martial 3.34.

96. *Epistulae* 40.2.

97. Plutarch *Antonius* 85.4 and Lucan 10.131-132; W. Pape, *Wörterbuch der griechischen Eigennamen*[3] (Brunswick 1863-1870) s.v. Εἰράς.

98. *Epigrammata* 41.9-10.

99. *Parentalia* 5.4-5.

100. For various divisions and tribes of Ethiopian peoples, see Chap. III.

Names of Ethiopians in the Greco-Roman World

1. For this and all other names included on the basis of color, see n. 94 *supra.*

2. Cf. n. 93 *supra*.
3. As to the race of Terence, G. Norwood (*Plautus and Terence* [New York 1932] 100) considered the playwright a native of Africa and apparently a mulatto or quadroon, and E. K. Rand (*The Building of Eternal Rome* [Cambridge, Mass. 1943] 100) stated that Terence's name suggests that he may have been of Negro extraction. J. W. Duff, *A Literary History of Rome*, vol. I: *From the Origins to the Close of the Golden Age*[3], ed. A. M. Duff (New York 1963) 148 regards "Afer" as suggesting Terence's belonging to a native tribe conquered by the Carthaginians. Commentators on this point, however, have not given sufficient consideration to the combination of the cognomen *Afer* and Terence's color ("colore fusco," Suetonius (*Vita Terenti*) 5 [Loeb II 460]), which, when considered in light of the most detailed anthropological description of a Negro from classical antiquity, has a special pertinence. It will be recalled that among the details provided by the author of the *Moretum* (31-35) in describing the Negroid Scybale were these: (1) "Afra genus," and (2) "fusca colore." The anthropological correspondence and the evidence for the presence of Negroes in Carthage, therefore, point to the possibility that Terence was of Ethiopian or Negroid extraction. The highly significant *Moretum* passage indicates clearly that *Afer* was used at times in the sense of Negro or Negroid. Helpis Afra, an occupant of a *caupona-lupanar* at Pompeii, is regarded by M. Della Corte, *Case ed abitanti di Pompei*[3] (Naples 1965) no. 544 as Greek but dark-complexioned on the basis of *Afra*. (In the first edition of the same work [Pompeii 1926] 85 Della Corte expressed the opinion that Helpis was Greek in name but black in color since the cognomen *Afra* seemed to indicate the country of her origin.) But since Helpis Afra was doubtlessly of slave origin, Della Corte's conclusion as to her Greek provenance is questionable in view of evidence which points to the frequent lack of relation between the provenance of a slave and his name, cf. Westermann, *The Slave Systems of Greek and Roman Antiquity* (Philadelphia 1955) 96. Although Domitius Afer et alii provide proof that the cognomen *Afer* by no means always implies Ethiopian extraction, there is no reason to exclude the possibility that Helpis Afra, like Scybale, "Afra genus," was Negroid.
4. For blacks perhaps included under the designation "Persian," see Chap. IV, note 40.
5. On the spelling of Troglodytes without λ, especially in papyri, see E. Mayser, *Grammatik der griechischen Papyri aus der Ptolemäerzeit*, I (Berlin and Leipzig 1923) 187; and W. L. Westermann, "Lamp Oil from the Estate of Apollonius," *CP* XIX (1924) 236.
6. The anthropological importance of black-skinned and woolly-haired (especially the hair, cf. n. 58 *supra*) in identifying the Ethiopian and Negroid type cannot be overlooked. Hence, since the Negro was known outside of Africa as early as Minoan times, the possibility

of Negroid extraction cannot be excluded from consideration in the question of Eurybates' race. F. E. Wallace, *Color in Homer and in Ancient Art: Preliminary Studies,* Smith College Classical Studies 9 (Northampton 1927) 20, without attempting to identify specifically racial origin, admits the possibility that Eurybates was a barbarian. See Chap. III.

II. The Physical Characteristics of the Ethiopians — the Archaeological Evidence

1. See E. Gjerstad, J. Lindros, E. Sjöquist, and A. Westholm, *The Swedish Cyprus Expedition, Finds and Results of the Excavations in Cyprus: 1927-1931,* vol. II. Plates (Stockholm 1935) plate CCXXXIX, figs. 2-6, nos. 1095, 1228; my Fig. 1 reproduces nos. 1095 and 1228. See also E. Gjerstad, *The Swedish Cyprus Expedition,* vol. IV, pt. 2: *The Cypro-Geometric Cypro-Archaic and Cypro-Classical Periods* (Stockholm 1948) 103-104, 466-467 for sixth-century Cypriote Negroes with contracted waists and *Moretum* 34 for a much later description of a Negroid type with narrow waist.

2. For the painting on the askos, depicting a dance which includes among the participants a phlyax, a menad, a satyr, and a nude Negro woman with pendulous breasts, see A. Furtwängler and K. Reichhold, *Griechische Vasenmalerei,* Series II, Text (Munich 1909) plate 80, no. 4, in which Furtwängler 107 regards the face of the naked dancer as a caricature — with its small, flat nose and large, ugly mouth. M. Bieber, *The History of the Greek and Roman Theater*[2] (Princeton: Princeton University Press 1961) 296 refers to "a nude old woman with grotesque features." The woman, however, is obviously Negroid as E. Romagnoli, "Nimfe e Cabiri," *Ausonia: Rivista della Società Italiana di Archeologia e Storia dell'Arte* II (1907) 165-166 and others have pointed out. See M. Jatta, "La Collezione Jatta e l'ellenizzamento della Peucezia," *Japigia* III (1932) 253-254 and figure 37; H. Kenner, *Das Theater und der Realismus in der griechischen Kunst* (Vienna 1954) 55, n. 15; H. Sichtermann, *Griechische Vasen in Unteritalien,* Bilderhefte des deutschen archäologischen Instituts Rom — drittes und viertes Heft (Tübingen 1966) no. 90, p. 56, and plate 146; and A. D. Trendall, *Phlyax Vases*[2], revised and enlarged, University of London, Institute of Classical Studies, Bulletin Supplement No. 19 (1967) p. 68 no. 135(130). See my Fig. 2 and compare woman on a fifth-century lekythos who has been interpreted as a Negro woman tortured by satyrs (Athens, National Museum, no. 1129), C. T. Seltman, "Two Heads of Negresses," *AJA* XXIV (1920) 14-15, C. H. E. Haspels, *Attic Black-Figured Lekythoi* (Paris 1936) plate 49b and my Fig. 89.

3. Petronius *Satyricon* 102. For a Roman terra cotta, probably

from the Fayum, with cicatrices on each cheek of a woman considered Sudanese or Ethiopian, see L. Keimer, "Une Petite Tête romaine en terre cuite représentant une Soudanaise à cicatrices faciales," *Bulletin de la société archéologique d'Alexandrie*, no. 40 (1953) 32-34 and fig. 2. Keimer notes that the terra cotta is evidence that the form of facial incisions known today as selukh goes back at least to the Roman period. See my Fig. 3. I purchased the terra cotta from a dealer in Cairo. The similarity between my figure and Keimer's is marked.

4. A. Dumont and J. Chaplain, *Les Céramiques de la Grèce propre*, I (Paris 1888) plate XVIII — fifth-century B.C.; J. D. Beazley, *Attic Red-Figure Vase-Painters*², I (Oxford 1963) 554, no. 82, attributed to the Pan Painter. For circumcision among Ethiopians, see Herodotus 2.104 and Josephus *Contra Apionem* 1.169 and for a bronze of an ithyphallic, circumcised Negro see A. Michaelis, "Eine alexandrinische Erzfigur der Goetheschen Sammlung," *Jahrbuch des (kaiserlich) deutschen archäologischen Instituts* XII (1897) 49-50, and figure on p. 50. For ithyphallic black pygmies, see Ctesias *Indica* 11 (pp. 67-68 in edition of R. Henry [Brussels 1947]), who places these pygmies in India. For ithyphallic Negroes in mosaics, see the Negro on the floor of the threshold of a *calidarium* at Pompeii, A. Maiuri, *La Casa del Menandro e il suo tesoro di argenteria*, I (Rome [1933]) 146-147 and fig. 68; a fisherman in the House of the Calendar at Antioch-on-the-Orontes, R. Stillwell, ed., *Antioch-on-the-Orontes*, II: *The Excavations, 1933-1936* (Princeton, London, The Hague 1938) plate 53, no. 72, Panel B; and a bath attendant on the threshold of floor of baths at Timgad, F. G. de Pachtere, *Inventaire des mosaïques de la Gaule et de l'Afrique*, III (Paris 1911) 22, no. 86; S. Reinach, *Répertoire de peintures grecques et romaines* (Paris 1922) 250, no. 11 and description thereof by A. Ballu in *Bulletin archéologique du comité des travaux historiques et scientifiques* [1906] 209. A. J. B. Wace, "Grotesque and the Evil Eye," *The Annual of the British School at Athens*, no. X (Session 1903-04) 110, in discussing the phallus as a potent charm against the evil eye, suggests that the bronze of the circumcised, ithyphallic Negro mentioned above, who makes a well-known gesture (placing the thumb between the first and second fingers of the closed hand, mentioned by Ovid *Fasti* 5.1.33), points to a belief among the ancients in the apotropaic powers of the Negro. D. Levi, *Antioch Mosaic Pavements*, I (Princeton, London, The Hague 1947) 33, 39-40 and in R. Stillwell, ed., *Antioch-on-the-Orontes*, III: *The Excavations 1937-1939* (Princeton, London, The Hague 1941) 224-226 and n. 80, suggests that ithyphallic Negroes depicted on the thresholds of baths (sometimes carrying fire shovels, probably objects of a prophylactic significance) appearing also in Nilotic scenes of Hellenistic inspiration, may, like the "lucky hunchback," have been regarded as having an apotropaic meaning. The apotropaic interpretation, especially in the absence of literary cor-

roboration with respect to Ethiopians, may be overdrawn. Perhaps R. M. Cook, *Greek Painted Pottery* (London 1960) had such interpretations in mind when he observed that archaeologists are too fond of invoking apotropaic magic (p. 364). In light of modern discussions of macrophallism among Negroes and curiosity as to the Negro's sexual potency (J. H. Lewis, *The Biology of the Negro* [Chicago 1942] 77, and J. Dollard, *Caste and Class in a Southern Town*[2] [New York 1949] 160-161) the classical depiction of ithyphallic Negroes may merely represent an ancient example of modern accounts and curiosity. An illustration of a scientific interest in this area appears in Aristotle's denial (*De generatione animalium* 2.2.736a and *Historia animalium* 3.22.523a) of the Herodotean statement (3.101) that the Ethiopian's semen was black.

5. R. Paribeni, "Ariccia — Rilievo con scene egizie," in *Notizie degli scavi di antichità* (1919) 106-112 and photograph opposite p. 106 and *Le Terme di Diocleziano e il Museo Nazionale Romano*[2] (Rome 1932) no. 103. For steatopygy among Negroes, especially Bushmen and Hottentots, see Lewis, *Biology* 22-23.

6. For this vase in the Museum of Fine Arts, Boston, see A. Fairbanks, *Catalogue of Greek and Etruscan Vases*, I: *Early Vases, Preceding Athenian Black-Figured Ware,* Museum of Fine Arts, Boston (Cambridge, Mass. 1928) plate LXX, no. 564 (no. 99.534) and M. H. Swindler, "A Terracotta Altar in Corinth," *AJA* XXXVI (1932) 517. For a modern note on the stomach of pygmies, see *Encyclopaedia Britannica*[11] (New York 1911) s.v. *Pygmy* 678, which notes that the protuberant abdomen of African pygmies is not found in Oceanic Negritoes.

7. "Tête de nègre de la Collection de Janzé au Cabinet des Médailles," *Gazette archéologique* IX (1884) 204-205 and plate 27. As early as 1879, E. de Chanot, "Bronzes antiques," *Gazette archéologique* V (1879) 209-210 foresaw the anthropological significance of classical representations of Negroes. He commented on the anthropological accuracy observable in two south Italian lamps and noted that the lamps would be important for the history of the relations of the Greco-Roman world with Africa at some future date if an anthropologist should undertake a study of the black races of Africa.

8. For blacks and Negroes in Crete, see A. Evans, *The Early Nilotic, Libyan and Egyptian Relations with Minoan Crete,* The Huxley Memorial Lecture for 1925 (London 1925) 27; *id., The Palace of Minos at Knossos,* I (London 1921) 310, fig. 230, a, b, c; 312, fig. 231; 525-526; *The Palace of Minos at Knossos,* vol. II, pt. II (London 1928) 755-757 and plate XIII.

9. See pertinent references in n. 1 *supra*.

10. M. J. Herskovits, *Encyclopaedia Britannica* XVI (1960) s.v. *Negro* 193.

11. For the mask, see P. Marconi, *Agrigento arcaica* (Rome 1933)

plate V, nos. 5-6, and pp. 53-54; B. Pace, *Arte e civiltà della Sicilia antica,* II (Milan, Genoa, Rome, Naples 1938) 109 and fig. 104; P. Griffo and G. Zirretta, *Il Museo Civico di Agrigento: un secolo dopo la sua fondazione* (Palermo [1964]) 61; R. A. Higgins, *Catalogue of the Terracottas in the Department of Greek and Roman Antiquities,* vol. I: Text Greek, 730-330 B.C. (London 1954) 323; for the sixth-century B.C. laver-handles, see *Ashmolean Museum Summary Guide: Department of Antiquities*[4] (Oxford 1931) 91.

12. For this vase in West Berlin, Staatliche Museen, see A. Furtwängler, *Beschreibung der Vasensammlung im Antiquarium — Königliche Museen zu Berlin* (Berlin 1885) 1021, no. 4049.

13. E. A. Hooton, *Up from the Ape,* rev. ed. (New York: The Macmillan Co. 1946) plate 28a.

14. C. S. Coon, *The Origin of Races* (New York: A. A. Knopf, Inc. 1963) plate IV.

15. See J. Sieveking, *Die Terrakotten der Sammlung Loeb,* I (Munich 1916) 21 and plate 29.

16. Xenophanes, *Frg.* 16 in H. Diels, *Die Fragmente der Vorsokratiker*[10] (Berlin 1961) and Chap. VIII.

17. The faience vase is in London, British Museum; E. Buschor, "Das Krokodil des Sotades," in *Münchner Jahrbuch der bildenden Kunst* XI (1919) 34. (For a study of hair of Negroes as treated by later artists who worked in marble and especially bronze, see R. Steiger, "Drei römische Bronzen aus Augst," in *Gestalt und Geschichte: Festschrift Karl Schefold,* Supplementary Volume 4, *Antike Kunst* [1967] 193-195 and plate 64.)

18. For my Figs. 12a-c, see J. D. Beazley, *Attic Red-Figure Vase-Painters*[2], II (Oxford 1963) 1534, no. 10; for Fig. 13, aryballos, head-vase from Greece, see Beazley, *Red-Figure*[2] II 1530, no. 2, the Epilykos Class; for Fig. 14, kantharos, Janiform heads of Negro and Heracles, see Beazley, "Charinos (Attic Vases in the Form of Human Heads)," *JHS* XLIX (1929) 60, the Vatican Group.

19. Brussels, Musées Royaux du Cinquantenaire, no. A 130; Ch. Lenormant and J. De Witte, *Elite des monuments céramographiques,* III (Paris 1858) plate LXVI, 136, 185 and F. Mayence, *Corpus Vasorum Graecorum* [Belgium, fasc. 1, Brussels, Musées Royaux du Cinquantenaire, fasc. 1] (Paris n.d.) III H e, plate 7, 1a regard the Negro as Memnon; J. D. Beazley, *Attic Black-Figure Vase-Painters* (Oxford 1956) 308, no. 82 considers the Negro an attendant of Memnon; Beazley, "Mid-Sixth-Century Black-Figure," *The Annual of the British School at Athens,* no. XXXII (Session 1931-32) 16 attributes the vase to the Swing Painter, mid-sixth century B.C.

20. This alabastron in West Berlin, Staatliche Museen, is one of some thirty alabastra of the fifth century B.C. depicting Negroes of similar types; Beazley, *Red-Figure*[2], I 269. For interpretations of these vases, see Chap. IV.

21. The kylix is from Poggio Sommavilla and is in Paris, in the Louvre. E. Pottier, *Catalogue des vases antiques de terre cuite, troisième partie, l'école attique*[2] (Paris 1929) 925; Beazley, *Red-Figure*[2], I 225, no. 4 considers the warrior a henchman of Memnon.

22. Hair of attendants of Memnon on black-figured neck-amphorae: (1) Beazley, *Black-Figure Vase-Painters,* p. 149, near Exekias; and (2) Beazley, *ibid.*, p. 144, no. 8, Exekias.

23. The vase (ca. 530 B.C.) is in Vienna, Kunsthistorisches Museum, cf. A. Furtwängler, and K. Reichhold, *Griechische Vasenmalerei,* Series I, Plates (Munich 1904) plate 51, and pp. 255-260.

24. The lekythos is in Naples, Museo Nazionale; *Monumenti Antichi* XXII, pt. 1 (Milan 1913) 507; H. Heydemann, *Die Vasensammlung des Museo Nazionale zu Neapel* (Berlin 1872) 864, no. RC 172.

25. The vase is Würzburg no. 302; cf. Furtwängler and Reichhold, *Griechische Vasenmalerei,* Series II, Plates (Munich 1908) plate 104; J. D. Beazley, "Kleophrades," *JHS* XXX (1910) 62 attributes the vase to the Kleophrades Painter; E. Langlotz, *Griechische Vasen,* I (Munich 1932) 101-102, no. 508 and plate 176 in accompanying volume of plates.

26. For the fifth-century B.C. sard scarab in Museum of Fine Arts, Boston, see J. D. Beazley, *The Lewes House Collection of Ancient Gems* (Oxford 1920) 49-50, no. 52; for the gold pendant in the form of a Negro head, see F. H. Marshall, *Catalogue of the Jewellery, Greek, Etruscan, Roman, in the Departments of Antiquities British Museum* (London 1911) 258, no. 2272 and plate XLV. For Negroes on coinage of Athens, Delphi, and Lesbos, see Chap. VI, n. 46; and for lead tesserae, see A. Engel, "Choix de tessères grecques en plomb tirées des collections athéniennes," *Bulletin de correspondance hellénique* VIII (1884) 13, nos. 99-100, and plate IV.

27. For the lekythos which is in East Berlin, Staatliche Museen, see R. C. Bosanquet, "Some Early Funeral Lekythoi," *JHS* XIX (1889) 173-177 and plate III; Beazley, *Red-Figure*[2], II, 1227, no. 9; for the hydria in the British Museum, see C. H. Smith, *Catalogue of the Greek and Etruscan Vases in the British Museum,* vol. III: *Vases of the Finest Period* (London 1896) 152-153; Beazley, *Red-Figure*[2], II 1062.

28. Hooton, *Ape* 483 and M. J. Herskovits, s.v. *Negro* 193.

29. Figs. 27a-b present views of a fifth-fourth century B.C. vase from Vulci in West Berlin, Staatliche Museen, A. Furtwängler, *Beschreibung der Vasensammlung im Antiquarium* 831, no. 2870; Fig. 28 is another fifth-fourth century B.C. head-vase, Paris, Bibliothèque Nationale; cf. T. Panofka, "Delphi und Melaine," *Winckelmannsprogramm* IX (Berlin 1849) 7, who suggested, on the basis of the stars on the headband, that the figure represented night.

30. My Fig. 29, a Negro-head oinochoe from near Viterbo (?),

fourth century B.C., is in New York, Metropolitan Museum of Art, G. M. A. Richter, *Handbook of the Etruscan Collection,* The Metropolitan Museum of Art (New York 1940) 46, figs. 134-135; the other fourth-century B.C. vases in form of Negro heads are Fig. 30, New York, Metropolitan Museum of Art; Fig. 31, Ferrara, Museo Archeologico Nazionale, S. Aurigemma and N. Alfieri, *Il Museo Nazionale Archeologico di Spina in Ferrara*[2] (Rome 1961) 23; and Fig. 32, Oxford, Ashmolean Museum, J. D. Beazley, *Etruscan Vase-Painting* (Oxford 1947) 187, 305.

31. For this vase, which is in London, British Museum, see H. B. Walters, *Catalogue of the Greek and Etruscan Vases in the British Museum,* vol. IV: *Vases of the Latest Period* (London 1896) 191, F 417.

32. The vase is in Ruvo, Jatta Collection, H. Sichtermann, *Griechische Vasen in Unteritalien* (Tübingen 1966), 63 and plates 166-167. For a similar vase, see Naples, Museo Nazionale, no. C.S.968.

33. Paris, south Italian lekythos, Louvre.

34. Oxford, Ashmolean Museum. H. B. Walters, "Odysseus and Kirke on a Boeotian Vase," *JHS* XIII (1892-93) 81 and plate IV; cf. G. M. A. Richter, *A Handbook of Greek Art* (New York 1959) 346 and fig. 464; E. Romagnoli, "Nimfe e Cabiri," *Ausonia* II (1907) 141-185, esp. 159-161. See Chap. VII.

35. Oxford, Ashmolean Museum; *Ashmolean Museum Summary Guide: Department of Antiquities* (Oxford 1931) 87.

36. New York, Metropolitan Museum of Art.

37. The gold phiale is in Plodiv (Bulgaria), the National Archaeological Museum, and is described by D. Tsonchev, "The Gold Treasure of Panagurishte," *Archaeology* VIII (1955) 218-227, with photographs on p. 223, figs. 9 and 10. Tsonchev 226 considers the work Greek of the second half of the fourth century B.C., probably from Attica. H. Hoffmann, "The Date of the Panagurishte Treasure," *Mitteilungen des deutschen archaeologischen Instituts, Roemische Abteilung* LXV (1958) 140 accepts a Hellenistic date for the phiale, though considering other objects of the treasury in the style of the Constantinian era. For a discussion of the identification of this phiale, see N. M. Kontoleon, "The Gold Treasure of Panagurischte," *Balkan Studies: A Biannual Publication of the Institute of Balkan Studies* III (1962) 185-200, plates VI and VII; D. von Bothmer, "A Gold Libation Bowl," *Bulletin of the Metropolitan Museum of Art* XXI (1962) 154-166; D. E. Strong, *Greek and Roman Gold and Silver Plate* (Ithaca 1966) 80, 97-98, 102. The Negroes are certainly not "almost caricatures," as von Bothmer states (161). The significance of the Negroes on this phiale is discussed in Chap. VI and notes 32 and 34.

38. See P. Perdrizet, *Les Terres cuites grecques d'Egypte de la Collection Fouquet,* I, Text and II, Plates (Nancy, Paris, Strasbourg

1921) I 139-140, II plates XCVI, XCVII, CI for Greco-Roman terra cottas; for examples from the first three centuries A.D., Ev. Breccia, *Terrecotte figurate greche e greco-egizie del Museo di Alessandria,* Monuments de l'Egypte gréco-romaine, vol. II, fasc. 1 (Bergamo 1930) nos. 396, 397, 420-424, 435, 440-449, 451, 453, 456, 470, 475 and plates XXVI, 11; XXVII, 2, 11; XXVIII, 4; XXIX, 2, 5, 7, 9; XXX, 1, 7, 8-9; XXXI, 8; XXXII, 3-4; XXXIV, 4; LI, 11; LIV, 19. *Id.*, vol. II, fasc. 2 (Bergamo 1934) p. 40 (nos. 216-217), p. 47 (nos. 292-293), p. 48 (no. 303), p. 50 (nos. 316-319), p. 51 (nos. 327-332), plates LXX (359), LXXI (362-363), LXXII (368), LXXIV (378-379), LXXXIV (440-441), LXXXV (445-446), C (567-568, 570, 571, 574-576).

39. Cf. L. Oschinsky, *The Racial Affinities of the Baganda and Other Bantu Tribes of British East Africa* (Cambridge, Eng. 1954) table LIX, appendix C, and photographs which follow.

III. Greco-Roman Acquaintance with African Ethiopians

1. Important for the India-Ethiopia question are the studies of A. Dihle: (1) "Der fruchtbare Osten," *Rheinisches Museum für Philologie* CV (1962) 97-110; (2) "The Conception of India in Hellenistic and Roman Literature," *Proceedings of the Cambridge Philological Association* CXC (n.s.10 1964) 15-23; and (3) "Frumentios und Ezana" and "Zur Geschichte des Aethiopennamens," in *Umstrittene Daten: Untersuchungen zum Auftreten der Griechen am Roten Meer* (Cologne and Opladen 1965), Wissenschaftliche Abhandlungen der Arbeitsgemeinschaft für Forschung des Landes Nordrhein-Westfalen, vol. XXXII esp. 36-54 and 65-79. Herodotus 3.98 says that of all the peoples of Asia the Indians lived farthest to the east and the sunrise. In classical literature, however, the number of references to Ethiopians in Asia is small (see F. Jacoby, *Die Fragmente der griechischen Historiker* III C (Leiden 1958) 308-309. In one instance (3.94) Herodotus says that the Paricanii and Ethiopians of Asia formed the seventeenth satrapy. In another passage (7.70) he mentions Ethiopians of the east who served with the Indians and stated that these eastern Ethiopians differed from the Ethiopians who lived near Egypt in speech and in appearance only with respect to the hair. The Ethiopians of the east were straight-haired, Herodotus informs us, whereas the Ethiopians of Libya were the most woolly-haired of all men. Strabo (2.3.8), however, notes that the Asian differed in no respect from the Libyan Ethiopians. Since Herodotus, like others who mention eastern Ethiopians, gives little or no information as to their location, it is not certain where the eastern branch lived. E. A. W. Budge, *The Egyptian Sudan: Its History and Monuments,* II (Philadelphia and London 1907) 107 believes that Herodotus used western

Ethiopians of the Negro tribes to the west of the white Nile and eastern Ethiopians of the light, red-skinned tribes of the eastern desert. For other views see R. W. Macan, *Herodotus,* I (London 1908) pt. I 94; C. F. Smith and A. G. Laird, *Herodotus: Books VII and VIII* (New York 1908) 157; A. D. Fraser, "The Panoply of the Ethiopian Warrior," *AJA* XXXIX (1935) 43-44; Ph.-E. Legrand, *Hérodote,* VII (Paris 1951) 98; and W. W. How and J. Wells, *A Commentary on Herodotus,* I (Oxford 1912) 285. Oldfather in a note on Diodorus 2.22 (Loeb 423) states that by eastern Ethiopians Herodotus probably meant Assyrians. Early versions of the Memnon story (Chap. VI) associated Memnon with the east and particularly with Susa, whereas Memnon at a later period was located in Africa and was described as black and Ethiopian. These two versions of Memnon's provenience may have contributed to the confusion in the minds of some between east and south. Some scholars, however, have argued that an eastern Memnon is evidence that the Greeks were acquainted with dark and Negroid populations known from archaeology (depiction of blacks on monuments at Susa) and anthropology (Negrito skulls in Elam) to have existed in Elam. When the Greeks found black peoples in the east, the argument goes, they naturally compared them with the Ethiopians whom they had known via Egypt. (H. Field, *Contributions to the Anthropology of Iran* [Anthropological Series, Field Museum of Natural History, vol. XXIX no. 1, Dec. 15, 1939, Publication 458] esp. 119-120, 126, 154-155; P. Sykes, *A History of Persia*[2], I [London 1921] 51-52, M. A. Dieulafoy, *L'Acropole de Suse* [Paris 1893] 27-28, 44-45.) Further, when the Greeks found that Indians were dark or black, it was natural for them to compare the inhabitants of India with those of Ethiopia whom they had known through contacts in Egypt and elsewhere. Hence, it was common for classical writers to compare India and Ethiopia as to climate, flora, fauna, and peoples; cf. A. Dihle, "Der fruchtbare Osten," 97-110. Strabo (15.1.25) refers to those who noted the similarity of India to Egypt and Ethiopia (cf. 15.1.19). The geographer (15.1.13) notes that the same animals are found in India as in Ethiopia and Egypt, that Indian rivers have all the river animals except the hippopotamus, and that southern Indians resemble Ethiopians in color, and northern Indians, the Egyptians (*supra,* for other comparisons of Indians and Ethiopians, and especially Arrian *Indica* 6.1-9, in which southern Indians are black like Ethiopians but not so flat-nosed or woolly-haired). When Alexander saw crocodiles in the Hydaspes (Strabo 15.1.25) and in the Indus (Arrian *Anabasis* 6.1.2), he thought he had found the sources of the Nile although he later concluded that the Indus had nothing to do with Egypt. E. De Saint-Denis ("Notes sur le livre IV des *Géorgiques,*" *Revue des études latines* XXVIII [1950] 204-209) believes that Vergil's reference to the Nile sweeping down from the colored Indians "coloratis amnis devexus ab Indis" (*Georgics*

4.293) was indicative of a confusion between south and east and in support of such an interpretation points out that, in spite of Roman penetration toward the south, the question of the Nile still remained very obscure; and that Roman penetration into Africa at the time of Augustus renewed interest in the legends of the region and in the accounts of the expeditions sent by Sesostris, Cambyses, Alexander et al. The interpretation of scholars, however, who maintain that *Indis* in the *Georgics* and Ovid's mention of Perseus bringing Andromeda from the black Indians, "Andromedan Perseus nigris portarit ab Indis" (*Ars amatoria* 1.53) are equivalents of African Ethiopians seems to be supported by the evidence. Apropos of the Ovid line, a comment of Philostratus (*Imagines* 1.29) suggests that although some in his day may have been confused as to south and east, *he* had no such misunderstanding. In his description of the Perseus-Andromeda myth Philostratus observes that it is not a question of the Red Sea nor of inhabitants of India but of Ethiopians and of a Greek man in Ethiopia. Despite increased geographical knowledge in Hellenistic and early Roman times and growth in Roman trade with India via Egypt and the Red Sea, the ecclesiastical writers present problems with respect to their usage of Ethiopia and India. Cf. F. Cabrol and H. Leclercq, *Dictionnaire d'archéologie chrétienne et de liturgie,* V (Paris 1922) s.v. *Ethiopie* 590-591; and A. Dihle's articles cited above: "The Conception of India in Hellenistic and Roman Literature," 16, 20-21 and "Frumentios und Ezana," 36-54. For a study of the blending of mythological Ethiopians with increased geographical knowledge, of attempts to reconcile eastern and western Ethiopians, and of a tendency to associate earlier myths with the peoples south of Egypt, see A. Lesky, "Aithiopika," *Hermes* LXXXVII (1959) 36-38. See also Chap. I and n. 10 and Chap. IX, notes 79-80.

2. For the Homeric references, see *Iliad* 1.423-4, 23.205-7; *Odyssey* 1.22-24; 4.84; 5.282, 287. T. D. Seymour, *Life in the Homeric Age,* new ed. (New York 1914) 62 suggests that the gods made twelve-day visits because evidently the Ethiopians lived so far from Greece that it was not worthwhile to visit for a single dinner or to make a brief call. Seymour states (63) that Homer's description of Memnon as most beautiful (*Odyssey* 11.522) without reference to color might show that he was at least not referring to the western Ethiopians of Herodotus. But Seymour overlooks the fact that Herodotus (3.20) called the Macrobian Ethiopians the most handsome men on earth.

3. Strabo 1.2.31.

4. For Eurybates as herald of Odysseus in *Iliad* and as one who accompanied him on the mission to Achilles, *Iliad* 2.184, 9.170; as black-skinned and woolly-haired in the description of Odysseus to Penelope, *Odyssey* 19.246-247. For a much later testimony as to a trumpeter of a very pronounced Negro type, see a fifth-century B.C. vase painting depicting a Negro on the shield of a Homeric warrior,

cited Chap. II, Fig. 22. For an interesting association of Odysseus with Negroes, see Negro Circe, Chap. VII.

5. *Odyssey* 2.15. T. D. Seymour, *Homeric Age* 63 says that the old man is called Aegyptius probably because he or his father had made a visit there.

6. *Iliad* 3.6. C. Préaux, "Les Grecs à la découverte de l'Afrique par l'Egypte," *Chronique d'Egypte* XXXII (1957) 290 states that the knowledge of pygmies could have come to the Greeks through Crete from Egypt. H. Thomas and F. H. Stubbings in A. J. B. Wace and F. H. Stubbings, ed., *A Companion to Homer* (London and New York 1963) 307-309 state that the Homeric Ethiopians were possibly located in Palestine. Though considering the pygmies, however, as "even . . . the real Pygmies of Africa, vaguely known by indirect accounts," these two scholars curiously regard the Ethiopians as on the borderline between fact and fiction. If vague accounts of pygmies could have reached the Greeks, the same certainly could have been true with respect to African Ethiopians. Professor Mabel L. Lang, who will publish the frescoes from the Palace of Nestor, has kindly provided me with a note on a fragmentary fresco from Pylos, depicting what was apparently a life-sized black, somewhat comparable to the "Captain of the Blacks" from Knossos: "On the most important piece there remains only the lower part of a naked black torso, a three-tiered girdle, and part of a kilt. The black man seems to belong to a procession in which white men wear lion skins but the black man wears a Minoan kilt." For ai-ti-jo-qo (Aithiops) in the Pylos tablets, see M. Ventris and J. Chadwick, *Documents in Mycenaean Greek* (Cambridge, Eng. 1959) 243-244, 248, 250-252 and for ai-ku-pi-ti-jo (Aigyptios) 98; J. Chadwick and L. Baumbach, "The Mycenaean Greek Vocabulary," *Glotta: Zeitschrift für griechische und lateinische Sprache* XLI (1963) 168; L. A. Stella, *La civiltà micenea nei documenti contemporanei* (Rome 1965) 210 for the view that the name ai-ti-jo-qo is evidence of contacts with Asiatics of dark color; and A. Dihle, *Umstrittene Daten* 68.

7. For modern views on the location of Homeric Ethiopians, see V. Bérard, *Les Phéniciens et l'Odyssée,* I (Paris 1902) 335, II (Paris 1903) 87; M. Cary and E. H. Warmington, *The Ancient Explorers* (London 1929) 46-47; H. E. Burton, *The Discovery of the Ancient World* (Cambridge, Mass. 1932) 21; and A. Rousseau-Liessens, *Géographie de l'Odyssée, la Phéacie* (Brussels 1961) 30, 32-33.

8. Hesiod, cited in Strabo 7.3.7, who was quoting Eratosthenes; for later groupings of Scythians and Ethiopians, see Chap. VIII.

9. *Opera et dies* 527; κυανέων ἀνδρῶν δῆμόν τε πόλιν.

10. *Hymnus ad Venerem* 225-227, Hesiod *Theogonia* 984-985. (Memnon in early Greek art is usually depicted as white, see Chap. VI.)

11. T. Bergk, *Poetae Lyrici Graeci*[4], II (Leipzig 1882) *Frg.* 145

[126] p. 428 and Athenaeus 4.167 d; cf. Chap. I for Αἰθίοψ as cognomen.

12. *Frg.* 8 (Loeb) 94.

13. Aeschylus *Prometheus Vinctus* 808-9. H. J. Rose, *A Commentary on the Surviving Plays of Aeschylus* (Amsterdam 1957) 304 states that the ποταμὸς Αἰθίοψ of this passage, whether a vaguely conceived Niger or simply the river of the black man's country, corresponds in Aeschylus' geography to the upper course of the Nile above the cataracts.

14. Herodotus 2.152, 154. For Egyptian dating I have in general followed W. S. Smith, *Ancient Egypt* [as represented in the Museum of Fine Arts, Boston], fourth edition fully revised (Boston 1960).

15. Strabo (17.1.18) says that Milesians in the time of Psammetichus I settled on the Bolbitine mouth of the Nile and later founded Naucratis. F. W. von Bissing, "Naukratis," *Bulletin de la société royale d'archéologie d'Alexandrie* XXXIX (1951) 47 states that the Greek settlement at Naucratis was the oldest on the site of any importance and that it goes back only to the time of Psammetichus II, after 594 B.C.; H. Kees, *Ancient Egypt: A Cultural Topography* (Chicago 1961) 207 believes that, on the basis of the finds at Naucratis, its foundation should be dated possibly in the reign of Psammetichus II. E. Paribeni in *Enciclopedia dell'arte antica,* V (Rome 1963) s.v. *Naukratis* 361 states that the evidence of pottery demonstrates conclusively that there was definite and consistent evidence of a Greek nucleus in Naucratis beginning with the middle of the seventh century B.C. and J. Boardman, *The Greeks Overseas* (Penguin Books 1964) 138 considers the ceramic evidence indicative of a substantial settlement before 600 B.C. For a modern cast of a pronounced Negroid type made from a mold of perhaps the fifth century B.C. found at Naucratis, see C. C. Edgar (Section G. Minor Antiquities) in D. G. Hogarth, H. L. Lorimer, and C. C. Edgar, "Naukratis, 1903," *JHS* XXV (1905) 132 for the observation that the manufacture of terra cottas at Naucratis is proved by the molds such as this of a Negro, now in Oxford, Ashmolean Museum, no. G96; G. M. A. Richter, *Greek Portraits, III,* Collection Latomus, vol. XLVIII (1960) 29 and plate XXII, figs. 106-107. For the probable Naucratic source of the Busiris legend, see R. I. Hicks, "Egyptian Elements in Greek Mythology," *Transactions of the American Philological Association* XCIII (1962) 106-107. For Amasis as Egyptian-born and brought up in Naucratis, see J. Boardman, "The Amasis Painter," *JHS* LXXVIII (1958) 1-3 and *Greek Overseas* 169 and esp. 129-169 for the effects of the presence of the Greeks on Egyptian soil. For Greeks in the army of Psammetichus II, see Chap. IV *infra*, n. 9.

16. *Frg.* 16, H. Diels, *Die Fragmente der Vorsokratiker*[10] (Berlin 1961).

17. M. N. Tod, *A Selection of Greek Historical Inscriptions*[2], I

(Oxford 1946) no. 4; A. Bernand and O. Masson, "Les Inscriptions grecques d'Abou-Simbel," *Revue des études grecques* LXX (1957) 1-42.

18. K. Freeman, *The Pre-Socratic Philosophers: A Companion to Diels,* Fragmente der Vorsokratiker[2] (Cambridge, Mass. 1959) 89 doubts the story of Xenophanes' visit to Egypt and notes that Xenophanes could have learned of Ethiopian religion without actual contact with the people of Ethiopia, for example. My interpretation provides a reasonable explanation for Xenophanes' anthropological details concerning Ethiopians.

19. See Chap. VII. C. Préaux, cited n. 6 *supra,* 291-298, among the possible sources for such information includes the expedition of Psammetichus II, the Ethiopian campaign of Cambyses, Persians who had been in Egypt, and Ethiopians who fought in the army of Xerxes against the Greeks.

20. 7.70.

21. 4.197.

22. 2.29.

23. Herodotus 2.29-32; 3.17-24; 4.183. The Asmach of Herodotus have been considered to be the same people as the Sembritae of later writers (e.g., Eratosthenes as cited by Strabo 17.1.2). Strabo (17.1.5) and other later writers reported Cambyses' expedition as dispatched against the Ethiopians of Meroë.

24. Herodotus 2.32; E. H. Bunbury, *A History of Ancient Geography*[2], with a new introduction by W. H. Stahl, I (New York 1959) 271.

25. 4.43; L. Casson, *The Ancient Mariners: Seafarers and Sea Fighters of the Mediterranean in Ancient Times* (New York 1959) 132. The meaning of Herodotus' mention of black-skinned, woolly-haired Colchians (2.104) is not as clear, but may point to a knowledge in the fifth century of Negroid peoples in the area. See Chap. IV, n. 3 and the references cited.

26. 4.42-43.

27. *Periplus* of Hanno, *GGM* I 1-14. For discussions of the *Periplus,* its date, and opinions as to the identification of regions mentioned, see R. Mauny, "La Navigation sur les côtes du Sahara pendant l'antiquité," *Revue des études anciennes* LVII (1955) 92-101; G. Germain, "Qu'est-ce que le *Périple d'Hannon?* Document, amplification littéraire ou faux intégral?" *Hespéris* XLIV (1957) 205-248; L. Casson, *Ancient Mariners* 133-136; B. H. Warmington, *Carthage,* revised edition (New York 1969) 70-76; G. and C. Charles-Picard, *Daily Life in Carthage at the time of Hannibal* (New York 1961) 222-236; G. Picard, *Carthage* (New York 1965) 89-90, 194. Some maintain that Hanno did not get beyond the coast of Morocco; but others argue that he sailed further south as far as Guinea or even Cameroon, depending upon whether the Chariot of the Gods mentioned in the *Periplus* is identified as Mt. Kakoulima or Cameroon Mountain.

28. Cerne has been identified by some modern scholars as Herne Island, a little north of the Tropic of Cancer; by others, as at the mouth of the Senegal River.

29. *Periplus* of Scylax, *GGM* I 94.

30. *De incredibilibus* 31 (32) in N. Festa's edition of *Mythographi Graeci*, III, 2 (Leipzig 1902).

31. Ephorus, as cited by Strabo 1.2.26, refers to a mountain Dyris (explained in Strabo 17.3.2 as the barbarian name for Atlas) as the limit of the Ethiopian migration. Some later illustrations of Ethiopians clearly regarded as inhabiting west or northwest Africa are these: Apollonius Rhodius *Argonautica* 3.1191-1192 (far away in the west beyond the furthest hills of the Ethiopians); Strabo 2.5.15 (speaks of western Ethiopians as the most remote peoples south of the Carthaginian regions); Strabo 3.4.3 (reference to the Lotos-eaters who lived beyond Maurusia next to the western Ethiopians); Strabo 17.3.5 (mentions western Ethiopians situated above Maurusia, on the outside sea); Pausanias 1.33.5 (Ethiopians who are neighbors of the Mauri and extend as far as the Nasamones); Isidore *Origines* 14.5.16 (two Ethiopias, one near the rising sun, the other near the setting sun in Mauretania); cf. F. Jacoby, *Die Fragmente* 305-308, and J. Desanges, *Catalogue des tribus africaines de l'antiquité classique à l'Ouest du Nil*, Publications de la section d'histoire, no. 4 (Dakar 1962) 247-248, where Desanges states that in his opinion *Aethiopes Hesperii* was a vague term designating certain Ethiopians living along the Ocean, in the south of present-day Morocco, and perhaps especially in the vicinity of Cape Noun.

32. Diogenes Laertius 9.35.

33. Pliny *Naturalis historia* 6.35.183, who cites Dalion in 6.35.194. E. Bevan, *A History of Egypt under the Ptolemaic Dynasty* (London 1927) 76 suggests that Dalion made his journey in the reign of Ptolemy II (283-246 B.C.).

34. The dates are those suggested by F. Jacoby, cited n. 1 *supra*, who (277-284) includes the materials relating to these writers of *Aethiopica*. For Charon of Lampsacus, see also Suidas (A. Adler's edition[4], (Leipzig 1935) s.v. Χάρων 791 and L. Pearson, *Early Ionian Historians* (Oxford 1939) 140 for 464 B.C. as the *floruit* for Charon.

35. Diodorus 3.6.3, 3.11.3 and Strabo 2.5.12. The Gymnosophists and kings of Ethiopia, according to Heliodorus (9.25), studied Greek.

36. Eratosthenes as cited by Strabo 17.1.2.

37. Strabo 2.3.4-5. For an evaluation of Posidonius' account of Eudoxus of Cyzicus and Strabo's treatment thereof, see M. Laffranque, "Poseidonius, Eudoxe de Cyzique et la circumnavigation de l'Afrique," *Revue philosophique* CLIII (1963) 199-222.

38. Agatharchides *De Mari Erythraeo* 23-29 (Diodorus 3.12-14) for gold mines; 31-46 (Diodorus 3.15-20) for Ichthyophagi and for nudity and wives in common; 57 (Diodorus 3.28) for Simi; 58

(Diodorus 3.29) for Acridophagi; 50 (Diodorus 3.23) for Rhizophagi; 51 (Diodorus 3.24) for Hylophagi and for nudity and wives in common; 57 (Diodorus 3.28) for Struthophagi; 63 (Diodorus 3.32-33) for Troglodytes; 52 (Diodorus 3.25) for tree-dwellers and archers (Cynegi); 53-56 (Diodorus 3.26-27) for methods of hunting elephants. For the passages from Agatharchides, see vol. I of *GGM*.

39. For Diodorus on his sources, see 3.11 and for the view that Diodorus' account (3.2-10) is probably for the most part derived from Agatharchides, see E. H. Bunbury, *Ancient Geography,* II 51-52. Diodorus may have supplemented his literary sources from his interviews with Ethiopian ambassadors resident in Egypt. For Diodorus' description of savage Ethiopians and "pure" Negroes, see esp. 3.8 and for more developed Ethiopians, 3.2-7.

40. See Chap. V for Roman military activity among the Ethiopians. For Roman coins in sub-Egyptian Ethiopia, see M. P. Charlesworth, "A Roman Imperial Coin from Nairobi," *The Numismatic Chronicle and Journal of the Royal Numismatic Society,* sixth ser. IX (1949) 107-110 and T. V. Buttrey, "Another Roman Coin from Africa," *ibid.,* seventh ser. IV (1964) 133-134. Charlesworth (108) expresses doubt about Roman coins found in or south of Rhodesia. For Constantius' interest in the Axumites, see Chap. IX.

41. Lepcis Magna — Negroid figures in mosaic of Villa del Nilo, 2nd century A.D., in S. Aurigemma, *L'Italia in Africa: Le scoperte archeologiche* (a.1911-a.1943), *Tripolitani*a, vol. I — *I monumenti d'arte decorativa, parte prima* — *I mosaici* (Rome 1960) plate 86, two Negroid figures, one seated, the other standing, both nude from waist up, and commentary on p. 48 and G. Guidi, "La Villa del Nilo," *Africa Italiana: Rivista di storia e d'arte a cura del Ministero delle Colonie* V (1933) 6-8 and figs. 3-4. J. M. C. Toynbee, *The Art of the Romans* (New York and Washington 1965) plate 78 and note on p. 259. Though these figures depict Nilotic scenes, the models for the Negroid figures could easily have been local Negroes. Hadrumetum — black marble statue of a Negro boy from Hadrumetum, second century A.D., Fig. 58; esp. J. W. Salomonson, *Mosaïques romaines de Tunisie: Catalogue* (Brussels 1964) 43, no. 43. Thysdrus — a Negro, one of five gladiators celebrating by drinking, third-century A.D. mosaic, Salomonson, *ibid.,* plate 19 and pp. 33-34. Carthage — black limestone herm of a Negro (Fig. 85) found in the Antonine baths, middle second century A.D., no doubt representing a Negro prisoner from among the Ethiopian tribes who lived together with Libyans in the Sahara, captured by the Romans, G. Picard, *Carthage* plate 2, and Salomonson, *Mosaïques* 43. This Ethiopian herm and that of a Libyan found also in the baths were symbols of the barbarian territory which extended along the frontier of the African province. A mosaic (fourth century A.D.) from Carthage represents a Negro whom G. Charles-Picard [*La Carthage de Saint Augustin* (Paris 1965) 73-77 and fig.

74] regards as one of the numerous Negroes who lived in the area then as now and interprets as a participant in a religious ceremony (see Chap. VIII *infra*). For Negroes in Carthage and environs, see G. & C. Charles-Picard, *Daily Life in Carthage* (New York 1961) 76, 129, 166, 214-216. Hippo — in a third or early fourth century A.D. mosaic in a Roman villa a black slave prepares a drink for his masters, F. G. de Pachtere, "Les nouvelles fouilles d'Hippone," *Mélanges d'archéologie et d'histoire de l'Ecole Française de Rome* XXXI (1911) 334-335. Thuburbo Maius — mosaic (not before second half of fourth century A.D.) depicting Negro camel-drivers, G. and C. Charles-Picard, *Daily Life in Carthage* 249-250, and G. Picard, *Carthage* plate 46. Thamugadi — Roman lamp in shape of a Negro, A. Ballu and R. Cagnat, *Musée de Timgad,* Musées de l'Algérie et de la Tunisie (Paris 1902) 28 and plate XII, no. 3; Negro in mosaic in baths at Timgad, probably employed as bath attendant, see Chap. II *supra*, n. 4.

42. See Chap. V.

43. See J. Desanges, *Catalogue* esp. 201-241.

44. *Ibid.*

45. Desanges, *Catalogue* 181-199 and 201-241.

46. For Garamantes as Ethiopians, see Solinus 30.2, Ptolemy *Geographia* 1.8.5 (described as for the most part Ethiopians), Isidore *Origines* 9.2.128; as distinguished from Ethiopians, Strabo 2.5.33, 17.3.19; Dionysius "Periegetes" *Orbis descriptio* 217-218 *GGM* III 114.

47. *Perusti,* Lucan 4.679 (cf. Pliny *Naturalis historia* 6.22.70 for *exusti* of Ethiopians; *furvi,* Arnobius *Adversus nationes* 6.5; *niger, Anthologia Latina* 155, no. 183.

48. S. Gsell, *Histoire ancienne de l'Afrique du Nord,* I[3], rev. (Paris 1921) 298.

49. G. and C. Charles-Picard, *Daily Life in Carthage* 215.

50. Sergi, in B. Pace, S. Sergi, and G. Caputo, *Monumenti antichi,* vol. XLI: *Scavi sahariani: Ricerche nell'Uadi el-Agial e nell'Oasi di Gat* (Rome 1951) 461-465, 480, 493-499.

51. J. Desanges, *Catalogue* 95, n. 4.

52. For Leucoe Aethiopes, see Pliny *Naturalis historia* 5.8.43; Leucoaethiopes, Mela *De chorographia* 1.4.23; and Ptolemy *Geographia* 4.6.6 and for Melanogaetuli, Ptolemy 4.6.5; O. Bates, *The Eastern Libyans: An Essay* (London 1914) 44, notes 1-2 and for Libyans resembling Ethiopians see Adamantius *Physiognomonica* 2.31 (p. 384 in vol. 1 [Leipzig 1893] of R. Foerster's *Scriptores Physiognomonici Graeci et Latini.*

53. J. Desanges, *Catalogue* 95 (n. 4), 219-220, 223.

54. Scholars differ on many points concerning the political and cultural history of the Ethiopian peoples south of Egypt. My account of aspects of these kingdoms relevant to this book is based on the standard sources. For a summary of the regions in question and the

relations of the peoples with the inhabitants of Egypt during the Ptolemaic and Roman periods, see M. I. Rostovtzeff, *The Social and Economic History of the Roman Empire*[2], rev. by P. M. Fraser, I (Oxford 1957) 298-307 and II 677-680 and the bibliography there cited. For a more up-to-date bibliography see F. F. Gadallah, "Meroitic Problems and a Comprehensive Meroitic Bibliography," *Kush: Journal of the Sudan Antiquities Service* XI (1963) 196-216 [hereafter abbreviated as *Kush*], and W. Y. Adams, "Post-Pharaonic Nubia in the Light of Archaeology. I" and "Post-Pharaonic Nubia in the Light of Archaeology. II," *The Journal of Egyptian Archaeology* L (1964) 102-120 and LI (1965) 160-169. On the designation of "Kush" for this region and preference of some modern scholars for this terminology, see D. M. Dixon, "The Origin of the Kingdom of Kush (Napata-Meroë)," *The Journal of Egyptian Archaeology* L (1964) 123. As to the chronology of the three periods, opinions differ (see Dixon, *ibid.*, n. 11). For the dating of this period I have also followed W. S. Smith (cited n. 14 *supra*).

55. The peoples south of Egypt had a long military tradition. For accounts of Egyptian use of southerners and blacks as auxiliaries and mercenaries of various types, see T. Säve Söderbergh, *Ägypten und Nubien: ein Beitrag zur Geschichte altägyptischer Aussenpolitik* (Lund 1941) 231-234; J. A. Wilson, *The Burden of Egypt: An interpretation of Ancient Culture* (Chicago 1951), esp. 136-138, 186-188, 292; R. O. Faulkner, "Egyptian Military Organization," *The Journal of Egyptian Archaeology* XXXIX (1953) 32-47; G. Posener, *Dictionary of Egyptian Civilization* (New York 1959) esp. articles on Army, Nubia, and Police; H. G. Fischer, "The Nubian Mercenaries of Gebelein during the First Intermediate Period," *Kush* IX (1961) 44-79; H. Kees, *Ancient Egypt* esp. 141-143, 218-219. Inasmuch as the Egyptian peasant, according to one view (Kees, *ibid.*, 141-142), never had the heart of a soldier, the Egyptians, in order to augment their regular standing army, increasingly used men from neighboring tribes as police in Egypt and as foreign mercenaries. For dark, bushy-haired (at times edged with painted dots to emphasize the kinky appearance) Nubian mercenaries on stelae of the First Intermediate Period (ca. 2258-2040 B.C.) in the Gebelein region of Upper Egypt, see Fischer, "Nubian Mercenaries" 44-79; Fischer believes that these mercenaries apparently enjoyed considerable prestige and in all likelihood were employed as mercenaries by groups who participated in conflicts preceding the reunification of Egypt. Southern troops were vividly represented by the wooden models of forty black archers found in a tomb of a prince of Assiut, G. Maspero, *Guide du visiteur au musée du Caire*[4] (Cairo 1915) 336-337 and nos. 3345-3346; J. H. Breasted, Jr., *Egyptian Servant Statues,* The Bollingen Series XIII (Washington 1948) 102, *The Egyptian Museum, Cairo: A Brief Description of the Principal Monuments* (Cairo 1963) 61; Posener, *Dictionary* 16 and

photographs on p. 17. (As to the date for these archers scholars vary from the Ninth-Tenth to the Twelfth Dynasty.) Breasted states that the almost black color of the men suggests they are to be identified with the traditional Nubian bowmen; Posener refers to them as black Nubian archers; and the recent Cairo guide, as Negroes. For five well-fed, corpulent Nubian mercenaries depicted in a recruitment scene from the tomb of an official of Tuthmosis IV (1423-1410 B.C.) see N. M. Davies and A. H. Gardiner, *Ancient Egyptian Paintings*, vol. III, *Descriptive Text* (Chicago 1936) 90-93 and plates XLV and XLVI (a Nubian drummer) in vol. I and A. Mekhitarian, translated by S. Gilbert, *Egyptian Painting* (Skira n.d.) 95-97.

56. About the character of the Ethiopian rule in Egypt, T. Säve Söderbergh (*Pharaohs and Mortals* [Indianapolis and New York 1961] 157) remarks that the dark-skinned conquerors did not act like foreign barbarians but considered themselves champions of the ancient religion and succeeded for a while in defending their former Egyptian rulers against the Assyrians.

57. For blacks and Negroes in the Egyptian population, see Posener, *Dictionary* s.v. *Race* 237-238 and A. M. El Batrawi, *Mission archéologique de Nubie 1929-1934: Report on the Human Remains* (Cairo 1935) 160-177. On the racial origins of the XXVth Dynasty, see A. Gardiner, *Egypt of the Pharaohs: An Introduction* (Oxford 1962) 340, Dixon, "Origin of the Kingdom of Kush" 127-132 and literature there cited and R. Oliver and J. D. Fage, *A Short History of Africa* (Penguin Books 1962) 40. P. L. Shinnie, *Meroe: A Civilization of the Sudan* (New York and Washington: Praeger 1967) 30 states that although the origins of the Napata rulers are not known, there is no reason to assume that they were not natives of the region.

58. Dixon, "Origin of the Kingdom of Kush" 130-132. J. Finegan, *Light from the Ancient Past: The Archaeological Background of Judaism and Christianity*[2] (Princeton 1959) fig. 80 and p. 215 considers the strongly Negroid figure as "doubtless" Taharqa. For the Taharqa head in the Cairo Museum see *The Egyptian Museum, Cairo* no. 1185, and for another head (my Fig. 79), see no. 44 in O. Koefoed-Petersen, *Egyptian Sculpture in the Ny Carlsberg Glyptothek* (Copenhagen 1962). For what is perhaps a fourth-century B.C. portrait of one of the last kings of Egypt, see the "Black Royal Head," no. 45 and p. 34, in Koefoed-Petersen, who regards the heavy lips as suggestive of Nubian blood. P. L. Shinnie, *Meroe* 154-155.

59. See Chap. V.

60. M. I. Rostovtzeff, *Roman Empire*[2] I 302-305. P. L. Shinnie, n. 57 *supra*, 99, for the view that Meroïtic art, like other aspects of the culture, has been passed over as "a provincial aberration of Egyptian art containing some extraneous elements," and 114-116.

61. W. Y. Adams, "Post-Pharaonic Nubia. I" 115-120; *id.*, "An Introductory Classification of Meroïtic Pottery," *Kush* XII (1964) 171.

62. W. B. Emery, *Nubian Treasure: An Account of the Discoveries at Ballana and Qustul* (London 1948) 26 says that the identification is not at all certain but that the balance of evidence points to an identification with the Blemmyes; for other views, including identification with Nobatae, Nobadae, and Nobades see L. P. Kirwin, *The Oxford University Excavations at Firka* (London 1939) 39-40 and literature there cited.

63. W. Y. Adams, "Post-Pharaonic Nubia. II" 160-161.

64. Theocritus 7.114. Theocritus uses only one "m"; a letter spelling "Blemmyes" is used in this text (for other variants, see *RE* III s.v. *Blemyes* 566-568).

65. *Scholia in Theocritum Vetera* 7.114a (C. Wendel's edition) 106 (ἔθνος Αἰθιοπικὸν μελανόχρουν); Dionysius "Periegetes," *Orbis descriptio* 220 *GGM* III 114 (αἰθαλέων Βλεμύων), the adjective being used, according to Eustathius (*Commentarii* 220 *GGM* IV 255) because, like Αἰθίοπες, it was derived from αἴθω; Avienus *Descriptio orbis terrae* 330 *GGM* III 180 ("nigri cute").

66. *Dionysiaca* 26.341 (οὐλοκόμων Βλεμύων). Although Nonnus' account of a black, woolly-haired "Blemys," a general of the Indian king Deriades, as one who gave his name to the Blemmyes may be completely worthless, his mention of woolly hair may point to an acquaintance with such a physical characteristic of the Blemmyes.

67. L. P. Kirwan, *Excavations at Firka* 48; A. J. Arkell, *A History of the Sudan from the Earliest Times to 1861,* 2nd ed. rev. (London 1961) 179.

68. 7.114.

69. Strabo 17.1.2.

70. 17.1.53.

71. See Chap. IV.

72. Pomponius Mela *De chorographia* 1.4.23.

73. Cf. C. L. Woolley and D. Randall-MacIver, *Karanòg: The Romano-Nubian Cemetery,* University of Pennsylvania Egyptian Department of the University Museum, Eckley B. Coxe Junior Expedition to Nubia: III, Text (Philadelphia 1910) 87-90 [hereafter abbreviated as Karanòg]; L. P. Kirwan, *Excavations at Firka* 46-48.

74. For other variants see *RE* XVII s.v. Νοῦβαι 1230 and Desanges, *Catalogue* 192-196. With respect to Nobatae and Nobades, Cosmas Indicopleustes *Topographia Christiana* 3.169C [p. 72 in E. O. Winstedt's edition (Cambridge, Eng. 1909)] and Procopius 1.19.28-36 use Νοβάται. Νουβάδες is found in Priscus 21 *Fragmenta Historicorum Graecorum* IV 100-101; in a papyrus describing the menace of the Blemmyes and Nobades in the time of Theodosius II, U. Wilcken, "Heidnisches und Christliches aus Ägypten," *Archiv für Papyrusforschung* I (1901) 399-400; on the stele of a Christian Silko, *Orientis Graeci Inscriptiones Selectae* I no. 201; Nobades and Nobadae, in John of Ephesus' Ecclesiastical History (4.6-4.7 and 4.49-4.52) in edi-

tion of E. W. Brooks, *Iohannis Ephesini Historiae Ecclesiasticae Pars Tertia, Scriptores Syri*, 3rd series, III, *Corpus Scriptorum Christianorum Orientalium* (Louvain 1936) 136-139, 175-179. J. G. Milne, *A History of Egypt under Egyptian Rule*[3], rev. (London 1924) 79, 99, 100, 110 and J. B. Bury, *History of the Later Roman Empire* (London 1931) I, 237 and II 328-330, 371 use Nobadae; M. I. Rostovtzeff, *The Social and Economic History of the Roman Empire*[2], rev. by P. M. Fraser (Oxford 1957) I 301, 305, 307, II 679, n. 57 uses Nobades; A. H. M. Jones, *The Later Roman Empire 284–602* (Norman, Oklahoma 1964) I 611, 656, Nobadae, and II 942 Nobades. In this book Nobades will be used.

75. Strabo 17.1.2.

76. 17.1.53.

77. *Naturalis historia* 6.35.192.

78. *Punica* 3.269.

79. Desanges, *Catalogue* 194.

80. Ptolemy *Geographia* 4.7.10 and 4.6.5 and Desanges, *Catalogue* 194-196 and 227-228. Desanges states that in general the ancients seem to have considered the Nubae and perhaps the Nobades as Libyans (cf. Stephanus of Byzantium s.v. Νοῦβαι).

81. Claudian *De consulatu Stilichonis* 1.254 and Procopius *De bello Persico* 1.19.28-29 and A. J. Arkell, *History of the Sudan*[2] 178-179.

82. For the history of this period, see C. L. Woolley and D. Randall-MacIver, *Karanòg*, III 85-98; U. Monneret de Villard, *Storia della Nubia cristiana* (Rome 1938) 24-52; L. P. Kirwan, *Excavations at Firka* 39-48; W. B. Emery, *Nubian Treasure* 26-32; 55, 59, 68, and plate 13; W. Y. Adams, "Post-Pharaonic Nubia. II" 160-172. For the study of the skeletons of the late Meroïtic period, see A. M. El Batrawi cited in n. 57 *supra*.

83. F. F. Gadallah, "Meroitic Problems" 196-197 states that although the classical account of sub-Egyptian Ethiopia is not always critical and at times reflects hearsay, much is based on a good knowledge of the country and contains a number of points which appear to be true. T. W. Africa, "Herodotus and Diodorus on Egypt," *Journal of Near Eastern Studies* XXII (1963) 258 concludes that unless confirmed by Egyptian sources no oral tradition preserved by Herodotus or Diodorus can be accepted without suspicion.

84. 2.29.

85. Herodotus 2.137-140; Manetho *Aegyptiaca* (Epitome) fragments 66-67 (Loeb 166-168); Diodorus 1.60, 65.

86. Strabo 15.1.6.

87. 3.2.4.

88. See Chap. V.

89. A. J. Arkell, *Early Khartoum: An Account of the Excavation of an Early Occupation Site Carried out by the Sudan Government*

Antiquities Service in 1944-5 (London, New York, Toronto 1949) 111-114, points out (a) that the early Khartoum people belonged to a Negroid race whose pottery and barbed stone spears seem in type to predate the earliest known in Egypt and that it is reasonable to think that they may have been passed on to predynastic Egypt; (b) that the tradition (preserved in Diodorus 3.2.1-4) of the southern origin of many Egyptian customs may contain some truth. H. J. Kantor, reviewing Arkell's book (*AJA* LV [1951] 414-415), considers Arkell's findings perhaps the first tangible evidence in support of those who have questioned the traditional concept that Nubia and Sudan merely received and perpetuated various elements of Egyptian culture. T. W. Africa, "Herodotus and Diodorus on Egypt" 254, n. 14 regards the view of Diodorus 3.3.2-7 that Egypt was a colony of Ethiopians as later propaganda justifying the conqueror Piankhi rather than a valid echo of earlier tradition.

90. See Chap. II.

91. Diodorus 3.8.2; Ptolemy *Geographia* 1.9.7.

92. R. Oliver and J. D. Fage, *Short History of Africa* 40.

93. *Ibid.*

IV. Greek Encounters with Ethiopian Warriors

1. G. H. Beardsley, *The Negro in Greek and Roman Civilization: A Study of the Ethiopian Type* (Baltimore and London 1929) 53. A. R. Burn, *The Pelican History of Greece* (Baltimore 1966) 175 questions the validity of the traditional doubts as to Xerxes' use of Ethiopian troops and notes the use of wild-looking barbarian auxiliaries in the Roman imperial army.

2. See Chap. III, n. 55.

3. Herodotus 2.103-104. The Sesostris of the classical authors has been interpreted as Ramesses II (1301-1234 B.C.) Loeb 389 and as a composite of Sety I (1313-1301 B.C.) and Ramesses II, *Encyclopaedia Britannica,* XX (Chicago, London, Toronto 1960) 377 s.v. *Sesostris.* F. Dvornik, *The Idea of Apostolicity in Byzantium and the Legend of the Apostle Andrew* (Cambridge, Mass. 1958) 174, n. 111 and P. T. English, "Cushites, Colchians, and Khazars," *Journal of Near Eastern Studies* XVIII (1959) 49-53. English holds that Herodotus was correct in his observations on Negroid Colchians. He argues that (1) there was no reason for Herodotus to confuse Negroes and Egyptians; (2) since Herodotus said that Colchians were black and woolly-haired, there is no reason to doubt his report; (3) Abkhazian Negroes living in almost the same area of which Herodotus wrote are a surviving remnant of the Negroid Colchians.

4. See Chap. III.

5. H. R. Hall, *The Civilization of Greece in the Bronze Age* (London 1928) 119-123 believes that the Cretan blacks must have come from Egypt, while A. Evans (*The Palace of Minos at Knossos,* II pt. II [London 1928] 755-756) states that North African terminals of caravan routes to Lake Chad and the Niger should also be considered as points of origins (see Evans, plate XIII for the Minoan blacks). A. R. Burn (n. 1 *supra*) 44 raises the question as to whether the blacks in the fresco are Nubian slaves purchased from Egypt by a "Minos" who could no longer trust his subjects.

6. Homer *Odyssey* 19.246-247 and Chap. III *supra.*

7. Memnon was considered king of the Ethiopians as early as Hesiod, but the loss of the *Aethiopis* of Arctinus creates a serious lacuna with respect to early Greek conceptions of Ethiopians as allies of the Trojans. For Greek views on Memnon and Ethiopians at Troy we must depend on later literary and artistic sources. See Chap. VI.

8. Herodotus 2.152, 154.

9. For the Abu Simbel inscriptions and discussions thereof, see M. N. Tod, *A Selection of Greek Historical Inscriptions*[2], I (Oxford 1946) no. 4 and A. Bernand and O. Masson, "Les Inscriptions grecques d'Abou-Simbel," *REG* LXX (1957) 1-42. For the suggestion that a phrase in the inscription refers to the region of the Fourth in the neighborhood of Dongola and not the Second Cataract, see S. Sauneron and J. Yoyotte, "La Campagne nubienne de Psammétique II et sa signification historique," *Bulletin de l'Institut Français d'archéologie orientale du Caire* L (1952) 157-207.

10. For the Cyprus statues, see E. Gjerstad, J. Lindros, E. Sjöquist, and A. Westholm, *The Swedish Cyprus Expedition, Finds and Results of the Excavations in Cyprus: 1927-1931,* vol. II, Plates (Stockholm 1935) plate CCXXXIX, nos. 1095 and 1228 and E. Gjerstad, *The Swedish Cyprus Expedition,* vol. IV: *The Cypro-Geometric Cypro-Archaic and Cypro-Classical Periods* (Stockholm 1948) 103-104, 356, 466-467. For the Greek view of Ethiopians in Cyprus, see Herodotus 7.90. Professor Gjerstad has called my attention to a Negro head of faience found in tomb 51 at Lapithos, dating from Middle Cypriote II-III, illustrated in P. Aström, *The Middle Cypriote Bronze Age* (Lund 1957) 158, fig. 18. For a human mask of a Negro in gold from a bronze-age tomb near Klaudia in the Larnaka district in Cyprus, see F. H. Marshall, *Catalogue of the Jewellery, Greek, Etruscan, and Roman, in the Departments of Antiquities, British Museum* (London 1911), no. 144, fig. 2 and pp. 14-15.

11. Herodotus 3.17-26.

12. Herodotus 7.69-70; P. Graindor, "Mélanges d'archéologie et d'épigraphie: Les vases au nègre," *Musée belge* XII (1908) 29-30, and "Mélanges d'archéologie," *Bulletin of the Faculty of Arts, University of Egypt,* vol. III, pt. 2 (Cairo 1955) 105-110.

13. Aeschylus, *Persae* 311-312. H. R. Hall, *The Cambridge Ancient*

History, vol. III: *The Assyrian Empire* (Cambridge, Eng. 1925) 315 in a discussion of the leaders of the Persian fleet as given by Aeschylus lists Arcteus as Ethiopian (Etearchus, Taharqa), comments on the prominence of Egyptian names included in the Persian navy, and suggests that although they were probably all fictitious, they were invented to give a general idea of the names of the foreign leadership in the battle of Salamis. H. J. Rose, *A Commentary on the Surviving Plays of Aeschylus,* I (Amsterdam 1957) 114 in commenting on πηγαῖς Νείλου of lines 311-312 states that if πηγαῖς is to be regarded with a view to geographical accuracy, persons living in this area would come from Upper Egypt, perhaps from Nubia, and that if Aeschylus is not using the phrase in such a sense, he may mean from somewhere up country.

14. Aeschylus *Persae* 315 and Chap. I, n. 94 *supra.*

15. To the bibliography and discussion of the vases appearing in G. H. Beardsley, *The Negro* 48-54 and nos. 74-99, add A. D. Fraser, The Panoply of the Ethiopian Warrior," *AJA* XXXIX (1935) 41-45; A. Bovon, "La Représentation des guerriers perses et la notion de barbare dans la 1re moitié du Ve siècle," *Bulletin de correspondance hellénique* LXXXVII (1963) 598; Beazley, *Attic Red-Figure Vase-Painters²*, I (Oxford 1963) 267-268, who lists thirty-one alabastra depicting a single Negro, one with two Negroes; two plates with a Negro; eight alabastra and one plate with Amazons, one with a Negro and Amazon on the same alabastron. G. Perrot, *Histoire de l'art de l'antiquité,* vol. X: *La Grèce archaïque: La céramique d'Athènes* (Paris 1914) 694 and A. D. Fraser, "Ethiopian Warrior," 41-45 hold that Negroes entered Greece in the army of Xerxes, whereas P. Graindor, "Les vases au nègre," 30 suggests that the Greeks in the Ionian expedition of 498 B.C. may have seen Negroes. Fraser has argued that the Negroes depicted were eastern Ethiopians mentioned by Herodotus 7.70, whereas Graindor maintained that the artist was concerned with Ethiopians of the Sudan. The Graindor view is supported by the obvious attempt of the artist to represent the hair characteristic of many types of African Negroes. The "dots" by which the hair is depicted resemble the style chosen by many Greek artists to portray the Negro's hair, noticed by Herodotus (7.70). (For the white figures, see D. von Bothmer, *Amazons in Greek Art* [Oxford 1957] 95, 152, 158 and for Negro and Amazon on the same alabastron, inv. 3382 Staatliche Museen Antiken-Abteilung, Berlin [Beazley, *Red-Figure²*, I 269] and for Negro on a plate, Taranto, Museo Nazionale, I.G. 4424 [Beazley, *Red-Figure²*, I p. 268, no. 34].) The Greek victory over a Persian army which included Ethiopians may explain the artist's choice of the Negro motif. But what would have motivated the artist to depict Amazons, similarly dressed and equipped, at times singly and, in one instance, on the same alabastra with a Negro? Perhaps the artist recalled that Ethiopians and Amazons had fought

as allies of the Trojans against the Greeks in an earlier Greco-Asian conflict. And such an evocation of the past, celebrated in epic, would have been even more fitting if the designers of the fifth-century vases were acquainted with the tradition, recorded by Diodorus (3.52.1-55.11), of African Amazons reported as inhabiting the western part of Libya near Ethiopia (and if Libyan Amazons lived near Ethiopians, why not dress and equip them alike?); cf. scholiast on Apollonius Rhodius 2, 963/65c (C. Wendel's second edition [Berlin 1958] 199), for the statement that Amazons lived in Ethiopia. In any case the artist, proud of a recent Greek victory over the Persians, perhaps reasoned as follows: just as in our epic past the Trojans, our eastern foes, suffered defeat in spite of foreign recruits from distant lands — Amazons and Ethiopians — so in our most recent encounter with inhabitants of Asia we have defeated the Persians, though reinforced by foreign troops — Libyans and Ethiopians — the latter, descendants of a people who once had conquered and ruled Egypt.

16. Pliny *Naturalis historia* 36.4.17 ascribes the Rhamnus Nemesis to Agoracritus, but Pausanias 1.33.2-3 assigns the sculpture to Phidias; cf. G. M. A. Richter, *The Sculpture and Sculptors of the Greeks* (New Haven and London 1929) 180-181. See J. G. Frazer, *Pausanias's Description of Greece* II (London 1898) 458; and C. Picard, "Pourquoi la Némésis de Rhamnonte tenait-elle à sa dextre une coupe ornée de têtes de nègres?" *Revue archéologique* (1958) 98-99, who suggests that the Ethiopian figures on the Rhamnus phiale, associated with the Ethiopians in the Persian army, were also reminiscent of an Egyptian practice of depicting in art heads of Negroes as a sign of Pharaonic triumphs.

17. For a discussion of the Panagurishte phiale see Chap. VI and notes 32-36 and bibliography there cited.

18. E. D. Ross, *The Persians* (Oxford 1931) 35; E. E. Herzfeld, *Iran in the Near East: Archaeological Studies Presented in the Lowell Lectures at Boston* (London and New York 1941) plate LXXXI; A. T. Olmstead, *History of the Persian Empire [Achaemenid Period]* (Chicago 1948) 244; and E. F. Schmidt, *Persepolis I: Structures. Reliefs. Inscriptions.* The University of Chicago Oriental Institute Publications, vol. LXVIII (Chicago 1953) 90 and plate 49, cf. Thronebearer described on p. 120. J. Leroy, "Les 'Ethiopiens' de Persépolis," *Annales d'Ethiopie* V (1963) 295 comments on the Negroid nose and hair of the Persepolis Ethiopians.

19. Herodotus 3.97. L. S. de Camp, "Xerxes' Okapi and Greek Geography," *Isis* LIV (1963) 123-125 considers the Negroid figures pygmies (they are shorter than the Persian leader, but such identification seems doubtful), suggests that the scene was inspired by an expedition sent by Xerxes to central Africa, within sight of the Ruwenzori range, and that later Greek references to Ethiopian snows and Aristotle's mention of Silver Mountain stemmed from informa-

tion which reached the Greeks as a result of the Xerxes expedition.

20. Frontinus *Strategemata* 1.11.18; S. Gsell, *Histoire ancienne de l'Afrique du nord* I[3] (Paris 1921) 303, n. 6 points out that we do not know where these blacks came from; and in II[2] (Paris 1921) 367 refers to them as doubtlessly Negroes, but adds that the report was perhaps a legend; however, scholars in their discussions of the Mediterranean use of black troops have too often overlooked the accumulation of evidence pointing to a long history of black mercenaries in the Aegean and Mediterranean world.

21. Diodorus 20.58.

22. G. M. A. Richter, *Catalogue of Engraved Gems, Greek, Etruscan, and Roman,* Metropolitan Museum of Art, New York (Rome 1956) plate XVI, no. 95 and p. 26.

23. M. I. Rostovtzeff, *The Social and Economic History of the Hellenistic World,* I (Oxford 1941) 381-383.

24. 1.37.5.

25. N. 9 *supra.*

26. C. Préaux, "Sur les communications de l'Ethiopie avec l'Egypte hellénistique," *Chronique d'Egypte* XXVII (1952) 261-263.

27. F. Preisigke, *Sammelbuch griechischer Urkunden aus Ägypten,* I (Strasbourg 1915) no. 302; D. Randall-MacIver and C. L. Woolley, *Buhen,* University of Pennsylvania Egyptian Department of the University Museum, Eckley B. Coxe Junior Expedition to Nubia: vol. VII, Text (Philadelphia 1911) 126. C. Préaux, "Communications," 263.

28. F. Preisigke, *Sammelbuch* no. 5111; E. Bevan, *A History of Egypt under the Ptolemaic Dynasty* (London 1927) 77; C. Préaux, "Communications" 264.

29. Diodorus 3.36.3; Strabo 16.4.7-8; 16.4.10; 16.4.13; 17.1.5; Pliny *Naturalis historia* 6.34.171. *Periplus Maris Erythraei* 3 *GGM* II 258-259.

30. Pliny *Naturalis historia* 6.35.183; E. Bevan, *History* 76.

31. Athenaeus 5.201.

32. 17.87; 7.113-114; and A. S. F. Gow, *Theocritus,* Edited with a Translation and Commentary, II (Cambridge 1950) 159-160.

33. Diodorus 3.36.3-4.

34. Diodorus 3.18.4.

35. *Orientis Graeci Inscriptiones Selectae,* I nos. 82, 86; Strabo 16.4.15 and E. Bevan, *History* 243.

36. For Ethiopian participation in Egyptian rebellions under the Ptolemies, see E. Bevan, *History* 260-261, 274, 293-294, 324; cf. C. Préaux, "Esquisse d'une histoire des révolutions égyptiennes sous les Lagides," *Chronique d'Egypte* XI (1936) esp. 535-536; M. I. Rostovtzeff, *History of the Hellenistic World,* II 709-719.

37. Agatharchides, *De Mari Erythraeo* 20 *GGM* I 119; E. Bevan, *History* 260.

38. M. I. Rostovtzeff, *History of the Hellenistic World* II, 712. Harmachis and Anchmachis, according to Bevan, *History* (260) may have been Egyptian or Ethiopian. P. W. Pestman, "Harmachis et Anchmachis, deux rois indigènes du temps des Ptolémées," *Chronique d'Egypte* XL (1965) 168 states that Nubians may have been among the insurgents but that we know little of the origin of the rebels or the revolt.

39. E. Bevan, *History* 293-294, 324-325; M. I. Rostovtzeff, *The Social and Economic History of the Roman Empire*, 2nd ed. rev. by P. M. Fraser, I (Oxford 1957) 303.

40. M. Launey, *Recherches sur les armées hellénistiques*, Bibliothèque des Ecoles Françaises d'Athènes et de Rome, I (Paris 1949) 59-60 and 598 and the sources there cited. Although Launey states that many blacks and desert dwellers, and Libyans in particular, may be concealed under the pseudo-ethnic "Persian," his opinion with respect to the Ptolemaic use of blacks is not supported by the evidence which reveals (1) that blacks had been regularly used by Egyptians both in Egypt and abroad, at some time as auxiliaries perhaps by the Cretans, and by the Persians against the Greeks; (2) that the Ethiopians had actually conquered and ruled Egypt; (3) that the military experience of the Ethiopians over a long period of time and their reputations as warriors were obviously the reasons for their use by the peoples mentioned. Further, an echo of Ptolemaic military experiences with Ethiopian warriors appears in Agatharchides *De Mari Erythraeo* 16 GGM I 118. It is highly probable that experience as soldiers can account for the presence of numerous blacks in Ptolemaic Egypt. For a study of the designation "Persian," see also J. F. Oates, "The Status Designation: Πέρσης, τῆς ἐπιγονῆς," *Yale Classical Studies* XVIII (1963) 1-129.

V. *Roman Encounters with Ethiopian Warriors*

1. *Punica* 3.265-9.

2. "L'Eléphant d'Annibal," *Revue numismatique* 3rd ser., XIV (1896) 1-13 and "L'Eléphant d'Annibal," *Mélanges numismatiques*, 3rd ser. (Paris 1900) 153-157 (note the excellent depiction of the Negroid features in the reproduction of the coin); P. R. Garrucci, *Le monete dell'Italia antica: Raccolta generale del P. Raffaele Garrucci*, pt. 2 (Rome 1885) 58, nos. 11-15 and plate LXXV, nos. 11-15; [R. S. Poole], *A Catalogue of the Greek Coins in the British Museum. Italy* (London 1873) p. 15, nos. 17-21.

3. C. T. Seltman, *Greek Coins: A History of Metallic Currency and Coinage down to the Fall of the Hellenistic Kingdoms*[2] (London 1960) 250.

4. H. H. Scullard, "Hannibal's Elephants," *The Numismatic Chronicle and Journal of the Royal Numismatic Society,* 6th ser. VIII (1948) 163; W. Gowers and H. H. Scullard, "Hannibal's Elephants Again," *The Numismatic Chronicle* X (1950) 279-280; cf. my note, "A Note on Hannibal's Mahouts," *The Numismatic Chronicle* XIV (1954) 197-198. S. Gsell, *Histoire ancienne de l'Afrique du Nord,* II[2] (Paris 1921) 408 and n. 6. Gsell (408) states, without an explanation, that he sees no reason that the Carthaginians should have employed Negroes as mahouts. Gowers and Scullard (271), however, point out that when the Ptolemies first used elephants from Ethiopia they imported Indian trainers, but that eventually Ἰνδοί was probably applied to mahouts irrespective of their origin. W. R. Paton in Loeb Polybius (1.40.15) translates Ἰνδοῖς as mahouts. On elephants in the Carthaginian army, see Daremberg-Saglio s.v. *Elephas* 538 and G. T. Griffith, *The Mercenaries of the Hellenistic World* (Cambridge, Eng. 1935) 214.

5. See Chap. VII.

6. *Tactica* 2.2 and 19.6. The Ethiopian king Hydaspes, according to Heliodorus (9.16, 18), employed tower-bearing elephants with crews of six archers each, the elephants being protected by iron armor.

7. F. Hintze, "Preliminary Report on the Excavations at Musawwarat Es Sufra, 1960-1," *Kush* X (1962) 184. Some reliefs were found on the Lion Temple, built between 235 and 221 B.C. with some restoration between 221 and 218 B.C., 125 kilometers northeast of Khartoum. For reproductions of these elephants, see Hintze, fig. 6, p. 180, plates LII and LVa and descriptions on pp. 180, 183-184. For a further discussion of elephants at Musawwarat-es Sofra, see P. L. Shinnie, *Meroe: A Civilization of the Sudan* (New York and Washington 1967) 93-94, 100-101 (for the belief that African war elephants used in Ptolemaic and Roman times were trained by Meroïtes), 111, 127-128, 146, fig. 27 for a relief of a king riding an elephant, fig. 48 for elephants engraved on a bronze beaker, and plate 20 for the wall terminating in the figure of an elephant. Although Cosmas Indicopleustes (*Topographia Christiana* 11.449D, p. 325, E. O. Winstedt's edition) wrote that Ethiopians did not know how to tame elephants, both the literary evidence and the recent archaeological finds indicate clearly that the Ethiopians were experienced in handling elephants.

8. *Poenulus* 1289-1291; cf. Paulus ex Festo (W. M. Lindsay's edition 26); P. Nixon, Plautus (Loeb) IV 131; G. E. Duckworth, *The Complete Roman Drama,* I (New York 1942) 777; *Oxford Latin Dictionary,* fasc. I (Oxford 1968) s.v. *Aegyptini* 63.

9. Naples, Museo Nazionale, no. 124845. A. Mau, "Ausgrabungen von Pompeji Insula VI 15," *Mitteilungen des deutschen archäologischen Instituts, Römische Abteilung* XIII (1898) 19-20 and A. Ruesch, *Guida illustrata del Museo Nazionale di Napoli* (Naples 1908) 145 and fig. 44. A. Levi, *Le terrecotte figurate del Museo Naz-*

ionale di Napoli (Florence 1926), plate XIII and no. 848 on pp. 196-197 describes the driver as "moro." J. D. Beazley, *Etruscan Vase-Painting* (Oxford 1947) 212 says that the driver looks like a Negro. An examination of the original, however, reveals that the driver of the Pompeiian elephant is pronouncedly Negroid, especially as to nose and lips. Gowers and Scullard (n. 4 *supra*) 281 point out that the elephant depicted is African, that in light of the Campanian provenance it may depict one of Hannibal's animals, and that Hannibal may have employed some Negro drivers for both African and Asian (the elephant on the bronze coinage is considered Asian) elephants. A tower-bearing elephant ridden by two warriors and a driver, all of whom are brown-colored, on a Villa Giulia plate has been interpreted as a reference to Pyrrhus' elephants, G. Q. Giglioli, *Corpus Vasorum Antiquorum, Italia: Museo Nazionale di Villa Giulia in Roma* (Rome, Milan n.d.) fasc. III, IV B, 9, plate 3, 1-3, no. 23949. The figures depicted on the Villa Giulia plate are of a dark brown color, but the indeterminate features make it impossible to identify the subjects more precisely.

10. Several studies have treated various aspects of Roman contacts with Ethiopians during this period. None, however, has considered this subject from the point of view of the classical image of the Ethiopian warrior or in the light of the long history of Ethiopian military and diplomatic relations with Greek and Roman inhabitants of Egypt.

11. C. L. Woolley and D. Randall MacIver, *Karanòg* 85-98; J. Lesquier, *L'Armée romaine d'Egypte d'Auguste à Dioclétien,* fasc. 1, Mémoires publiés par les membres de l'Institut Français d'Archéologie Orientale du Caire, XLI (Cairo 1918) 9-15, 458-475; U. Monneret de Villard, *Storia della Nubia cristiana, Orientalia Christiana Analecta,* CXVIII (Rome 1938) 7-60; W. B. Emery, *Nubian Treasure: An Account of the Discoveries at Ballana and Qustul* (London 1948) 25-32; L. P. Kirwan, "Rome Beyond the Southern Egyptian Frontier," *The Geographical Journal* CXXIII (1957) 13-19; M. I. Rostovtzeff, *The Social and Economic History of the Roman Empire*[2], rev. by P. M. Fraser, II (Oxford 1957) 303-308.

12. 17.1.53.

13. *CIL* III 14147[5]; H. Dessau, *Inscriptiones Latinae Selectae,* III (Berlin 1916) no. 8995; N. Lewis and M. Reinhold, *Roman Civilization,* Selected Readings Edited with an Introduction and Notes, Vol. II: *The Empire* (New York 1955) 45-46.

14. The title "Candace," according to Pliny (*Naturalis historia* 6.35.186), was passed on through a succession of Meroïtic queens for many years; see *Acts* 8:27 for the Ethiopian eunuch, a minister of Candace, the queen of the Ethiopians, whom Philip baptized and Ps.-Callisthenes *Historia Alexandri Magni* 3.18 (pp. 115-116 in W. Kroll's edition [Berlin 1926]) for Candace, queen of Meroë, report-

edly visited by Alexander the Great. Though the exact significance of "Candace" is not clear, the title seems to suggest its application to Queen Mothers, perhaps at times to the mother of a reigning king. See D. Dunham, *The Royal Cemeteries of Kush,* vol. IV, *Royal Tombs at Meroë and Barkal* (Boston 1957) 8.

15. 17.1.53-1.54; cf. Dio Cassius 54.5.4-6 and Pliny *Naturalis historia* 6.35.181-182. S. Jameson, "Chronology of the Campaign of Aelius Gallus and C. Petronius," *The Journal of Roman Studies* LVIII (London: Society for the Promotion of Roman Studies 1968) pts. I and II 71-84 argues for a date before the spring or early summer of 24 B.C. for Petronius' first campaign, and for 22 B.C. as the probable date for the conclusion of the second; and examines several plausible reasons for the Ethiopian expeditions (punitive reprisals against Ethiopian brigandage, economic gain, and territorial expansion).

16. Strabo at one point states that the Ethiopians who lived in the south and in the direction of Meroë were not numerous, did not band together, and were ill-equipped for warfare. If this picture of isolated, poorly armed peoples was an accurate description of the Ethiopians, how then did Strabo explain the fact that the Ethiopians were able to capture several cities and enslave the inhabitants? His explanation is that it was by a surprise attack at a time when the Roman garrison in Egypt was undermanned, there being three cohorts at Syene (the only figures mentioned here). When Petronius counterattacked, however, figures become more precise in the Strabo account — a Roman force of fewer than 10,000 infantry and 800 cavalry routed 30,000 Ethiopians. At another time, however, when the Ethiopians threatened Premnis, Strabo says that Candace had advanced with many thousands of men. At this point, Petronius agreed to a summit conference between Candace's ambassadors and Augustus, who granted all the Ethiopian requests.

17. *Naturalis historia* 6.35.182.

18. F. Ll. Griffith, "Meroïtic Studies IV," *JEA* IV (1917) 159-168 states that a Meroïtic version of the encounter seems to indicate that prisoners were captured in three campaigns and "a fair number" in one; and Rostovtzeff, *History of the Roman Empire*[2], II 679, n. 56 comments that the peace terms of Augustus demonstrate that Strabo probably exaggerated the Roman victory and that there is some truth in claims made in Meroïtic inscriptions. Cf. R. Paribeni, *L'Italia imperiale, da Ottaviano a Teodosio* (Milan n.d.) 92. The *Monumentum Ancyranum* 5.26.22 records that the Roman army penetrated Ethiopia up to *oppidum Nabata . . . cui proxima est Meroe.* Noting the great distance between Napata and Meroë, Monneret de Villard, *Storia* 10-11 concludes that either the geographical error or the boasting was great. Jameson, "Chronology" 82 states: "The sources throughout smack of apologia. Augustus was aiming at territorial expansion and failed."

19. J. Garstang, A. H. Sayce, and F. Ll. Griffith, *Meroë: The City of the Ethiopians* (Oxford 1911) plate XXXIII 3 and Monneret de Villard, *Storia* 12.

20. R. West, *Römische Porträt-Plastik* (Munich 1933) plate XXIX, no. 120; P. L. Shinnie, *Meroe* 48.

21. 17.1.54.

22. *Allard Pierson Museum. Algemeene Gids* (Amsterdam 1937) 50 no. 465 and plate XXV and M. I. Rostovtzeff, *The Social and Economic History of the Hellenistic World,* II (Oxford, Clarendon Press 1941) 900 and plate CI, fig. 2.

23. The Graeco-Roman Museum at Alexandria, nos. 23099, 19505, and 23211. E. Breccia, *Terrecotte figurate greche e greco-egizie del Museo di Alessandria,* Monuments de l'Egypte gréco-romaine, vol. II, fasc. 2 (Bergamo 1934) plate LXXI, nos. 362-363, p. 50, nos. 317-318.

24. K. A. Neugebauer, "Aus der Werkstatt eines griechischen Toreuten in Aegypten," in *Schumacher Festschrift* (Mainz 1930) 236 and plate 23, East Berlin, Staatliche Museen, nos. Misc. 10485-86.

25. *CIG* III 5080.

26. F. Ll. Griffith, *Karanòg: The Meroitic Inscriptions of Shablûl and Karanòg,* University of Pennsylvania Egyptian Department of the University Museum, Eckley B. Coxe Junior Expedition to Nubia: Vol. VI (Philadelphia 1911) no. 112. W. K. Simpson reports that the 1961-62 excavations of the University of Pennsylvania and Yale University in Egyptian Nubia discovered a Meroïtic tomb stele which mentions two envoys to Rome, in "The Pennsylvania-Yale Excavations in Nubia," *AJA* LXVII (1963) 217.

27. F. Ll. Griffith, *Meroitic Inscriptions Part II,* Napata to Philae and Miscellaneous (London 1912) 54-55, no. 129.

28. F. Ll. Griffith, *Catalogue of the Demotic Graffiti of the Dodecaschoenus,* Vol. I, Text (Oxford 1937), Ph. 416, pp. 11, 114-119. For a discussion of this and other inscriptions pertinent to relations between the Romans and the Blemmyes in the third century A.D., see D. G. Haycock, "Later Phases of Meroïtic Civilization," *JEA* LIII (1967) 112-118; D. Dunham, *Royal Cemeteries of Kush* (cited n. 14 *supra*) 186 (21-3-375) and fig. 122 for an amphora with a Latin stamp found in a tomb of Teqērideamani.

29. *CIG* IV 4915 C (p. 1224); F. Ll. Griffith, *Meroitic Inscriptions* 47; *Catalogue of Demotic Graffiti* 11, 116, 118; and Dunham, *Royal Cemeteries of Kush* 3 who suggests that Teqērideamani ruled at least from A.D. 246 to 266.

30. Haycock, "Later Phases of Meroïtic Civilization" 118.

31. J. Baillet, *Inscriptions grecques et latines des tombeaux des rois ou syringes,* Mémoires publiés par les membres de l'Institut Français d'Archéologie Orientale du Caire, XLII (1926) 242, no. 1094.

32. Garstang, Sayce, and Griffith, *Meroë* 4. Kirwan, "Rome" 18.

33. *CIL* III 83. For the several interpretations of this inscription, which has been dated as early as the first century A.D. and as late as 600 A.D., see J. De Decker, "Le Culte d'Isis à Méroé en Ethiopie," *Revue de l'instruction en Belgique* LIV (1911) 293-310; F. Hintze, *Studien zur meroitischen Chronologie und zu den Opfertafeln aus den Pyramiden von Meroe* (Berlin 1959) = *Abhandlungen der deutschen Akademie der Wissenschaften zu Berlin, Klasse für Sprachen, Literatur und Kunst,* 1959, no. 2, 29; P. L. Shinnie, "A Late Latin Inscription," *Kush* IX (1961) 284-286 and plate XXXV; J. Leclant in his review of Hintze's *Studien* in *Orientalia* XXXII (1963) 104; and F. Hintze, "The Latin Inscription from Musawwarat Es Sufra," *Kush* XII (1964) 296-298.

34. Pliny 6.35.181; Seneca *Quaestiones naturales* 6.8.3.

35. For views on Nero's Ethiopian interests, see Woolley and Randall-MacIver, *Karanòg* 86; J. G. Milne, *A History of Egypt under Roman Rule*[3], rev. (London 1924) 22-23; J. G. C. Anderson in *The Cambridge Ancient History,* X (Cambridge, Eng. 1934) 778-779; M. I. Rostovtzeff, *History of the Roman Empire*[2], rev. by P. M. Fraser, I 303; Kirwan, "Rome" 16; and Hintze, *Studien* 28-29. For a dissertation on Greco-Roman contacts with eastern Africa, especially the Auxumite kingdom, see S. Hable-Selassie, *Beziehungen Äthiopiens zur griechisch-römischen Welt,* Habelts Dissertationsdrucke: Reihe Alte Geschichte, Heft 2 (Bonn 1964).

36. A. Vogliano, *Un papiro storico greco della Raccolta Milanese e le campagne dei romani in Etiopia* (Milan 1940) 1-24. Several inscriptions from a temple in the Thebaid record the thanks of those saved from the fury of the Troglodytes, W. Dittenberger, *Orientis Graeci Inscriptiones Selectae,* I (Leipzig 1903) nos. 70-71.

37. E. G. Turner, "Papyrus 40 'della Raccolta Milanese,'" *JRS* XL (1950) 57-59.

38. Kirwan, "Rome" 17 who sees an inconsistency in a military operation conducted by an exploring party which required a military escort from Meroë.

39. 3.2.4-3.1.

40. Strabo 17.1.54.

41. Many problems concerning the details, particularly the chronology, of this period, have been covered by several scholars. For reconstructions of the period and for Roman relations with the Blemmyes and Nobades, see Woolley and Randall-MacIver, *Karanòg* 90-98; J. G. Milne, *History of Egypt* 70, 76, 79, 100, 104, 110-111; J. B. Bury, *History of the Later Roman Empire,* I (London 1931) *passim;* Emery, *Nubian Treasure* 26-32.

42. *Chronicon Paschale* in *Corpus Scriptorum Historiae Byzantinae,* I (Bonn 1832) 504-505.

43. Scriptores Historiae Augustae [hereafter abbreviated as SHA] *Tyranni Triginta* 22.6-7. L. Mussius Aemilianus had been prefect of

Egypt as early as 257 A.D., see J. G. Milne, "Aemilianus the 'Tyrant,'" *JEA* X (1924) 80-82 and A. Alföldi in *The Cambridge Ancient History,* XII (Cambridge, Eng. 1939) 173-174, and 186.

44. F. Ll. Griffith, *Catalogue of Demotic Graffiti* 83, Ph. 252.

45. SHA, *Aurelianus* 33.4; *Firmus* 3 notes that Aurelian crushed Firmus, who had maintained the closest relations with the Blemmyes.

46. *Ibid., Probus* 17.2, 19.2. For the confusion in the record of these counteroffensives and the problems of the identity of Probus, see Woolley and Randall-MacIver, *Karanòg* 91 and Loeb SHA, *Probus* 370, n. 2.

47. Procopius *De bello Persico* 1.19.29-35; cf. A. H. M. Jones, *The Later Roman Empire 284-602: A Social Economic and Administrative Survey,* I (Norman: University of Oklahoma Press 1964) 611 on Roman system of alliances with tribes and use of periodic gifts and regular subsidies to gain support as buffer states. For a Diocletianic coin found in the Sudan, see Chap. III and n. 40.

48. Olympiodorus 37 *Fragmenta Historicorum Graecorum* IV 66.

49. Bury, *Later Roman Empire,* I 237; U. Wilcken, "Heidnisches und Christliches aus Ägypten," *Archiv für Papyrusforschung* I (1901) 399-400.

50. Evagrius *Historia ecclesiastica* 1.7.259-260; Emery, *Nubian Treasure* 29 suggests 429 A.D. as the date for raids on the Kharga settlements and Bury, *Later Roman Empire,* I 238 suggests the early years of Marcian's reign.

51. U. Wilcken, n. 49 *supra.*

52. Priscus 21 *Fragmenta Historicorum Graecorum,* IV 100-101. L.-A. Christophe, "Sanctuaires nubiens disparus," *Chronique d'Egypte* XXXVIII (1963) 17-29, commenting on Maximin's concession to the Blemmyes, argues that the existence of twenty and perhaps twenty-one Nubian temples in the Dodekaschoinos can be accounted for only by the desire of each Nubian village to enjoy for a few hours the divine presence of Isis.

53. Jordanes *Romana* 333 (ed. T. Mommsen, *Monumenta Germaniae Historica* [Berlin 1882] 43); cf. Evagrius *Historia ecclesiastica* 2.5.

54. For an account of the relations between the Blemmyes and the Romans during the reign of Justin I, see A. A. Vasiliev, *Justin the First* [*An Introduction to the Epoch of Justinian the Great*] (Cambridge, Mass. 1950) 285-288. For the papyrus, see J. Maspero, ed., *Catalogue général des antiquités égyptiennes du Musée du Caire: Papyrus grecs d'époque byzantine,* I, fasc. 1 (Cairo 1910) 16-18, no. 67004. On the civil and military powers of the *dux* of the Thebaid in the fifth and sixth centuries A.D., see A. H. M. Jones (cited in n. 47 *supra*) 656-657.

55. J. Maspero, *Catalogue* 36-39, no. 67009.

56. *Blemyomachiae Fragmenta* in A. Ludwich, *Eudociae Augus-*

tae, Procli Lycii, Claudiani Carminum Graecorum Reliquiae. Accedunt Blemyomachiae Fragmenta (Leipzig 1897) 190-195 for the fragments and 183-189 for views on the date and the relevance of the fragments to the Roman difficulties with the Blemmyes; Bury, *Later Roman Empire* I 238; Vasiliev, *Justin* 42, 285-286.

57. L. Mitteis and U. Wilcken, *Grundzüge und Chrestomathie der Papyruskunde,* I (Leipzig and Berlin 1912) no. 7, pp. 13-14; F. Bilabel, *Sammelb.* III (Berlin and Leipzig 1926) no. 6257, p. 39. Mitteis and Wilcken date the letter about the sixth century; J. B. Bury, *History of the Later Roman Empire,* II (London 1931) 330 suggests as probable dates the reign of Anastasius I (491-518 A.D.) or Justin I (518-527 A.D.); and *RE* III s.v. *Blemyes* 567, the sixth to the eighth century.

58. See Chap. IX.

59. Procopius *De bello Persico* 1.19.37.

60. J. Maspero, "Un Dernier Poète grec d'Egypte: Dioscore, fils d'Apollôs," *REG* XXIV (1911) 426-427, 430-431; Vasiliev, *Justin* 288.

61. *CIG* III no. 5072; *Orientis Graeci Inscriptiones Selectae,* I no. 201. R. M. Haywood's statement in *The Myth of Rome's Fall* (New York 1958) 16 of the peoples south of Roman Egypt as uncivilized nomads and the weakness of their military potential seems to overlook the prolonged difficulties of the Romans with the southerners.

62. Ptolemy *Geographia* 1.8.4. M. Cary and E. H. Warmington, *The Ancient Explorers* (London 1929) 182 date the expedition of Septimius Flaccus about 70 or 80 A.D. E. H. Warmington (*Oxford Classical Dictionary*) s.v. *Libya* 504 lists the date of Maternus' mission as A.D. 100(?) and states that Maternus reached the Sudanese steppe, probably near Lake Chad. Cary and Warmington 182 state that in any case Maternus emerged from the Sahara to the Sudanese steppe. R. Syme in *The Cambridge Ancient History,* XI (Cambridge, Eng. 1936) 145 suggests that Julius Maternus was perhaps a merchant rather than a soldier and that the Romans reached Lake Chad; *RE* X 676 refers to Maternus as a Roman officer. B. E. Thomasson, *Die Statthalter der römischen Provinzen Nordafricas von Augustus bis Diocletianus,* II (Lund 1960) 160 considers Septimius Flaccus *leg. Aug. pro pr. leg. III Aug.*, a possibility which J. Desanges recognizes, "Note sur la datation de l'expédition de Julius Maternus au pays d'Agisymba," *Latomus: REL* XXIII (1964) 723 and who (713-725) argues for a time between 85 and 87, probably 86 A.D., as the date of Septimius Flaccus' expedition (accepted by *Prosopographia Imperii Romani,* II pt. IV, fasc. 3 [Berlin 1966] 414) and places Maternus' mission between 87 and 90 A.D.

63. For Lepcis' trans-Saharan trade, see R. M. Haywood "Roman Africa" in *An Economic Survey of Ancient Rome,* IV (Baltimore 1938) 62 who states that Lepcis and other cities may have been the

terminals of caravan routes coming from the interior and that products such as ivory, gems, slaves, beasts for games, and perhaps gold dust must have been the principal objects of caravan commerce.

64. G. Charles-Picard, "Tunisia" s.v. Archaeological News: Classical Lands, *AJA* LII (1948) 498 and plate XLVI; G. and C. Charles-Picard, *Daily Life in Carthage at the Time of Hannibal* (New York 1961) 216 and G. Picard, *Carthage* (New York 1965) plate 2, p. 18.

65. L. Foucher, *Hadrumetum:* Publications de l'Université de Tunis, Faculté des Lettres — 1ère Série: *Archéologie. Histoire* — vol. X (Paris 1964) 170-171 makes this observation with reference to a marble of a second-century A.D. Negro boy found at Hadrumetum.

66. SHA, *Septimius Severus* 22.4-5.

67. Cf. G. L. Cheesman, *The Auxilia of the Roman Imperial Army* (Oxford 1914) 86-89. Mr. Anthony R. Birley of Leeds University has called to my attention a *numerus Maurorum* stationed at a third-century A.D. garrison at Aballava (Burgh-by-Sands) and has suggested that the Ethiopian in the army of Septimius Severus was serving in that fort. For the inscription attesting the presence of a *numerus Maurorum* at Aballava, see R. G. Collingwood and R. P. Wright, *The Roman Inscriptions of Britain* I (Oxford 1965) 626, no. 2042.

68. For photographs of the soldier, see the figure to the right with the conical shaped helmet in F. Castagnoli, *Foro Romano* (Milan 1957) plate 42, and R. Brilliant, *The Arch of Septimius Severus in the Roman Forum* (Rome 1967) = volume XXIX Memoirs of the American Academy in Rome, plates 78 c, d. Brilliant (247) refers to the figures in question as "full, fleshy profiles, large curving noses with well defined nostrils, full lips and strong heavy chins."

69. For Lusius Quietus as full-blooded black Ethiopian, see articles by W. Den Boer, cited in n. 87, Chap. I.

70. H. P. L'Orange, "Maurische Auxilien im Fries des Konstantinsbogens," *Symbolae Osloenses* XIII (1934) 105-113 and "Una strana testimonianza finora inosservata nei rilievi dell'Arco di Costantino: Guerrieri etiopici nelle armate imperiali romane," *Roma: Rivista di studi e di vita romana* XIV (1936) 217-222. A poem, though punning on *niger* and *candidus* by referring to a "Niger dux" and black soldiers, may point to black troops, *Poetae Latini Minores,* ed. E. Baehrens, V (Leipzig 1883) 370, Carmen LXIV, 1-2.

71. Lucian *De saltatione* 18; Heliodorus *Aethiopica* 9.16, 19; Claudian *De tertio consulatu Honorii* 20-21; *XII Panegyrici Latini,* no. XI (III) 17.4 (R. A. B. Mynors' edition [Oxford 1964]). Lucian refers to the warriors as Ethiopians; Heliodorus, as Troglodytes and those who lived near the cinnamon country; and Claudian, as the people of Meroë. For photographs of the figures with the unusual headdress on the Arch of Constantine, see A. Giuliano, *Arco di Costantino* (Milan 1955) 37-38.

72. L'Orange, 21 in the *Roma* article cited in n. 70 *supra.*

VI. The Ethiopians in Classical Mythology

1. *Iliad* 1.423-424; cf. Diodorus 1.97.8-9 for myths concerning a journey of Zeus and Hera to the Ethiopians.
2. *Odyssey* 1.22-25. T. D. Seymour, *Life in the Homeric Age,* new ed. (New York 1914) 62.
3. *Iliad* 23.205-207.
4. The Homeric statements about the Ethiopian and the Olympian gods may echo a report circulated in the same manner as accounts of pygmies as given in Homer; see C. Préaux, "Les Grecs à la découverte de l'Afrique par l'Egypte," *Chronique d'Egypte* XXXII (1957) 290.
5. J. H. Breasted, *Ancient Records of Egypt,* IV (Chicago, London, Leipzig 1906) 419-444.
6. *Egypt of the Pharaohs: An Introduction* (Oxford 1962) 340; cf. H. R. Hall, *The Cambridge Ancient History,* III: *The Assyrian Empire* (Cambridge, Eng. 1954) 271, who notes that the stele is lacking in the bombastic and often meaningless phraseology which characterizes many royal documents.
7. E. Mireaux, *Les Poèmes homériques et l'histoire grecque,* I (Paris 1948) discusses the piety of the 25th Dynasty (Ethiopian) in Egypt (78-82) and suggests that reports of the events of this Dynasty could not have reached the Greeks before 730 B.C.
8. 2.137 and 139. Manetho lists three Ethiopian kings for the 25th Dynasty: Sabacôn, Sebichôs, and Tarcos/Taracos (Tirharqa in the Old Testament).
9. 3.21 and 25. Some scholars have suggested that there may have been some connection between Homer's allusion to the feasts of the gods with the Ethiopians and the Macrobian "Table of the Sun" described by Herodotus 3.18, the Macrobian practice of exposing in a meadow boiled meat on which passers-by might feast the next day. C. L. Woolley and D. Randall-MacIver, *Karanòg* 56 state that a scene on a piece of Nubian pottery is reminiscent perhaps of the Herodotean "Table of the Sun."
10. 1.65.1-8.
11. 1.60.2-5. For Actisanes as a possible double of Sabacos, see Loeb Diodorus 207, n. 2.
12. 3.2.2-3.3.1. (Translation by C. H. Oldfather in Loeb edition.)
13. Diodorus 3.11.3.
14. *De ira* 3.20.2.
15. 17.1.54.
16. *Thebais* 5.426-428. For red Ethiopians see Chap. I.
17. *Juppiter Tragoedus* 37; see also Lucian's *Prometheus* 17.

18. *De sacrificiis* 2; cf. Ps.-Lucian, *Philopatris* 4.
19. 1.33.4.
20. Philostratus, *Vita Apollonii* 6.21.
21. *De natura animalium* 2.21.
22. *Aethiopica* 9.20.
23. *Ibid.*, 10.39.
24. *Ibid.*, 9.21.
25. *Ibid.*, 9.26.
26. *Orbis descriptio* 559-561 *GGM* III 139.
27. *Adversus nationes* 6.4.
28. 4.2.25 in C. Wachsmuth and O. Hense's edition IV (Berlin 1909) 157.
29. Stephanus Byzantius s.v. Αἰθίοψ.
30. *Commentarii in Thebaida* 5.427 (R. Jahnke's ed. [Leipzig 1898]) 284.
31. *Inscriptiones Graecae* 2^2 no. 1425, col. I, line 25 (p. 38) and no. 1443, col. II, line 127 (p. 58); cf. Kontoleon (cited n. 32 *infra*) n. 16, pp. 191-192.
32. For this phiale, see D. Tsonchev, "The Gold Treasure of Panagurishte," *Archaeology* VIII (1955) 218-227 and figs. 9-10 on p. 223; H. Hoffmann, "The Date of the Panagurishte Treasure," *Mitteilungen des deutschen archäologischen Instituts, Römische Abteilung*, LXV (1958) 121-141; E. Simon, "Der Goldschatz von Panágjuriste — eine Schöpfung der Alexanderzeit mit einem Beitrag von Herbert A. Cahn," *Antike Kunst* III (1960) 3-26; N. M. Kontoleon, "The Gold Treasure of Panagurischte," *Balkan Studies* III (1962) 185-200 and bibliography there cited; D. von Bothmer, "A Gold Libation Bowl," *Bulletin of the Metropolitan Museum of Art*, XXI (1962) 154-166.
33. D. von Bothmer, "Bowl" 162, 164, fig. 17; cf. Jacopi, "Lorrikà," *Presenza* (Periodico di cultura e di informazioni) I (1947) 239 and figs. 1-2.
34. D. von Bothmer, "Bowl" 164. Von Bothmer (161) considers the heads on the phiale "almost caricatures," revealing "little of the Homeric spirit" which represented Ethiopians living at the extremities of the earth in an exalted spirit and as friends of the gods. There is no proof, however, that the artist intended the Negroes as caricatures. On the contrary, the variety of expressions and the features of the Negroes indicate that the artist was well acquainted with the physical characteristics of Negroes. Although some classical representations of Negroes, especially in Kabeiric scenes, were caricatures, both Greeks and Romans most often selected blacks as subjects because they found them artistically and scientifically interesting.
35. *Opera et dies* 232-233.
36. See N. M. Kontoleon (n. 32 *supra*) 190, who considers it impossible that the artist of the phiale would have ignored such a

famous piece of sculpture as the Rhamnus Nemesis, described by Pausanias 1.33.2-3. Pausanias was able to offer no explanation of the Ethiopians and was unwilling to accept the opinion of those who believed that the Ethiopians appeared because they lived near Ocean, the father of Nemesis. Kontoleon 200 interprets the presence of the Ethiopians as symbolizing the pervasiveness of the influence of Nemesis, whose power extends all over the world, like Ethiopians who inhabit the ends of the earth, both in the east and the west.

37. For Ethiopians among the descendants of the son of Kronos, see Hesiod, *Frg.* 40A (Loeb 604, 11. 15-19). A. S. Hunt and B. P. Grenfell, *The Oxyrhynchus Papyri, Part XI* (London 1915) no. 1358, *Frg.* 2, and p. 50 state that lines 16-19 apparently trace the origin of the Ethiopians and others (mentioned in the preceding lines) from Zeus. T. Reinach in his review of Grenfell and Hunt in *REG* XXIX (1916) 120 makes them descendants of Poseidon. H.-J. Newiger in *Lexikon des frühgriechischen Epos* s.v. Αἰθίοπες col. 298 writes that verses 16-19 represent the Ethiopians as descendant "from Zeus (or Poseidon?)." For Zeus Αἰθίοψ, see Lycophron *Alexandra* 535-537, Tzetzes (edition of E. Scheer cum scholiis II [Berlin 1958] 191), and A. W. Mair in Loeb Callimachus and Lycophron 539, n. k.

38. *Commentarii ad Homeri Odysseam* 1.22.1385. Interesting is a statement by C. T. Seltman, *Greek Coins: A History of Metallic Currency and Coinage Down to the Fall of the Hellenistic Kingdoms*[2] (London 1955) 183 and plate XLII, 6 that the countenance of Zeus Ammon on the coinage of Cyrenaica has such a cast of countenance and such curly hair as to suggest Negro blood. E. S. G. Robinson, *Catalogue of the Greek Coins of Cyrenaica* (Bologna 1965) xxxiii says that the figure on the coins has been taken for a Negro but that it lacks the thick lips and flattened nose of a Negro and shows the characteristic frizzled hair of the Libyan. Fusion of Negro and Libyan stocks, however, was not uncommon, see O. Bates, *The Eastern Libyans* (London 1914) 39, 43-44, 69 and Chap. III *supra* for Leucaethiopes and Melanogaetuli.

39. The sarcophagus is in Baltimore, Walters Art Gallery, no. 23.31, *Handbook of the Collection* (Baltimore 1936) 40; K. Lehmann-Hartleben and E. C. Olsen, *Dionysiac Sarcophagi in Baltimore* (Baltimore 1942) 10, 12, 26-28, 72 (the authors date the sarcophagus ca. 180-200 A.D.). For examples of Nubians on sarcophagi, see G. Kaschnitz von Weinberg, *Sculture del magazzino del Museo Vaticano* I, text (Vatican City 1937), plates (1936) 116, no. 254 and plate XCIII, limestone head of a Nubian boy, second half of second century A.D., perhaps from a relief on a sarcophagus; 234, no. 548 and plate LXXXVI, marble head of Nubian, fragment of a sarcophagus, first half of third century A.D.; 234, no. 549, and plate LXXXV, marble, upper part of marble figure of a Nubian, from side of a sarcophagus of first half of third century A.D.

40. 3.64.7-3.65.3.

41. Perhaps, as L. Vivien de Saint-Martin has suggested (*Le Nord de l'Afrique dans l'antiquité grecque et romaine, étude historique et géographique* [Paris 1863] 2-4), the mystery of the Nile may have served to enhance the reputation of the Ethiopians as pious and just. The river of grandeur whose floods occurred so regularly during seasons when rivers in Greece were receding or becoming dry fascinated the Greeks; curiosity about the river carried over to the people — the country of the mysterious Nile was also the country of the mysterious black, just people. On Greek admiration for the distant Ethiopians and for stories of their manners and their virtue, see also D. Mallet, *Les Rapports des grecs avec l'Egypte,* Mémoires publiés par les membres de l'Institut Français d'Archéologie Orientale du Caire (Cairo 1922) 11-12, 181.

42. *Scholia in Aeschyli Eumenides* 2 in W. Dindorf's edition (Oxford 1851) 129; Ovid *Metamorphoses* 6.120; cf. J. Fontenrose, *Python: A Study of Delphic Myth and Its Origins* (Berkeley and Los Angeles 1959) 47.

43. *Scholia in Euripidis Orestem* 1094, E. Schwartz's edition (Berlin 1887) 204; Pausanias 10.6.3-4.

44. P. Graindor, "Mélanges d'archéologie," *Bulletin of the Faculty of Arts, University of Egypt,* III, pt. 2 (Cairo 1955) 108 rejects the Delphos identification largely on the basis of the fact that μέλας never means Αἰθίοψ, Negro; but see evidence to the contrary, Chap. I and C. T. Seltman, *Athens: Its History and Coinage before the Persian Invasion* (Cambridge, Eng. 1924) 97.

45. H. Diels, *Die Fragmente der Vorsokratiker,* I[10] (Berlin 1961) Musaeus, *Frg.* 13, p. 25.

46. For reproductions of the coins and for identification, see T. Panofka, "Delphi und Melaine," *Winckelmannsprogramm* IX (Berlin 1849) 6-9; E. Babelon, *Traité des monnaies grecques et romaines,* (Paris 1907) 1000-1001; B. V. Head, *Historia Numorum,* new and enlarged edition (Oxford 1911) 340; Seltman, *Athens* 97. W. M. Leake, *Numismata Hellenica: A Catalogue of Greek Coins* (*European Greece*) (London 1854) 45 considers the Negro head a depiction of Aesop based on descriptions of Aesop as Negroid; cf. B. E. Perry, *Aesopica* (Urbana 1952) I 35, 81, 111. P. Graindor, "Mélanges d'archéologie" 108 believes that the coins, like the series of alabastra depicting Negroes (*supra*), refer to the Ethiopian troops in the Persian army and the Athenian victory. Seltman, *Athens* 97 considers unfounded the doubts of Waser (*RE* IV s.v. *Delphos* 2700.63) as to the Delphos attribution of the Delphic coinage. A Negro on several coins of Lesbos has also been interpreted as a representation of Delphos. At any rate, whomever it represents, a Negro type, wearing a stephane, appears on the reverse of a Lesbos coin, the obverse of which carries a head of Hera, W. Wroth, *Catalogue of the Greek Coins*

of Troas, Aeolis, and Lesbos (London 1894) 163, no. 71; cf. 153, no. 41. A Negro appears on the obverse of other coins found at Lesbos (Babelon, *Traité* 355-358, nos. 595-599). A Negro woman also appears on a coin of Lycia, E. Babelon, *Les Perses Achéménides* (Paris 1893) cxii, 81, no. 549. E. Pottier, "Epilykos: Etude de céramique grecque," *MonPiot* IX (1902) 144, n. 3 states that he can only suggest, without being able to do so precisely, a political or some other reason for giving a place of special prominence to a Negro in fifth-century Attic art.

47. Hesiod *Theogonia* 985-986.

48. Herodotus 5.53-54 and 7.151; Aeschylus, cited in Strabo 15.3.2; cf. *Persae* 17, 118.

49. 2.22. On eastern and western Memnon, see G. Goossens, "Memnon était-il éthiopien ou susien?" *Chronique d'Egypte* XIV (1939) 337-338.

50. 15.3.2; 17.1.42 and 46.

51. 4.8.3.

52. *Orationes* 11.114; cf. 31.92, where Dio Chrysostom places the colossal statue of Memnon in Egypt.

53. 15.680b.

54. *Aethiopica* 4.8 and 10.6.

55. Pliny *Naturalis historia* 36.11.58; Dio Chrysostom *Orationes* 31.92; Juvenal 15.5; Lucian *Toxaris* 27 and *Philopseudes* 33; Philostratus *Imagines* 1.7.3, *Vita Apollonii* 6.4; Pausanias 1.42.3; Callistratus *Statuarum descriptiones* 1.5 and 9.2. The "voice" has been explained as resulting from sudden changes in temperature and humidity at dawn, G. Posener, S. Sauneron, and J. Yoyotte, *Dictionary of Egyptian Civilization* (New York 1959) s.v. *Memnon (Colossi of)*.

56. *Statuarum descriptiones* 9.2. For the statue of the "Egyptian Memnon," see A. and E. Bernard, *Les Inscriptions grecques et latines du colosse de Memnon*, Institut Français d'Archéologie Orientale (Bibliothèque d'étude) XXXI (1960) and A. Gardiner, "The Egyptian Memnon," *JEA* XLVII (1961) 91-99.

57. Philostratus *Heroicus* 3.4 (pp. 167-168, C. L. Kayser's edition, Leipzig 1886).

58. For white Memnon and Negro followers, see J. D. Beazley, *Attic Black-Figure Vase-Painters* (Oxford 1956) no. 8 (p. 144), p. 149, no. 207 (p. 375), no. 3 (p. 390), no. 11 (p. 392). Beazley considers no. 82 (p. 308) the Negro between two Amazons as an attendant of Penthesilea and Memnon. Ch. Lenormant and J. DeWitte, *Elite des monuments céramographiques,* III (Paris 1858) 185 and plate LXVI and E. Gerhard, *Auserlesene griechische Vasenbilder,* I (Berlin 1840) 167 consider the Negro Memnon himself (my Figs. 15a–b); and Museo Nazionale, Naples, no. 86339, my Fig. 21. The kneeling Negro warrior depicted on a red-figured kylix may be a portion of the Memnon episode, E. Pottier, *Catalogue des vases antiques de terre cuite, troisième partie, l'école attique*[2] (Paris 1929) 925.

59. 10.31.7.
60. *Imagines* 2.7.2.
61. *Imagines* 1.7.
62. *Carmina* 66.52: "Memnonis Aethiopis." Laevius, as cited by Aulus Gellius 19.7.6, described Memnon as "nocticolorem."
63. *Aeneid* 1.489: "nigri Memnonis."
64. *Agamemnon* 212: "Memnon niger."
65. *Amores* 1.8.3-4: "nigri Memnonis"; cf. *Epistulae ex Ponto* 3.3.96-97, *Amores* 1.13.33-34; cf. 3.5.43-44 and H. Fraenkel, *Ovid: A Poet between Two Worlds*, Sather Classical Lectures, vol. XVIII (Berkeley and Los Angeles 1945) 14 and 178. For other examples of Memnon as black, see Manilius *Astronomica* 1.767: "Auroraeque nigrum partum"; Corippus *Johannis* 1.186: "niger Memnon" (p. 7, J. Partsch's edition in *MGH*); *Anthologia Latina* no. 189, in which Memnon's assistance to Priam is referred to as "nigrum . . . auxilium," and no. 293, in which Memnon appears as a synonym for Ethiopian or Negro in a poem celebrating a famed black charioteer: "Dum Memnon facie es, non tamen es genio."
66. *Vita Apollonii* 6.4 and *Heroicus* 3.4.
67. Vergil *Aeneid* 1.489.
68. Cf. A. Bataille, *Les Memnonia*, Publications de l'Institut Français d'Archéologie Orientale du Caire (1952) esp. 14, 20-21.
69. Pliny *Naturalis historia* 6.35.182 and Tacitus *Historiae* 5.2; cf. J. Fontenrose, *Python* 279 and n. 7.
70. Strabo 16.2.28.
71. Pliny *Naturalis historia* 5.14.69; Josephus *Bellum Judaicum* 3.420-421.
72. Jerome *In Jonam prophetam* 1.3 *PL* 25.1123A; cf. Pausanias 4.35.9.
73. Apollodorus *Bibliotheca* 2.4.3.
74. *Naturalis historia* 6.35.182.
75. 4.6.78.
76. Ovid *Metamorphoses* 4.669.
77. *Bibliotheca* 2.4.3. and Lucian *Dialogi marini* 14.323.
78. Ovid *Metamorphoses* 4.669, 764, 5.1; Propertius 4.6.78 and Fraenkel, *Ovid* 178 who suggests *Cepheno* as an emendation for *Cephalio* in line 31 of the *Amores* passage.
79. *Heroides* 15.35-36; *Ars amatoria* 3.191; *Metamorphoses* 4.676.
80. *Ars amatoria* 1.53.
81. *Imagines* 1.29.
82. 3.7.4.
83. *Aethiopica* 4.8.
84. *Naturalis historia* 6.35.187.
85. Apollodorus *Bibliotheca* 2.1.5 and Chap. VII.
86. See Chap. VII and note 25.
87. See Chap. VII and note 28.

88. S. Reinach, *Répertoire des vases peints, grecs et étrusques,* I (Paris 1899) 396.

89. For this scene appearing on a fifth-century B.C. lekythos, Athens, National Museum, no. 1129, see M. Mayer, "Noch einmal Lamia," *AthMitt* XVI (1891) 300-312 and plate XII and C. T. Seltman, "Two Heads of Negresses," *AJA* XXIV (1920) 14-15 who suggest that the Negro woman is Lamia, though E. Buschor, "Die Affen-Inseln," *AthMitt* LII (1927) 230-232 connects the scene with Pausanias 1.23.5-6. For a reproduction, see C. H. E. Haspels, *Attic Black-Figured Lekythoi* (Paris 1936) plate 49b. Also see the discussion of this scene, Chap. VII, and for reference to Negroid features of satyrs. A squatting Dionysus has been interpreted as a youthful god — a conflation of a squatting Negro and the youthful Dionysus. R. A. Higgins, *Catalogue of the Terracottas in the Department of Greek and Roman Antiquities, British Museum,* II (London 1959) no. 1712, p. 65, and plate 41. T. B. L. Webster, *JHS* LXXXI (1961) 227 states that the peak of hair is not at all Negroid. Mr. Higgins' interpretation may be correct, although in this study I have classified art objects as Negroid only if there are present at least two Negroid physical characteristics.

VII. Ethiopians in the Theater and Amphitheater

1. For the treatment of foreigners in Greek tragedy, see H. H. Bacon, *Barbarians in Greek Tragedy* (New Haven 1961).

2. Aeschylus *Prometheus Vinctus* 807-812.

3. Aeschylus, *ibid., Frg.* 328 (Nauck[2]) for an Ethiopian tongue (Αἰθίοπα φωνήν); *Frg.* 329 for a reference to an Ethiopian woman; cf. Euripides, *Frg.* 228 for black Ethiopians living in Africa.

4. Aeschylus *Supplices* 559-561, *Frg.* 300; Euripides *Helena* 1-3, Frg. 228; cf. Diodorus 1.38.4-7, who cites Euripides and questions the likelihood of snow in Ethiopia.

5. *Persae* 315: ἵππου μελαίνης . . . τρισμυρίας; *Frg.* 328 for Ethiopian tongue; and *Frg.* 370 for μελανστέρφων γένος.

6. *Supplices* 719-720: μελάγχιμος is used here as well as in 745; cf. 887-888, where the herald of the sons of Aegyptus is referred to as a black dream.

7. *Ibid.*, 154-155. Here Aeschylus uses μελανθὲς ἡλιόκτυπον. In *Prometheus Vinctus* 851 Epaphus, the distant ancestor of the Danaïdes, is described as κελαινός, the adjective used in the same play (808) of the black men who live by the fountains of the sun and the river Aethiops.

8. *Supplices* 279-285.

9. For Ethiopians in Cyprus, see Chapters II and IV and for Libyan Amazons living near western Ethiopians, see Diodorus 3.53.4.

10. *Supplices* 496; μορφῆς δ'οὐχ ὁμόστολος φύσις are the words of Danaüs, commenting on physical differences between Nilotic and Argive races. On the question of Danaüs as a purely Argive personage or an immigrant of Africa and on the origin and development of the widely accepted view that Danaüs was of Egyptian origin, see C. Bonner, "A Study of the Danaid Myth," *Harvard Studies in Classical Philology* XIII (1902) 130-131, 138-141. R. I. Hicks, "Egyptian Elements in Greek Mythology," *Transactions of the American Philological Association* XCIII (1962) 100 in commenting on the dark coloring of the Danaïdes observes that the girls, though of Greek ancestry, were conceived as being Egyptianized as a result of the family's long residence in Egypt.

11. For Danaüs' seven daughters by an Ethiopian woman, see Apollodorus *Bibliotheca* 2.1.5.

12. See H. C. Baldry, *The Unity of Mankind in Greek Thought* (Cambridge, Eng. 1965) 18: "it is notable that here, as elsewhere in ancient literature, there is no suggestion of antipathy based specifically on colour: darkness of skin is only one of the elements in the strangeness of the picture as a whole."

13. Cf. H. H. Bacon, *Barbarians* 26. For fragments of the *Memnon* and of the *Psychostasia* (in which Zeus weighed the souls of Memnon and Achilles) of Aeschylus, see Nauck[2] *Frgs.* 127-130, 279-280; of the *Aethiopes* of Sophocles, *Frgs.* 25-30.

14. *Ibid.*, for the fragments of the *Andromeda* of Sophocles, *Frgs.* 122-132, of Euripides, *Frgs.* 114-156.

15. S. Birch, "On a Vase Representing an Adventure of Perseus," *Archaeologia* XXXVI (1855) 53-70 and plate 6; E. Petersen, "Andromeda," *JHS* XXIV (1904) 99-112 and plate V, who suggests that the central figure is Phineus, and argues that the scene represents Sophocles' version of the story; H. B. Walters and E. J. Forsdyke, *Corpus Vasorum Graecorum*, Great Britain, fasc. 7, British Museum, fasc. 5 (London 1930) 12, who consider untenable the suggestion that the central figure is an effete Phineus rather than Andromeda; and H. H. Bacon, *Barbarians* 89-92. K. M. Phillips, Jr., "Perseus and Andromeda," *AJA* LXXII (1968) 6 and note 46 also rejects Petersen's identification of the central figure as Phineus.

16. H. Hoffmann, "Attic Red-figured Pelike from the Workshop of the Niobid Painter, ca. 460 B.C.," *Bulletin of the Museum of Fine Arts, Boston* LXI (1963) 108-109, no. 63.2663.

17. M. Bieber, *The History of the Greek and Roman Theater*[2] (Princeton 1961) 31-32, figs. 110 and 111a.

18. A. Furtwängler and K. Reichhold, *Griechische Vasenmalerei* Series I. Plates (Munich 1904) plate 51; M. H. Swindler, *Ancient Painting* (New Haven and London 1929) 125.

19. *Real Museo di Napoli,* XII (Naples 1856) plate XXXVIII and B. Quarante's commentary on p. 2; H. Heydemann, *Die Vasen-*

sammlungen des Museo Nazionale zu Neapel (Berlin 1872) 333, no. 2558. For vases on the Busiris legend, see F. Brommer, *Vasenlisten zur griechischen Heldensage*[2] (Marburg 1960) 26-29.

20. For the scene on the red-figured stamnos, see J. D. Beazley, *Corpus Vasorum Antiquorum,* Great Britain, fasc. 3, Oxford, fasc. 1 (Oxford, London, Paris 1927) 22-23, plates XXVI, 1-4, and XXXI, 5 who states that the style of the vase resembles that of Hermonax; *Ashmolean Museum Summary Guide, Department of Antiquities*[4] (Oxford 1931) 87; cf. P. Gardner, "Vases added to the Ashmolean Museum," *JHS* XXIV (1904) 307; B. Philippaki, *The Attic Stamnos* (Oxford 1967) 38 attributes the vase to a late follower of the Berlin Painter. For the red-figured column-krater, see J. D. Beazley, *Attic Red-Figure Vase-Painters*[2], I (Oxford 1963) 574 no. 9 (9).

21. See J. D. Beazley, *Etruscan Vase-Painting* (Oxford 1947) 188, 305.

22. C. H. E. Haspels, *Attic Black-Figured Lekythoi,* II (Paris 1936) plate 49b; Haspels, *ibid.,* I (Paris 1936) 140 questions whether the woman is Negroid and interprets the scene as representing servants taking revenge on a hard mistress; M. Mayer, "Noch einmal Lamia," *AthMitt* XVI (1891) 300-312 and C. T. Seltman, "Two Heads of Negresses," *AJA* XXIV (1920) 14-15 suggest that the Negro woman is Lamia while Buschor, "Die Affen-Inseln," *AthMitt* LII (1927) 230-232 connects the painting with Pausanias 1.23.5-6; H. Kenner, *Das Theater und der Realismus in der griechischen Kunst* (Vienna 1954) 24.

23. See A. Furtwängler and K. Reichhold, *Griechische Vasenmalerei* Series II, Text (Munich 1909) 106-107 where mention is made of the woman's flat nose and extraordinarily large mouth; E. Romagnoli, "Nimfe e Cabiri," *Ausonia: Rivista della Società Italiana di Archeologia e Storia dell'Arte* II (1907) 164 and fig. 19, 164-166 and reference to his views on Negro women in Kabeiric vases; F. Weege, *Der Tanz in der Antike* (Halle 1926) 110 and fig. 162; M. Bieber (n. 17 *supra*) 296, n. 82 describes the nude dancer as an old woman with grotesque features. "Grotesque" has too often been used by archaeologists who have failed to realize the anthropological intent of classical artists. The woman in question is clearly Negroid, as H. Kenner, *Theater* 55 points out; *Moretum* 31-35. Particularly worthy of note are the pendulous breasts mentioned in the *Moretum,* which are also a characteristic of the woman tortured by the satyrs.

24. E. M. W. Tillyard, *The Hope Vases* (Cambridge, Eng. 1923) 71, no. 121, plate 19.

25. G. Perrot, "Le Triomphe d'Hercule, caricature grecque d'après un vase de la Cyrenaïque," *Monuments grecs publiés par l'Association pour l'Encouragement des Etudes Grecques en France,* no. 5 (Paris 1876) 25-51 and plate III; H. Metzger, *Les Représentations dans la céramique attique du IV*[e] *siècle* (Paris 1951) = (fasc. 172 of the

Bibliothèque des écoles françaises d'Athènes et de Rome) 212, no. 35; M. Bieber, *Die Denkmäler zum Theaterwesen im Altertum* (Berlin and Leipzig 1920) 137-138, and fig. 125 points out that although the vase is perhaps Attic, it may also be Cyrenaic. See also T. B. L. Webster, *Art and Literature in Fourth Century Athens* (London 1956) 33; and Beazley, *Red-Figure*², II 1335, no. 34 who attributes the vase to the Nikias Painter.

26. For the dating of the Kabeiric vases, see P. E. Arias, *Enciclopedia dell'arte antica,* II (Rome 1959) s.v. *Cabirici, Vasi* 241.

27. 9.25.5.

28. M. H. Swindler, *Ancient Painting* 298 mentions the Negroid characteristics of Circe's profile in the first skyphos described, located in the British Museum. H. B. Walters, "Odysseus and Kirke on a Boeotian Vase," *JHS* XIII (1892-3) 77-87 and plate IV comments (79) on the snub nose and protruding lips of the Circe in the second vase, although G. M. A. Richter, *A Handbook of Greek Art*⁵ (London 1967) 346 and fig. 464 makes no reference to Circe's racial identity. See also P. Gardner, *Catalogue of the Greek Vases in the Ashmolean Museum* (Oxford 1893) plate 26, no. 262 and p. 19.

29. S. Reinach, *Monuments nouveaux de l'art antique,* I (Paris 1924) 123 describes the Mitos-Pratolaos scene as strange. E. Romagnoli, "Nimfe e Cabiri," 141-185 but esp. 164-166 argues that the Kabeiric vases depict Negro women. P. Wolters and G. Bruns, *Das Kabirenheiligtum bei Theben* (Berlin 1940) 96, n. 5 state a belief that Romagnoli is mistaken in seeing Negroid elements in some characters in these vases. A first-hand examination of the several Kabeiric vases in the National Museum in Athens, however, has convinced me, in light of the many representations of Negroes which I have studied, that the artist's intent was to depict certain figures as Negroid in Kabeiric vases.

30. G. Becatti, in *Enciclopedia dell'arte antica,* V (Rome 1963) s.v. *Negro* 398 and VI (Rome 1965) s.v. *Pigmei* 168 comments on the role of Negroes in Kabeiric vases. For the skyphos depicting a non-Greek and possibly Negroid Hera and Aphrodite, see A. Fairbanks, *Catalogue of Greek and Etruscan Vases,* I: *Early Vases, Preceding Athenian Black-Figured Ware* (Cambridge, Mass. 1928) 196, no. 562, and plate LXIX. Three of four figures appearing on a black-figure skyphos in a private London collection may represent caricatures. The scene depicts a reclining, wreathed male figure (a god or hero) who offers a wreath to one of three standing female figures, two of whom are fully dressed and one half-naked. P. Levi, "A Kabirion Vase (Plates V-VI)" *JHS* LXXXIV (1964) 155-156 observes that the subject matter of these vases is often mysterious and that in this case as in others we are left in melancholy ignorance; and concludes that the scene (plate VI) must be an allusion to a well-known Boeotian story and could be a burlesque of any heroic couple in mythology.

31. P. Marconi, *Agrigento arcaica* (Rome 1933) 53-54 and plate V, nos. 5-6.

32. R. A. Higgins, *Catalogue of the Terracottas in the Department of Greek and Roman Antiquities, British Museum,* Vol. I: Text Greek: 730-330 B.C., Vol. I: Plates (London 1954) no. 1195, plate 63.

33. Lipari, Il Museo Archeologico Eoliano, L. Bernabò Brea, *Il Castello di Lipari e il Museo Archeologico Eoliano* (Palermo n.d.) 78-79, *id., Musei e monumenti in Sicilia* (Novara 1958) 84; T. B. L. Webster, *Monuments Illustrating Tragedy and Satyr Play*^{2}, University of London, Institute of Classical Studies, Bulletin Supplement, no. 20 (1967) 71. The closed mouth of the mask suggests to Webster that the Negro nurse was intended as a mute.

34. L. Bernabò Brea, *Museen und Kunstdenkmäler in Sizilien* (Munich 1959) 78 and P. E. Arias, *A History of Greek Painting,* trans. and rev. by B. B. Shefton (London 1962) 390-391 and fig. 240.

35. R. Bartocinni and A. De Agostino, *Museo di Villa Giulia: Antiquarium e collezione dei vasi castellani* (Milan n.d.) and fig. XIV, no. 52393.

36. C. Grandjouan, *The Athenian Agora,* vol. VI: *Terracottas and Plastic Lamps of the Roman Period* (Princeton 1961) 62, no. 606 and plate 15.

37. For terra-cotta masks of Negroes from Lower Egypt, see P. Perdrizet, *Les Terres cuites grecques d'Egypte de la Collection Fouquet,* I (Text) and II (Plates) (Nancy, Paris, Strasbourg 1921) 140, no. 372 and plate XCVI; and for a gold mask, with the hair indicated by raised dots, from the Roman period of the 3rd or 4th century A.D., see F. H. Marshall, *Catalogue of the Jewellery, Greek, Etruscan, and Roman in the Departments of Antiquities, British Museum* (London 1911) 369, no. 3094 from excavations at Benghasi and Teuchira.

38. C. Drago, *Il Museo Nazionale di Taranto* (Rome 1956) 25 and 65. G. M. A. Hanfmann, *Classical Sculpture* (Greenwich, Conn. 1967) 332 and plate 252 dates the figure 4th-3rd cent. B.C.; E. Langlotz, *L'Arte della Magna Grecia* (Rome 1968) 311-312 and plate 159 dates a pair of terra-cotta dancers from Taranto executing a dance similar to that of the Negro phlyax as 2nd-1st cent. B.C.

39. C. Grandjouan, *Athenian Agora* no. 1052 and plate 29.

40. Plautus *Poenulus* 1112-1113.

41. *Eunuchus* 165-167 and 470-471.

42. Cicero (*Pro Caecina* 10.27) referred to a witness, Sextus Clodius Phormio, as not less black or less bold than the Phormio of Terence — noticed also by Quintilian (*Institutio oratoria* 6.3.56) H. E. Butler (Loeb, n. 3, p. 468) in commenting on the Quintilian passage states that the reference must be to Phormio's stage makeup since there is nothing in the play to suggest the epithet "black."

43. Suetonius *Caligula* 57.4.

44. *Scholia ad Persium* 5.9 (E. Kurz's edition [Burgdorf 1889]).

45. *Epitome* LXII 63.3 (Loeb 140); cf. J. Beloch, *Campanien*[2] (Breslau 1890) 137-138 = Rome (1961) reprint (*Studia Historica* 11).

46. G. M. A. Richter, "Grotesques and the Mime," *AJA* XVII (1913) 149-156.

47. *Tristia* 2.497-500; W. Beare, *The Roman Stage: A Short History of Latin Drama in the Time of the Republic* (Cambridge, Mass. 1951) 148, 232; J. Lindsay, *Daily Life in Roman Egypt* (London 1963) 179-182.

48. See Chap. VIII.

49. N. 57 *infra* and Chap. VIII, n. 131.

50. 1.19b.

51. A. Köster, *Die griechischen Terrakotten* (Berlin 1926) 89-90 and plate 101; M. Bieber (n. 17 *supra*) 249 and fig. 830.

52. *De saltatione* 18.

53. *Aethiopica* 9.19.

54. S. Reinach, *Répertoire de la statuaire grecque et romaine,* IV (Paris 1913)[2] 354, no. 1; R. Fleischer, *Die römischen Bronzen aus Österreich,* Römisch-germanisches Zentralmuseum zu Mainz (Mainz am Rhein 1967) 152-153, plate 108, no. 205.

55. For the bronze dancer see D. K. Hill, *Catalogue of Classical Bronze Sculpture in the Walters Art Gallery, Baltimore* (Baltimore 1949) 71, no. 149, and plate 5.

56. For the Herculaneum bronze see *'De bronzi di Ercolano e contorni incisi con qualche spiegazione,* R. Accademia Ercolanese di Archeologia, II (Naples 1771) plate XC and commentary on 359-360; H. Roux and L. Barré, *Herculanum et Pompéi,* VI (Paris 1876) 199 and plate 104, 1 and 3; S. Reinach, *Répertoire de la statuaire grecque et romaine,* II 2 (Paris 1898) 563, no. 4.

57. R. Paribeni, "Ariccia — Rilievo con scene egizie," *Notizie degli scavi* (1919) 106-112 and photograph opposite p. 106; *id., Le Terme di Diocleziano e Il Museo Nazionale Romano*[2] (Rome 1932) no. 103. For a comparison of certain movements in these dances — twisting of the body, bending of the knees, and rhythmic clapping of the hands — with older Nubian dances depicted in Egyptian monuments, see H. Wild, "Une Danse nubienne d'époque pharaonique," *Kush* VII (1959) 76-92.

58. F. Winter, *Die Typen der figürlichen Terrakotten,* III 2 (Berlin and Stuttgart 1903) 449, no. 6.

59. See Chap. VIII, n. 131.

60. See Chap. III, n. 41 and Chap. VIII, n. 131 for this scene appearing in a mosaic from the Villa del Nilo near Lepcis Magna.

61. Rome, Museo Nazionale, no. 66176; J. Winckelmann, *Monumenti antichi inediti,* II, pt. 2 (Rome 1821) 245, and plate 188; S. Reinach, *Répertoire,* II 2 563, no. 6.

62. *Naturalis historia* 7.12.51.

63. H. B. Walters, *Catalogue of the Terracottas in the Department of Greek and Roman Antiquities, British Museum* (London 1903) D84 and D85, 310-311.

64. Martial 6.39.8-9. For much earlier evidence on Negro wrestlers, see H. B. Walters, *Catalogue of Terracottas* 258, C 617 for fragments of a group of wrestlers, one with his arms locked around the neck of the other, from Naucratis.

65. *Naturalis historia* 8.38.92-93.

66. A. H. Smith, *A Catalogue of Sculpture in the Department of Greek and Roman Antiquities, British Museum,* III (London 1904) 114-115, no. 1768. The British Museum acrobat is poised on a crocodile; the other is not.

67. 17.1.44.

68. W. B. McDaniel, "A Fresco Picturing Pygmies," *AJA* XXXVI (1932) 260-271.

69. Pliny *Naturalis historia* 8.40.96.

70. Dio Cassius 55.10.8.

71. Pliny *Naturalis historia* 8.54.131.

72. *Epistulae* 85.41.

73. 1.104.9-10.

74. Achilles Tatius 4.4.6. Cf. Martial 6.77.8: "quaeque vehit similem belua nigra Libyn" and O. Ker, "Some Explanations and Emandations of Martial," *The Classical Quarterly* XLIV (1950) 19, who suggests *minimum . . . Libyn* for *similem . . . Libyn* and compares the passage with *minimus Aethiops* in the Seneca passage cited above in n. 72.

75. J. P. Peters and H. Thiersch, *Painted Tombs in the Necropolis of Marissa* [Marêshah] (London 1905) 26; M. H. Swindler, *Ancient Painting* 349-351; E. R. Goodenough, *Jewish Symbols in the Greco-Roman Period,* vol. I: *The Archaeological Evidence from Palestine,* Bollingen Series XXXVII (New York 1953) 68.

76. *Anthologia Latina* (A. Riese's edition) 277-278, nos. 353-354.

77. J. W. Salomonson, ed., *Mosaïques romaines de Tunisie: Catalogue* (Brussels 1964) no. 29, pp. 33-34.

78. SHA, *Probus* 19.8.

79. D. K. Hill, *Catalogue* xvi; G. M. A. Richter, *Handbook* 166 and fig. 239.

80. G. M. A. Richter, *ibid.,* and H. Gallet de Santerre, *Bulletin de correspondance hellénique* LXXIV (1950) 291 for a description of this still unpublished relief found not far from Colonus.

81. *Real Museo di Napoli,* VI (Naples 1838) plate XXIII and commentary by G. Finati; S. Reinach, *Répertoire de reliefs grecs et romains,* III (Paris 1912) p. 94, no. 1.

82. No. 10228 (limestone) in the Graeco-Roman Museum at Alexandria.

83. *Anthologia Latina* (A. Riese's edition) 251, no. 293. Among

the horsemen who appear in the Carthaginian "Mosaic of the Horses" from the Imperial period is a Negro easily identifiable from his hair and nose, J. W. Salomonson, *La Mosaïque aux chevaux de l'antiquarium de Carthage* (The Hague 1965) = Etudes d'archéologie et d'histoire ancienne publieés par l'Institut Historique Néerlandais de Rome: I, Tableau 4 (fig. 8, pl. LVIII, 2) described on pp. 95-96.

VIII. Greco-Roman Attitude toward Ethiopians — Theory and Practice

Note: Much of the material in Chapters VIII and IX I have discussed in an earlier article, "Some Greek and Roman Observations on the Ethiopian," *Traditio* XVI (1960) 19-38.

1. *The Relations of the Advanced and the Backward Races of Mankind* (Oxford, London 1902) 18.
2. The Earl of Cromer [E. Baring], *Ancient and Modern Imperialism* (London 1910) 131.
3. *The Anthropology of the Greeks* (London 1914) 88.
4. *The Greek Commonwealth* (The Modern Library, New York n.d.) 330, n. 1.
5. "Slavery and the Elements of Freedom," *Quarterly Bulletin of the Polish Institute of Arts and Sciences* I (1943) 346.
6. *The Stranger at the Gate* (Oxford 1948) 299.
7. *Anthropology and the Classics* (Providence 1961) 34, 42.
8. *The Unity of Mankind in Greek Thought* (Cambridge, Eng. 1965) 4.
9. For classical concepts of non-Greek and non-Roman peoples, see J. Jüthner, *Hellenen und Barbaren: Aus der Geschichte des Nationalbewusstseins* (*Das Erbe der Alten,* New Series, VIII (Leipzig 1923); Haarhoff (n. 6 *supra*); M. Hammond, "Ancient Imperialism: Contemporary Justifications," *Harvard Studies in Classical Philology* LVIII-LIX (1948) 137-139; W. L. Westermann, *The Slave Systems of Greek and Roman Antiquity* (Philadelphia: The American Philosophical Society 1955); M. Hadas, *Hellenistic Culture: Fusion and Diffusion* (New York 1959) esp. 11-19; H. C. Baldry (n. 8 *supra*). Although the basic theme of A. N. Sherwin-White's *Racial Prejudice in Imperial Rome* (Cambridge, Eng.: Cambridge University Press 1967) is the Roman opinion of northerners, the author notes the common assertion that the ancient world knew nothing of the color bar, and finds no color prejudice but something "akin to colour bar" in what the author considers a Roman allergy to the tall stature and huge size of northern Europeans (57-58). As to the Roman opinion of northerners, Sherwin-White concludes that, in spite of the existence of the "raw material and basic attitudes of racial and cultural prejudice," in actuality such attitudes were "occasional"

and "potential"; that there was an aversion to certain traits of northern barbarians but that a conscious technical and military superiority "negatived the potential forces that might have worked up steam in different circumstances" (101). Sherwin-White, in my opinion, attaches too much significance to Roman comments on the stature and size of northerners but assesses properly the Roman's awareness of cultural differences (what W. G. Sumner called ethnocentrism, in *Folkways: A Study of the Sociological Importance of Usages, Manners, Customs, Mores, and Morals* [New York 1960] 27-29) and his sense of cultural superiority.

10. A. Diller, *Race Mixture among the Greeks before Alexander,* Illinois Studies in Language and Literature, no. 20 (Urbana 1937) 56. See Chap. VI, *supra* for Delphos and Chap. VII *supra* for the Danaïdes.

11. Hippocrates περὶ ἀέρων ὑδάτων τόπων (=*Aër.*); see notes 30, 31 *infra.*

12. For the Greek attitude toward the Scythians, see Ephorus cited by Strabo 7.3.9. A. M. Armstrong, "Anacharsis the Scythian," *Greece and Rome* XVII (1948) 18-23, has collected pertinent references to the classical image of the Scythians. For Herodotus' attitude toward non-Greeks, especially Persians, see Haarhoff (n. 6 *supra*) 20-26.

13. *Respublica* 5.470C-D.

14. *Panegyricus* 50.

15. *Politica* 1.2.3-6, 1.2.11-19.

16. Eratosthenes as cited by Strabo, 1.4.9; cf. Plutarch *De Alexandri Magni fortuna aut virtute* 1.6.

17. Cf. Westermann (n. 5 *supra*) 79, n. 43.

18. Cf. Haarhoff (n. 6 *supra*) 216-221.

19. *Epistulae* 47.10.

20. *Dissertationes* 1.3.1.

21. Dio Chrysostom *Orationes* 15.29-32.

22. Rom. 1.14; Col. 3.11 (RSV).

23. British Museum, no. A 1233 (1220); E. Buschor, "Das Krokodil des Sotades," *Münchner Jahrbuch der bildenden Kunst* XI (1919) 34 and fig. 50; G. H. Beardsley, *The Negro in Greek and Roman Civilization: A Study of the Ethiopian Type* (Baltimore 1929) 15. Although Mrs. Beardsley does not relate the Janiform vases to the environment theory, she does detect an interest more scientific than humorous in certain ointment vases contrasting an Ethiopian and an Asiatic (22).

24. *Frg.* 16 in H. Diels, *Die Fragmente der Vorsokratiker*[10].

25. Hesiod, cited in Strabo 7.3.7, who was quoting Eratosthenes.

26. N. 24 *supra.*

27. 2.22.

28. Aeschylus *Prometheus Vinctus* 709.

29. *Ibid.*, 807-809.
30. Hippocrates *Aër.*, esp. chap. xii and xxiv and, for Scythian-Egyptian contrast, xvii-xxiii.
31. Hippocrates περὶ διαίτης 2.37.
32. 4.20-21.
33. Polybius 4.21.2.
34. *A Study of History*, I (London, New York, Toronto: Oxford University Press 1935) 252-253. For Scythians and Ethiopians as north-south extremes, see K. Reinhardt, *Poseidonius* (Munich 1921) 67-87, esp. 72; for east-west extremes of India and Iberia, see Strabo 1.1.13; Seneca *Quaestiones naturales* 1 Praef. 13.
35. Cited in Strabo 1.2.28. Cf. Lucretius 6.1106-1113, who mentions the differences between the climate in Britain and Egypt and between that in Pontus and Gades "usque ad nigra virum percocto saecla colore" (right on to the races of black men with their scorched color); then points out that as we see these four climates to be diverse under the four winds and regions of the sky, so the inhabitants differ widely in color, features, and in their susceptibility to particular diseases.
36. *De generatione animalium* 5.3.782b.
37. Cited in Strabo 2.3.7.
38. 1.1.13.
39. 1.2.27.
40. 3.34.7-8.
41. *Naturalis historia* 2.80.189.
42. *Ibid.*, 6.22.70. For Posidonius, see n. 37 *supra*, and for Manilius, *Astronomica* 4.723-725 (ed. A. E. Housman, IV, 2nd ed. [Cambridge, Eng. 1937] 94-95).
43. *De architectura* 6.1.3-4; cf. Strabo 15.1.24 for deficiency of moisture on the skin-surface resulting from scorching of the sun as the cause of the Ethiopian's black complexion and woolly hair.
44. N. 39 *supra*.
45. *Tetrabiblos* 2.2.56.
46. *Adversus mathematicos* xi.43.
47. Ps.-Galen φιλόσοφος ἱστορία 133 (H. Diels, *Doxographi Graeci* [Berlin 1879] 648).
48. *De ira* 3.26.3.
49. Julius Firmicus Maternus *Mathesis* 1.2.1; cf. 1.5.1-2.
50. Boethius *In librum Aristotelis* περὶ ἑρμηνείας *commentarii* 2.7 (K. Meiser's edition[2] [Leipzig 1880]) 169.
51. *Adversum paganos* 1.10.19.
52. *Contra Galilaeos* 143D-E.
53. "Race Mixture," in *The Race Question in Modern Science* (New York: UNESCO 1956) 344.
54. Although Toynbee (n. 34 *supra*) finds both the environment and the race theory of the geneses of civilizations intellectually vul-

nerable (253), he considers the environment theory more imaginative, more rational, more human, and above all unprejudiced and possessing none of the repulsiveness of the race theory. The Greeks explained obvious physical differences, Toynbee adds, "as being the effects of diverse environments upon a uniform Human Nature, instead of seeing in them the outward manifestations of a diversity that was somehow intrinsic in Human Nature itself" (250).

55. For the history of the Europe-Asia antithesis originating in the opposition of Greeks to Persians and modifications in the Greek outlook, see G. Pugliese Carratelli, "Europa ed Asia nella storia del mondo antico," *La parola del passato,* XL (1955) 5-19.

56. *Frg.* 612 (A. Koerte, Leipzig 1959 = *Frg.* 533 in T. Kock, *Comicorum Atticorum Fragmenta,* III [Leipzig 1888] 157), as translated by F. G. Allinson in the Loeb Menander, 481. See H. C. Baldry's comment on the significance of the Menander passage in *The Unity of Mankind in Greek Thought* 138-140.

57. Antiphon, *Frg.* 44 in Diels, *Vorsokr*[10] II (352-353).

58. *Frg.* 95 (Kock [n. 56 *supra*] II 508).

59. *De Mari Erythraeo* 16 *GGM* I 118.

60. Pointing out that the Romans evinced no preoccupation with racial purity, R. Syme, *Colonial Elites: Rome, Spain and the Americas* (London, New York, Toronto 1958) 17 cites Cicero *Pro Balbo* 22.51 (esp. "[imperatores] hominum ignobilium virtutem persaepe nobilitatis inertiae praetulerunt") for this Roman attitude.

61. Frontinus *Strategemata* 1.11.17-18.

62. *Anthologia Latina* (A. Riese's edition) 277, no. 353.

63. Ps.-Callisthenes *Historia Alexandri Magni* 3.18.6 in W. Kroll's edition I (Berlin 1926) 116 = L. Bergson, *Der griechische Alexanderroman Rezension* β, Studia Graeca Stockholmiensia, III (Stockholm, Göteborg, Uppsala 1965) 3.18.10-11, p. 153.

64. C. Schmidt, "Eine griechische Grabinschrift aus Antinoë," *Aegyptiaca: Festschrift für Georg Ebers* (Leipzig 1897) 100. For later printings of this inscription see J. Geffcken, *Griechische Epigramme* (Heidelberg 1916) no. 371; W. Peek, *Griechische Vers-Inschriften* (Berlin 1955) no. 1167.

65. Westermann (n. 9 *supra*) 104.

66. *Adversus mathematicos* xi. 43; cf. Philostratus *Vita Apollonii* 2.19, who suggests that white is less esteemed than black among Indians because they themselves are black. The Philostratus reference and the usual Greco-Roman attitude toward the Ethiopian's color, in my judgment, do not support a suggestion which has been made for a difficult line in Elder Pliny *Naturalis historia* 6.35.190. D. Detlefsen (Berlin 1866) reads *Hypsodores* (one of several Ethiopian peoples whom Pliny locates south of the Macrobii); K. Mayhoff (Leipzig 1906) reads *hi pudore,* followed by H. Rackham (Loeb). If the latter reading is correct, Pliny would be explaining the Ethiopians'

practice of painting their bodies with red clay because they were ashamed of their black color.

67. 3.20.

68. *Imagines* 1.29.

69. Ps.-Callisthenes 3.18.2 (n. 63 *supra*) 115, p. 153 (Bergson).

70. Philodemus in *Anthologia Palatina* 5.121 (1.184 Loeb).

71. Asclepiades *ibid.,* 5.210 (1.232 Loeb); cf. Meleager *ibid.,* 12.165 (4.366 Loeb).

72. *CIL* IV 1520, 1523, 1526, 1528; P. Gusman, *Pompéi, la ville, les mœurs, les arts,* rev. ed. (Paris 1906) 63. The first line of the distich is an echo of Propertius 1.1.5: "donec me docuit castas odisse puellas"; the second, of Ovid *Amores* 3.11.35: "Odero, si potero; si non, invitus amabo." In fact, M. Della Corte, *Amori e amanti di Pompei antica* (Cava dei Tirreni n.d.) 59 reads the graffito as Ovid, which may have been the intent of the scribbler, rather than "Odero si potero, sed non invitus amabo." A. W. Van Buren in his translation of Della Corte's work (*Loves and Lovers in Ancient Pompeii* [Cava dei Tirreni 1960]) 61 translates the distich: "The Blonde suggested: despise the brunette! I will hate her . . . if I can! If not, even unwilling . . . I shall love her!" In the setting of the "grand *lupanar*" from which the graffito comes, "black and white girls" seems to be more appropriate than "blonde and brunette," particularly in light of *CIL* IV 6892, discussed in n. 149 *infra.*

73. *Amores* 2.8.

74. 1.115.4-5.

75. *Anthologia Latina* (A. Riese's edition) 277-278, no. 353.

76. Latin passages suggesting preference for a *candidus* type: Lucretius 4.1160; Ovid *Ars amatoria* 2.657-658, cf. 3.270, *Remedia amoris* 327, *Fasti* 3.493; (it should be noted, however, that in spite of these Ovidian expressions of preference for *candidae puellae,* Ovid wrote passionately of love for *fusca Cypassis* — hence, for Ovid, as for Propertius, color makes no difference); Martial 1.72.5-6, 4.62, 7.13; *Scholia ad Persium* 5.116 (O. Jahn's edition [Leipzig 1843] 333); Augustine *Enarrationes in Psalmos* 33.15 (*CCL* 38.292). Passages suggesting preference for a *niger* type (other than those cited in notes 69-76 *supra*): Theocritus 10.26-29; Vergil *Eclogues* 2.16-18, 10.38-39; Martial 7.29.7-8; *CIL* IV 6892. A reference in Petronius *Satyricon* 102 to "labra . . . tumore taeterrimo implere" seems to imply an "undesirable" lip-thickness in the Ethiopian described.

77. 2.25.41-42; cf. Ovid *Amores* 2.4.39-40.

78. [Aristotle] *Physiognomonica* 6.812a.

79. Appian *Bella civilia* 4.17.134; Florus 2.17.7.7-8; Plutarch *Brutus* 48 (all three refer to the same incident). For black associated with death and the underworld, see J. André, *Etude sur les termes de couleur dans la langue latine* (Paris 1949) 57, 362-364; and for black as the color of evil, F. J. Dölger, *Die Sonne der Gerechtigkeit und der*

Schwarze; Eine religionsgeschichtliche Studie zum Taufgelöbnis, Liturgiegeschichtliche Forschungen, II (Münster 1918) 57-64.

80. SHA, *Septimius Severus* 22.4-5.

81. *Anthologia Latina* (ed. A. Riese) 157-158 no. 189.

82. Agatharchides (cited in n. 59 *supra*) and Seneca (cited in n. 48 *supra*) may have had some such belief in mind when they commented on the insignificance of color and other physical characteristics. In spite of a belief that black was ominous, some Greeks and Romans, we have seen, preferred *nigri* to *candidi.* Since the total evidence demonstrates that as a whole the Greeks and Romans ignored color in evaluating men aesthetically, morally, or intellectually, the observations of some modern scholars should be re-examined. T. D. Seymour (*Life in the Homeric Age,* new ed. [New York 1914] 63), for example, in his discussion of what Homer meant by Ethiopians writes: "That Memnon is called the most beautiful of men, with no reference to his complexion, might show that he was at least not one of Herodotus' western Aethiopians." The inference that "black" cannot be considered "beautiful" is amply contradicted by the ancient evidence cited in this book. See Beardsley (n. 23 *supra*) 8 for statement "as Memnon because of his great beauty was evidently white." G. Highet (*Juvenal the Satirist: A Study* [Oxford: Clarendon Press 1954] 255, n. 17) in a discussion of Terence's race states that it is not possible to tell whether Terence was a Negro or a Berber but since he was freed *ob ingenium et formam* and since "Romans did not think Negro features handsome," it might be inferred that Terence was a frail Berber. W. G. Waddell's (*Selections from Menander* [Oxford: Clarendon Press 1927] 152) commentary on Menander *Frg.* 533 Kock has the following note on Αἰθίοψ: "contemptuously, like 'blackamoor,' 'nigger': cf. the proverb Αἰθίοπα σμήχειν, 'wash a blackamoor white' . . . and *Dacus et Aethiops,* Hor. *C.* iii.6.14." Waddell's interpretation, as my discussions of the Menander passage and the proverb have demonstrated, is not supported by the evidence. On the contrary, the long history of both the Menander sentiment and the proverb shows clearly a remarkable absence of color prejudice and nothing of contempt. Horace by his use of *Aethiops,* though he may include some Ethiopians, is using the term loosely for Egyptians and, furthermore, is thinking of the Egyptians and Dacians as military inferiors of the Romans. "Aethiopem albus," the last two words of Juvenal 2.23 — "loripedem rectus derideat, Aethiopem albus" (Let the straight-legged man laugh at the bandy-legged, the white man at the Ethiopian) — are simply an illustration of the proverbial *ater* (*Aethiops*)-*albus* (see Chap. I, n. 16) and many similar black-white contrasts which have no overtones of racial bias. Further, Juvenal's attitude toward Greeks and Orientals certainly suggests that the poet, had he been disposed, would have spoken more caustically and explicitly than he does here or elsewhere. Mrs. Beardsley

(119-120), in my judgment, therefore, is wrong in her conclusion that Juvenal summed up the Roman attitude toward the Ethiopian which crystallized into racial feeling. For a discussion of this point, see my article "The Negro in Classical Italy," *AJP* LXVIII (1947) 288-289.

83. Ptolemy *Tetrabiblos* 2.2.56.

84. As cited in Strabo 7.3.9. For Ephorus' use of the Scythians in this instance and his praise of distant countries for didactic purposes, see L. Edelstein, *The Idea of Progress in Classical Antiquity* (Baltimore 1967) 67-68.

85. Diodorus 3.8.2-4.

86. 3.2.2-4. H. Frankfort, *Kingship and the Gods: A Study of Ancient Near Eastern Religion as the Integration of Society and Nature* (Chicago 1948) 163-165, 348 (n. 4), 383 (n. 22) suggests that certain features common to ancient Egyptian and African culture may have ultimately been derived from an old, widespread "Hamitic substratum."

87. *De astrologia* 3.

88. *Naturalis historia* 2.80.189; Plutarch *Septem sapientium convivium* 151B-C mentions a contest in wisdom between Amasis, king of the Egyptians, and the king of the Ethiopians.

89. *Odyssey* 19.246-248.

90. See Chap. VI.

91. *Aethiopica* 9.21.

92. See E. Babelon, "Tête de nègre de la collection de Janzé au Cabinet des Médailles," *Gazette archéologique* IX (1884) 205-206, plate 27 for the statement that a Roman bronze head breathes nobility and intelligence. The terra-cotta Negro Spinario is regarded by Beardsley, *The Negro* 81 as an outright instance of the comic but R. A. Higgins, *Greek Terracottas* (London 1967) 120 finds the same terra cotta, inspired by a famous sculpture, transformed into a human document through a sympathetic study of the Negro boy; and Beardsley, *ibid.*, 37-38, detects in the use of a popular subject of a Negro seized by a crocodile a keen sense of the comic interest of the Ethiopians. For the prophylactic interpretation of Negroes, see Chap. II.

93. *Enciclopedia dell'arte antica* V (Rome 1963) s.v. *Negro* 353-400.

94. "Charinos," *JHS* XLIX (1929) 39.

95. See Chap. VI.

96. M. Collignon, "L'Afrique personnifiée: Statuette provenant d'Egypte acquise per Jean Maspero," *MonPiot* XXII (1916) 163-173 and plate XVI.

97. F. Cumont, "Tête de marbre figurant la Libye," *MonPiot* XXX (1932) 41-50.

98. E.g., R. H. Barrow, *Slavery in the Roman Empire* (London 1928) 15-21, 208-229; A. M. Duff, *Freedmen in the Early Roman Empire* (Cambridge, Eng. 1958) 1-11; W. L. Westermann, *Slave*

Systems 97; M. Hadas and the editors of Time-Life Books, *Imperial Rome* (New York 1965) 50. For an understanding of the significance of the Negro element in the population of the ancient world, see F. Cumont, cited in n. 97 *supra,* 46-50. Further, M. I. Rostovtzeff, *The Social and Economic History of the Roman Empire*[2] (rev.), I (Oxford 1957) 66 notes that the Bedouins of the Sahara may have exported large numbers of Negro slaves. One of the reasons that scholars have not properly evaluated the Ethiopian element in the population is that they have failed to consider the archaeological as well as the literary and papyrological evidence.

99. 5.201a.

100. Strabo 17.1.54.

101. Pliny *Naturalis historia* 8.54.131.

102. Dio Cassius *Epitome* LXII, 63.3 (Loeb 140).

103. *Spectacula* 3.10.

104. For the emporium of Adulis, see Pliny *Naturalis historia* 6.34.172-173; for Ethiopian slave-dealers, see F. Preisigke, "Ein Sklavenkauf des 6. Jahrhunderts," *Archiv für Papyrusforschung* III (Leipzig 1906) 415-424.

105. See P. Perdrizet, *Les Terres cuites grecques d'Egypte de la Collection Fouquet,* I Text and II Plates (Nancy, Paris, Strasbourg 1921); and Ev. Breccia, *Terrecotte figurate greche e greco-egizie del Museo di Alessandria,* II (Bergamo 1930) fasc. 1 and (Bergamo 1934) fasc. 2 and *passim.* One leaves the Graeco-Roman Museum in Alexandria with the feeling that one has been face-to-face with the motley population of ancient Alexandria and the impression that the Negroid element was sizeable and resembled many of the blacks seen on the streets in Alexandria today. Ev. Breccia (fasc. 2) 51 comments on the presence of Negroes in Egyptian population from ancient times and of the propensity of Greco-Roman artists for depicting the Negroid type.

106. *De lingua Latina* 8.20.38, 8.21.41; 9.30.42.

107. 4.50.63; for Negroes in baths, see Chap. II, n. 4.

108. 31-35.

109. Diodorus 3.8.2; Pliny *Naturalis historia* 2.80.189; Petronius 102.

110. Eusebius *De vita Constantini* 4.7. (*PG* 20.1156.)

111. Diodorus 3.6.3-4.

112. Diogenes Laertius 2.86. On the problem of identifying the Aristippus referred to, see Loeb 215, n. b.

113. C. C. Vermeule, "Greek, Etruscan, and Roman Bronzes Acquired by the Museum of Fine Arts, Boston," *CJ* LV (1960) 198 and fig. 7.

114. *Art Treasury of Turkey,* circulated by the Smithsonian Institution, 1966-1968 (Washington 1966) 93, no. 145.

115. For examples of the occupations cited, see: *bootblack* — S.

Reinach, *Répertoire de la statuaire grecque et romaine,* III (Paris 1904) 158, no. 3, H. B. Walters, *Catalogue of the Bronzes, Greek, Roman, and Etruscan in the Department of Greek and Roman Antiquities, British Museum* (London 1899) 269, no. 1676; *cook* — *Moretum* 31, cf. also Martial 6.39.7; *courtesan* — *CIL* IV 1520, 1523, 1526, 1528, SHA, *Elagabalus* 32.5.6; *diver* — S. Reinach, *Statuaire grecque et romaine* III 158, no. 6, H. B. Walters 169, nos. 1674, 1675; *laborer* — (bronze) Alexandrian, standing figure seems to be making an effort as if to pull a cable — E. Babelon and J. A. Blanchet, *Catalogue des bronzes antiques de la Bibliothèque Nationale* (Paris 1895) fig. 1010 and pp. 440-441; (terra cotta) after 30 B.C., a laborer working Archimedean screw with his feet and standing among vines; *lamp-* or *lantern-bearer* — Helenos, an Ethiopian lamp-bearer mentioned in Zenon papyri — C. C. Edgar, *Zenon Papyri,* IV (Cairo 1931) 59782 (a), 69; Athenaeus 4.148b, who says that Cleopatra's departing guests were provided with Ethiopian lamp-bearers; F. Poulsen, *Sculptures antiques de musées de province espagnols* (Copenhagen 1933) 58, plate LVIII, fig. 90-92, Roman bronze after Alexandrian model, found near Tarragona; London, British Museum bronze, no. 1908-5-15-1, H. B. Walters, *Select Bronzes, Greek, Roman, and Etruscan, in the Department of Antiquities,* British Museum (London 1915) plate LXVIII; J. Szilágyi, *Aquincum* (Budapest 1944) plate X; Roman bronze found at Reims (Marne), F. Braemer, *L'Art dans l'occident romain. Trésors d'argenterie. Sculptures de bronze et de pierre* (Ministère d'Etat Affaires Culturelles — Palais du Louvre, Galerie Mollien, July–October 1963) no. 484, p. 109; S. Reinach, *Statuaire grecque et romaine,* II 2 vols. in 1 (Paris 1897) 561, no. 5; and terra cotta from Graeco-Roman Museum, Alexandria; *personal attendant* — slave accompanying his weary master home, a terra cotta, after 30 B.C.

116. E. Babelon, "Tête de nègre" 205-206, plate 27.

117. [S. A.] Morcelli, [C.] Fea, [P. E.] Visconti, *La Villa Visconti (ora Torlonia) descritta* (Imola 1870) 38, no. 209. W. Helbig, *Guide to the Public Collections of Classical Antiquities in Rome,* II, trans. by J. F. and F. Muirhead (Leipzig 1896) 86, no. 847. Although the nose is restored, the woolly hair and thick lips leave no doubt as to the Negroid characteristics.

118. R. T. Günther, *Pausilypon, the Imperial Villa near Naples* (Oxford 1913) 260; and D. Faccenna, "Rappresentazione di negro nel Museo di Napoli," *Archeologia Classica* I (1949) 188-195 and plates LIV and LV. The statue was found in the Gaiola Region near Posillipo.

119. Philostratus, *Vita Apollonii* 3.11, and *Vitae Sophistarum* 2.558. P. Graindor, *Un Milliardaire antique: Hérode Atticus et sa*

famille (Cairo 1930) 114-116 (= *Université Egyptienne, Recueil de travaux publiés par la Faculté des Lettres,* fasc. 5).

120. Z. A. Glava, *A Study of Heliodorus and His Romance, the Aethiopica,* abridged (New York 1937) 1 suggests that Heliodorus may be referring to his Ethiopian descent when in 10.41 he describes himself as of the race of the sun. M. Hadas, *Heliodorus: An Ethiopian Romance,* translated with an Introduction (Ann Arbor 1957) ix states that the romance is a glorification of a dark-skinned race and that it is easy to believe the author a colored man.

121. *Römertum und Latinität* (Stuttgart 1964) 319.

122. Diodorus 3.9.2; cf. Strabo 17.2.3. I have treated Ethiopian and Isiac Worship in *L'Antiquité classique* XXV (Brussels 1956) fasc. 1, pp. 112-116.

123. Diodorus 3.3.1.

124. The so-called king is in Copenhagen, Ny Carlsberg Glyptotek; the queen (?) in Edinburgh, the Scottish Museum. H. Garstang, A. H. Sayce, and F. Ll. Griffith, *Meroë: The City of the Ethiopians* (Oxford 1911) 19 and plate XVIII, nos. 2-3; G. Posener et al., *Dictionary of Egyptian Civilization* (New York 1959) 191 dates the figure of the king ca. 100 B.C.; O. Koefoed-Petersen, *Egyptian Sculpture in the Ny Carlsberg Glyptothek* (Copenhagen 1962) 37-38, considers the two figures a Meroïtic king and his spouse and dates the figures 3rd or 2nd centuries B.C., and fig. 50; and P. L. Shinnie, *Meroe: A Civilization of the Sudan* (New York and Washington 1967) 102-103 sees nothing in the so-called queen's statue to suggest that it represents a female, considers it a male royal figure, and dates the statues tentatively in the 2nd cent. A.D. The building in which the statues were found has been identified as a temple of Isis on the basis of two small figures of Isis also discovered on the site.

125. E. A. W. Budge, *The Egyptian Sudan,* I (London 1907) 407 and fig. on p. 403.

126. F. Ll. Griffith, *Catalogue of the Demotic Graffiti of the Dodecaschoenus,* Vol. I, Text (Oxford 1937) 11; and especially Philae 416 (pp. 114-119), Philae 417 (pp. 119-121), Philae 421 (pp. 121-122).

127. Procopius *De bello Persico* 1.19.27-37.

128. F. Poulsen, "Tête de prêtre d'Isis trouvée à Athènes," *Mélanges Holleaux* (Paris 1913) 221 and plate VI. The date of the head is given as first century B.C. or first half of the next century; Ch. Picard, *La Sculpture antique de Phidias à l'ère byzantine* (Paris 1926) 306, like Poulsen, suggests that the head came from the temple of Isis at Piraeus.

129. Ch. Picard, "Le Nain bossu au coq de Strasbourg, et les lagynophories alexandrines," *Gallia* XVI (1958) 93-94 and fig. 5; K. T. Erim "De Aphrodisiade," *AJA* LXXI (1967) 237-239 suggests that the figure represents a slave or bath attendant. The figure is in Versailles, Gaudin Collection.

130. M. Rostovtzeff, *A History of the Ancient World,* vol. II: *Rome* (Oxford, reprint 1938) plate XC, no. 2 and commentary on p. 342.

131. E. Guimet, "L'Isis romaine," in *Académie des Inscriptions et Belles-lettres,* Comptes rendus des séances de l'année 1896, 4th ser., XXIV (1896) plate IX and commentary considers the central figure an Ethiopian; C. M. Dawson, *Romano-Campanian Mythological Landscape Painting,* Yale Classical Studies, IX (1944) 9-10; K. Schefold, *Pompejanische Malerei, Sinn und Ideengeschichte* (Basel 1952) plate 42. W. von Bissing, "Notes on Some Paintings from Pompeii Referring to the Cult of Isis," in *Transactions of the Third International Congress for the History of Religions* I (Oxford 1908) 225-228 considers the central figure not a Negro but a dancing priest playing the role of Bes. Von Bissing argues that the face of the dancer resembles the mask of an animal rather than a human being and that the body, forehead, and arms are covered with hair. After a careful examination of the fresco, however, I am convinced that von Bissing is incorrect in his interpretation. The face of the figure, in my judgment, is as human as the others represented. Von Bissing's interpretation of the strokes of light paint as hair is also erroneous. The strokes of paint bear no resemblance whatsoever to hair but apparently represent an Ethiopian practice noted by Herodotus (7.69) and Pliny the Elder (6.35.190) of painting the body. Certain similarities between two of the figures in the Herculaneum fresco and two Negroid figures in a mosaic from Lepcis Magna deserve comment. The north African mosaic presenting an allegory of the fertilizing Nile includes two Negroid figures, both of whom wear on their heads a band from which two leaves of marsh reeds rise like horns. The headdress of the Herculaneum dancer is apparently a variation of that worn by the Lepcis Negroes and one of several used in Nilotic rituals which symbolize the regions of the Sudan, like Egypt, a beneficiary of the Nile. In both scenes there are standing figures playing a similar musical instrument. For the Lepcis mosaic, see S. Aurigemma, *L'Italia in Africa,* I (Rome 1960) plate 86, and p. 48 and G. Guidi, "La Villa del Nilo," *Africa Italiana* V (1933) 6-8 and figs. 3-4 cited in Chap. III *supra,* n. 41. V. Tran Tam Tinh, *Essai sur le culte d'Isis à Pompéi* (Paris 1964) 102 accepts von Bissing's interpretation but presents no additional evidence.

132. Suetonius *Caligula* 57.4; cf. Petronius *Frg.* XIX (Loeb 332).

133. A. D. Nock, *Conversion* (Oxford 1933) 124.

134. R. Paribeni, "Ariccia — Rilievo con scene egizie," in *Notizie degli scavi* (1919) 106-112 and photograph opposite 106; *idem, Le Terme di Diocleziano e il Museo Nazionale Romano*^{2}, (Rome 1932) no. 103.

135. *Philopseudes* 34, and see Chap. I s.v. *Pancrates.*

136. 6.526-529.

137. *CIL* III 83. J. De Decker, "Le Culte d'Isis à Méroé en Ethiopie," *Revue de l'instruction publique en Belgique* LIV (1911) 293-310 gives the following reading of the inscription: "Bona fortuna! Dominae Reginae in multos annos feliciter! Venit e urbe, mense aprile die XV vidi(t) Tacitus" (301). Although De Decker (306) states that *urbe* may refer also to Alexandria, he believes Rome was intended. Cf. G. Highet, *Juvenal* 242-243.

138. *Metamorphoses* 11.4.

139. Cf. F. Hiller von Gärtringen, *Inschriften von Priene* (Berlin 1906) 138, no. 195.

140. *Metamorphoses* 11.26.

141. G. Charles-Picard, *La Carthage de saint Augustin* (Paris 1965) 71-77, figure of Negro (74).

142. Herodotus 2.30. Plutarch *De exilio* 601 E adds a moral note not present in Herodotus.

143. Josephus *Antiquitates Judaicae* 2.252-253.

144. *Moretum* 32-35.

145. I have found no reference to this bust (second half of the second century A.D.) in the literature.

146. *Anthologia Palatina* 5.121, 210 and *supra* notes 70-71; cf. G. Luck, *The Latin Love Elegy* (New York 1960) 48.

147. Martial 7.29.7.

148. *CIL* IV 1520, 1523, 1526, 1528, 1536 and SHA, *Elagabalus* 32.5. A. Furtwängler in A. Furtwängler and K. Reichhold, *Griechische Vasenmalerei,* Series II. Text (Munich 1909) 107 considers the Negroid nude dancer in a scene from a south Italian vase perhaps a hetaira of a low type.

149. *CIL* IV 6892 reads, "Quisquis amat nigra(m) nigris carbonibus ardet./Nigra(m) cum video, mora libenter (a)ed (e)o." M. Della Corte, *Amori e amanti* 60 and M. D'Avino, *The Women of Pompeii,* trans. by M. H. Jones and L. Nusco (Naples: Loffredo 1967) 66 both read *Nigram,* rather than *nigram.* This graffito, which seems to have an erotic meaning and to pun on blackness, has puzzled commentators and has evoked several questionable interpretations. For a summary of the various interpretations, see G. Zottoli, "Lusus Pompeianus," *Atene e Roma* XI (1908) 357-360. Zottoli sees the erotic aspect of the graffito but, like Della Corte, translates *nigram* as "bruna." Zottoli (358), however, adds that it makes no difference whether "nigram" is an allusion to all brown girls in general or to a particular girl, named Nigra and exceedingly black, a well-known "black but comely" Pompeiian. Zottoli prefers to read *Nigra,* a cognomen, as does D'Avino, who translates the graffito as follows: "Whoever loves *Nigra* burns as upon black coals. When I see *Nigra* I could easily eat blackberries."

150. J. P. Mahaffy and J. G. Smyly, ed., *The Flinders Petrie Papyri,* III (Dublin 1904) no. II; W. Peremans and E. Van't Dack,

Prosopographia Ptolemaica, V (Louvain 1963) nos. 14403, 14305. The name Melaenis particularly in an Egyptian context has significance for Negroid extraction.

151. 6.39.6-7, and 18.

152. 6.595-601.

153. *Declamationes* 2 (G. Lehnert's edition [Leipzig 1903]).

154. *Hebraicae quaestiones in Genesim* 30,32.33, *CCL* 72.38.

155. *Aethiopica* 4.8.

156. Aristotle *De generatione animalium* 1.18.722a and *Historia animalium* 7.6.586a; cf. Antigonus *Mirabilia* 112 (122); Aristophanes *Historiae animalium epitome* 2.272.

157. Pliny *Naturalis historia* 7.12.51.

158. *De sera numinis vindicta* 21 (563).

159. In addition to illustrations included in this book as examples of types interpreted as descendants of black-white crosses, the following should be noted: (1) the thick lips and beard have suggested to some that the head of an African from Cyrene from the end of the fourth century B.C. (H. B. Walters, *Select Bronzes* plate XV, Beardsley, *The Negro* 75 and G. Becatti, *Enciclopedia* 398) represented a person of Negroid blood; (2) limestone head of a man, head bald, thick lips, snub-nose, called an Egyptian or Libyan, perhaps a priest, 1st cent. B.C. no. 747, Syracuse, Museo Nazionale (N. Bonacasa, *Ritratti greci e romani della Sicilia* [Palermo 1964] 25-26, no. 27, plate XII 1-2); (3) marble head of a man described as an African or Asiatic, snub-nose, prominent lips, very short hair, second half of 1st cent. B.C., Agrigento, Museo Nazionale, no. AG. 498 (Bonacasa, *ibid.,* 26, no. 28, and plate XII, 3-4); (4) an Isiac mulatto priest of the first century B.C. or first half of the first century A.D. from Athens whom F. Poulsen ("Tête de prêtre d'Isis trouvée à Athènes" 221 and plate VI) regards as a person "evidently of a mixed race"; and (5) L. D. Caskey, *Catalogue of Greek and Roman Sculpture,* Museum of Fine Arts, Boston (Cambridge, Mass. 1925) 215-216, no. 127 considers the features of a little girl from Corinth and dating from the Flavian or Trajanic eras suggestive of a "strain of Negro blood."

160. Among modern concepts, the attitude of Brazilians toward miscegenation follows the spirit of the Greco-Roman tradition. On miscegenation in Brazil, see F. Tannenbaum, *Slave and Citizen: The Negro in the Americas* (New York 1947) 120-126, esp. 121; G. Freyre, *New World in the Tropics: The Culture of Modern Brazil* (New York 1959) 118 and 121, and *The Mansions and the Shanties: The Making of Modern Brazil* (New York 1963) 400-431. For a vastly different modern approach to miscegenation in the United States, see W. D. Zabel, "Interracial Marriage and the Law," *Atlantic Monthly* CCXVI (1965) 75.

161. See C. Stern, "The Biology of the Negro," *Scientific American* CXCI.4 (1957) 85 for the estimate that if random mating with no

regard to racial differences were to take place in the United States, the darker shades of Negro pigmentation would be virtually eliminated and that the few thousand black people left would have straight hair, narrow noses, and thin lips; T. F. Pettigrew, *A Profile of the Negro American* (Princeton, Toronto, New York, London 1964) 62-63; cf. H. L. Shapiro, "Race Mixture" 342: "If race mixture enjoyed complete acceptance in the modern world, its offsprings would ultimately be absorbed by the society into which they were born and consequently no problem would exist."

IX. Early Christian Attitude toward Ethiopians — Creed and Conversion

1. Origen *De principiis* 2.9.5-6 (Rufinus' translation), *Die griechischen christlichen Schriftsteller der ersten drei Jahrhunderte,* Origen 5.169-170.
2. Col. 3.11, RSV. For literary echoes of Menander in Paul, see W. A. Oldfather and L. W. Daly, "A Quotation from Menander in the Pastoral Epistles?" *CP* XXXVIII (1943) 202-204 and R. M. Grant, "Early Christianity and Greek Comic Poetry," *CP* LX (1965) 157-163.
3. *Oratio de incarnatione Verbi,* Migne, *Patrologiae Cursus Completus, Series Graeca* [hereafter abbreviated as *PG*] 25.188.
4. *Carmina* 5.2.7-10 in *Monumenta Germaniae Historica* IV [Auctores Antiquissimi] pt. 1, p. 104. Similarly St. Jerome *Epistulae* 107.2, after mentioning the arrival of monks from India, Persia, and Ethiopia, had stated that the cold Scythians were warmed by the glow of the faith.
5. *Vita S. Moysis Aethiopis* 1, in V. Latyšev, *Menologii Anonymi Byzantini Saeculi X Quae Supersunt* (St. Petersburg 1912) fasc. 2, p. 330.
6. *Corpus Fabularum Aesopicarum* (edition of Hausrath, Haas, and Hunger [Leipzig 1959] no. 274).
7. Jer. 13.23.
8. *Epistulae* 69.6.7-8; cf. Gregory of Nazianzus *Orationes* 4 (*Contra Julianum* 1) 62 (*PG* 35.584-585) and Basil *Epistulae* 130.
9. Lucian *Adversus indoctum* 28.
10. Dio Chrysostom *Spuria* (*Sermo in Sanctos duodecim Apostolos*) *PG* 59.495.
11. Gregory of Nyssa *Commentarius in Canticum Canticorum* (1,5) oratio 2 (*PG* 44.792 = W. Jaeger's edition VI [Leiden 1960] 48-49). The Greek reads: λαμπροὺς ποιῆσαι τοὺς μέλανας. λαμπρός is used of garments, especially white ones, and λάμπω is used in II Cor. 4.6 of the light of God.
12. *Vita S. Moysis Aethiopis* 6, in V. Latyšev, *Menologium* (cited in n. 5 *supra*) 332.

13. Cf. Origen *Commentarius in Canticum Canticorum* 2.367 (*GCS,* Origen 8.118); Origen *Homiliae in Numeros* 6.4 (*GCS,* Origen 7.36); Irenaeus *Contra haereses* 4.20.12 (*PG* 7.1042); Jerome *Commentarii in Sophoniam prophetam* 3.10 (*PL* 25.1380); Theodoret *Quaestiones in Exodum,* interrogatio 4 (*PG* 80.228); Cyril of Alexandria *Glaphyra in Numeros* 1.1-2 (*PG* 69.593-596); Faustus of Riez *Sermones* 8 *CSEL* 21.253.

14. 8.5, translated as the verse reads in the Septuagint. Origen *Homiliae in Jeremiam* 11.5 (*GCS,* Origen 3.84-85).

15. *Commentarius in Canticum Canticorum* 2.377 (*GCS,* Origen 8.125-126); cf. Paulinus of Nola *Carmina* 28.249-251, *CSEL* 30.302: "Aethiopum populos non sole perustos/sed vitiis nigros et crimine nocticolores" ("Ethiopian peoples burnt not by the sun but black with vices and dark with sin").

16. *Commentarius in Canticum Canticorum* 2.379 (*GCS,* Origen 8.127).

17. 1.5 which reads μέλαινά εἰμι καὶ καλή ("I am black and beautiful") in the Septuagint and "Nigra sum, sed formosa" ("I am black but beautiful") in the Vulgate. Origen *Commentarius in Canticum Canticorum* 2.360 (*GCS,* Origen 8.113) writes: " 'Fusca sum et formosa . . .' In aliis exemplaribus legimus: 'nigra sum et formosa.' " (" 'I am dark and beautiful . . .' In some copies we read: 'I am black and beautiful.' "). The reading μέλαινα or *nigra* was the one appearing most often in the early commentators: Origen *Homiliae in Jeremiam* 11.6 (*GCS,* Origen 3.84: μέλαινά εἰμι καὶ καλή; Origen *Homiliae in Canticum Canticorum* 1.6 (*GCS,* Origen 8.35): "nigra sum et speciosa"; Gregory of Nyssa *Commentarius in Canticum Canticorum* (1,5) oratio 2 (*PG* 44.788-789): μέλαινά εἰμι καὶ καλή = W. Jaeger (Leiden 1960) 42-45; Jerome *Epistulae* 22.1.3-4: "nigra sum et speciosa," alters the text of the Vulgate (as F. A. Wright in Loeb edition [*Select Letters of St. Jerome*] 54, n. 4 points out), but in *Commentarii in Sophoniam prophetam* 1.1 (*PL* 25.1339) follows the Vulgate "nigra sum, sed speciosa"; Augustine *Enarrationes in Psalmos* 73.16 (*CCL* 39.1014): "Nigra sum, et speciosa"; Arator *De Actibus Apostolorum* 1.698 (*CSEL* 72.54): "Fuscam pulchramque."

18. Song of Sol. 1.5-6 as the passage reads in the Septuagint. The Septuagint 1.6 reads in part παρέβλεψέν με ὁ ἥλιος; in the Vulgate, "decoloravit me sol." The Jerusalem Bible translates the verb as "has burnt"; the King James Version, as "hath looked upon"; the RSV, as "has scorched." L. Koehler and W. Baumgartner, ed., *Lexicon in Veteris Testamenti Libros* II (Leiden and Grand Rapids 1953) s.v. *shāzaph* 959 give "make brown, burn" as the meaning in Song of Sol. 1.6 and as "catch sight of" in Job 20.9, 28.7; F. Brown, S. R. Driver, and C. A. Briggs, *A Hebrew and English Lexicon of the Old Testament* (Oxford 1955) 1004 under the same entry give only the meaning "catch sight of" or "look on." Commentators have pointed out that

the Hebrew verb *shāzaph* is used elsewhere in the Old Testament in the sense of "see," "catch sight of," or "look on" only in Job 20.9 and 28.7 (in all three cases the Septuagint uses παρέβλεψε and the Vulgate renders the Song of Sol. verb as *decoloravit;* the verb in the first Job reference, as *viderat;* and the second as, *intuitus est*); that the Septuagint by its use of παρέβλεψέν με ("looked askance on me") is following the Hebrew verb in the sense of "see" etc.; and that the *decoloravit* of the Vulgate is an interpretation influenced by the context rather than a translation. Some commentators have argued that the Hebrew verb of Song of Sol. 1.6 is not the equivalent of *shāzaph* in Job 20.9 and 28.7 ("to see or to catch sight of") but rather *shādhaph* appearing in Gen. 41.6, 23, 27, which is used of wheat reddened and dried by the burning east wind and, hence, in the Song of Sol. 1.6 should be translated as "burned," the meaning rendered by the συνέκαυσέ με of Aquila and the περιέφρυξέ με of Theodotion (F. Field, *Origenis Hexaplorum Quae Supersunt* II [Oxford 1875] 412); see F. Delitzsch, *Commentary on the Song of Songs and Ecclesiastes,* trans. by M. G. Easton (Edinburgh 1885) 26-27; P. Jouon, *Le Cantique des Cantiques* (Paris 1909) 134; and A. Robert and R. Tournay, *Le Cantique des Cantiques* (Paris 1963) 72-73. Since the Septuagint used παρέβλεψε in all three instances (Song of Sol. 1.6, Job 20.9 and 28.7) [these last two cases obviously in the sense of "see" (*video, intueor*)], it is not necessary to rule out the possibility that the intent of the Septuagint was similar in the Song of Sol. passage, i.e., the sun has looked upon me ("with its discoloring and burning rays" to be understood from the context); see J. F. Schleusner, *Novus Thesaurus Philologico-Criticus sive Lexicon in LXX ac Reliquos Interpretes Graecos ac Scriptores Apocryphos,* pt. IV (Leipzig 1821) s.v. παραβλέπω 185-186.

19. *Homiliae in Canticum Canticorum* 1.6 (*GCS,* Origen 8.36). F. J. Dölger, *Die Sonne der Gerechtigkeit und der Schwarze* 62 includes this passage from Origen in his discussion of the imagery of blackness and sin in early Christian writers and concludes that Christianity continued the classical view of black as the color of evil.

20. Origen *Commentarius in Canticum Canticorum* 2.360-362 (*GCS,* Origen 8.113-115). Origen's comments on "the black and beautiful" woman unable to boast the noble blood of Abraham, Isaac, and Jacob as well as those on the eunuch Abdimelech described as "iste alienigena et obscurae gentis homo et degeneris" (that foreigner of a dark and ignoble race) referred to in notes 50 and 51 *infra,* should be compared with Menander (Kock 533 — Koerte 612 — Loeb 481), who says that it is not γένος which is important but intrinsic worth which determines the εὐγενής. The Christian commentators here as elsewhere echo familiar Greek language and concepts. Mary = Miriam in RSV.

21. Gregory of Nyssa *Commentarius in Canticum Canticorum*

(1, 5-6) oratio 2 (*PG* 44.788-792) = W. Jaeger VI (Leiden 1960) 42-51.

22. Romans 5.8.

23. In this commentary on the Song of Solomon, Gregory contrasts the appropriate forms of λαμπρός and μέλας. Paul, says Gregory, had become λαμπρὸς ἐκ μέλανος, Gregory, *Commentarius in Canticum Canticorum PG* 44.792 = Jaeger VI 48-49.

24. Χριστὸς εἰς τὸν κόσμον ἦλθε λαμπροὺς ποιῆσαι τοὺς μέλανας Gregory, *ibid.*

25. γίνονται . . . λαμπροὶ οἱ Αἰθίοπες Gregory, *ibid.*

26. Psalms 71.9. (Septuagint reading and numbering = 72.9 in RSV.)

27. Psalms 73.14. (Septuagint reading and numbering = 74.14 in RSV.)

28. Cf. Sophonias 2.12; Cyril of Alexandria *Expositio in Psalmos* 73.14 (*PG* 69.1188). Cf. Ambrosius *De paradiso* 3.16; Paulinus of Nola *Carmina* 28.249-251 (*CSEL* 30.302); Cassiodorus *Expositio in Psalterium,* 73.13 (*PL* 70.531); cf. Hesychius of Jerusalem *De temperantia et virtute* 1.23 (*PG* 93.1488).

29. *Epistulae* 22.1 (*CSEL* 54.145).

30. Cf. Sophonias 2.12.

31. Cf. Jer. 13.23.

32. Cf. Song of Sol. 8.5 (Septuagint reading).

33. *Commentarii in Sophoniam prophetam* 2.12ff (*PL* 25.1367-1369).

34. *Vita S. Moysis Aethiopis* 2, in V. Latyšev *Menologium* 330.

35. *Apophthegmata Patrum* [hereafter abbreviated as *Apophth. Patrum*], *De abbate Mose* 4 (*PG* 65.284).

36. *Commentarius in Canticum Canticorum* 2.362-378 (*GCS,* Origen 8.114-126).

37. Cf. Num. 12.1-16.

38. Cf. Matt. 12.42 and I Kings 10.1-10.

39. Psalms 68.31.

40. Cf. Sophonias 3.10.

41. Cf. Jer. 38.7-13. Abdimelech = Ebedmelech in RSV.

42. *Commentarius in Canticum Canticorum* 2.366-367 (*GCS,* Origen 8.117-118).

43. Cf. Num. 12.7-8.

44. The frequent commentaries on the marriage of Moses to the Ethiopian woman, with few exceptions, make similar points: Philo *Legum allegoria* 2.67 points out that it was God Himself who wedded the Ethiopian woman to Moses and that Moses deserved high praise for having married the Ethiopian woman, the nature, tested by fire, that cannot be changed. Cf. Origen *Homiliae in Canticum Canticorum* 1.6 (Origen 8.36-37); Origen *Homiliae in Numeros* 6.4 (*GCS,* Origen 7.35-36) and 7.2 (*GCS,* Origen 7.38-41); Irenaeus *Contra haereses,*

4.20.12 (*PG* 7.1042-1043); Jerome *Commentarii in Sophoniam prophetam* 2 (*PL* 25.1369); Theodoret *Quaestiones in Numeros,* interrogatio 22 (*PG* 80.373-376) and *Quaestiones in Exodum,* interrogatio 4 (*PG* 80.228); Cyril of Alexandria *Glaphyra in Numeros* 1.1-2 (*PG* 69.592-596); Arator *De Actibus Apostolorum* 1.692-694 (*CSEL* 72.53).

45. *Homiliae in Numeros* 7.2 (*GCS,* Origen 7.39).

46. *Commentarius in Canticum Canticorum* 2.367-370 (*GCS,* Origen 8.118-121). Josephus *Antiquitates Judaicae* 8.165 refers to the "Queen of Sheba" as "the Queen of Egypt and Ethiopia" and, hence, points to a tradition which regarded the Queen as Ethiopian rather than as Arabian. A note in the Loeb edition (pp. 660-661) states that Josephus was probably acquainted with some native Egyptian or Ethiopian tradition which connected the Queen of the Arabian kingdom with Egypt and Ethiopia. E. Ullendorff, "The Queen of Sheba," *Bulletin of the John Rylands Library* XLV (1962-63) 491-492 notes that the Josephus passage apparently referred to Nubia-Meroë rather than Abyssinia proper and concentrates on an African rather than an Arabian origin.

47. Origen, *ibid.,* 2.372-373 (*GCS,* 8.122-123); cf. Psalms 67.32.

48. Cf. Sophonias 3.10.

49. Cf. Rom. 11.25 (RSV).

50. *Commentarius in Canticum Canticorum* 2.373-374 (*GCS,* Origen 8.123).

51. Abdimelech's humble origin is similar to that of the black woman of ignoble birth as presented in discussions of the Song of Solomon (n. 20 *supra*).

52. *Commentarii in Sophoniam prophetam* 2.12 ff. *PL* 25.1368; *Epistulae* 69.6.7-8.

53. *De Actibus Apostolorum* 1.673-707 (*CSEL* 72.52-54).

54. Psalms 73.14 (Septuagint = 74.14 RSV).

55. Eph. 5.8.

56. Augustine *Enarrationes in Psalmos* 73.16 [*Corpus Christianorum, Series Latina,* hereafter abbreviated as *CCL*] 39.1014.

57. *Enarrationes in Psalmos* 71.12 (*CCL* 39.980); cf. Augustine, *ibid.,* 67.40 (*CCL* 897): "Aegypti, vel Aethiopiae nomine, omnium gentium fidem significavit, a parte totum" ("Under the name of Egypt or Ethiopia he has signified the faith of all nations, from a part the whole").

58. *Enarrationes in Psalmos* 71.12 (*CCL* 39.980). The phrases "eam . . . gentem . . . *quae in finibus terrae est*" and "Aethiopes *extremos . . . hominum*" ("that nation which is at the ends of the earth" and "the remotest of men") in this passage are strikingly similar to Homer's Ethiopians — τηλόθ' ἐόντας,/Αἰθίοπας τοὶ διχθὰ δεδαίαται, ἔσχατοι ἀνδρῶν ("The far-off Ethiopians who live divided, the most remote of men") (*Odyssey* 1.22-23) — and, in a manner

similar to Menander and Origen, leave no doubt as to the comprehensiveness and meaning of Augustine's concept, particularly since Augustine by the Homeric reminiscence takes the reader back to the beginning of recorded classical literature which dscribed as ἔσχατοι ἀνδρῶν a people used frequently in later authors as one type of physical extreme unlike the Greeks and the Romans.

59. Hab. 3.7.

60. *De civitate Dei* 16.8 as translated by E. M. Sanford and W. M. Green in Loeb edition.

61. *Enarrationes in Psalmos,* 67.41 (*CCL* 39.898).

62. *Commentarius in Canticum Canticorum* (1,5) oratio 2 *PG* 44.792 = Jaeger VI 48-49.

63. Acts 8.26-40. For a reader of Acts, ἀνὴρ Αἰθίοψ or *vir Aethiops,* as the eunuch was described, would mean a black man, perhaps a Negro, from the region above Egypt. That the commentators regarded the eunuch as a black is obvious, for example, from Jerome's statement that the baptism of the eunuch is proof that though it is against nature the Ethiopian does change his skin (*Epistulae* 69.6.7-8) and from Arator's inclusion of the eunuch in his exegesis of Scriptural passages referring to the Ethiopian, *De Actibus Apostolorum* 1.673-707 (*CSEL* 72.52-54). For discussions of the identity of the Ethiopian eunuch and related problems, see J. Hastings, *A Dictionary of the Bible* I (Edinburgh and New York 1904) s.v. *Ethiopian Eunuch* 790 and III (Edinburgh and New York 1904) s.v. *Philip the Evangelist* 836; E. S. Bucke, ed., *The Interpreter's Dictionary of the Bible: An Illustrated Encyclopaedia* II (New York and Nashville 1962) s.v. *Ethiopian Eunuch* 177-178; I. Singer, ed., *The Jewish Encyclopedia,* V (New York and London 1916) s.v. *Eunuch* 266; F. Vigouroux, *Dictionnaire de la Bible* II (Paris 1912) s.v. *Candace* 129-131.

64. Irenaeus *Contra haereses* 3.12.8 (*PG* 7.901-902), 4.23.2 (*PG* 7.1048-49); Eusebius *Historia ecclesiastica* 2.1 (*PG* 20.137); Jerome *Commentarii in Isaiam prophetam* 14.53 (*PL* 24.527-528).

65. *Epistulae* 69.6.7-8.

66. Cf. Psalms 67.32 (Septuagint numbering = RSV 68.31) as cited by Theodoret *Interpretatio in Psalmos* 67.32 (*PG* 80.1397).

67. Jerome *Epistulae* 69.6.7-8, *Commentarii in Sophoniam prophetam* 1.1 (*PL* 25.1339) and Arator *De Actibus Apostolorum,* 1.673-707 (*CSEL* 72.52-54).

68. J. Hastings, *A Dictionary,* I 790.

69. *Ibid.,* III 836.

70. *Commentarii in Sophoniam prophetam* 1.1 (*PL* 25.1339).

71. *Homiliae in Epistulam Primam ad Corinthios* 36.6 (*PG* 61.314-315).

72. John Chrysostom *Homiliae in Matthaeum* 1.6 (*PG* 57.21).

73. Theodosius *De situ Terrae Sanctae* 5 (*CSEL* 39.139).

74. Eusebius *Historia ecclesiastica* 2.1 (*PG* 20.137); Jerome

Commentarii in Isaiam prophetam 14.53.7 (*PL* 24.527-528); Irenaeus *Contra haereses* 3.12.8 (*PG* 7.902) and 4.23.2 (*PG* 7.1048-49) *Synaxarium Ecclesiae Constantinopolitanae* 788.6-9 (edition of H. Delehaye [Brussels 1902]).

75. *Historia ecclesiastica* 2.1 (*PG* 20.137).

76. Psalms 71.9 (Septuagint numbering = 72.9 RSV) cited by Justin (*Dialogus cum Tryphone Judaeo* 34 (*PG* 6.548).

77. Rufinus *Historia ecclesiastica* 1.9 (*PL* 21.478); Socrates *Historia ecclesiastica* 1.19 (*PG* 67.125); Gelasius of Cyzicus, *Historia ecclesiastica* 3.9.2 (*GCS*, 28.148); Venantius Fortunatus *Carmina* 5.2.9 (*MGH* IV pt. 1, p. 104). It was Thomas who baptized the Ethiopians in one account (Dio Chrysostom, *Spuria* [*Sermo in Sanctos duodecim Apostolos*] *PG* 59.495).

78. *Commentariorum series in Matthaeum* 39 (*GCS*, Origen 11.76).

79. Rufinus *Historia ecclesiastica* 1.9 (*PL* 21.478-480); Socrates *Historia ecclesiastica* 1.19 (*PG* 67.125-139); Sozomen *Historia ecclesiastica* 2.24 (*PG* 67.996-1000); Gelasius *Historia ecclesiastica* 3.9.3-17 (*GCS*, 28.148-150). For discussions of the Frumentius mission, see E. A. W. Budge, *A History of Ethiopia, Nubia, and Abyssinia,* I (London 1928) 147-153, 242-259; A. H. M. Jones and E. Monroe, *A History of Abyssinia* (Oxford 1935) 24-25, 28-29; K. S. Latourette, *A History of the Expansion of Christianity,* I: *The First Five Centuries* (London 1944) 236; and C. P. Groves, *The Planting of Christianity in Africa* (London and Redhill 1948) = Lutterworth Library, vol. XXVI, 52-53; and A. Dihle, "Frumentios und Ezana," in *Umstrittene Daten: Untersuchungen zum Auftreten der Griechen am Roten Meer* (Cologne and Opladen 1965) 36-64.

80. For India in the terminology of the ecclesiastical writers, see A. Dihle (n. 79 *supra*) and especially the following points of relevance to the assignment of Frumentius to Axum: the frequent application (up to the fifth century) of "Indians" to the inhabitants of the coastal regions of the Red Sea and to the Axumites (but not to Ethiopians from Meroë to Napata); the gradual abandonment in the sixth century of this practice by the educated and the application of "Ethiopians" to the Axumites and of "Indians" to the inhabitants of India proper; and Abyssinia as the country intended in the reports of the area which Frumentius proselytized.

81. Athanasius *Apologia ad Constantium* 31 (*PG* 25.636-637).

82. For Theophilus as Indian, see Philostorgius *Historia ecclesiastica* 2.6 (*PG* 65.469) Epitome of Photius; as Blemmys, Gregory of Nyssa *Contra Eunomium* 1 (*PG* 45.264 = Jaeger I 38). For views on the identity and location of the island of Divus, see J. Desanges, "Une Mention altérée d'Axoum dans l'*Expositio Totius Mundi et Gentium,*" *Annales d'Ethiopie* VII (1967) 146-148.

83. Philostorgius *Historia ecclesiastica* 3.4-6 (*PG* 65.481-488); cf.

E. O. Winstedt, *The Christian Topography of Cosmas Indicopleustes* (Cambridge, Eng. 1909) 346 and F. Cabrol and H. Leclercq, *Dictionnaire d'archéologie chrétienne et de liturgie,* V, pt. 1 (Paris 1922) s.v. *Ethiopie* 590-592.

84. Cabrol and Leclerq, *ibid.,* argue that the designation of Theophilus as a Blemmys by Gregory and as a Libyan by the Council of Constantinople proves what "Indian" means in this instance and that Theophilus was born in Ethiopia, an origin supported by the facts in the biography of Theophilus and in the religious controversies of the day. A. Dihle, however, (n. 79 *supra*) n. 52, p. 50 attaches no importance to Gregory's designation of Theophilus as Blemmys. Desanges (n. 82 *supra*) p. 148, n. 1 expresses the opinion that there is not necessarily a contradiction in Philostorgius' and Gregory's usage and that perhaps for Gregory, Theophilus was an Indian in a kind of "sub-Egyptian" sense.

85. Jerome *Epistulae* 46.10.1-2, *CSEL* 54.339-40; E. Cerulli *Etiopi in Palestina* I (Rome 1943) notes that the correspondence of Jerome was written between 386 and 412 A.D.

86. *Epistulae* 107.2.3 (*CSEL* 55.292). The date of the letter is 402/403 A.D. Cerulli, *Etiopi* 2-3 comments on the traditional format of the two passages, i.e., a catalogue of peoples including Indians, Persians, Ethiopians, and Scythians, and notes the difficulty of determining the precise regions from which the Ethiopians came. Cf. O. Meinardus, "The Ethiopians in Jerusalem," *Zeitschrift für Kirchengeschichte* LXXVI (1965) 116.

87. Palladius *Historia Lausiaca* 52 (*PG* 34.1145C; Rufinus of Aquileia *Historia monachorum, de Apollonio* 7.151 (*PL* 21.415).

88. For sources on the life of Father Moses, see Palladius *Historia Lausiaca* 22 (*PG* 34.1065-1068); Sozomen *Historia ecclesiastica* 6.29 (*PG* 67.1376-1381); *Acta Sanctorum,* August, VI, 199-212; *Apophth. Patrum* (*PG* 65.281-290); Joseph-Marie Sauget in *Bibliotheca Sanctorum,* IX (Rome 1967) s.v. *Mosè di Scete o l'Etiope* 652-654.

89. The date of his death has been placed between 391 and 409; cf. H. G. Evelyn-White, *The Monasteries of the Wâdi'N Natrun,* Part II: *The History of the Monasteries of Nitria and of Scetis* (New York 1932) 154-156.

90. Palladius *Historia Lausiaca* 22 (*PG* 34.1065-1068).

91. *Apophth. Patrum* 6 (*PG* 65.284).

92. *Ibid.,* 8 (*PG* 65.285).

93. *Ibid.,* 4 (*PG* 65.284).

94. *Ibid.,* 2 (*PG* 65.281-284).

95. *Ibid.,* 9-10 (*PG* 65.285).

96. Evelyn-White (n. 89 *supra*) 155, n. 5; J.-M Sauget, "Mosè di Scete" (cited in n. 88 *supra*) 652.

97. *Collationes* 3.5 (*PL* 49.563-564).

98. *Historia ecclesiastica* 6.29 (*PG* 67.1377B-D).

99. *Vita S. Moysis Aethiopis,* in V. Latyšev *Menologium* fasc. 2, pp. 330-334.

100. Cited in n. 93 *supra.*

101. Although the role of Father Moses in the later history of the Church falls outside this book, it should be noted that his body has been venerated at Dair-el-Baramus monastery in Egypt. For commemoration of Moses in the Coptic, Greek, and Latin Churches, see Evelyn-White (n. 89 *supra*) 155 and F. G. Holweck, *A Biographical Dictionary of the Saints* (St. Louis and London 1924) 723; and H. Thurston and D. Attwater, *Butler's Lives of the Saints* III (London 1956) 435-436.

102. For St. Menas, see M. A. Murray, "St. Menas of Alexandria," *Proceedings of the Society of Biblical Archaeology* XXIX (1907) 25-30, 51-60, 112-122, plates I-II for Negro head on *ampullae;* C. M. Kaufman, *Zur Ikonographie der Menas-Ampullen* (Cairo 1910) 123-128, and fig. 63 (opposite p. 123) for a fourth-century Menas as a Negro; Kaufmann argues (124) that the Negroid type originated (perhaps as a concession to the black race) after the basic type had been stamped and that the resemblance to Negroes in the prototypal image of Menas, especially on medium-sized *ampullae,* is a result of imperfect stamps or stylistic characteristics of the artist; *id., Die Menasstadt und das Nationalheiligtum der altchristlichen Aegypter in der westalexandrinischen Wüste* (Leipzig 1910) plate 96 for *ampullae* with Negro type; F. L. Cross, ed., *The Oxford Dictionary of the Christian Church* (London, New York, Toronto 1958) s.v. *Menas, St.* 885-886; L. Réau, *Iconographie de l'art chrétien,* III: *Iconographie des saints II G-O* (Paris 1958) s.v. *Ménas d'Alexandrie* 948-949; M. C. Celletti in *Bibliotheca Sanctorum* IX (Rome 1967) s.v. *Menna (Menas)* 324-343. For much later representations, especially in German art, of St. Maurice and St. Gregory the Moor as Negroes, see L. Réau, *Iconographie* s.v. *Maurice d'Agaune* 935-939 and s.v. *Grégoire le Maure* 616.

103. Fulgentius *Epistulae* 11-12 (*PL* 65.378-392).

104. *Ibid.,* 11.2 (*PL* 65.378).

105. Relevant Greek and Latin sources for the efforts of the Axumite king Elesboas to halt the persecution of the Himyarites are Procopius, *De bello Persico* 1.20.1-9; Cosmas Indicopleustes, *Topographia Christiana* 2.101C (p. 72 in E. O. Winstedt's edition [Cambridge, Eng. 1909]); and *Acta Martyrii Arethae, Acta Sanctorum,* October, X, 743, 747, 761-762. For discussions of the episode and other sources, see A. Moberg, *The Book of the Himyarites* (Lund, London, Paris, Leipzig 1924); J. B. Bury, *History of the Later Roman Empire,* II (London 1931) 322-327; and A. A. Vasiliev, *Justin the First* 288-297, the details of whose reconstruction (based on Greek, Arabian, and Syriac sources) of the incident I have followed. On the question of the name of the Axumite king, see Moberg, pp. xli-xlii

and Vasiliev, 291 — variants — Ellatzbaas, Hellestheaeus, Elesboas, Elesbaas, Elesbas, Caleb (Kaleb).

106. *Topographia Christiana* 3.169 C (p. 119 E. O. Winstedt's edition).

107. A basic source for the sixth-century Christian missionary efforts in Nubia herein discussed is the Ecclesiastical History of John of Ephesus (or Asia) ca. 507-586 A.D. See 4.6-4.8 and 4.48-4.53 in R. Payne Smith, *The Third Part of the Ecclesiastical History of John, Bishop of Ephesus* (Oxford 1860); E. W. Brooks, *Iohannis Ephesini Historiae Ecclesiasticae Pars Tertia, Scriptores Syri,* 3rd series, III, *Corpus Scriptorum Christianorum Orientalium* (Louvain 1936). For discussions of this period of Christian activity in Nubia, see J. Kraus, *Die Anfänge des Christentums in Nubien* (Mödling 1931), *passim* but esp. 54-93 and K. S. Latourette, *A History of the Expansion of Christianity,* II: *The Thousand Years of Uncertainty* (London 1939) 231-236.

108. *CIG* III 5072; *Orientis Graeci Inscriptiones Selectae* I no. 201.

109. E. A. W. Budge, *The Egyptian Sudan: Its History and Monuments,* II (Philadelphia and London 1907) 297.

Index of Names and Subjects

Index of Sources

(For more detailed bibliographical information, see pages cited)